CONTENTS

D0394588

LIST OF MAPS

ABOUT THE AUTHOR

Jennifer Eveland spent part of her childhood in Singapore, has studied in Hong Kong, lived for a spell in Bangkok, and has traveled extensively throughout East and Southeast Asia. In addition to *Frommer's Singapore & Malaysia,* she has authored previous editions of *Frommer's Thailand* and contributes to *Frommer's Southeast Asia.* In 1999 she returned to Singapore, where she has been based as a full-time freelance writer. She writes regularly for *The International Herald Tribune* and contributes travel, finance, and lifestyle stories to numerous local and international magazines, newspapers, and books. She lives near Little India with her husband, a Singaporean musician and producer, their toddler son, and their three cats.

ACKNOWLEDGMENTS

I am indebted to Susy Atkinson for her research assistance and valuable insight for traveling in Singapore. Susy grew up in hotels, with parents employed in the hospitality industry in her native UK. A freelance writer, she has co-authored a travel guidebook on Singapore. Her travels have taken her throughout the region, but she is now settled in Singapore with her husband, who is a journalist and historian, and their twin toddler sons.

I would also like to thank David Bowden, who provided research and expert travel advice for the Malaysia chapters. An Australian, David is an award-winning freelance photojournalist specialising in travel, food, wine, and the environment who has been based in Asia for over a decade. He's penned children's books, travel books and guides, and articles. He is currently based in KL with his wife and daughter.

As always I am grateful to the Singapore Tourism Board and to the Malaysia Tourism Board for their continued support for this project.

—Jennifer Eveland

AN INVITATION TO THE READER

In researching this book, we discovered many wonderful places—hotels, restaurants, shops, and more. We're sure you'll find others. Please tell us about them, so we can share the information with your fellow travelers in upcoming editions. If you were disappointed with a recommendation, we'd love to know that, too. Please write to:

Frommer's Singapore & Malaysia, 6th Edition
Wiley Publishing, Inc. • 111 River St. • Hoboken, NJ 07030-5774

AN ADDITIONAL NOTE

Please be advised that travel information is subject to change at any time—and this is especially true of prices. We therefore suggest that you write or call ahead for confirmation when making your travel plans. The authors, editors, and publisher cannot be held responsible for the experiences of readers while traveling. Your safety is important to us, however, so we encourage you to stay alert and be aware of your surroundings. Keep a close eye on cameras, purses, and wallets, all favorite targets of thieves and pickpockets.

Other Great Guides for Your Trip:

Frommer's Southeast Asia
Frommer's Thailand
Frommer's Hong Kong
Frommer's China

FROMMER'S STAR RATINGS, ICONS & ABBREVIATIONS

Every hotel, restaurant, and attraction listing in this guide has been ranked for quality, value, service, amenities, and special features using a **star-rating system.** In country, state, and regional guides, we also rate towns and regions to help you narrow down your choices and budget your time accordingly. Hotels and restaurants are rated on a scale of zero (recommended) to three stars (exceptional). Attractions, shopping, nightlife, towns, and regions are rated according to the following scale: zero stars (recommended), one star (highly recommended), two stars (very highly recommended), and three stars (must-see).

In addition to the star-rating system, we also use **seven feature icons** that point you to the great deals, in-the-know advice, and unique experiences that separate travelers from tourists. Throughout the book, look for:

(Finds)	Special finds—those places only insiders know about
(Fun Facts)	Fun facts—details that make travelers more informed and their trips more fun
(Kids)	Best bets for kids and advice for the whole family
(Moments)	Special moments—those experiences that memories are made of
(Overrated)	Places or experiences not worth your time or money
(Tips)	Insider tips—great ways to save time and money
(Value)	Great values—where to get the best deals

The following **abbreviations** are used for credit cards:

AE	American Express	DISC	Discover	V	Visa
DC	Diners Club	MC	MasterCard		

FROMMERS.COM

Now that you have this guidebook to help you plan a great trip, visit our website at **www.frommers.com** for additional travel information on more than 4,000 destinations. We update features regularly to give you instant access to the most current trip-planning information available. At Frommers.com, you'll find scoops on the best airfares, lodging rates, and car rental bargains. You can even book your travel online through our reliable travel booking partners. Other popular features include:

- Online updates of our most popular guidebooks
- Vacation sweepstakes and contest giveaways
- Newsletters highlighting the hottest travel trends
- Podcasts, interactive maps, and up-to-the-minute events listings
- Opinionated blog entries by Arthur Frommer himself
- Online travel message boards with featured travel discussions

What's New in Singapore & Malaysia

SINGAPORE

From 2009 onward, Singapore's downtown will look like a completely different place. In November 2008, the city completed the **Marina Barrage,** a giant dam project at the mouth of Marina Bay, which transformed the bay into a freshwater reservoir. Located in the heart of the city, the bay will support water sports and entertainment, and will be surrounded by parks and promenades that will enhance Singapore's waterfront lifestyle feel. The Marina Barrage also includes The Sustainable Singapore Gallery, a high-tech museum devoted to showcasing Singapore's efforts toward environmental sustainability.

A huge parcel of reclaimed land is currently being developed with wide avenues and futuristic infrastructure to support office towers, luxury high-rise condominiums, and a new financial center. An extension of the Shenton Way business district, the new area is being developed as a 'round-the-clock hub for working, living, and playing.

The centerpiece of the new downtown development is the **Marina Bay Sands**, Singapore's first casino, built by Las Vegas Sands, which has invested S$5 billion (US$3.4 billion/£2.3 billion). The huge complex will also feature 110,000 sq. m (1,184,029 sq. ft.) of meeting and convention space, two 2,000-seat theaters, three hotel towers, an **ArtScience** museum, luxury retail outlets, dining venues in floating pavilions on the bay, plus innovative public spaces that include a rooftop park with a 360-degree city view, an ice skating rink, and indoor canals. The complex will open in stages from late 2009.

Towering above the Marina Bay, the **Singapore Flyer** (p. 124), the world's largest observation wheel, has good views of all the construction.

There are also plans to join two landmark buildings within the Historic District—City Hall and the old Supreme Court building—and convert them into a large exhibition space for contemporary arts in Singapore and Southeast Asia, with visiting exhibits from around the world. The new art gallery, alongside **The Arts House** at the Old Parliament (p. 183) and The Esplanade–Theatres on the Bay, will turn the former colonial administrative heart of Singapore into a vibrant arts hub.

On Sentosa Island, a second casino complex, **Resorts World at Sentosa**, is being developed by Genting International and Star Cruises, who will invest S$5.2 billion (US$3.5 billion/£2.3 billion) to build an enormous facility on Sentosa Island. Geared toward family and leisure activities, the casino will be supported by spa resort accommodations, restaurants, and bars, plus retail and entertainment outlets. Perhaps the most exciting part of the package will be the addition of **Universal Studios Singapore,** promised to be Asia's largest, with 22 attractions in themed "worlds," including "Journey to Madagascar," and a DreamWorks Digital Animation Studio. Also in the works is the **Quest Marine Life Park,** with the largest single marine tank in the world, and an interactive dolphin habitat. The **Equarius Water Park** will feature water rides and a maritime museum. Three amphitheaters will have international entertainment, including a resident show from the creators of **Cirque du Soleil.** Resorts World at Sentosa is scheduled to open in stages starting in 2010.

MALAYSIA

Like Singapore, Malaysia also has an observation wheel. First opened in Kuala Lumpur in 2007, the **Eye on Malaysia** (p. 237) reopened in its permanent location in Melaka, at the mouth of the Melaka River, in November 2008. The observation wheel sits on 1.6 hectares (4 acres) of land, which is currently being developed to include a light and sound giant waterscreen showcase, a laser light show that uses a screen made from flowing water, and the **Malaysian International Space Adventure (MISA),** with interactive education exhibits celebrating Malaysia's first astronaut in space. Both of these projects are expected to open in late 2009.

This guide also includes a few new hotels. **The Majestic Malacca** (p. 236) is a welcome addition to the Melaka hotel scene, where accommodations tend to be either bland international chain hotels or tiny guesthouses. The Majestic is a luxurious property built within a charming 1920s mansion located along the newly cleaned Melaka River.

Tioman Island, along Malaysia's east coast, has hosted only one international-class resort for ages, but with the opening of **JapaMala** (p. 261), visitors now have a choice of accommodations on the idyllic island. JapaMala is a five-star resort that has rustic charm, built into the jungle, with a gorgeous beach. Better still, it's open year-round, as its location is somewhat protected from the monsoon.

The Best of Singapore & Malaysia

A fascinating mix of contrasts, Singapore lies at the crossroads of East and West, and as a result, it hums with a unique culture that is equal parts oriental and occidental. Founded by an adventurer who was searching for the epicenter of global trade, early Singapore drew waves of immigrant traders, investors, laborers, and adventurers from all corners of the world. Some 200 years later, Singapore is still fulfilling its original role, with one of the busiest shipping ports on Earth, a multicultural native population, and fresh waves of new immigrants and expatriates from countries far and wide. True to its heritage, Singapore has always been, and will always be, a nation that blends the best of all worlds into one nation.

It is understandable for a visitor to feel as if Singapore has sold its Asian soul in exchange for a Western lifestyle. On the surface, the terrain is distinctly consumer driven; its rows of shiny shopping malls flank wide, manicured avenues dotted with McDonald's and Starbucks. At rush hour, the flow of office workers forms an endless river of black business suits and Blackberries through the Mass Rapid Transit system into the downtown Central Business District. A modern metropolis, Singapore is a city on the move, with places to go and people to see.

But for those who pause to take a closer look, Singapore's cultural heart is alive and well beneath the polished veneer. Singapore's Chinese are still driven by ancient values that respect the family, authority, and success merited by hard work. Its Malays share openly their warm ideals of generosity, hospitality, and joy among friends and family. And the city's Indians possess a culture steeped in thousands of years of traditional beauty and passion for life. Add to this the spirit of Arabs and Armenians, Bugis and British, various Europeans and Eurasians, and many more—a multitude of cultures that, combined, defines what it means to be Singaporean.

Singapore strives to honor its past while keeping one eye firmly focused on the future. Amid its efforts to grow the nation's economy and its people's standard of living are huge plans for tourism development. Already it hosts stellar world-class institutions, such as the Asian Civilisations Museum, the Singapore Arts Museum, and the award-winning Singapore Zoo and Night Safari. In recent years, the city has completely revamped the Singapore History Museum and has added the Singapore Flyer to its repertoire. All of these attractions, and many more, are detailed within the pages of this guide.

Major changes are on the horizon. In the coming years, visitors can look forward to The Marina Bay Sands, which comprises a Las Vegas-style casino supported by a convention center, three hotel towers topped by an interconnected skypark, "floating" pavilions on the bay, an ArtScience Museum, a luxury shopping mall, celebrity chef restaurants, theaters, and nightclubs. The complex is slated for opening in stages from the end of 2009.

The following year another casino complex will be launched on Sentosa, Singapore's leisure destination island, just minutes from the downtown area. Resorts World at Sentosa will include, in addition to a casino, Universal Studios Singapore, Marine Life Park,

Southeast Asia

TAIWAN
Bashi Channel
0
500 mi
0
500 km
N
National Capital
Luzon
Bagio City
Philippine Sea
Manila
PHILIPPINES
PACIFIC OCEAN
Puerto Galera
Mindoro
Samar
Panay
Cebu
Cebu City
Negros
Bohol
Sulu Sea
PALAU
Mindanao
Isabela
Celebes Sea
Makassar Strait
Molucca Sea
Halmahera
MOLUCCAS
Sorong
Sulawesi (Celebes)
Ceram Sea
Jayapura
New Guinea
Buru
Seram
N E S I A
Banda Sea
Sea
Flores
Dili
EAST TIMOR
Arafura Sea
Timor
Timor Sea
Darwin
AUSTRALIA

Maritime Xperiential Museum, Equarius Water Park, six hotels, conference facilities, a kids' club, a world-class spa, plus shopping, dining, and entertainment. This complex will open in stages starting in 2010.

Singapore's tireless drive for growth is contrasted by Malaysia's laid-back atmosphere, where in some places it can seem as if time stands still. In fact, many Singaporeans look to their northern neighbor for the perfect vacation, exploring its rich national forests and marine parks, unwinding on picture-perfect beaches at sophisticated resorts, taking in the down-to-earth culture of its small towns, shopping for inexpensive handicrafts, and eating some of the most delicious food in Southeast Asia. But despite its exotic and world-class holiday offerings, Malaysia lacks the hoards of tourists that beat feet for Singapore and Thailand. Because Malaysia remains comparatively quiet, it's easy to enjoy a holiday without the tacky trappings of the tourist trade.

My favorite part of Malaysia, however, is the warmth of its people. I have yet to travel in this country without collecting remarkable tales of hospitality, openness, and generosity. I've found the Malaysian people to be genuine in their approach to foreign visitors, another fine byproduct of the underdeveloped tourism industry. For those who want to find a nice little corner of paradise, Malaysia could be your answer.

I've crept down alleys, wandered the streets of cities and towns, combed beaches, and trekked jungles to seek out the most exciting things that Singapore and Malaysia have to offer. In this book I've presented the sights and attractions of these countries with insight into historical, cultural, and modern significance to bring you a complete appreciation of all you are about to experience. I've peeked in every shop door, chatting up the local characters inside. I've eaten local food until I can't move. I've stayed out all night. I've done it all and written about it here. I can only hope you will love Singapore and Malaysia as much as I do.

1 FROMMER'S FAVORITE SINGAPORE EXPERIENCES

- **Sipping a Singapore Sling at the Long Bar:** Ahhhh, the Long Bar, home of the Singapore Sling. I like to come here in the afternoons, before the tourist rush. Sheltered by long jalousie shutters that close out the tropical sun, the air cooled by lazy *punkahs* (small fans that wave gently back and forth above), you can sit back in old rattan chairs and have your saronged waitress serve you sticky alcoholic creations while you toss back a few dainty crab cakes. Life can be so decadent. Okay, so the punkahs are electric, and, come to think of it, the place is air-conditioned (not to mention that it costs a small fortune), but it's fun to imagine the days when Somerset Maugham, Rudyard Kipling, or Charlie Chaplin would be sitting at the bar sipping Slings and spinning exotic tales of their world travels. Drink up, my friend; it's a lovely high. See p. 179

- **Witnessing Ceremonial Gore:** By midnight, the air surrounding Sri Perumal Temple is thick with burning incense. A sea of people is lit by bare bulbs. Family and friends gather around men who are bare-chested and rigid, with eyes focused forward. They are in deep spiritual meditation following 40 days of a strictly guided diet and prayer regimen to prepare their bodies for physical torture all night long.

It's the start of the Thaipusam festival, an annual Hindu religious occasion to express gratitude to Lord Subramaniam for granting their wishes in the previous year. To do this, they will carry *kevadis,* steel racks hung with fruits and flowers, held onto their bodies with skewers that dig into their flesh. Others will have rows of hooks piercing the thick skin on their backs—the hooks attached to long leather straps that are pulled hard. Still others drive skewers through both cheeks and pierce their tongues.

Once ready, they will parade en masse, in full torture regalia, through the streets of Little India and Singapore's downtown to the Sri Thandayuthapani Temple.

Singapore's Hindus celebrate Thaipusam every January into February, and like many other cultural and religious celebrations, foreign visitors are welcome to come and (respectfully) observe. If you're not in town for this unusual festival, you can catch ceremonial gore at annual events like Thimithi, the Birthday of the Monkey God, and the Festival of the Nine Emperor God later in the year. See chapter 3 for details.

- **Checking Out the Orchard Road Scene:** You can't find better people-watching than on Orchard Road every Saturday afternoon, when it seems like every Singaporean crawls out of the woodwork to join the parade of shoppers, strollers, hipsters, posers, lovers, geeks, and gabbers. Everybody is here, milling around every mall, clustered around every sidewalk bench, checking everybody else out. At the corner of Scotts Road and Orchard, just below the Marriott, there's an alfresco cafe where you'll find local celebrities hanging out to see and be seen. International celebrities and models have been spotted here on occasion, too. In the mix, you're bound to see most every tourist on the island, coming around to see what all the excitement is about.

The malls are filled with mobs of groovy teenagers kicking around, trying to look cool, and watching the music videos in the front window of the HMV music store in the Heeren. Moms and dads also have half-days at the office, so the strip takes on the feel of an obstacle course as all the parents race around wielding strollers, trying to run errands while they have the chance. Meanwhile, outside in the shady areas, you can see crowds of domestic maids and workers relaxing and catching up on the latest news on their free afternoon.

For some, the scene is a madhouse to be avoided; for others, it's a chance to watch life on a typical Saturday afternoon in downtown Singapore.

2 FROMMER'S FAVORITE MALAYSIA EXPERIENCES

- **Letting the Sea Wash Away All Your Stress:** This is paradise. Lying flat, arms outstretched across the surface of the water, I felt the rays of the sun warming my back and the cool ripples of salty sea beneath me. Through the clear water I could see the seabed at the bottom of the bay and all assortment of creatures swimming in and out of corals. My snorkel guide pointed in the shadows to the silhouette of a meter-long shark, too shy to approach.

Back near the beach, I stood in the shallows feeding bread crumbs to the smaller fish. Within minutes I was surrounded by a swarm of brilliant colors—vivid Day-Glo flashes of saltwater fish, thousands of them, dozens of species, swirling around me and plucking bread from my fingertips.

On the beach, my friends and I lazed under the shade of a tree, digging our feet into the soft and powdery sand. One friend climbed a coconut palm and twisted a giant nut off its stem. Using a cleaver from the kitchen, we hacked it open and poured the coconut water over ice in a glass, then picked the sweet flesh from the inside the shell. After a day of this, I was ready to tear up my return ticket.

This kind of paradise is everywhere in Malaysia, and you can find it within an hour's flight from Kuala Lumpur (KL), if you visit Langkawi, Tioman, and Redang, or, if you have more time, in Sabah.

- **Experiencing *Kampung* Hospitality:** Pakcik (uncle) was just slightly older than his ancient Mercedes, but his price was right, so I hired him for the day to drive me around Kota Bharu. Sometime after lunch, during a stop at the kite-maker's house, I spotted a beautiful *gasing*, a wood-and-steel Malay top. It would be the perfect gift for my brother! I just had to have one.

Well, the kite-maker didn't want to give his up, but Pakcik had a few ideas. After coming up empty at the local shops, he took on my quest with personal conviction. Off we drove through the outskirts of town, the sights becoming increasingly rural. He turned down a dirt road, past grazing water buffaloes lazing near rice

paddies. Soon the fields turned to jungle, and a small *kampung* (village) appeared in the trees. I watched out the window as we passed traditional wooden stilt houses where grannies fanned themselves on the porch watching the children chase chickens in the yard. Beside each house, colorful batik sarongs waved from clotheslines in the breeze.

The path wound to the house of Pakcik's nephew. I was welcomed inside with curiosity, perhaps the first foreigner to visit. They offered me a straw mat, which I used to join the others resting comfortably on the floor. Within minutes, an audience of neighbors gathered around, plucking fruits from the trees in the yard for me. I listened as Pakcik told them of my search for a gasing. That afternoon I was offered every gasing in the village.

My afternoon in Pakcik's kampung is one of my most cherished memories and a most meaningful experience. As Southeast Asia becomes increasingly affluent and globalized, this way of life becomes steadily endangered. It's a lifestyle that for many urban Malaysians captures the spirit of the good life—simple days when joy was free. And everyone will be proud to show you; all you need is an open heart and a big smile. Malaysian hospitality never ceases to amaze me.

3 THE BEST SMALL TOWNS & VILLAGES

- **Any Kampung (Tioman Island, Malaysia):** Even though Tioman was developed for the tourism industry, you'll never think this place is overdeveloped. The casual and rustic nature of the island's tiny beach villages holds firm, and those who seek escape rarely leave disappointed. See p. 258.

- **Melaka (Malacca, Malaysia):** As the oldest trading port in Malaysia, this town hosted a wide array of international traders: Arabs, Portuguese, Dutch, English, Indian, and Chinese, all of whom left their stamp. See p. 233.

- **Kuching (Sarawak, Malaysia):** Renegade adventure-seeker James Brooke thumbed his nose at London's colonial office so that he could claim Sarawak for his own and rule as the region's first White Raja. He built a cozy little capital with quaint tropical-colonial architecture, picturesque back streets, and a pretty riverfront. See p. 276.

4 THE BEST BEACHES

- **Sentosa Island (Singapore):** The three beaches on Sentosa are just about the best you'll find in Singapore, which isn't really known for its beaches. They're lively, with watersports and beach activities plus food and drink. Every so often you'll find an all-night dance party here. (See p. 152.) However, if you really need pristine seclusion, you'll have to head for Malaysia.
- **The Four Seasons (Langkawi, Malaysia):** Perhaps the most stunning beach in Malaysia, this wide gorgeous stretch of white sand looks out onto crystal-clear, deep-blue waters. Even if you can't afford a room at the resort, I highly recommend a cocktail at their deliciously exotic beachside bar so you can get a chance to enjoy the view. See p. 254.
- **Kampung Juara (Tioman Island, Malaysia):** This beach is what they mean when they say isolated. Be prepared to live like Robinson Crusoe—in tiny huts, many with no electricity at all. But, oh, the beach! Most visitors don't get to this part of the island, so many times you can have it all to yourself. See p. 262.
- **Cherating (Malaysia):** If you're a leatherback turtle, you'll think the best beach in the world is just north of Cherating. Every spring and summer, these giant sea creatures come ashore to lay their eggs, so if you're in town from May to June you might catch a look at the hatchlings. Meanwhile, during the turtles' off season, international windsurfing and water-board enthusiasts gather annually for competitions at this world-famous spot. See p. 264.

5 THE MOST EXCITING OUTDOOR ADVENTURES

- **Trekking in Taman Negara (Malaysia):** With suitable options for all levels of comfort and desired adventure, peninsular Malaysia's largest national park opens the wonders of primary rainforest and the creatures who dwell in it to everyone. From the canopy walk high atop the forest to night watches for nocturnal life, this adventure is as stunning as it is informative. See p. 229.
- **Sungei Buloh Wetland Reserve (Singapore):** Every year during the winter months, flocks of migrating birds from as far north as Siberia vacation in the warm waters of this unique mangrove swamp park. Easily traversed by a wooden walkway, the park will never disappoint for glimpses of stunning wildlife. See p. 149.

1

6 THE MOST FASCINATING TEMPLES, CHURCHES & MOSQUES

- **Thian Hock Keng (Singapore):** One of Singapore's oldest Chinese temples, it is a fascinating testimony to Chinese Buddhism as it combines with traditional Confucian beliefs and natural Taoist principles. Equally fascinating is the modern world that carries on just outside the old temple's doors. See p. 132.
- **Armenian Church (Singapore):** Although not the biggest Christian house of worship in the city, it is one of the most charming in its architectural simplicity, tropical practicality, and spiritual tranquillity. See p. 115.
- **Hajjah Fatimah Mosque (Singapore):** I love this mosque for its eclectic mix of religious symbols and architectural influences. To me, it represents not just the Singaporean ability to absorb so many different ideas, but also a Muslim appreciation and openness toward many cultures. See p. 136.
- **Jalan Tokong, Melaka (Malaysia):** This street, in the historical heart of the city, supports a Malay mosque, a Chinese temple, and a Hindu temple existing peacefully side by side—the perfect example of how the many foreign religions that came to Southeast Asia shaped its communities and learned to coexist in harmony. See p. 238.

7 THE MOST INTERESTING MUSEUMS

- **National Museum of Singapore. (Singapore):** This historic museum recently underwent a S$132.6 million ($88.8 million/£59.7 million) renovation and is now expanded to more than twice its original size, featuring state-of-the-art multimedia exhibits. They've done a fantastic job. See p. 121.
- **Asian Civilisations Museum (Singapore):** This extremely well-presented museum documents the evolutionary and cultural history of the region's major ethnic groups. A very informative afternoon. See p. 115.
- **Penang Museum and Art Gallery (Penang, Malaysia):** A slick display of Penang's colonial history and multicultural heritage, this place is chock-full of fascinating tidbits about the people, places, and events of this curious island. Plus, it doesn't hurt that the air-conditioning works very well! See p. 249.
- **State Museums of Melaka (Malaysia):** This small city has more museums than any other city in the country, with some unusual displays such as kites and Malaysian literature. See p. 237.

8 THE BEST LUXURY RESORTS & HOTELS

- **Raffles Hotel (Singapore):** For old-world opulence, Raffles is second to none. It's pure fantasy of the days when tigers still lurked around the perimeters. See p. 72.
- **Shangri-La Hotel (Singapore):** What sets this hotel apart from other city properties is its sprawling grounds. Shang is a meticulously landscaped tropical oasis, with lush garden views

from every angle. Three individual wings give you a choice of accommodations styles: urban contemporary, natural resort style, and Oriental opulence. See p. 81.

- **Hilton Kuala Lumpur (Kuala Lumpur, Malaysia):** The coolest of the cool stay at the new Hilton. Rooms feel like suites, all decorated in slickety-slick contempo style with the latest entertainment and IT built in—even in the bathrooms. See p. 221.
- **Tanjong Jara Resort (Terengganu, Malaysia):** Traditional Malay-style chalets furnished in natural woods and local textiles blend gorgeously with the tropical gardens of this seaside resort. The people here will bend over backward to make sure your stay is perfect. See p. 268.
- **Four Seasons Langkawi (Langkawi, Malaysia):** Raising the bar, this resort is an exotic Moorish paradise on the most gorgeous beach in Malaysia. Rooms and public areas drip with the ambience of the Arabian Nights. Three words: To. Die. For. See p. 254.

9 THE BEST HOTEL BARGAINS

- **Perak Hotel (Singapore):** This family-run budget hotel on the edge of Little India is full of charm and friendly people. It's easy to meet fellow backpackers in the cozy lobby cafe and share stories and travel tips. See p. 77.
- **Traders Hotel Singapore (Singapore):** Value-for-money is the name of the game here. All sorts of promotional packages, self-service launderettes, vending machines, and a checkout lounge are just a few of the offerings that make this the most convenient hotel in the city. See p. 86.
- **Swiss-Inn (Kuala Lumpur, Malaysia):** Location, location, location! Right in the center of Kuala Lumpur's bustling Chinatown, the Swiss-Inn is the perennial favorite for travelers here. A comfortable choice, plus it's so close to everything. See p. 223.
- **Heeren House (Melaka, Malaysia):** This boutique hotel in the heart of the old city is the place to stay in Melaka if you want to really get a feel of the local atmosphere. See p. 235.
- **Telang Usan Hotel (Kuching, Malaysia):** An informal place, Telang Usan is homey and quaint, and within walking distance of many major attractions in Kuching. See p. 279.

10 THE BEST LOCAL DINING EXPERIENCES

- **Hawker Centers (Singapore and Malaysia):** Think of them as shopping malls for food—great food. For local cuisine, who needs a menu with pictures when you can walk around and select anything you want as it's prepared before your eyes? See chapters 6, 13, 14, and 15.
- **Imperial Herbal (Singapore):** In the Chinese tradition of yin and yang, dishes are prepared under the supervision of the house doctor, a traditional healer who will be glad to "prescribe" the perfect cure for whatever ails you. See p. 109.

- **Chili Crab at UDMC Seafood Centre (Singapore):** A true Singaporean favorite, chili crabs will cause every local to rise up in argument over where you can find the best in town. Head out to UDMC to try the juicy crabs cooked in a sweet chili sauce. Prepare to get messy! See p. 110.

- **Gurney Drive (Penang, Malaysia):** Penang is the king of Asian cuisine, from Chinese to Malay to Indian and everything else in between. This large hawker center by the sea is a great introduction to Penang. See p. 248.

11 THE BEST MARKETS

- **Arab Street (Singapore):** Even though Singapore is a shopper's paradise, it could still use more places like Arab Street. Small shops selling everything from textiles to handicrafts line the street. Bargaining is welcome. See p. 169.
- **Central Market (Kuala Terengganu, Malaysia):** This huge bustling market turned me into a shopping freak. All of the handicrafts Terengganu is famous

for come concentrated in one exciting experience: batik, songket cloth, brassware, basket weaving—the list goes on. See p. 269.
- **Petaling Street (Kuala Lumpur, Malaysia):** This night market gets very, very crowded and crazy with all who come for watches, handbags, computer software, DVDs, and all manner of blatant disregard for international copyright laws. See p. 227.

12 THE BEST SHOPPING BARGAINS

- **Batik (Singapore and Malaysia):** While most of the batiks you find in Singapore come from Indonesia, many in Malaysia are made at factories that you can often tour. The Indonesian prints usually show traditional motif and colors, while Malaysian designs can be far more modern. Look for batik silk as well. See chapters 8, 13, and 14.
- **Knockoffs and Pirated Goods (Malaysia):** Check out how real those watches look! And so cheap! You can find them at any night market. Ever dream of owning a Gucci? Have I got a deal for you! Can I tell you about pirate DVDs and computer software without getting

my book banned? Uh, okay, whatever you do, don't buy these items! See chapters 8 and 13.
- **Silver Filigree Jewelry (Malaysia):** This fine silver is worked into detailed filigree jewelry designs to make brooches, necklaces, bracelets, and other fine jewelry.
- **Pewter (Malaysia):** Malaysia is the home of Selangor Pewter, one of the largest manufacturers of pewter in the world, and their many showrooms have all sorts of items to choose from. For locations in Kuala Lumpur, Penang, Malacca, and Johor, call the company hotline at (℡) **03/422-1000.**

13 THE BEST NIGHTLIFE

- **Singapore, the whole city:** Nightlife is becoming increasingly sophisticated in

Singapore, where locals have more money for recreation and fun. Take the time to choose the place that suits your personality. Jazz club? Techno disco? Cocktail lounge? Wine bar? Good old pub? The city has it all. See p. 175.

- **Bangsar (near Kuala Lumpur, Malaysia):** Folks in Kuala Lumpur know to go to Bangsar for nighttime excitement. A couple of blocks of concentrated restaurants, cafes, discos, pubs, and wine bars will tickle any fancy. Good people-watching, too. See p. 229.

Singapore in Depth

A little red dot in the center of Southeast Asia, Singapore is a cosmo-politan city built on the backs of immigrants from across Asia and the four corners of the world. The nation's cultural mix continues to expand, thanks to continuing migrations of foreign talent—one in three people in Singapore today has come from elsewhere. This cultural diversity is refreshing, but not nearly as refreshing as the sense of openness and harmony that exists between races and religions.

Singapore Inc. runs like clockwork. Over 40 decades of political stability have seen the seeds of development take hold and grow at an impressive rate. The government is a well-oiled machine that operates like the executive board of a massive company, carefully plotting deliberate steps for economic growth and building a safe and orderly country. Even its detractors concede: Singapore works.

I'll confess, many travelers complain to me about how Westernized Singapore is. For some, a vacation in Asia should be filled with culture shock and bizarre sights. Today's travel philosophy seems to be that the more underdeveloped and obscure a country is, the more "authentic" the travel experience will be. But with all its shopping malls, imported fashion and steel skyscrapers, Singapore looks like any other contemporary city in any other part of the world. But to peel through the layers is to understand that life here is more complex. While the outer layers are startlingly Western, just underneath lies a curious area where East blends with West in language, cuisine, attitude, and style. At the core, you'll find a sensibility rooted in the cultural heritage of values, religion, superstition, and memory.

For me, this is where the fascination begins. Like the rows of historic shophouses that line the city's oldest streets, if you look closely you'll see a jumble of influences from colonial architectural mandates to Chinese superstitions and Malay finery. Even the local language is a blend: "Singlish," the unofficial local tongue, combines English language with Chinese grammar, common Malay phrases, and Hokkien slang to form a Patois unique to this part of the world. It's a cultural convergence that's been ongoing for almost 200 years. So, in a sense, Singapore is no different today than it was a century ago. And in this I find my "authentic" experience.

1 SINGAPORE TODAY

Who would have believed that Singapore would rise to such international fame and become the vaunted "Asian Tiger" it has in recent decades? This small country's political stability and effective government have inspired many other nations to study its methods, and former prime minister (and current minister mentor) Lee Kuan Yew is counted among the most respected political figures in the world. When asked to explain how Singapore's astounding economic, political, and social success was made possible, Lee always takes the credit—and deservedly so—but in the face of international criticism for dictatorial policies, absolutist law enforcement, and human rights violations, he also stands first in line to take the heat.

THE SINGAPOREAN PEOPLE

Many tourists come to Singapore for the shopping or the sights, but I love the people. Most often, when you travel in foreign lands, the people you meet are other international travelers. In Singapore, however, the friends you make are many times Singaporean—perhaps it's because of the common language, perhaps because Singaporeans are very open to Western culture.

The median age of the population is around 35, with most Singaporeans struggling to juggle work and family responsibilities the same as in any other post-industrialized country. While most Singaporeans of both sexes tend to focus on educational and career goals, most also marry later and have children later, a trend that has left the government worried about a declining birth rate. Yet even with these demands, your average Singaporean never loses sight of "Asian family values" that encourage children to live with and care for their aging parents—many households are multigenerational.

There's an ever-present image consciousness fuelled by heavy consumerism. Fashion, cars, and social scenes are "in." Money is in. Success is in. Young Singaporeans strive for what they call the 5Cs—career, condo, car, cash, and credit cards—and it sometimes seems they'll stop at nothing to achieve them.

As with any modern culture, while the younger generations are busy finding their niche in the world, it is the older generations who keep traditional cultures alive. Singapore's resident population, measured at 3.64 million people, is a mix of Chinese (75%); Malays (13.7%); Indians (8.7%); and others (2.6%), including Eurasians. (The total population is 4.84 million, which includes foreigners living and working in Singapore.) Though the country is overwhelmingly Chinese, the government has embraced all local heritage, recognizing religious holidays and festivals and promoting racial harmony in its policies as part of its plan to foster a single national identity molded from the disparate cultural backgrounds of the Singaporean populace.

Unfortunately, this government social planning may have contributed to one of the common problems that plague Singapore's younger generations today: a lack of identity. No longer solely immersed in the traditions of their own ethnic groups and with traditional values being rapidly replaced by commercialism, it's not surprising to hear so many young people ask, "Who am I?"

The Chinese

When Raffles opened Singapore's port for free trade, junkloads of Chinese immigrated to find their fortunes. Most were poor workers from China's southern regions who brought with them different cultures and dialects from their respective places of origin. Of the mix, the Hokkiens from Fujian Province are the largest percentage of Chinese in Singapore, at 42%, followed by the Teochews, of Guangdong province, the Cantonese, also from Guangdong; the Hakkas, from central China; and finally the Hainanese, from Hainan island (near Hong Kong), at 6%.

The Chinese are over 50% Buddhist, following the dharma of the Buddha, who taught that all life is suffering and the only

---

(Fun Facts)   **The Little Red Dot**

Singapore is the second most densely populated county in the world, behind Monaco.

ⓘ Tips   Etiquette: The Right Hand

While in Singapore, try to use only your right hand in social interaction. Why? Because in Indian and Muslim society, the left hand is used only for bathroom chores. Not only should you eat with your right hand and give and receive all gifts with your right hand, but you should make all gestures, especially pointing (and especially in temples and mosques), with your right hand. By the way, you should also try to point with your knuckle rather than your finger, to be more polite.

way to relieve suffering is to dispel desire. Early immigrants brought Buddhism from China with them, of a sect called Mahayana, or the Greater Vehicle, the branch of Buddhism that also claims Tibetan and Zen Buddhist traditions.

Despite religious affiliation, almost every Chinese is Taoist to some degree. Tao is a philosophy as opposed to religion. Tao, meaning "the way," follows the belief in an energy source, "chi," that permeates all living and nonliving creatures and objects in the universe. This energy force links everything, shifting from place to place, sometimes flowing freely to create positive energy and sometimes stagnating to create bad vibes.

Tao is the philosophy behind feng shui, or Chinese geomancy, laws of nature that dictate how buildings and spaces should be situated and the furnishings placed inside, as well as the reasoning behind Chinese traditional medicine that uses herbs and natural remedies to keep good chi flowing throughout the body.

Chinese tradition is also filled with rich tales of heroes and heroines, gods and goddesses, who watch over the physical world. In Singapore you find statues in temples for Ma Cho Po, the Mother of Heavenly Sages, who protects sailors and other travelers, and Kuan Yin, the Goddess of Mercy—these are only two of a number of gods and goddesses of Chinese legend who still play important roles in the everyday lives of local Singaporeans.

Characteristically, the Chinese are very superstitious, with numbers playing a critical role in everyday decisions, preferring auspicious numbers for automobile license plates and choosing dates that contain lucky numbers for business openings. Here's another superstition—don't leave your chopsticks sticking up in your rice bowl; it invites hungry ghosts.

The Malays

When Raffles arrived, Malays had already inhabited the island, fishing the waters and trading with other local seafaring people, and many more were to migrate from the mainland in the decades to follow.

Although Singapore's Malay population is very low in numbers today, the language on the street is Malay, some of the best-loved local dishes are Malay, and even the national anthem is sung in Malay. The shame is that while Malays are recognized as the original inhabitants, they constantly feel marginalized by the dominant Chinese culture and policy. In addition, this group represents an unbalanced percentage of the lower-income classes, with the lowest levels of education and the highest number of criminal offenders. The government prides itself on policies to promote racial harmony, but it is widely accepted that Malays occupy jobs on the low end of the pay scale. Even in the military, while there are many Malays in the enlisted troops, there are almost none in the officer ranks.

Good Vibrations

Chinese geomancy, also known as *feng shui,* has made a mark on the Singapore landscape. Nowhere is this practice more evident than at Suntec City. The combined convention center, shopping mall, and office space occupies five towers. Placed in a semicircle, the towers represent the five digits of an open hand. In the center, an unusual round fountain, the largest fountain in the world, sprays water inward. As water means wealth, the fountain is a symbol of money flowing into a hand.

On a positive note, it is widely understood that the Malays have the greatest sense of community in Singapore. Families still congregate around the neighborhood mosque, and there's a greater sense of charity and commitment to helping those less fortunate.

Virtually every Malay is Muslim, either practicing or nonpracticing, following the teachings of the Islamic prophet Muhammad. Most Singaporeans are quite moderate in their beliefs and very open toward those of other faiths. You will, however, notice that quite a few eat only *halal* food, prepared according to strict Islamic dietary laws. And while some women choose to wear a *tudung,* a scarf to cover their heads, it is purely voluntary here. Actually, Malay women have a great sense of style; their *kurau baju,* long flowing tunics, often show off lively colors. But don't be surprised if you see younger Malays in the clubs drinking alcohol.

The Peranakans

Until recently, you didn't hear much about the Peranakans, also called Straits Chinese, a subculture of the colonial era that grew out of intermarriage between the Chinese and Malays. But recent trends to embrace Singapore's heritage has rekindled interest in this small yet influential group who are unique to Singapore and Malaysia.

In the early days of Singapore, immigration of Chinese women was forbidden, so many Chinese men found wives within the native Malay population. The resultant ethnic group combined characteristics of each culture but found a middle ground in language and religion, which tended to be English and Christianity, respectively. This mixed heritage allowed them to become strong economic and political players, often serving as middlemen between Chinese, Europeans, and other locals. Singapore's early *towkays* (big bosses) were mostly Peranakan, and, in fact, Minister Mentor Lee Kuan Yew himself is of this cultural background.

Peranakan literally means "Straits-born," so technically speaking, all people born in Singapore and Malaysia can argue they are Peranakan, and in a lot of literature you may see the term used broadly. Today, though, with many Singaporeans able to trace their heritage to this ethnic group, a heritage society has developed to support their interests and keep their culture alive.

The Indians

Many Indians were aboard Raffles's ship when it first landed on the banks of the Singapore River, making this group one of Singapore's earliest recorded immigrants. In the following decades, many more Indians would follow to find work and wealth. Some found positions in the government as clerks, teachers, policemen, and administrators, following the English colonial administration set by the British Raj in India. Others were moneylenders and financiers. Still more were laborers who came to make a buck.

Chew on This

Contrary to popular belief, it's perfectly legal to chew gum in Singapore, and you can bring in small quantities for personal consumption with no problems. It is, however, illegal to import and sell it. The story goes that after the multibillion-dollar Mass Rapid Transit (MRT) system opened, vandals brought the network to a halt when they disposed of chewed gum by jamming the trains' door sensors. The ban took effect in 1992.

In 1825, hundreds of Indians who had been imprisoned in Bencoolen (in Sumatra) were transferred to Singapore, where they worked as laborers. These convicts built many of the government buildings and cathedrals—for instance, St. Andrew's Cathedral, Sri Mariamman Temple, and the Istana—and worked on heavy-duty municipal projects. Eventually, they served their sentences and assimilated into society, many remaining in Singapore.

While most Indian immigrants were from the southern regions of India, there is still great diversity within the community. The largest group by far is the Tamils, but you'll also find Malayalis, Punjabis, and Gujaratis. So despite Little India's reputation as an Indian enclave, the Indian population is actually split into groups based on social divisions and settled in pockets all over the city. The Indians were also divided by religious affiliation, with factions split between Islam and Hinduism, which revolves around the holy trinity of Shiva, Vishnu, and Brahma but includes many, many other deities; other groups include Sihks and Christians as well. Interestingly, while the Buddha and Buddhism originally came from India, few Indians follow his teachings in India and around the world.

The Indians tend to be an informal and warm people, adding their own brand of casual ease to Singapore life. But any Singaporean will tell you that one of the most precious contributions the Indians made is their cuisine. Indian restaurants are well patronized by all ethnic groups because the southern Indian vegetarian cooking is the only food that can be enjoyed by all Singaporeans no matter what cultural or religious dietary laws they may have.

Recently Indians have become somewhat discontented with life in Singapore, feeling overwhelmed by a Chinese government they feel promotes Chinese culture. Indians are some of the most open critics of government practices.

THE GOVERNMENT

Since Lee's election, and without debate, his unfailing vision of a First World Singapore has inspired the policies and plans that created the political and economic miracle we see today. During his tenure, he mobilized government, industry, and citizens toward fulfilling his vision, establishing a government almost devoid of corruption, a strong economy built from practically no resources except labor, and a nation of racial and religious harmony from a multiethnic melting pot.

Both critics and admirers refer to Lee Kuan Yew as a strict yet generous "father" to the "children" of Singapore, raising them to a high position on the world stage yet dictating policies that have cost citizens many of their personal freedoms. You'll find that the average Singaporean expresses some duality about this: He or she will be outwardly critical of the government's invasion of privacy and disregard for personal freedoms and of policies that have driven up the cost of housing and healthcare, but will also recognize all that Lee has done to raise Singaporeans' standard of living, expand their opportunities for the future, and ensure tranquillity at home—achievements for which many are willing to sacrifice a certain amount of freedom to enjoy. By and large, they wish to see the current government continue its work.

Lee stepped down from the prime minister's chair in 1990, assuming the position of senior minister. He was replaced by Goh Chok Tong, who for 14 years continued the long-term policies driven by Lee and the PAP. Goh was a popular leader, who, in addition to initiating increased citizen participation in the political process, supported local visual and performing arts.

In August 2004, Goh passed the prime minister's baton to Lee Hsien Loong, Lee Kuan Yew's son. The resulting cabinet shift created a new position for Lee Kuan Yew as minister mentor, with Goh filling the senior minister seat.

THE CENSORSHIP QUESTION

One infamous feature of Singapore's government is its control over media, both domestic and international. All national news publications have ties to the government, whose philosophy holds that the role of the media is to promote the government's goals. Articles are censored for any content that might threaten national security, incite riot, or promote disobedience or racism. Pornographic materials are also prohibited. Offenders face stiff fines.

It doesn't stop at the print media, either. Television is also censored, as is cable television content, and satellite dishes are banned. The Internet provided Singapore with a tough dilemma. By design, the Net promotes freedom of communication, which is taken advantage of by, among others, every political dissident and pornographer who can get his hands on a PC. This thought so concerned the Singapore government that it debated long and hard

about allowing access to its citizens. However, the possibilities for communications and commerce and their implications for the future of Singapore's economy won.

THE ECONOMY

Singapore's economy is a bizarre marriage between free trade and government control. Lee Kuan Yew's vision and resulting policies have created annual national growth rates of between 7% and 9% going on 3 decades. Singapore survived the East Asian Economic Crisis that began in July 1997 because of its firm bank-lending regulations and transparent government and business dealings. Unfortunately, Singapore limped through the economic slump that plagued the globe in the years to follow, and in 2003 suffered from the SARS outbreak. The biggest moneymakers are the electronics industry, financial and business services, transportation and communications, petroleum refining and shipping, construction, and tourism. Seventy-six percent of Singapore's exports (not counting oil exports) go to the United States, Malaysia, the European Union, Hong Kong, and Japan.

In January 2009, in the face of a global recession, the Singapore government revised its GDP growth forecast for the year to between –5.0 and –2.0 percent. Days later, it unveiled a S$20.5 billion (US$13.7 billion/£9.2 billion) economic stimulus package designed to help keep the country afloat. The move was unprecedented, as it was the first time the government has ever loosened its tight grip on its coffers. The money will be spent to preserve jobs; stimulate bank lending; improve infrastructure, education, and health sectors; and provide both tax measures to help cash flow and tax rebates to bolster households.

Singaporeans enjoy a high standard of living, with average annual incomes reaching S$49,900 (US$33,433/£22,455), according to 2007 estimates.

TOURISM

The Singapore Tourism Board has far-reaching influence that has helped to turn Singapore into a veritable machine for raising foreign cash. In 2008, 10.1 million tourists visited Singapore, spending S$14.8 billion (US$9.9 billion/£6.7 billion) during their stays.

Not content to rest on its laurels, Singapore has big plans to dramatically increase these numbers over the next few years with the building of two casinos built into integrated resorts, abbreviated locally as IRs. The Marina Bay Sands, located in the heart of Singapore's downtown business district, will include a casino, hotel rooms, convention facilities, and leisure facilities—it's slated to open in stages from the end of 2009. On Sentosa Island, to the south of the business district, Resorts World at Sentosa will include, in addition to a casino, a Universal Studios theme park plus countless family-oriented attractions and resort-style accommodations.

A landmark move by the Singapore government, the establishment of legalized gambling marks the end of a conservative era in the history of this notoriously squeaky-clean city-state.

2 LOOKING BACK AT SINGAPORE

By the 1800s, European powers had already explored much of the world, staking their authority over major trade routes. Southeast Asia's initial attraction was its position between two seasonal monsoons—one half of the year saw winds that carried sailing vessels from China to Southeast Asia, while the other half of the year favored ships coming from India and Arabia. The English, Dutch, Portuguese, French, and Spanish, recognizing Southeast Asia's advantage, scrambled to set up trading posts to receive valuable tea, opium, silk, spices, and other goods from China.

The British East India Company, in its rivalry with the Dutch East Indies Company, sought to control the Straits of Malacca, the narrow passage between Indonesian Sumatra and the Malay peninsula. They already had a port at Penang, an island in the north of the Straits, but it was proving an economic failure. The company charged one of its officers, Sir Stamford Raffles, with the task of locating a new post. Raffles, who knew the area well, had his heart set on a small island at the tip of the Malay peninsula.

A SLEEPY BACKWATER

At the time of its "discovery," Singapore was occupied by about 1,000 people, mainly Malay residents, *orang laut* (sea nomads), a handful of Chinese farmers, plus assorted pirates in hiding. The island had little known historical significance. An early settlement on the island, called Temasek, had been visited regularly by Chinese merchants, and later the settlement came under the rule of the far-reaching Srivijaya Empire (9th–13th c. A.D.), which was based in Palembang in Sumatra. It was the Srivijayas who named the island Singapura, or Lion City, after its leader claimed to have seen a lion on its shores. However, the Srivijayas were eventually overtaken by a neighboring power, the Java-based Majapahits. Sometime around 1390, a young Palembang ruler, Iskander Shah (aka Parameswara), rebelled against the Majapahits and fled to Singapura, where he set up independent rule. The Majapahits were quick to chase him out, and Iskander fled up the Malay peninsula to Melaka (Malacca), where he founded what would be one of the most successful trading ports in the region at the time.

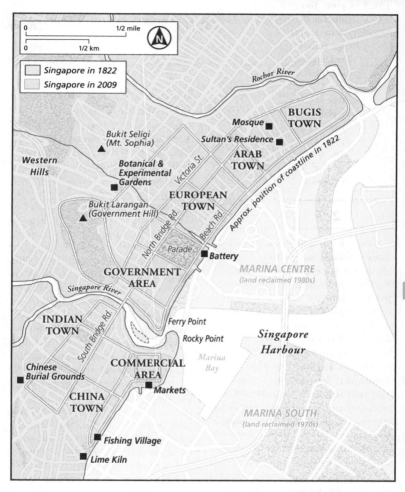

THE BRITISH EAST INDIA COMPANY ARRIVES (1819–1827)

When Raffles arrived in 1819, Singapura had been asleep for nearly 400 years under the rule of the sultan of Johor, of the southernmost province in Malaya, with local administration handled by a temenggong, or senior minister. It was Temenggong Abdu'r Rahman who, on February 6, 1819, signed a treaty with Raffles to set up a trading post on the island in return for an annual payment to the Sultanate. After this, Raffles didn't stay around for too long, handing over the Residency of the port to his friend and colleague, Col. William Farquhar.

When Raffles returned 3 years later, Singapore was fast becoming a success story. The ideally situated port was inspired

Impressions

If no untimely fate awaits it, Singapore promises to become the emporium and pride of the East.

–Sir Stamford Raffles, 1823

by Raffles's own dream of free trade and Farquhar's skill at orderly administration. The population had grown to more than 11,000—Malays, Chinese, Bugis (from Celebes in Indonesia), Indians, Arabs, Armenians, Europeans, and Eurasians. The haphazard sprawl convinced Raffles to draft the Town Plan of 1822, assigning specific neighborhoods to the many ethnic groups that had settled. These ethnic enclaves remain much the same today—Singapore's Chinatown, the administrative center or Historic District, Kampong Glam, and other neighborhoods are still the ethnic centers they originally were (of course, with many modern alterations).

This would be the last trip Raffles would make to the island that credits him with its founding. His visit in 1822 was merely a stop on his way back to London to retire. Raffles had big plans for his career with the East India Company but never witnessed any of his ambitions come to fruition. In 1826 he died before he was even recognized for the role he played in the expansion of the British Empire—he died penniless. He remains, however, a hero to modern-day Singaporeans.

In 1824, the Dutch finally signed a treaty with Britain acknowledging Singapore as a permanent British possession, and Sultan Hussein of Johor ceded the island to the East India Trading Company in perpetuity. Three years later, Singapore was incorporated, along with Malacca and Penang, to form the Straits Settlements. Penang was acknowledged as the settlements' seat of government, with direction from the Presidency of Bengal in India.

EARLY IMMIGRANT COMMUNITIES

Singapore's first 40 years were filled with all the magic of an oriental trading port. Chinese coolie laborers came to Singapore in droves to escape economic hardship at home. Most were from one of four major dialect groups: Hokkien, Teochew, Cantonese, and Hakka, all from southern China. Living in crowded bunks in the buildings that sprang up behind the go-downs, or warehouses, these immigrants formed secret societies, social and political organizations made up of residents who shared similar ancestry or Chinese home-towns. These clan groups helped new arrivals get settled and find work, and carried money and messages back to workers' families in China. But it was the secret societies' other contribution—to gambling, street crime, and violence—that helped fuel Singapore's image as a lawless boomtown, filled with all the excitement and danger of a frontier town in America's Wild West. Surrounded by boundless opportunity, many Chinese immigrants found great success, building fortunes as businessmen and traders.

Indians were quick to become Singapore's second-largest community. Most were traders or laborers, but many others were troops carried with the Brits. Most came from southern India, from the mainly Tamil-speaking population, including the Chettiars, Muslim moneylenders who financed the building of several places of worship in the early neighborhoods. After 1825, the British turned over possession of Bencoolen on Sumatra to the Dutch, transferring the thousands of

Resource Scarcity

Entrepôt trade is the term given when imported commodities are processed, graded and repackaged, and then exported at a markup. For a resource-scarce city like Singapore, entrepôt trade has been a lifeline: In the late 19th century, Singapore was the world's largest tin-smelting center. Today Singapore is the third-largest petroleum refiner, importing oil from Malaysia and Indonesia.

Indian prisoners incarcerated there to Singapore, where they were put to work constructing the buildings and clearing the land that the fledgling settlement needed. After they'd worked off their sentences, many stayed in Singapore to work their trade as free men.

During this period, the Istana Kampong Glam was built in Raffles's designated Malay enclave, along with the Sultan Mosque. The surrounding streets supported a large but modest Malay settlement of businesses and residences.

THE BOOMTOWN YEARS (1827–1942)

Despite early successes, Singapore was almost entirely dependent on entrepôt trade, which was literally at the whim of the winds. Dutch trading power still threatened its economic health, and the opening of Chinese trading ports to Western ships placed Singapore in a precarious position. The soil on the island barely supported a small sago palm industry, and with the lack of natural resources, Singapore had to constantly look to trade for survival. True economic stability wouldn't arrive until the 1860s.

Major changes around the globe had an enormous effect on Singapore in the second half of the 19th century. In 1869, the Suez Canal opened, linking the Mediterranean and the Red Sea and putting Singapore in a prime position on the Europe–East Asia route. In addition, steamship travel made the trip to Singapore less dependent on trade winds. The

shorter travel time not only saw entrepôt trade leap to new heights, but also allowed leisure travelers to consider Singapore a viable stop on their itinerary.

The blossoming Industrial Revolution thirsted for raw materials, namely tin and rubber. Malaya was already being mined for tin, much of which changed hands in Singapore. Rubber didn't enter the scene until 1877, when "Mad" Henry Ridley, director of the Botanic Gardens, smuggled the first rubber seedlings from Brazil to Singapore. After developing a new way to tap latex, he finally convinced planters in Malaya to begin plantations. To this day rubber remains a major industry for Malaysia.

WORLD WAR II

Although the British maintained a military base of operations on the island, Singapore was virtually untouched by World War I. Just before the Great Depression, however, Britain bowed to U.S. pressure and broke off relations with Japan due to the latter's increasing military power. At this time, Singapore's defense became a primary concern; however, the British, believing any invasion would come by sea, installed heavy artillery along the southern coastline, leaving the north of the island virtually unprotected.

In 1941, on the night of December 7, the Japanese attacked Pearl Harbor, invaded the Philippines and Hong Kong, landed in southern Thailand, and dropped the first bombs on Singapore.

Made in Singapore

Tiger Balm is one of Singapore's most endearing global brands. The herbal ointment, which comes in tiny glass pots covered in colorful postage-stamp paper scrawled with Chinese characters and a leaping tiger, was actually invented in Burma in the late 1800s by Aw Chu Kin. In 1920, his two sons, Aw Boon Haw and Aw Boon Par, moved the business to Singapore, where it has been based since.

Japanese Lieut. General Yamashita, emerging from battles in Mongolia, saw a definite advantage in Singapore's unprotected northern flank and stealthily moved three divisions—almost 20,000 troops—down the Malay Peninsula on bicycles. On the evening of February 8, 1942, the army quietly invaded the island. For days, the British tried to hold off their attackers, but lost ground. Within days, the Japanese were firmly entrenched.

The occupation brought terrible conditions to multiethnic Singapore, as the Japanese ruled harshly and punished any word of dissent with prison or worse. Mass executions were commonplace, prisoners of war were tortured and killed, and it was said that the beaches at Changi ran red with blood. Some prisoners that survived were sent to Thailand to work on the railway. Conditions were worst for the island's Chinese, many of whom were arrested indiscriminately simply because of their ethnicity, rowed out to sea, and dumped overboard. Little information from the outside world, save Japanese propaganda, reached Singapore's citizens during this time. Poverty, sickness, and starvation became a daily reality.

Mercifully, the Japanese surrender came before Singapore became a battleground once again. On September 5, 1945, British warships arrived, and a week later, the Japanese officially surrendered to Lord Louis Mountbatten, supreme Allied commander in Southeast Asia.

THE POSTWAR YEARS

Under British rule once again, Singapore spent the following 10 years revitalizing itself, while efforts to become a fully self-governing nation were tantamount. Living conditions were terrible and food was scarce, but the British helped with post-occupation reconstruction to clean up the port and harbor and return them to civilian control, restore public utilities, and overhaul the police force. However, resentment against the British was very strong for the way they'd lost the island to the Japanese in 1941.

THE RISE OF LEE KUAN YEW & SINGAPOREAN INDEPENDENCE

In 1949, Lee Kuan Yew, a third-generation Straits Chinese and a law student at Cambridge, formed a discussion group in London aimed at bringing together Malayan overseas students. Upon his return to Singapore, his education completed, Lee made a name for himself as an effective courtroom lawyer. Around this time, Chinese in Malaya were forming the Malaya Communist Party, inspired by mainland China's break from Western hegemonic powers, as a path toward national independence. Although Lee secretly detested communist politics, he recognized the strength of their numbers. Backed by local communists, he formed the People's Action Party (PAP).

By 1957, Malaya had gained independence, and Singapore was granted permission to establish its own fully elected,

51-seat Legislative Assembly. In the first elections for this body, in 1959, the popular PAP swept 43 of the seats and Lee Kuan Yew became the city-state's first prime minister. It wasn't until after his election that it became evident that Lee's politics were not in line with communist ideals.

After his election, it was Lee's wish to see Singapore and Malaya unite as one nation, but the Malayan government was fearful of Singapore's dominant Chinese influence and fought to keep the city-state out. In 1963, however, they broke down

and admitted Singapore as a member. It was a short-lived marriage. When the PAP began to expand its influence throughout Malaysia, as the new union was renamed, the latter became distrustful and demanded Singapore be expelled. On August 9, 1965, Singapore found itself an entirely independent country. Lee's tearful television broadcast announcing Singapore's expulsion from Malaysia and simultaneous gain of independence is one of the most famous in Singapore's history. In 1971, the last British military forces left the island.

3 SINGAPORE IN POPULAR CULTURE

BOOKS

If you're having trouble finding nonfiction books about Singapore in bookstores where you live, I suggest you wait until you arrive, then browse local shelves, where you'll find tons of books about the country and its history, culture, arts, food, along with local fiction. For interesting and informative reads that you can find (or order) through your neighborhood bookstore, here's a good place to start:

From Third World to First: The Singapore Story: 1965–2000, by Lee Kuan Yew (HarperCollins), details the history and policies behind Singapore's remarkable economic success, written by the man who was at the helm.

The Singapore Story: Memoirs of Lee Kuan Yew, by Lee Kuan Yew (Prentice Hall). An intimate account of Minister Mentor Lee's personal journey, this book will give insight into one of the world's most talked-about leaders.

Crossroads: A Popular History of Malaysia & Singapore, by Jim Baker (Times Books International). A readable history of Singapore and Malaysia from a longtime resident and expert.

The Singapore Grip, by J. G. Farrell (Knopf). A highly enjoyable work of historical fiction written by a Booker Prize

winner takes you back to Singapore on the brink of World War II to examine the last days of the British Empire.

King Rat, by James Clavell (Dell). In this novel set in Singapore during the Japanese Occupation, an American POW struggles to outwit the system in a harsh prison camp.

Lord Jim, by Joseph Conrad (Penguin Classics). Written in 1900, this classic narrative tells the story of a man's struggle to find redemption in a Southeast Asian post.

West from Singapore, by Louis L'Amour (Bantam). Few knew that Mr. L'Amour was a Merchant Marine in Southeast Asia. In this novel, he creates his brand of fascinating American West storytelling, only this tale takes place in the waters around pre–World War II Singapore.

Rogue Trader, by Nick Leeson (Time Warner). The subtitle says it all: "How I Brought Down Barings Bank and Shook the Financial World," written by Singapore's most notorious expatriate.

FILM

Few major motion pictures have been shot in or are about Singapore. Of note is Peter Bogdanovich's *Saint Jack* (1979), the only American film to have been shot entirely in Singapore. It was banned by the Singapore government, as it had been filmed secretly, capturing the city's seedy underbelly. The film is based on a (currently out-of-print) novel by Paul Theroux of the same name. Ben Gazarra plays the title character, who is a pimp in 1970s Singapore. In 2008, the film was finally removed from the black list.

Nick Leeson's autobiographical work *Rogue Trader* was made into a movie of the same name in 1999 starring Ewan McGregor.

While Singapore has a small fledgling local film industry, one director has received top honors at film festivals around the world for his excellent homegrown Singapore films. Director Eric Khoo's most recent project *My Magic* (2008) was nominated for the Golden Palm at the 61st Cannes Film Festival, where the film's screening prompted a 15-minute standing ovation.

4 EATING AND DRINKING IN SINGAPORE

Singaporeans pride themselves in their local cuisine, many times traveling to far corners of the island just to seek out the perfect wonton or the most succulent chili crab. The true local eating experience is the open-air hawker center, where tiny cooking stalls are operated by families who hand secret recipes down through generations—the best stalls can attract long lines daily. Choose from traditional Chinese, Malay, and Indian favorites under one roof. A meal at a hawker center is undoubtedly one of the truest Singaporean encounters.

Excellent cuisine from around the world can also be found in restaurants that range from moderately priced cafes and small venues to veritable palaces of gastronomy.

Connoisseurs may be interested to visit Singapore either in April, during the **World Gourmet Summit** (www.worldgourmetsummit.com), or in July, during the **Singapore Food Festival** (www.singaporefoodfestival.com).

CHINESE CUISINE

The large Chinese population in Singapore makes this obviously the most common type of food you'll find, and by right, any good description of Singaporean food should begin with the most prevalent Chinese regional styles. Many Chinese restaurants in the West are lumped into one category—Chinese—with only mild acknowledgment of Sichuan and dim sum. But China's a big place, and its size is

---

ⓘ Tips   How to Handle Your Asian Meal

You'll notice that not all Asians use chopsticks. The Chinese, Japanese, Koreans, and Vietnamese use them, while the Thais, Malays, and Indians do not (except for some noodle dishes). How can you tell who uses what? If your rice is served in a bowl, use chopsticks. If it's served on a flat plate, use a combination fork and spoon (the spoon is the actual eating utensil, the fork used only to push the food around).

Southern Indians and Malays also eat with their hands. If you choose to try this traditional style of eating, make sure to wash your hands before and after your meal, and use only your right hand for the task.

Don't stick them upright in any dish, don't gesture with them, and don't suck on them. Dropped chopsticks are also considered bad luck.

reflected in its many different tastes, ingredients, and preparation styles.

A lot of hawker center fare is inspired by regional Chinese home cooking. Local favorites like carrot cake (white radishes that are steamed and pounded until soft, then fried in egg, garlic, and chili), Hokkien *bak ku teh* (boiled pork ribs in an herbal soup), Teochew *kway teow* (stir-fried rice noodles with egg, prawns, and fish), and the number-one favorite for foreigners, Hainanese *chicken rice* (poached sliced chicken breast served over rice cooked in chicken stock). See section 8, "Hawker Centers," in chapter 6 for more on the hawker food scene.

Fusion cuisine has been hitting the market hard as globalization takes control of Singaporean palates. Also called "East meets West" or "New Asia," this cuisine combines Eastern and Western ingredients and cooking styles for a whole new eating experience. Some of it works, some of it doesn't, but true gourmet connoisseurs consider it all a culinary atrocity.

CANTONESE CUISINE Cantonese-style food is what you usually find in the West: Your stir-fries, wontons, and sweet-and-sour sauces all come from this southern region. Cantonese cooks emphasize freshness of ingredients, and typical preparation involves quick stir-frying in light oil or steaming for tender meats and crisp, flavorful vegetables. These are topped with light sauces that are sometimes sweet. Cantonese-style food also includes roasted meats like suckling pig and the red-roasted pork that's ever present in Western Chinese dishes. Compared to northern styles of Chinese cuisine, Cantonese food can be bland, especially when sauces and broths

are overthickened and slimy. Singaporean palates demand the standard dish of chili condiment at the table, which sometimes helps the flavor. One hearty Cantonese dish that has made it to local cuisine fame is **clay pot rice,** which is rice cooked with chicken, Chinese sausage, and mushrooms, prepared in—you guessed it—a clay pot.

Shark's fin soup can be found on the menu of many Cantonese restaurants, but if you have an interest in animal welfare, you may wish to steer clear, as it's considered to be endangering the world's shark population.

The Cantonese are also responsible for *dim sum* (or *tim sum,* as you'll sometimes see it written around Singapore). Meaning "little hearts," dim sum is a variety of deep-fried or steamed buns, spring rolls, dumplings, meatballs, spareribs, and a host of other bite-size treats. It's a favorite in Singapore, especially for lunch. At a dim sum buffet, dishes are offered from table to table and you simply point to what appeals. Food is served in small portions, sometimes still in the steamer. Take only one item on your plate at a time and stack the empty plates as you finish each one. Traditionally, you'd be charged by the plate, but sometimes you can find great all-you-can-eat buffets for a good price.

BEIJING CUISINE Beijing cuisine, its rich garlic and bean-paste flavoring betraying just a touch of chili, comes to us from the north of China. Heavier sauces allow for greater selections of beef and mutton, rarely found on southern Chinese menus. The most famous Beijing-style dish is **Beijing duck** (also known as Peking duck). The crispy skin is pulled away and

One from Column A, One from Column B . . .

Western cuisine serves each diner a plate with a complete meal for one. Not so with the Asians, where, even in the finest restaurants, Chinese, Indian, and every other kind of Asian fare is served "family style." To fully appreciate the experience, order a meat dish, a seafood dish, and a vegetable dish to share between two or three people. With your rice bowl in front of you, take only small servings of each dish at a time. For a larger party, add on a soup dish, plus other meat, seafood, and veggie selections for a variety of tastes to go around.

cut into pieces, which you then wrap in thin pancakes with spring onion and a touch of sweet plum sauce. The meat is served later in a dish that's equally scrumptious.

SHANGHAINESE CUISINE Shanghainese cuisine is similar to its Beijing counterpart but tends to be more oily. Because of Shanghai's proximity to the sea, Shanghainese recipes also include more fish. The exotic **drunken prawns** and the popular **drunken chicken** are both from this regional style, as is the mysterious **bird's nest soup,** made from swift's nests.

SICHUAN CUISINE Sichuan cuisine, second only to Cantonese in the West, also relies on the rich flavors of garlic, sesame oil, and bean paste, but is heavier on the chilies than Shanghainese cuisine—*much* heavier on the chilies. Sugar is also sometimes added to create tangy sauces. Some dishes can really pack a punch, but there are many Sichuan dishes that are not spicy. Popular are **chicken with dried chilies** and **hot-and-sour soup.** Another regional variation, **Hunan cuisine,** is also renowned for its fiery spice and can be distinguished from Sichuan style by its darker sauces.

TEOCHEW CUISINE Teochew cuisine uses fish as its main ingredient and is also known for its light soups. Many dishes are steamed, and in fact **steamboat,** which is a popular poolside menu item in hotels, gets its origins from this style. For steamboat, boiling broth is brought to the table, and you dunk pieces of fish, meat, and

vegetables into it, a la fondue. Other Teochew contributions to local cuisine are the **Teochew fish ball,** a springy ball made from pounded fish served in a noodle soup, and the traditional Singaporean breakfast dish *congee* (or *moi*), which is rice porridge served with fried fish, salted vegetables, and sometimes boiled egg. Also, if you see **braised goose** on the menu, you're definitely in a Teochew restaurant.

HOKKIEN CUISINE Although the Hokkiens are the most prevalent dialect group in Singapore, their style of cuisine rarely makes it to restaurant tables, basically because it's simple and homey. Two dishes that have become local cuisine favorites, however, are the **oyster omelet,** flavored with garlic and soy, and *Hokkien mee,* thick wheat noodles with seafood, meat, and vegetables in a heavy sauce.

MALAY CUISINE

Malay cuisine combines Indonesian and Thai flavors, blending ginger, turmeric, chilies, lemon grass, and dried shrimp paste to make unique curries. Heavy on coconut milk and peanuts, Malay food can at times be on the sweet side. The most popular Malay curries are *rendang,* a dry, dark, and heavy coconut-based curry served over meat; *sambal,* a red and spicy chili sauce; and *sambal belacan,* a condiment of fresh chilies, dried shrimp paste, and lime juice.

The ultimate Malay dish in Singapore is *satay,* sweet barbecued meat kabobs dipped in chili peanut sauce. Most Malay food is served as **Nasi padang**—a big pile of rice surrounded by meat, egg, vegetable, tofu, and condiments smothered in tasty, spicy gravy.

PERANAKAN CUISINE

Peranakan cuisine came out of the Straits-born Chinese community and combines such mainland Chinese ingredients as noodles and oyster sauces with local Malay flavors of coconut milk and peanuts. **Laksa lemak** is a great example of the combination, mixing Chinese rice flour noodles into a soup of Malay-style spicy coconut cream with chunks of seafood. Another favorite, **popiah,** is the Peranakan version of a spring roll, combining sweet turnip, chopped egg, chili sauce, and prawns in a delicate wrap. **Otak-otak** is very unique. It's toasted mashed fish with coconut milk and chili, wrapped in a banana leaf and grilled over flames.

INDIAN CUISINE

SOUTHERN INDIAN CUISINE Southern Indian food is a super-hot blend of spices in a coconut milk base. Rice is the staple, along with thin breads such as *prata* and *dosai,* which are good for curling into shovels to scoop up drippy curries. Vegetarian dishes are abundant, a result of Hindu-mandated vegetarianism, and use lots of chickpeas and lentils in curry and chili gravies. **Vindaloo,** meat or poultry in a tangy and spicy sauce, is also well known.

Banana leaf restaurants, surely the most interesting way to experience southern Indian food in Singapore, serve up meals on banana leaves cut like place mats. It's very informal. Spoons and forks are provided, but if you want to act local, use your hands. Remember to use your right hand only, as that is the proper etiquette, and don't forget to wash up before and after at the tap.

One tip for eating very spicy foods is to mix a larger proportion of rice to gravy.

Don't drink in between bites, but eat through the burn. Your brow may sweat, but your mouth will build a tolerance as you eat, and the flavors will come through more fully.

NORTHERN INDIAN CUISINE Northern Indian food combines yogurts and creams with a milder, more delicate blend of herbs and chilies than is found in its southern neighbor. It's served most often with breads like fluffy nans and flat chapatis. Marinated meats like chicken or fish, cooked in the tandoor clay oven, are the highlight of a northern Indian meal.

Northern Indian restaurants are more upmarket and expensive than the southern ones, but although they offer more of the comforts associated with dining out, the southern banana leaf experience is more of an adventure.

Some Singaporean variations on Indian cuisine are **mee goreng,** fried noodles with chili and curry gravy, and **fish head curry,** a giant fish head simmered in a broth of coconut curry, chilies, and fragrant seasonings.

Muslim influences on Indian food have produced **roti prata,** a humble late-night snack of fried bread served with chickpea gravy, and **murtabak,** a fried prata filled with minced meat, onion, and egg. Between the Muslims' dietary laws *(halal)* forbidding pork and the Hindus' regard for the sacred cow, Indian food is the one cuisine that can be eaten by every kind of Singaporean.

JAPANESE CUISINE

Japanese food is very popular in the city, and not only with the Japanese expat population. Singaporeans love the focus on quality fresh ingredients, as well as the ease with which you can grab sushi on a break from the office or shopping. Quality and price ranges from supermarket refrigerator sushi, to conveyer-belt restaurant chains, right up to the epicurean shrines that fly their ingredients freshly from

Tokyo's Tsujiki fish market every day. Other than sushi, plenty of places specialize in cooked foods including noodles, delicately fried tempura, and hearty dishes like *tonkatsu* (breaded, fried pork, rather like Wienerschnitzel).

SEAFOOD

One cannot describe Singaporean food without mentioning the abundance of fresh seafood. But most important is the uniquely Singaporean **chili crab,** chopped and smothered in a thick tangy chili sauce. **Pepper crabs** and **black pepper crayfish** are also a thrill. Instead of chili sauce, these shellfish are served in a thick black-pepper-and-soy sauce.

FRUITS

A walk through a wet market at any time of year will show you just what wonders the Tropics can produce. Varieties of banana, fresh coconut, papaya, mango, and pineapple are just a few of the fresh and juicy fruits available year-round; in addition, Southeast Asia has an amazing selection of exotic and almost unimaginable fruits. From the light and juicy star fruit to the red and hairy rambutan, they are all worthy of a try, either whole or juiced.

Dare to try it if you will: The fruit to sample—the veritable king of fruits—is the **_durian,_** a large green, spiky fruit that, when cut open, smells worse than old tennis shoes. The "best" ones are in season every June, when Singaporeans go wild over them. In case you're curious, the fruit has a creamy texture and tastes lightly sweet and deeply musky.

One interesting note on fruits: The Chinese believe that foods contain either yin or yang qualities with corresponding "heaty" and "cooling" effects. According to Traditional Chinese Medicine (TCM) practitioners, fried and oily foods are heaty, producing heat in the body, and, therefore, should be kept to a minimum in the Tropics, and the same is true for some fruits. Whereas watermelon, star fruit, and oranges are cooling, mangoes, litchi, and durians are heaty. Taking too many heaty foods is believed to result in a fever, aches, and sore throat, for which the best remedy is to take Chinese tea.

3

Planning Your Trip to Singapore

The seasoned traveler typically has as many travel nightmares as he has glorious experiences—the luggage gets sent to Timbuktu, the hotel reservations get lost, and the taxi driver takes the $500 scenic route to nowhere. The good news about traveling to Singapore? This place works. A seamless communications infrastructure means that you can plan your own trip, without a travel agent, and still have everything go as smoothly as if you were on an organized coach tour. Reliable phone lines, fax technology, and Internet presence make advance planning a breeze. Of course, it helps that so many Singaporeans speak English. Additionally, the Singapore Tourism Board (STB) is a wealthy and well-oiled machine that has anticipated the needs of travelers.

The STB is perhaps one of the most visible government agencies in Singapore, and it's impossible for any tourist to get out of the country without encountering at least one of its many publications or postings or coming face-to-face with one of its innumerable representatives. If you have access to one of its offices before your trip, it's a great source of information. (More information on STB is listed under "Visitor Information," below.)

In this chapter, I'll run through the nuts and bolts of travel to Singapore, letting you in on everything from how much your money will buy to the best time of year to travel, what to wear, how to get here, and how to find your way around. For additional help in planning your trip and for more on-the-ground resources in Singapore, please turn to the "Fast Facts," appendix on p. 290.

1 VISITOR INFORMATION

The long arm of the **Singapore Tourism Board (STB)** reaches many overseas audiences through its branch offices, which will gladly provide brochures and booklets to help you plan your trip, and through its detailed website, at **www.visitsingapore. com**.

After you arrive in Singapore, several visitor centers are staffed to assist, beginning with information desks at the Arrival Halls in Terminals 1, 2, and 3 at Changi Airport, open daily from 6am to 2am. Other visitor centers are located in the city as follows: at the junction of Orchard and Cairnhill roads (cater-cornered from the Meritus Mandarin Hotel), open daily from 9:30am to 10:30pm; in Little India at the InnCrowd Backpackers' Hostel, at 73 Dunlop Street, open daily from 10am to 10pm; and at Suntec Galleria, open from 10am to 6pm daily.

STB operates an information hotline from 8am to 9pm daily that is toll-free within Singapore at ✆ **800/736-2000**. Generally, STB has up-to-date information, but if you need accurate information about travel timetables, I recommend you call airlines, ferry services, bus companies, or train stations directly.

PASSPORTS

For information on how to get a passport, go to "Passports" in the "Fast Facts: Singapore" appendix (p. 293)—the websites listed provide downloadable passport applications as well as the current fees for processing passport applications. For an up-to-date, country-by-country listing of passport requirements around the world, go to the "Foreign Entry Requirement" Web page of the U.S. State Department at **http://travel.state.gov**.

VISAS

To enter Singapore, you must have a passport valid for at least 6 months from your date of entry. Leisure travelers from the United States, Canada, Australia, New Zealand, and the United Kingdom are not required to obtain a visa prior to arrival. A Social Visit Pass (with combined social and business status) good for up to 30 days (up to 90 days for U.S. visitors) will be awarded upon entry for travelers arriving by plane, or for 14 days if your trip is by ship or overland from Malaysia or Indonesia. Children traveling with parents from countries that qualify for a Social Visit Pass upon arrival can obtain entry with their own passport (provided it's valid for at least 6 months). Infants can enter on their parents' passports.

MEDICAL REQUIREMENTS

Singapore does not require any vaccinations to enter the country, unless you've been traveling in Africa or South America within 6 days of arrival, in which case you'll need a certificate that shows you've been vaccinated against yellow fever.

CUSTOMS
What You Can Bring into Singapore

There's no restriction on the amount of currency you can bring into Singapore.

For those over 18 years of age who have arrived from countries other than Malaysia and have spent more than 48 hours outside Singapore, allowable duty-free concessions are 1 liter of spirits; 1 liter of wine; and 1 liter of either port, sherry, or beer, all of which must be intended for personal consumption only. There are no duty-free concessions on cigarettes or other tobacco items. If you exceed the duty-free limitations, you can bring your excess items in upon payment of goods and services tax (GST) and Customs duty.

Prohibited Items

It is important to note that Singapore has some very unique prohibitions on the import of certain items. While pretty much every country in the world, including Singapore, prohibits travelers from bringing items like plutonium, explosives, and firearms through Customs—the same goes with agricultural products such as live plants and animals, controlled substances, and poisons—Singapore adds to the list any type of printed or recorded pornography; pirated movies, music, or software; and toy or decorative guns, knives, or swords. A detailed rundown of prohibited items can be found on the Net at the Ministry of Home Affairs home page: **www.mha.gov.sg**.

Singapore's Drug Policy

With all of the publicity surrounding the issue, Singapore's strict drug policy shouldn't need recapitulation, but here it is: Importing, selling, or using illegal narcotics is absolutely forbidden. Punishments are severe, up to and including the death penalty (automatic for morphine quantities exceeding 30 grams, heroin exceeding 15 grams, cocaine 30 grams, marijuana 500 grams, hashish 200 grams, opium 1.2 kilograms, or methamphetamines 250 grams). If you're carrying smaller sums (anything above: morphine 3 grams, heroin 2 grams, cocaine 3 grams, marijuana 15 grams, hashish 10 grams, opium 100 grams, or methamphetamines 25 grams), you'll still be considered to have intent to traffic and may face the death penalty if you can't prove otherwise. If you're crazy enough to try to bring these things into the country and you are caught, no measure of appeal to your home consulate will grant you any special attention.

What You Can Take Home from Singapore

U.S. Citizens: For specifics on what you can bring back and the corresponding fees, download the invaluable free pamphlet *Know Before You Go* online at **www.cbp. gov**. (Click on "Travel," and then click on "Know Before You Go! Online Brochure.") Or contact the U.S. Customs & Border Protection (CBP), 1300 Pennsylvania Ave. NW, Washington, DC 20229 (© **877/ 287-8667**) and request the pamphlet.

Canadian Citizens: For a clear summary of Canadian rules, write for the booklet *I Declare,* issued by the Canada Border Services Agency (© **800/461- 9999** in Canada, or 204/983-3500; www. cbsa-asfc.gc.ca).

U.K. Citizens: For information, contact **HM Customs & Excise** at © **0845/ 010-9000** (from outside the U.K., 020/ 8929-0152), or consult their website at **www.hmce.gov.uk**.

Australian Citizens: A helpful brochure available from Australian consulates or Customs offices is *Know Before You Go.* For more information, call the **Australian Customs Service** at © **1300/363-263,** or log on to **www.customs.gov.au**.

New Zealand Citizens: Most questions are answered in a free pamphlet available at New Zealand consulates and Customs offices: *New Zealand Customs Guide for Travellers, Notice no. 4.* For more information, contact **New Zealand Customs,** The Customhouse, 17–21 Whitmore St., Box 2218, Wellington (© **04/473-6099** or 0800/428-786; **www.customs.govt.nz**).

3 WHEN TO GO

A steady supply of business travelers keep occupancy rates high year-round in Singapore. However, some hotels report that business travel gets sluggish during the months of July and August, when they target the leisure market more aggressively. This is probably your best time to negotiate a favorable rate. Peak season for travel falls between December and June, with "super-peak" beginning in mid-December and lasting through the Chinese Lunar New Year, which falls in January or February, depending on the moon's cycle. During this season, Asian travel routes are booked solid and hotels are maxed out. Favorable deals are rare because much of Asia takes annual leave at this time.

As for weather, because Singapore is 137km (85 miles) north of the Equator, you can pretty much guarantee that it's hot. In terms of seasonal variations, you've got some months that are not as warm as others, but for the most part, they're all still hot.

What does vary greatly is rainfall. Singapore lies between two monsoon winds. The Northeast Monsoon arrives the beginning of November and stays until mid-March, when temperatures are slightly cooler, relatively speaking, than other times of the year. The heaviest rainfall occurs between November and January, with daily showers that sometimes last for long periods of time; at other times, it comes down in short, heavy gusts and goes quickly away. Wind speeds are rarely anything more than light. The Southwest Monsoon falls between June and September. Temperatures are much higher and, interestingly, it's during this time of year that Singapore gets the *least* rain (with the very least reported in July).

By and large, year-round temperatures remain uniform, with a daily average of 81°F (27°C), afternoon temperatures reaching as high as 87°F (31°C), and an average sunrise temperature as low as 75°F (24°C). Relative humidity often exceeds 90% at night and in the early morning. Even on a "dry" afternoon, don't expect it to drop much below 60%. (The daily average is 84% relative humidity.)

HOLIDAYS

There are 11 official public holidays (**Note:** The following dates, with regard to religious holidays, are estimates, as each date is subject to a different religious calendar. Dates provided here are for rough planning only. Please check with the STB prior to your trip to verify holidays that fall during your stay.): New Year's Day (Jan 1), Chinese New Year or Lunar New Year (Feb 14–15, 2010), Good Friday (Apr 2, 2010), Labour Day (May 1), Vesak Day (May 9, 2009; May 21, 2010), National Day (Aug 9), Hari Raya Puasa (Eid al-Fitr; Sept 20, 2009; Sept 8, 2010), Deepavali (Nov 15, 2009; Nov 5, 2010), Hari Raya Haji (Eid al-Adha; Nov 27, 2009; Nov 14, 2010), and Christmas Day (Dec 25). On these days, expect government offices, banks, and some shops to be closed.

CALENDAR OF PUBLIC HOLIDAYS & EVENTS

For an exhaustive list of events beyond those listed here, check http://events.frommers.com, where you'll find a searchable, up-to-the-minute roster of what's happening in cities all over the world.

JANUARY/FEBRUARY

New Year's Day. The first day of the calendar year is celebrated in Singapore by all races and religions. New Year's Eve in Singapore is always cause for parties similar to those in the West. Look for special events at restaurants and nightclubs, but don't expect to find a taxi when you need one. January 1.

Lunar New Year or Chinese New Year. If you want to catch the biggest event in the Chinese calendar and in Singapore, come during Chinese New Year for parades and festivals. In 2010 it begins on February 14, Valentine's Day.

Thaipusam Festival. If you're lucky enough to be in Singapore during this event, you're in for a bizarre cultural treat. This annual festival is celebrated by Hindus to give thanks to Lord Subramaniam, the child god who represents virtue, youth, beauty, and valor. During Thaipusam, male Hindus who have made prayers to Subramaniam for special wishes must carry *kavadis* in gratitude. These huge steel racks are decorated with flowers and fruits and are held onto the men's bodies by skewers and hooks that pierce the skin. Carrying the *kavadis,* the devotees parade from Sri Perumal Temple in Little India to the Sri Thandayuthapani Temple, where family members remove the heavy structures. For an additional spectacle, they will pierce their tongues and cheeks with skewers and hang fruits from hooks in their flesh. The devotees have all undergone strict diet and prayer before the festival, and it is reported that, afterward, no scars remain. Late January/early February.

Good Friday. Churches and cathedrals hold special services on this Christian holiday to remember the crucifixion of Christ. St. Joseph's on Victoria Street holds an annual candlelight procession. Late March/early April.

Qing Ming (All Souls' Day). Qing Ming, or All Souls' Day, was originally a celebration of spring. On this day, Chinese families have picnics at ancestral graves, cleaning the graves and pulling weeds, lighting red candles, burning joss sticks and "hell money" (paper money that, when burned, ascends to the afterworld to be used by ancestors), and bringing rice, wine, and flowers for the deceased in a show of ancestral piety. Early April.

The Singapore International Film Festival. This event showcases critically acclaimed works, including international films and Singaporean short productions. It's become a renowned showcase for Asian films, which constitute 40% of those featured. The festival includes competitions, workshops, and tributes to filmmakers. Schedule and ticketing information can be obtained from its website at www.filmfest.org.sg. April.

MAY

Vesak Day. Buddhist shrines and temples are adorned with banners, lights, and flowers; and worshipers gather to observe the birth, enlightenment, and death of the Buddha, which all occurred on this day. Good places to watch the festivities are the Temple of a Thousand Lights in Little India or Thian Hock Keng Temple in Chinatown. On this day, Buddhists will refrain from eating meat, donate food to the poor, and set animals (especially birds) free to show kindness and generosity. It falls on the full moon of the fifth month of the lunar calendar—which means somewhere around mid-May.

Singapore Arts Festival. During this month-long festival, premier local, regional, and international music and dance performances are staged in a number of venues. The cultural performances, some modern and some traditional, are always excellent and are highly recommended. Check out www.singaporeartsfest.com. Late May to mid-June.

JUNE

Singapore World Invitational Dragon Boat Races. The annual dragon boat races are held to remember the fate of Qu Yuan, a patriot and poet during the Warring States period in Chinese history (475–221 B.C.) who threw himself into a river to end his suffering at watching his state fall into ruin under the hands of corrupt leadership. The people searched for him in boats shaped like dragons, beating gongs and throwing rice dumplings into the water to distract the River Dragon. Today the dragon boat races are an international event, with rowing teams from up to 20 countries coming together to compete. Drums are still beaten, and rice dumplings are still a traditional favorite. Contact the STB for information. Late June/early July.

The Great Singapore Sale. This is a month-long promotion to increase retail sales, and most shops will advertise huge savings for the entire month. It's well publicized with red banners all over Orchard Road. June into July.

JULY

The Singapore Food Festival. Local chefs compete for honors in this month-long exhibition of international culinary delights. It's a good time to be eating in Singapore, as restaurants feature the brand-new creations they have entered in the events. Contact the STB for details. July.

Maulidin Nabi. Muslims celebrate the birth of the Prophet Mohammed on this day. Sultan Mosque is the center of the action for Muslims who come to chant in praise. July 17.

AUGUST

National Day. On August 9, 1965, Singapore separated from the Federation of Malaysia, becoming an independent republic. Patriotism is celebrated with a big parade held on a floating platform in Marina Bay with live performances, music, and fireworks. Tickets are available only through lottery, so few short-term visitors ever get the chance to see it live. August 9.

Festival of the Hungry Ghosts. The Chinese believe that once a year the gates of Purgatory are opened and all the souls inside are let loose to wander among the living. To appease these restless spirits and prevent evil from falling upon themselves, the Chinese burn joss, hell money, and paper replicas of luxury items, the latter two meant to appear in the afterworld for greedy ghosts to use. The main event is on the 15th day of the 7th month of the lunar calendar and is celebrated with huge feasts. At markets, altars offer mountains of goodies for hungry ghosts as well. Chinese operas are performed throughout the month to entertain the spirits and make them more docile. Nowadays, with Chinese Opera becoming a dying art, a lot of the street performances are karaoke acts. Mid-August/mid-September.

SEPTEMBER

The Mooncake and Lantern Festivals. Traditionally called the Mid-Autumn Festival, it was celebrated to give thanks for a plentiful harvest. The origins date from the Sung Dynasty (A.D. 970–1279), when Chinese officials would

exchange round mirrors as gifts to represent the moon and symbolize good health and success. Today the holiday is celebrated by eating moon cakes, which are sort of like little round hockey pucks filled with lotus seed paste or red bean paste and a salted duck egg yolk. Children light colorful plastic or paper lanterns shaped like fish, birds, butterflies, and, more recently, cartoon characters. There's an annual lantern display and competition out at the Chinese Garden, with acrobatic performances, lion dances, and night bazaars. Late September/early October.

Birthday of the Monkey God. In the Chinese temples, ceremonies are performed by mediums who pierce their faces and tongues and write prayers with the blood. In the temple courtyards, you can see Chinese operas and puppet shows. The Tan Si Chong Su Temple on Magazine Road, upriver from Boat Quay, is a good bet for seeing the ceremonies. Contact the STB for information. Late September/early October.

OCTOBER/NOVEMBER

Hari Raya Puasa. Hari Raya Puasa marks the end of Ramadan, the Muslim month of fasting during daylight hours. During Ramadan, food stalls line up around the Sultan Mosque in Kampong Glam, ready to sell tasty Malay goodies at sundown. Hari Raya Puasa is a 3-day celebration (though only the first day is a public holiday) of thanksgiving dinners, and non-Muslims are often invited to these feasts, as the holiday symbolizes an openness of heart and mind and a renewed sense of community. During the course of the 3 evenings, Geylang is decorated with lights and banners and the whole area is open for a giant *pasar malam,* or night market. In 2009 and 2010, the holiday falls in September.

Pilgrimage to Kusu Island. During this month-long period, plan your trips to Kusu Island wisely, as the place becomes a mob scene. Throughout the month (the lunar month, that is), Chinese travel to this small island to visit the temple there and pray for another year of health and wealth. See chapter 7 for more information on Kusu. October/November.

Festival of the Nine-Emperor God. During this celebration, held over the first 9 days of the ninth month of the lunar calendar (to the Chinese, the double nines are particularly auspicious), temples are packed with worshipers, hawkers sell religious items outside, and Chinese operas are performed for the Nine-Emperor God, a composite of nine former emperors who control the prosperity and health of worshipers. At the height of the festival, priests write prayers with their own blood. On the ninth day, the festival closes as the Nine-Emperor God's spirit, contained in an urn, is sent to sea on a small decorated boat. Contact the STB for information. Late October.

Navarathiri Festival. During this 9-day festival, Hindus make offerings to the wives of Shiva, Vishnu, and Brahma. The center point in the evenings is Sri Thandayuthapani Temple, where dances and musical performances are staged. Performances begin around 7:30pm. Contact the STB for information. Late October/early November.

Deepavali. Hindus and Sikhs celebrate Deepavali (also called Diwali) as the first day of their calendar. The new year is ushered in with new clothing, social feasts, and gatherings. It's a beautiful holiday, with Hindu temples aglow from the tiny earthen candles placed in crevices in the sides of walls. Hindus believe that the souls of the deceased come to earth during this time, and the candles help to light their way back to heaven. During the celebration, Serangoon Road in Little India is a mesmerizing display of colored lights and decorative arches. The dates quoted earlier in this section are estimates only, as Hindu officials had not released dates at the time of writing.

Thimithi Festival. Thimithi begins at the Sri Perumal Temple in Little India and makes its way in parade fashion to the Sri Mariamman Temple in Chinatown. Outside the temple, a bed of hot coals is prepared and a priest will lead the way, walking first over the coals, to be followed one at a time by devotees. Crowds gather to watch the spectacle, which begins around 5pm. Make sure you're early so you can find a good spot. Contact the STB for information. Late October/early November.

Christmas Light-Up. Orchard Road is brilliant in bright and colorful streams of Christmas lights and garlands. All of the hotels and shopping malls participate, dressed in the usual Christmas regalia of nativity scenes and Santa Clauses.

DECEMBER

Hari Raya Haji. One of the five pillars of Islam involves making a pilgrimage to Mecca at least once in a lifetime, and Hari Raya Haji (Eid al-Adha) is celebrated the day after pilgrims make this annual voyage to fulfill their spiritual promise. Muslims who have made the journey adopt the title of Haji (for men) and Hajjah (for women). After morning prayers, sheep and goats are sacrificed and their meat is distributed to poor families. In 2009 and 2010, this holiday falls in November.

Christmas Day. On this day, Christian Singaporeans celebrate the birth of Christ. December 25.

GETTING TO SINGAPORE
By Plane

Singapore's award-winning **Changi International Airport** is a major transportation hub for many of the world's largest passenger airlines, so flights from all corners of the globe are convenient.

In my experience, the best deals are offered through Asian carriers. Compare fares at Japan Airlines (www.jal.co.jp), Korean Air (www.koreanair.com), Cathay Pacific Airways (www.cathaypacific.com), Malaysia Airlines (www.malaysiaairlines.com), and Thai Airways International (www.thaiair.com). Otherwise, I've listed information for a few major airlines below.

Singapore's national carrier, **Singapore Airlines** (© **800/742-3333** in the U.S. and Canada, © 0844/800-2380 in the U.K., © 131011 in Australia, © 0800/808-909 in New Zealand, or © 65/6223-8888 in Singapore; www.singaporeair.com), is arguably one of the finest airlines in the world, with reliable service that is second to none. It's the most luxurious way to fly to Singapore, but sometimes the most expensive as well. It connects major cities in North America, Europe, Australia, and New Zealand to Singapore with daily flights.

From North America, **United Airlines** (© **800/864-8331** in the U.S. or 65/6873-3533 in Singapore; www.ual.com) and **Northwest Airlines** (© **800/225-2525** in the U.S. or 65/6336-3371 in Singapore; www.nwa.com) link all major destinations in the U.S. with Singapore.

From the U.K. and Australia, **British Airways** and **Qantas** collaborate to provide flights to Asia Pacific from major cities in the U.K. and Australia. (British Airways: © **0844/493-0787** in the U.K., © 1300/767-177 in Australia, or © 65/6622-1747 in Singapore; www.british

airways.com. Qantas: © **0845/774-7767** in the U.K., © 131313 in Australia, or © 65/6415-7373 in Singapore; www.qantas.com.)

From New Zealand, **Air New Zealand** has discontinued direct flights to Singapore. Contact **Singapore Airlines** (© **0800/808-909** in New Zealand, or © 65/6223-8888 in Singapore; www.singaporeair.com) for daily flights from Auckland and Christchurch.

Getting into Town from the Airport

Most visitors to Singapore will land at Changi International Airport, which is located toward the far eastern corner of the island. Compared to other international airports, Changi is a dream come true, providing clean and very efficient facilities. Expect to find in-transit accommodations, restaurants, duty-free shops, moneychangers, ATMs, car-rental desks, accommodations assistance, and tourist information all marked in English with clear signs. Three terminals are connected by a Skytrain system. When you arrive, keep your eyes peeled for the many Singapore Tourism Board brochures that are so handily displayed throughout each terminal.

The city is easily accessible by public transportation. A taxi trip to the city center will cost around S$22 to S$25 (US $15–US $17/£9.90–£11), which is the metered fare plus an airport surcharge, usually S$3 to S$5 (US$2–US$3.35/£1.35–£2.25), depending on the time of pickup. It takes around 30 minutes to reach the city. You'll traverse the wide Airport Boulevard to the Pan-Island Expressway (PIE) or the East Coast Parkway (ECP), past public housing estates and other residential neighborhoods in the eastern part of the island, over causeways, and into the city center.

If you've got a lot of people and luggage, **CityCab** offers a six-seater maxicab to anywhere in the city for a flat rate of S\$35 (US\$23/£16). You can inquire at the taxi queue or call ℂ **65/6542-8297.**

There's an **airport shuttle,** a coach that traverses between the airport and all major hotels. Booking counters at all three terminals are open daily from 6am to midnight. When you book your trip into town, you can also make an advance reservation for your departure. Pay S\$9 (US\$6.05/£4.05) for adults or S\$6 (US\$4/£2.70) for children at Terminal 1, ℂ **65/6543-1985;** Terminal 2, ℂ **65/6546-1646;** or Terminal 3, ℂ **65/6241-3818.**

The **MRT,** Singapore's subway system (see map, inside back cover), operates to the airport, linking you with the city and areas beyond. STB will tell you the trip takes 30 minutes, but really, give yourself at least an hour, because you'll need time to wait for the train to arrive, then you'll have to transfer trains at Tanah Merah station, and if you're arriving in Terminal 1, you'll need to hop on yet another train—a shuttle between terminals. After you get to your station in town, you'll still have to find your way, with your luggage, to your hotel. Personally, I think it's a pain in the neck, but hey, it costs only about S\$2.70 (US\$1.80/£1.20) to town. Trains operate roughly from 6am to midnight daily.

A couple of **buses** run from the airport into the city as well. SBS bus no. 36 is the best, with an express route to the Historic District and along Orchard Road. Pick up the bus in the basement of any terminal. The trip will take over an hour, and you'll need to get exact change before you board. A trip to town will be roughly S\$2 (US\$1.35/90p).

For arrival and departure information, you can call **Changi International Airport** at ℂ **65/6542-4422.**

By Train

While most visitors to Singapore will arrive by air, some will come via train from Malaysia. The Keretapi Tanah Melayu (KTM) operates a rail system that connects Singapore all the way up the Malay peninsula, with stops in Kuala Lumpur, Penang, and even connections to service in Thailand to Bangkok. Train passengers will stop for immigration at the checkpoint at Woodlands, just across the strait from Malaysia, but will not alight until they reach the **Singapore Railway Station** on Keppel Road (ℂ **65/6222-5165**), not far from Singapore's Shenton Way downtown financial district. Taxis to most major hotels will cost under S\$10 (US\$6.70/£4.50).

For train information from Kuala Lumpur, call **KL Sentral** railway station at ℂ **603/2267-1200.** In Bangkok, call the **Hua Lamphong Railway Station** at ℂ **622/223-7010.**

By Bus

Buses from Malaysia will drop off passengers at any number of points around the city, depending on the bus operator—there is no proper inbound bus station. For bus service from major Malaysian cities, refer to bus listings in each section. Operators will be able to tell you where you will be dropped off.

GETTING AROUND SINGAPORE

The many inexpensive mass transit options make getting around Singapore pretty easy. Of course, taxis always simplify the ground transportation dilemma. They're also very affordable and, by and large, drivers are helpful and honest, if not downright personable. The **Mass Rapid Transit (MRT) subway service** has lines that cover the main areas of the city and out to the farther parts of the island. Buses present more of a challenge because there are so many routes snaking all over the island, but they're a great way to see the country while getting where you want to go.

Of course, if you're just strolling around the urban limits, many of the sights within the various neighborhoods are within walking distance, but walking between the different neighborhoods can be a hike, especially in the heat. The STB Visitors' Centres carry a variety of free city maps and walking tour maps of individual neighborhoods to help you find your way around.

Stored-value EZ-Link fare cards can be used on both the subway and buses, and can be purchased at TransitLink offices in MRT stations. These save you the bother of trying to dig up exact change for bus meters. The card does carry a S$5 (US$3.35/£2.25) initial cost and a S$3 (US$2/£1.35) deposit—for a S$15 (US$10/£6.75) initial investment, you'll get S$7 (US$4.70/£3.15) worth of travel credit.

A better deal is the **Singapore Tourist Pass,** a card that allows unlimited travel on MRT trains and public buses for 1, 2, or 3 days. The cost is S$8 (US$5.35/£3.60) per day, with a refundable S$10 (US$6.70/£4.50) deposit. Passes can be purchased at the following MRT stations: Changi Airport, Orchard, Chinatown, City Hall, Raffles Place, Harbourfront, and Bugis, and at the STB Visitors' Centres at Changi Airport and Orchard Road.

I recommend purchasing the latest edition of the *TransitLink Guide* for about S$2 (US$1.35/90p) at the TransitLink office where you buy your card. This tiny book details both MRT and bus routes with maps of each MRT station surroundings, and it indicates connections between buses and MRT stations. It also tells you fares for each trip.

By Taxi

Taxis are by far the most convenient way to get around Singapore. Fares are cheap, cars are clean, and drivers speak English. Taxi stands can be found at every hotel, shopping mall, and public building; otherwise, you can flag one down from the side of the road. Most destinations in the main

parts of the island can be reached fairly inexpensively, while trips to the outlying attractions can cost from S$10 to S$15 (US$6.70–US$10/£4.50–£6.75) one-way. That said, I caution against becoming too dependent on them. During the morning and evening rush, you can wait a maddeningly long time in the line, and sometimes if you're at a destination outside the main city area, they're few and far between. If it's raining, you might as well stay put; you'll never get a cab.

If you do find yourself stranded, there are a few things you can do. If you're at an attraction or a restaurant, you can ask the cashier or help desk to call a taxi company and book a cab for you. If you're near a phone, you can make your own booking: **CityCab** (© **65/6552-2222**), **Comfort** (© **65/6552-1111**), and **TIBS** (© **65/6555-8888**). There's an extra charge for the booking, anywhere between S$2.50 and S$3.50 (US$1.65–US$2.35/£1.10–£1.55).

Taxis charge the metered fare, which is from S$2.80 to $3 (US$1.85–US$2/£1.25–£1.35) for the first kilometer ($^6/_{10}$ mile) and S20¢ (US10¢/5p) for each additional 300–400m (984–1,312 ft.) or 45 seconds of waiting. Extra fares are levied on top of the metered fare, depending on where you're going and when you go. At times, figuring your fare seems more like a riddle. Here's a summary:

Trips during peak hours: Between the hours of 7 and 9:30am Monday to Friday, and 5 and 8pm Monday to Saturday, meters tack on an additional 35%. If you're traveling within the Central Business District (CBD) from 5pm till midnight Monday through Saturday, you also pay an additional S$3 (US$2/£1.35) surcharge. (To accurately outline the boundaries of the CBD, I'd need to fill a couple of encyclopedia volumes, so for this purpose, let's just say it's basically Orchard

Rd., the Historic District, Chinatown, and Shenton Way.)

Additional charges rack up each time you travel through an Electronic Road Pricing (ERP) scheme underpass. On the Central Expressway (CTE), Pan-Island Expressway (PIE), and selected thoroughfares in the CBD, charges from S50¢ to S$3 (US35¢–US$2/25p–£1.35) are calculated by an electronic box on the driver's dashboard. The driver will add this amount to your fare.

And for special torture, here's some more charges: From midnight to 6am, add 50% to your fare. From 6pm on the eve of a public holiday to midnight the following day, you pay an additional S$1 (US65¢/45p). From Changi Airport, add S$5 (US$3.35/£2.25) if you're traveling Friday, Saturday, or Sunday between 5pm and midnight. Other times, it's S$3 (US$2/£1.35). And for credit card payments (yes, they take plastic!), add 10%.

By Trolley

For sightseeing trips around town, your best bet is the **SIA Hop-on bus.** Plying between Suntec City, the Historic District, the Singapore River, Chinatown, Orchard Road and the Singapore Botanic Gardens, Little India, and Sentosa, the Hop-on comes every 30 minutes between the hours of 9am and 10pm daily. Unlimited rides for 1 day cost S$12 (US$8.05/£5.40) adults and S$6 (US$4/£2.70) children. If you flew Singapore Airlines to get here, you have to pay only S$6 (US$4/£2.70) adults and S$3 (US$2/£1.35) children if you flash your boarding pass. Buy your tickets from the bus driver when you board. For info, call **SH Tours,** ✆ **65/6734-9923.**

By Mass Rapid Transit (MRT)

The MRT is Singapore's subway system. It's cool, clean, safe, and reliable, providing service around the central parts of the city, extending into the suburbs around the

island. There are stops along Orchard Road into the Historic District, to Chinatown and Little India—chances are, there will be a stop close to your hotel (see the map on the inside back cover for specifics).

Fares range from S70¢ to S$2 (US45¢–US$1.35/30p–90p), depending on which stations you travel between. System charts are prominently displayed in all MRT stations to help you find your appropriate fare, which you pay with an EZ-Link fare card. Single-fare cards can be purchased at vending machines inside MRT stations. See above for information on stored-fare cards for multiple trips. (**One caution:** A fare card cannot be used by two people for the same trip; each must have his own.)

MRT operating hours vary between lines and stops, with the earliest train beginning service daily at 5:15am and the last train ending at 12:47am. For more information, call the **TransitLink Hot Line** at ✆ **1800/225-5663** (daily 24 hr.).

By Bus

Singapore's bus system comprises an extensive web of routes that reach virtually everywhere on the island. Use an EZ-Link stored-value card to pay for your trips, and a TransitLink Guide to find your way around (see above for more details). All buses have a gray machine with a sensor pad located close to the driver. Tap your EZ-Link card when you board and alight, and the fare will be automatically deducted. It'll be anywhere between S80¢ and S$1.80 (US55¢–US$1.20/35p–80p). If you're paying cash, be sure to have exact change; place the coins in the red box by the driver and announce your fare to him. He'll issue a ticket, which will pop out of a slot on one of the TransitLink machines behind him. If you're not sure how much your fare should be, the driver can assist.

For more information, contact either of the two operating bus lines during standard business hours: **Singapore Bus Service**

(SBS; ✆ 800/287-2727) or the **Trans-Island Bus Service** (TIBS; ✆ 800/482-5433).

By Rental Car

Visitors to Singapore rarely rent cars for sightseeing, because it's just not convenient. Local transportation is excellent and affordable, you don't have to adjust to local driving rules and habits, plus there's no need to worry about where to park. Still, if you must, contact **Avis** at ✆ 800/373-1668; they operate counters in all three Changi Airport terminals daily 7am to 11pm.

5 MONEY & COSTS

Compared to its Southeast Asian neighbors, Singapore is considered expensive; however, visitors from the West will find their money still goes quite far. *The Economist* came up with a clever way to compare the standard of living from country to country. The Big Mac Index is a surprisingly credible way to consider the value of the exact same item as it differs from place to place around the globe. For example, according to the August 2008 Big Mac Index, the average price of a Big Mac in the United States is $3.57. In Singapore, the same burger is S$3.95. Convert that into U.S. dollars, and it's US$2.92—meaning, in Singapore you'll pay about U.S.65¢ less for a Big Mac. How much do you pay for your Big Mac at home? How about the U.K., at £2.29 per burger (US$4.57)? Or Australia, at A$3.45 (US$3.36)?

CURRENCY FOR SINGAPORE

The local currency unit is the **Singapore dollar.** It's commonly referred to as the "Sing dollar," and retail prices are often marked as S$ (a designation I've used throughout this book). Notes are issued in denominations of S$2, S$5, S$10, S$50, S$100, S$500, and S$1,000. S$1 bills exist but are rare. Notes vary in size and color from denomination to denomination. Coins are issued in denominations of S1¢, S5¢, S10¢, S20¢, S50¢, and the fat, gold-colored S$1. Singapore has an interchangeability agreement with Brunei Darussalam, so don't be alarmed if you receive Brunei currency with your change, as it's legal tender.

At the time of this writing, exchange rates on the Singapore dollar were as follows: US$1 = S$1.49, C$1 = S$1.22, £1 = S$2.17, A$1 = S$1, NZ$1 = S¢82. The exchange rate used throughout this book is US$1 = S$1.49, which was the average rate during late 2008/early 2009. Before you begin budgeting your trip, you can obtain the latest currency rates on the Internet at www.xe.com.

It's not an absolute necessity to buy Singapore dollars before your trip, because you can find ATMs that accept cards from the Cirrus and Plus networks at the Arrival Halls of all Changi Terminals as you exit the baggage claim area. If you do need currency changed, each terminal has money-changing services that operate 'round-the-clock.

In town, it's best to exchange currency or traveler's checks at a local authorized moneychanger, found in most shopping malls throughout the city. They'll give you the best rate. You'll lose money with the high rates at banks, hotels, and shops.

ATMS

The easiest and best way to get cash away from home is from an ATM (automated teller machine). The **Cirrus** (www.master

What Things Cost in Singapore	S$	US$	UK£
Taxi from the airport to city center	22.00	14.74	9.90
MRT from Orchard to Chinese Garden stations	1.60	1.07	0.72
Local telephone call (3 min.)	0.10	0.07	0.05
Double room at an expensive hotel	300.00	201.00	135.00
Double room at a moderate hotel	200.00	134.00	90.00
Double room at an inexpensive hotel	120.00	80.40	54.00
Dinner for one at an expensive restaurant	60.00	40.20	27.00
Dinner for one at a moderate restaurant	25.00	16.75	11.25
Dinner for one at an inexpensive restaurant	5.00	3.35	2.25
Glass of beer	9.00	6.03	4.05
Coca-Cola	1.10	0.74	0.50
Cup of coffee at common coffee shop	0.70	0.47	0.32
Cup of coffee at Starbucks, Coffee Club, and so on	2.80	1.88	1.26
Roll of 36-exposure color film	4.50	3.02	2.03
Admission to the Asian Civilisations Museum	10.00	6.70	4.50
Movie ticket	9.00	6.03	4.05

card.com) and **PLUS** (www.visa.com) networks span the globe; look at the back of your bank card to see which network you're on, then call or check online for ATM locations at your destination—in Singapore you will never be far from a machine that accepts either of these cards. It's a good idea to check your daily withdrawal limit before you depart. *Note:* Remember that banks impose a fee every time you use a card at another bank's ATM, and that fee can be higher for international transactions (up to US$5 or more) than for domestic ones (where they're rarely more than US$2). In addition, the bank from which you withdraw cash may charge its own fee. For international withdrawal fees, ask your bank.

CREDIT CARDS

Credit cards are another safe way to carry money. They also provide a convenient record of all your expenses, and they generally offer relatively good exchange rates. You can withdraw cash advances from your credit cards at banks or ATMs, provided you know your PIN. Keep in mind

that you'll pay interest from the moment of your withdrawal, even if you pay your monthly bills on time. Also note that many banks now assess a 1% to 3% "transaction fee" on **all** charges you incur abroad (whether you're using the local currency or your native currency). In Singapore, American Express, Visa, MasterCard, Diners Club, and JCB (Japan Credit Bureau) are accepted at virtually all major hotels, restaurants, nightclubs, and shopping centers. Even taxis accept payment by credit card. Smaller food and retail merchants generally don't accept plastic, and be advised, if you are trying to negotiate a discount with a vendor, you will always get a better price with good old-fashioned cash. Some retailers will insist on adding a credit card "service charge" to your bill. While it is true that the credit card companies charge the retailers a small fee each time a customer uses a card, it is a cost the retailers are supposed to bear themselves. If anyone tries to foist this charge onto you, sadly, your only recourse is to report him to your credit card company.

Singapore Dollar Conversion Chart		
S$	**US**	**$UK£**
0.10	0.07	0.05
0.20	0.13	0.09
0.50	0.34	0.23
1.00	0.67	0.45
2.00	1.34	0.90
5.00	3.35	2.25
10.00	6.70	4.50
20.00	13.40	9.00
50.00	33.50	22.50
100.00	67.00	45.00
500.00	335.00	225.00
1,000.00	670.00	450.00

TRAVELER'S CHECKS

You can buy traveler's checks at most banks. They are offered in denominations of $20, $50, $100, $500, and sometimes $1,000. Generally, you'll pay a service charge ranging from 1% to 4%.

American Express, Thomas Cook, Visa, and **MasterCard** offer **foreign currency traveler's checks,** which are accepted at moneychangers, banks, and hotels in Singapore, but are rarely accepted at shops and smaller establishments. You will be asked to produce your passport each time you cash one.

If you carry traveler's checks, keep a record of their serial numbers separate from your checks, in the event that they are stolen or lost. You'll get a refund faster if you know the numbers.

6 HEALTH

STAYING HEALTHY

As some intrepid travelers are so fond of accusing Singapore of being overly "squeaky-clean," *sane* travelers who don't want to spend their holiday infirm can rest assured that they are safe from most of the tropical world's nastiest scourges in sanitary Singapore. Food is clean virtually everywhere, tap water is potable, restaurants and food vendors are regulated by the government, and many other airborne, bug-borne, and bite-borne what-have-yous have been eradicated.

Singapore doesn't require that you have any vaccinations to enter the country but recommends immunization against diphtheria, tetanus, hepatitis A and B, and typhoid for anyone traveling to Southeast Asia in general. If you're particularly worried, follow their advice; if not, don't worry about it.

COMMON AILMENTS

TROPICAL ILLNESSES It seems inevitable for travelers from the West to suffer some sort of Montezuma's revenge or Delhi-belly when they visit the Tropics. If you suffer a bout of **diarrhea,** it could be from many causes: weakness from jet lag, adjustments to the climate, new foods, spices, or an increase in physical activity. Always carry Immodium, or a comparable antidiarrheal, but most important, don't forget to drink plenty of water to avoid dehydration. If symptoms include painful cramps, fever, or rash, seek medical attention immediately; otherwise, it'll probably just clear up by itself.

Singapore's climate guarantees heat and humidity year-round; you should remember to take precautions. Give yourself plenty of time to relax and regroup on arrival to adjust your body to the new climate (and to the new time, if there is a time difference for you). Also drink plenty of water. Avoid overexposure to the sun. The tropical sun will burn you like thin toast in no time at all. You may also feel more lethargic than usual. This is typical in the heat, so take things easy and you'll be fine. Be careful of the air-conditioning, though. It's nice and cooling, but if you're prone to catching a chill, or find yourself moving in and out of air-conditioned buildings a lot, you can wind up with a horrible summer cold.

BUG BITES Although you have no risk of contracting malaria in Singapore (the country's been declared malaria-free for decades by the World Health Organization), there is a similar deadly virus, **dengue fever,** that's carried by mosquitoes and for which there is no immunization. A problem in the Tropics around the world, dengue fever is controlled in Singapore with an aggressive campaign to prevent the responsible mosquitoes from breeding. Still, each year cases of infection are reported, almost all of them occurring in suburban neighborhoods and rural areas. Symptoms of dengue fever include sudden fever and tiny red, spotty rashes on the body. If you suspect you've contracted dengue, seek medical attention immediately (see the listing of hospitals under "Fast Facts: Singapore," in Appendix A). If left untreated, this disease can cause internal hemorrhaging and even death. Your

best protection is to wear insect repellent that contains DEET, especially if you're heading out to the zoo, bird park, or any of the gardens or nature preserves, especially during the daytime.

A newer threat, **chikunguniya**, also a mosquito-borne virus, has also posed a danger here in recent years. Symptoms are similar to those of dengue fever.

VIRAL INFECTIONS On February 25, 2003, Singapore reported its first case of Severe Acute Respiratory Syndrome, more commonly known as **SARS.** What exploded into an epidemic affecting almost 8,500 people worldwide was quickly brought under control in the island state due to immediate and effective actions taken by the Ministries of Health and Education and the media, combined with the tireless vigilance of Singaporeans themselves. After 3 months of battle, SARS had claimed the lives of 33 people in Singapore but had mobilized the entire country to take daily precautions against the spread of the disease in an effort that was highly lauded by the World Health Organization (WHO). The respiratory infection is passed on through droplets when an infected person sneezes or coughs; however, most SARS infections are transmitted only through very close contact. Today casual travelers face no threats of contracting this disease in Singapore.

Also in the news, cases of **Asian bird flu,** or Avian influenza, have been reported all over Asia Pacific, with countries culling over 100 million poultry to contain outbreaks. Avian influenza is an acute viral infection affecting birds and poultry. Cross-infection to humans is rare; however, it does happen among people who have come in contact with sick or dead birds. To protect the country, Singapore keeps a close watch on its poultry farms and has developed safe channels for the import of all poultry products to make sure infected meats and eggs don't cross its borders.

WHAT TO DO IF YOU GET SICK AWAY FROM HOME

If you require hospitalization, the centrally located **Mount Elizabeth Hospital** is near Orchard Road at 3 Mount Elizabeth (✆ **65/6737-2666;** for accidents and emergencies, call ✆ 65/6731-2218). You can also try **Singapore General Hospital,** Outram Road (✆ **65/6222-3322;** for accidents and emergencies, call ✆ 65/6321-4311).

Any foreign consulate can provide a list of area doctors who speak English. If you get sick, consider approaching your hotel's front desk, as many hotels have a general practitioner on call. You can also try the emergency room at a local hospital. Many hospitals also have walk-in clinics for emergency cases that are not life-threatening; you may not get immediate attention, but you won't pay the high price of an emergency room visit. We list **hospitals** and **emergency numbers** under "Fast Facts: Singapore," p. 290.

If you suffer from a chronic illness, consult your doctor before your departure. Pack **prescription medications** in your carry-on luggage, and carry them in their original containers, with pharmacy labels—otherwise they won't make it through airport security. Carry the generic name of prescription medicines, in case a local pharmacist is unfamiliar with the brand name.

7 SAFETY

Singapore is an extremely safe place by any standard. There's very little violent crime, even late at night. If you stay out, there's little worry about making it home safely. There is virtually no political or social unrest. Women travelers are treated with respect.

In recent years, some pickpocketing has been reported. Hotel safe-deposit boxes are the best way to secure valuables, and traveler's checks solve theft problems in a jiff.

Before you go, always check the U.S. State department website to see if any warnings have been issued in this region: **http://travel.state.gov/travel/cis_pa_tw/tw/tw_1764.html**.

8 SPECIALIZED TRAVEL RESOURCES

TRAVELERS WITH DISABILITIES

Most disabilities shouldn't stop anyone from traveling. While planning your trip, check out **www.disability.org.sg** to learn about accessibility issues facing those with disabilities, plus practical information about how to get around the city on public transportation.

Most hotels have accessible rooms, and some cab companies offer special van services. Almost all of the newer buildings are constructed with access ramps for wheelchairs, but older buildings are very problematic, especially the shophouses, with narrow sidewalks and many uneven steps.

For more on organizations that offer resources to disabled travelers, go to www.frommers.com/planning.

GAY & LESBIAN TRAVELERS

The conservative Singaporean government doesn't recognize or support alternative lifestyles; however, gay and lesbian culture

Frommers.com: The Complete Travel Resource

Planning a trip or just returned? Head to **Frommers.com,** voted Best Travel Site by *PC Magazine.* We think you'll find our site indispensable before, during, and after your travels—with expert advice and tips; independent reviews of hotels, restaurants, attractions, and preferred shopping and nightlife venues; vacation giveaways; and an online booking tool. We publish the complete contents of over 135 travel guides in our **Destinations** section, covering over 4,000 places worldwide. Each weekday, we publish original articles that report on **Deals and News** via our free **Frommers.com Newsletters.** What's more, **Arthur Frommer** himself blogs five days a week, with cutting opinions about the state of travel in the modern world. We're betting you'll find our **Events** listings an invaluable resource; it's an up-to-the-minute roster of what's happening in cities everywhere—including concerts, festivals, lectures, and more. We've also added weekly **podcasts, interactive maps,** and hundreds of new images across the site. Finally, don't forget to visit our **Message Boards,** where you can join in conversations with thousands of fellow Frommer's travelers and post your trip report once you return.

is alive and well here. What you'll find is that older gays and lesbians are more conservative and, therefore, less open to discussion, while the younger generations have very few qualms about describing the local scene and their personal experiences in Singapore.

There are tons of websites on the Internet for gays and lesbians in Singapore. Start at **www.utopia-asia.com**, an extremely comprehensive insider collection of current events, meeting places, travel tips, topical Web discussions, and links to resources.

For more gay and lesbian travel resources, visit www.frommers.com/planning.

SENIOR TRAVEL

In Singapore, you'll find very few hotels that offer senior citizen discounts; however, virtually every attraction with an entrance fee offers a special discounted rate, and some tour companies will quote you a better rate as well. Be warned that in

Singapore you're considered a senior citizen at the age of 55—you either love it or hate it!

Upon request, the STB can also help plan your trip and can offer its own advice for senior travelers. Regarding this service, here's my advice: If you work out your itinerary with the help of STB, make sure you're firm about time constraints. Many of the tours and daily itineraries are rushed, with little time for a rest here and there. A common complaint is exhaustion by the end of just 1 day. In the heat, this is not only uncomfortable, but dangerous as well.

For more information and resources on travel for seniors, see www.frommers.com/planning.

FAMILY TRAVEL

Because of their focus on business travelers, hotels in Singapore are not especially geared toward children. You can get extra beds in hotel rooms (this can cost anywhere from S$15–S$50/US$10–US$34/£6.75–£23), and most hotels will arrange a babysitter for you on request, though most ask for at least 24 hours notice. While almost all hotels have pools to keep the kiddies cool and happy, none have lifeguards on duty, and only one hotel, Shangri-La's Rasa Sentosa Resort, has activity programs specifically for children. See chapter 5 for more information on these hotels.

Children have their own special rates of admission for just about every attraction and museum. The cutoff age for children is usually 12 years of age, but if your kids are older, be sure to ask if the attraction has a student rate for teens. If the kids get antsy during the cultural aspects of your trip, the best places to take them are the Singapore Zoo and Night Safari, the Singapore Science Centre, Underwater World on Sentosa, and Escape Theme Park and Wild Wild Wet, all of which are covered in chapter 7. I can almost guarantee that your teen(s) (and you) will have a great time at any of these attractions.

To locate accommodations, restaurants, and attractions that are particularly kid friendly, refer to the "Kids" icon throughout this guide.

For a list of more family-friendly travel resources, visit www.frommers.com/planning.

9 SUSTAINABLE TOURISM

Sustainable tourism, meaning supporting tourism efforts that are protective of the environment and respectful to indigenous cultures, has become important to many travelers. Since Singapore is a very small nation that is almost entirely defined by its urban core, it has few natural resources to either exploit or defend and virtually no native cultures to speak of. However, travelers who are environmentally conscious may find Singapore interesting in surprising ways. The government is responsive to the call of environmentalists and has designed and implemented a number of innovative ways to solve the very real environmental and resource management issues that plague countless urban centers around the world.

Local legend has it that a prominent monk warned (then) Prime Minister Lee Kuan Yew that as Singapore develops, he must be careful to protect the forests. According to the monk, Singapore, whose name in Sanskrit means "Lion City," gets its power from the lions that once supposedly roamed here. To take away the trees will destroy the lion's habitat and force him to move elsewhere. It is a lesson in feng shui that Lee took to heart, as evidenced by the trees, shrubs, and flowering plants that have been incorporated into the urban design at almost every turn.

To learn about Singapore's unique approach to environmental sustainability, start at the **Marina Barrage,** 260 Marina Way (© **65/6514-5959;** www.pub.gov.sg/marina), the massive hydrodam that is transforming Singapore's downtown city core into the world's largest urban reservoir. The dam can be toured, but equally interesting is the Sustainable Singapore Gallery located within the dam, a brilliant display that outlines the government's efforts toward environmental sustainability. The gallery is open Monday to Friday 9am–6pm, but is closed on Tuesday. On Saturday and Sunday it's open 10am to 8pm. Admission is free and there is a free shuttle to the Barrage from Marina Bay MRT.

In addition to water resource and waste management, the Singapore government has initiated monetary incentives for land developers that incorporate green technology into the design and construction of all new buildings, and to those who renovate older buildings to similar standards. There are talks to make green buildings mandatory in the near future.

Outside the city center, Singapore also has a number of nature reserves that are outlined in chapter 7 of this guidebook. Of particular interest is **Bukit Timah Nature Reserve**—Singapore is one of only two cities in the world with *primary* rainforest located within city limits—and **Sungei Buloh Wetland Reserve,** a mangrove forest that protects an awesome number of migrating birds. The National Parks Board has guided tours by park specialists on selected weekends. Check out the schedule at **www.nparks.gov.sg**.

The **Singapore Zoo** has also been affected by global environmental concerns and has decided that, though it will support its current polar bear and Arctic exhibits, once these animals have lived their lives, they will not be replaced, and the zoo will focus on wildlife native to warmer climates.

Animal rights have a way to go when it comes to the rights of sharks. Shark's fin soup is still a delicacy and is a staple in every Chinese restaurant here. Be warned.

10 PACKAGES FOR THE INDEPENDENT TRAVELER

Package tours are simply a way to buy the airfare, accommodations, and other elements of your trip (such as car rentals, airport transfers, and sometimes even activities) at the same time and often at discounted prices.

Because Singapore is compact and efficient and most people speak English, few travelers feel the need for a travel operator to hold their hand during their stay. Still, package tour operators can get you better deals on travel and hotel stays. One company I recommend is **Absolute Asia** (15 Watts St., 5th Floor, New York, NY 10013; © **800/736-8187;** fax 212/627-4090; www.absoluteasia.com), with packages that give you plenty of free time to explore on your own and innovative itineraries that combine Singapore with one or more if its Southeast Asian neighbors. **Asia Transpacific Journeys** (2995 Center Green Court, Boulder, CO 80301; © **800/642-2742;** fax 303/443-7078; www.southeastasia.com) is another great operator, specializing in customized tours with particular attention to cultural and ecological sensitivity.

Travel packages are also listed in the travel section of your local Sunday newspaper. Or check ads in the national travel magazines such as *Arthur Frommer's Budget Travel Magazine, Travel + Leisure, National Geographic Traveler,* and *Condé Nast Traveler.*

For more information on Package Tours and for tips on booking your trip, see www.frommers.com/planning.

11 SPECIAL-INTEREST TRIPS

MEDICAL TRAVEL

Singapore's internationally accredited hospitals and specialist centers are staffed with medical professionals educated at some of the world's top schools, furnished with state-of-the-art diagnostic and procedural equipment, and administered with an efficiency that Singapore is famous for. International patients choose to receive medical care in Singapore for a number of reasons: because of insufficient medical facilities in their home countries, to cover gaps in medical insurance coverage, or for privacy for sensitive procedures and recovery. Singapore's international hospitals can provide health screening and cosmetic surgery, usually at a greater cost compared to competitor hospitals in Malaysia and Thailand, but many prefer the peace of mind that comes from Singapore's reputation as a first-world city. It has also nurtured a reputation for high-end surgical procedures and care in specialist areas like cardiology, neurology, obstetrics and gynecology, oncology, ophthalmology, orthopedics, and pediatrics.

The Singapore government has teamed up with the top hospitals for **www. singaporemedicine.com**, a portal that answers every question for prospective patients. Hospitals have specialized departments that handle everything from travel arrangements, accommodations, specialists appointments, and even tours during your recovery—they really handle everything soup to nuts.

MEDICAL SPAS

Medical spas blur the line between cosmetic medicine for beauty and rejuvenation, and spa treatments for relaxations and well-being. Medical treatments for the face and body are combined with indulgent amenities and services of a luxury spa. The top medical spas in Singapore are: **The MedSpa,** 1 Orchard Blvd., #12-03/05, Camden Medical Centre (*©* **65/ 6887-3087;** www.medspa.com.sg); and **DRx Medispa,** 3 Temasek Blvd., #03-52 Suntec City Mall (*©* **65/6836-1555**), or 583 Orchard Rd., #11-01, Forum (*©* **65/ 6223-1555;** www.drxmedispa.com).

COOKING CLASSES

The **Raffles Culinary Academy** at Raffles Hotel, 1 Beach Rd. (*©* **65/6412-1256;** www.raffles.com), has daily cooking classes taught by chefs from Raffles Hotel staff. Individual classes on Asian herbs and spices, kids' cuisine, Italian, Chinese, Indian, Japanese, and Thai, plus desserts and pastries, range from 2 to 4 hours and are suitable for professionals and hobbyists alike. Bookings can be made online.

12 STAYING CONNECTED

TELEPHONES

Hotels, with the exception of backpacker hostels, all have in-room telephones with International Direct Dialing (IDD) service. This is the most convenient way to make international calls, but is also the most expensive, as the hotel will always add its own surcharge to your telephone bill.

Public telephones can be found in booths on the street or back near the toilets in shopping malls, public buildings, or hotel lobbies. Because most Singaporeans now carry mobile phones, public phones aren't always properly maintained. Local calls cost S10¢ (US7¢/5p) for 3 minutes at coin- and card-operated phones. International calls can be made only from public phones designated specifically for this purpose. International public phones will accept either a stored-value phone card or a credit card. Phone cards for local and international calls can be purchased at Singapore Post branches, 7-Eleven convenience stores, or moneychangers—make sure you specify local or international phone card when you make your purchase.

To call Singapore from the United States, dial 011 (the international access code), then 65 (Singapore's country code), and then the eight-digit number. The whole number you'd dial would be 011-65-XXXX-XXXX.

To make international calls from Singapore, first dial 001 and then the country code (U.S. or Canada 1, U.K. 44, Ireland 353, Australia 61, New Zealand 64). Next, dial the area code and number. For example, if you wanted to call the British Embassy in Washington, D.C., you would dial © 001-1-202/588-7800.

To call Malaysia from Singapore, it is not necessary to use IDD service, as there is a trunk cable between Singapore and peninsular Malaysia. To place a call, dial 02 to access the trunk cable, then the area code *with the zero prefix,* followed by the seven- or eight-digit local number. For example, to call the Malaysia Tourist Centre in Kuala Lumpur, dial © 02-03-2164-3929. For calls to Malaysian Borneo, you must still use IDD.

For directory assistance within Singapore, dial © **100.** Dial © **104** for assistance with numbers in other countries.

For operator assistance in making a call, dial © **104** if you're trying to make an international call and © **100** if you want to call a number in Singapore.

For toll-free numbers, be aware that numbers beginning with 1800 within Singapore are toll free, but calling a 1-800 number in the States from Singapore is not toll free. In fact, it costs the same as an overseas call.

CELLPHONES

Cellphones in Singapore operate on two mobile phone networks, GSM900 and GSM1800—GSM, or Global System for Mobile Communications, is a seamless network that makes for easy cross-border cellphone use throughout the world. Call your wireless operator and ask for international roaming to be activated on your account, but expect to pay premium charges for all calls.

There are three mobile service providers in Singapore: SingTel (http://home.sing tel.com), M1 (www.m1.com.sg), and Star-Hub (www.starhub.com). To save money on calls, you can purchase a prepaid Subscriber Identity Module, or SIM card, which will assign you a local number while

in Singapore. Before you do this, be sure that your mobile handset is able to accept an alien SIM card, as many phones are locked by providers. If your cellphone is locked, you can always find someone who will unlock it for a few bucks on the sly at either Sim Lim Square or Lucky Plaza shopping malls. Cellphones, both new and used, are reasonably priced here. Consider buying a new handset before paying exorbitant rental fees to an international rental firm.

FYI: Singaporeans call their cellphones "handphones," and the local term for text messaging is "SMS."

VOICE-OVER INTERNET PROTOCOL (VOIP)

If you have Web access while traveling, consider a broadband-based telephone service (in technical terms, **Voice-over Internet protocol,** or **VoIP**) such as Skype (www.skype.com) or Vonage (www.von age.com), which allow you to make free international calls from your laptop or in a cybercafe. Neither service requires the people you're calling to also have that service (though there are fees if they do not). Check the websites for details.

INTERNET & E-MAIL
With Your Own Computer

Major hotels all supply high-speed broadband Internet access in-room, usually at extra cost. Some newer and more expensive hotels will have Wi-Fi, wireless Internet connections, in room, while others will support Wi-Fi throughout certain public spaces.

In 2007, the Infocomm Development Authority initiated the Wireless@SG program, where surfers can enjoy free seamless wireless broadband access with speeds of up to 512kbps at most public areas. As of July 2008, there were more than 7,400 Wi-Fi hotspots in Singapore. To connect to the Wireless@SG wireless broadband network, a user just needs a Wi-Fi-enabled device, such as a laptop computer or a

PDA, a Web browser, and a registered Wireless@SG account. The scheme is open to tourists and business travelers; register at the www.ida.gov.sg site. This site also lists hotspots across the island.

In addition, several cafes and restaurants, such as McDonald's and Starbucks, offer Wi-Fi access to customers.

Without Your Own Computer
To find cybercafes in your destination, check **www.cybercaptive.com** and **www.cybercafe.com**.

Aside from formal cybercafes, most **backpacker guesthouses** have Internet access. Avoid **hotel business centers** unless you're willing to pay exorbitant rates.

Most major airports now have **Internet kiosks** scattered throughout their gates. These give you basic Web access for a per-minute fee that's usually higher than cybercafe prices.

13 TIPS ON ACCOMMODATIONS

Singapore's hotels enjoy high occupancy rates year round, and as a result, they require early booking whenever possible, especially from December through Chinese New Year in January or February, considered the island's peak season. Most of the time, hotels are occupied by business travelers and, as such, are outfitted with amenities to accommodate working guests, especially international hotel chains such as Hilton, Grand Hyatt, Marriott, Sheraton, Carlton, InterContinental, The Regent, Four Seasons, Conrad, and the Ritz-Carlton. Leisure travelers can find better value at hotels that don't soak up resources for business centers, conference facilities, and high-profile power-lunch restaurants.

A major complaint among visitors to Singapore is the relative lack of decent budget accommodations. High real estate prices make budget hotels hard to sustain, but a few hotels offer comfortable rooms at value prices, the best of which are reviewed in this book.

Almost all hotels are located within the city limits and near to public transportation, making getting around exceptionally convenient.

For detailed tips about accommodations in Singapore, see chapter 5.

Suggested Itineraries Singapore

If you've made it all the way to Southeast Asia, you'll likely be on a limited schedule—especially if you've arrived via a long-haul flight from Europe or North America. The good news is that Singapore is easy. It's such a small place that virtually every sight is relatively close. Still, with so many to choose from, it can be tough to whittle down the must-sees. In this chapter I've done that job for you, identifying the best and more important sights and working them into even the shortest stay.

1 THE REGIONS IN BRIEF

On a world map, Singapore is nothing more than a speck nestled in the heart of Southeast Asia, at the tip of the Malaysian peninsula. In the north, it's linked to Malaysia by two causeways over the Straits of Johor, which are its only physical connection to any other body of land. The country is made up of 1 main island, Singapore, and around 60 smaller ones, some of which—like Sentosa, Pulau Ubin, Kusu, and St. John's Island—are popular retreats. The main island is shaped like a flat, horizontal diamond, measuring in at just over 42km (26 miles) from east to west and almost 23km (14 miles) north to south. With a total land area of only 693 sq. km (270 sq. miles), Singapore is shockingly tiny.

Singapore's geographical position, sitting approximately 137km (85 miles) north of the Equator, means that its climate features uniform temperatures, plentiful rainfall, and high humidity.

Singapore is a city-state, which basically means the city *is* the country. The urban center starts at the Singapore River at the southern point of the island. Within the urban center are neighborhoods that are handy for visitors to become familiar with: the Historic District, Chinatown, Orchard Road, Kampong Glam, and Little India.

Beyond the central urban area, you'll find older suburban neighborhoods such as Katong, Geylang, or Holland Village, neighborhoods that feature prewar homes with charming architectural details. Travel farther and you'll find New Towns, such as Ang Mo Kio or Toa Payoh, which are clusters of government-subsidized housing that have sprung up around the island, supported by their own shopping malls, schools, and clinics, many of them connected by the subway system.

THE CITY: URBAN SINGAPORE

The urban center of Singapore spans quite far from edge to edge, so walking from one end to the other—say, from Kampong Glam to Chinatown—will be too much for a relaxed walk. But within each neighborhood, the best way to explore is by foot, wandering along picturesque streets, in and out of shops and museums.

The main focal point of the city is the Singapore River, which on a map is located at the southern point of the island, flowing west to east into Marina Bay. It's along the banks of this river that Sir Stamford Raffles landed and built his settlement for the East India Trading Company. As trade prospered, the banks of the river were expanded to handle commerce, behind which neighborhoods and administrative offices took root. In 1822, Raffles developed a Town Plan which allocated neighborhoods to each of the races who'd come in droves to find work and begin lives. The lines drawn then remain today, shaping the major ethnic enclaves held within the city limits.

CHINATOWN

On the south bank of the river, go-downs, or warehouses, lined the water-side. Behind, offices and residences sprang up for the Chinese community of merchants and "coolie" laborers who worked the river- and sea-trade. Raffles named this section Chinatown, a name that stands today.

TANJONG PAGAR

Neighboring Chinatown to the south-west is Tanjong Pagar, a small district where wealthy Chinese and Eurasians built plantations and manors. With the development of the steamship, Keppel Harbour, a deep natural harbor just off the shore of Tanjong Pagar, was built up to receive the larger vessels. Tanjong Pagar quickly developed into a com-mercial and residential area filled with workers who flocked there to support the industry.

In the early days, both Chinatown and Tanjong Pagar were amazing sights of city activity. Row houses lined the streets with shops on the bottom floors and homes on the second and third. Chinese coolie laborers commonly lived 16 to a room, and the area flourished with gambling casinos, clubs, and opium dens for them to spend their spare time and money. Indians also thronged to the area to work on the docks, a small reminder that although races had their own areas, they were never exclusive communities.

As recently as the 1970s, a walk down the streets in this area was an adventure: The shops housed Chinese craftsmen and artists. On the streets, hawkers peddled food and other mer-chandise. Calligrapher scribes set up shop on sidewalks to write letters for a fee. Housewives would bustle, running their daily errands. Overhead, laundry hung from bamboo poles.

Today both of these districts are sleepy in comparison. New Towns offer-ing affordable housing have siphoned residents off to the suburbs, and though the government has renovated many of the old shophouses in an attempt to preserve history, they're now tenanted by law offices and architectural, public relations, and advertising firms. The only time you'll see this place hustle anymore is during weekday lunchtime when all the professionals dash out for a bite.

HISTORIC DISTRICT

The north bank was originally reserved for colonial administrative buildings and is today commonly referred to as the Historic District. The center point was the Padang, the field on which the Euro-peans would play sports and hold out-door ceremonies. Around the field, the Parliament Building, Supreme Court, City Hall, and other municipal build-ings sprang up in grand style. Govern-ment Hill, the present-day Fort Canning Hill, was home of the governors. The Esplanade along the waterfront was a center for European social activities and music gatherings, when colonials would don their finest Western styles and walk the park under parasols or cruise in horse-drawn carriages. These days, the Historic District is still the center of most of the government's operations and

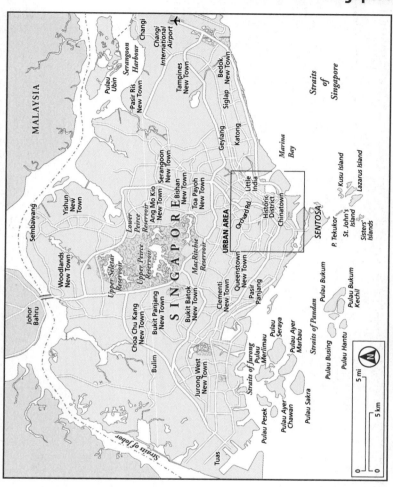

home to numerous high-rise hotels and shopping malls. The area on the bank of the river is celebrated as Raffles's landing site.

ORCHARD ROAD

To the northwest of the Historic District, in the area along Orchard and Tanglin roads, a residential area was created for Europeans and Eurasians. Homes and plantations were eventually replaced by apartment buildings and shops, and in the early 1970s luxury hotels ushered tourism into the area in full force. In the 1980s, huge shopping malls were erected along the sides of Orchard Road, turning the Orchardscape into the shopping hub it continues to be. The Tanglin area is home to most of the foreign embassies in Singapore.

Urban Singapore Neighborhoods

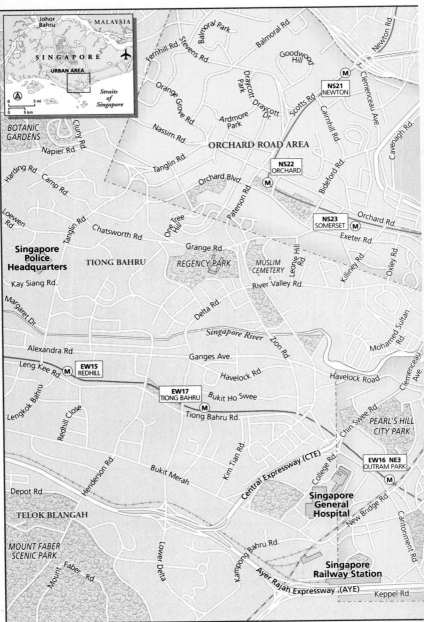

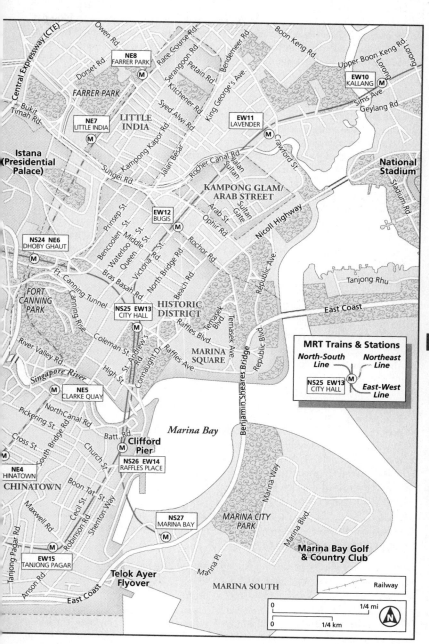

4

LITTLE INDIA

The natural landscape of Little India made it a natural location for an Indian settlement. Indians were the original cattle hands and traders in Singapore, and this area's natural grasses and springs provided their cattle with food and water while bamboo groves supplied necessary lumber for their pens. Later, with the establishment of brick kilns, Indian construction laborers flocked to the area to find work. Today many elements of Indian culture persist, although Indians make up a small percentage of the current population. Shops, restaurants, and temples still serve the community, and on Sundays Little India is a true mob scene, when all the workers have their day off and come to the streets here to socialize and relax.

KAMPONG GLAM

Kampong Glam, neighboring Little India, was given to Sultan Hussein and his family as part of his agreement to turn Singapore over to Raffles. Here he built his *Istana* (palace) and the Sultan Mosque, and the area subsequently filled with Malay and Arab Muslims who imported a distinct Islamic flavor to the neighborhood. The area is still a focal point of Muslim society in Singapore, thanks to Sultan Mosque, and the Istana has become a new exhibit celebrating Malay culture. Arab Street is a regular draw for both tourists and locals who come to find deals on fabrics and local and regional crafts.

SHENTON WAY: DOWNTOWN

Two areas of the city center are relatively new, having been built atop huge parcels of reclaimed land. Where the eastern edges of Chinatown and Tanjong Pagar once touched the water's edge, land reclamation created the present-day downtown business district that is named after its central thoroughfare, Shenton Way. This Wall Street–like district is home to the skyscrapers that grace Singapore's skyline and to the banks and businesses that have made the place an international financial capital. During weekday business hours, Shenton Way is packed with scurrying businesspeople—after-hours and on weekends, it's nothing more than a quiet forest of concrete, metal, and glass.

MARINA BAY

The Marina Bay area will soon be the new focal point for the city. With the Shenton Way financial district on one side, the Historic District on another, and Suntec convention center on yet another, the bay is humming with activity. In the coming years, with construction of one of Singapore's new casino integrated resorts, new office towers, and luxury condominiums on a tract of reclaimed land, Marina Bay will become a vibrant district of arts and entertainment where Singaporeans and foreign residents can work and also live.

SUBURBAN SINGAPORE

With rapid urbanization in the 20th century, plantations and farms turned into suburban residential areas, many with their own ethnic roots.

KATONG

To the east of the city is Katong, a famous residential district inhabited primarily by Peranakan (Straits Chinese) and Eurasian families. Its streets were, and still are, lined with Peranakan-style terrace houses, a residential variation of the shophouse found in commercial districts. The Peranakans and Eurasians were tolerant groups, a result of interracial marriages and multicultural family life, who created a close-knit community that's carried over to the present day. Main streets are still lined with Peranakan restaurants as well as many Catholic churches and schools that served the Eurasians.

GEYLANG

As public transportation opened up the eastern sections of the island, neighborhoods extended farther out. Geylang, the neighborhood just beyond Katong, was and still is primarily a Malay district. Joo Chiat and Geylang roads were once lined with antiques shops and restaurants where halal foods, in accordance with Islamic laws, were served. Today a lot of the shophouses are being renovated, but it's still a good area to find housewares, fabrics, and modern furniture shops. At night, parts of Geylang are notorious for partially regulated prostitution.

CHANGI VILLAGE

Also to the east is Changi Village, at the far eastern tip of the island. It was built as the residential section of a British military post, but the Brits are gone now and Changi is pretty quiet, with not much to see other than a large hawker center with some great seafood and a public beach from which you can see Singapore's northern islands, Malaysia, and Indonesia. The one notable aspect of the place is that it's where you pick up ferries to Pulau Ubin.

TIONG BAHRU

To the west is an old neighborhood, Tiong Bahru. Its original inhabitants were Chinese from the Chinatown and Tanjong Pagar district, and the neighborhood remains largely Chinese today. In the 1960s, the government replaced small homes and makeshift housing with high-rise public apartment housing. The

younger generations have since moved on to bigger housing in the New Towns, leaving the place mostly populated by the elderly.

HOLLAND VILLAGE

Located to the west of the city, Holland Village is another famous neighborhood that's become a tourist attraction in its own right. Its nucleus of shops carries merchandise catering to the wants and needs of Westerners, many of whom reside in the vicinity. Despite Western customers, there aren't necessarily Western goods here, but rather the kind of rattan furnishings, baskets, pottery, and other regional gifts and housewares that add Asian touches to otherwise Western-style homes.

THE NEW TOWNS

In the 1960s, to deal with the growing Singapore populations, the government created a scheme to build residential areas along an imaginary circle around the center of the island. These New Towns consist of blocks of high-rise public apartments around which shops, markets, schools, and clinics settled to support the residents. Villages, farms, and orchards were leveled; swamps were drained; and local streams were turned into concrete channels to make way for towns such as Bedok, Tampines, Pasir Ris, Toa Payoh, Bishan, Ang Mo Kio, Yishun, Woodlands, and Clementi. One trip on the subway, and all these names become familiar, as the Mass Rapid Transit (MRT) system was brought into the scheme to provide affordable transportation to all the towns.

Since 1960, almost one million government-subsidized apartments have been built, allowing over 80% of Singapore's population to own their own homes. But however appealing this housing scheme sounded at first, residents in New Towns have their complaints. The apartments have become

Kampong Life

When the stress of modern society gets them down, many Singaporeans look back with longing to the days when life was simple, before the government housing schemes shifted everyone out of their kampongs.

Kampongs, Malay for "villages" (and spelled *kampung* in Malaysia), were, once upon a time, home to most of Singapore's population. Chinese, Malays, and Indians lived side by side in small clusters of houses that were built from wood and *attap* thatch and raised on stilts. Built along the shores of the island and close to jungles, the houses and buildings were nestled against backdrops of idyllic greenery surrounded by banana and coconut groves and marshes. Homes had land for chicken coops and kitchen gardens, and backyards in which children could play. The kampongs had central wells, provision shops, and sometimes temples and mosques. Despite their poverty, the kampong villages represented community.

The 1950s and 1960s were the heyday of kampong life. Later the houses were improved with corrugated metal, concrete, and linoleum, all of which rusted and rotted over time, making the kampongs look more like slums than the homey villages they once were. Inside, modernization brought government-mandated running water, plumbing, and even electrical appliances like TVs, refrigerators, and telephones. Still, all in all, life was hardly opulent. Today this entire way of life is just a memory. Every last kampong has been razed, the inhabitants relocated by the government to public housing estates. Many former kampong inhabitants have had a difficult time adjusting to life in concrete high-rises with no front porch or backyard and neighbors who are too busy to remember their names. Despite the truth that kampong life reflected poverty and struggle, its memory remains a link to older days that, however irrelevant to the modern world, still warm the hearts of many Singaporeans.

extremely expensive, and long waiting lists are filled with couples who want to buy their first homes and families who need to upgrade to larger digs. Beyond questions of expense, though, there's the fact that the New Towns are singularly characterless, with high-rises looming overhead and compartmentalized living creating an urban anonymity among the many inhabitants.

2 THE BEST OF SINGAPORE IN 1 DAY

Perhaps you're in Singapore only overnight en route. Here's how to make the best of it. Since the city is compact, you can take in some sights fairly easily and still make it to the airport for your flight out. If your time is very limited, I recommend you bypass the museums and head straight for the streets, where you'll find a "living museum" of sorts, with local people, food, shops, and places of worship, plus a couple of interesting cultural displays. Do yourself a favor and stop first at a **Singapore Tourism Board (STB) Visitors'**

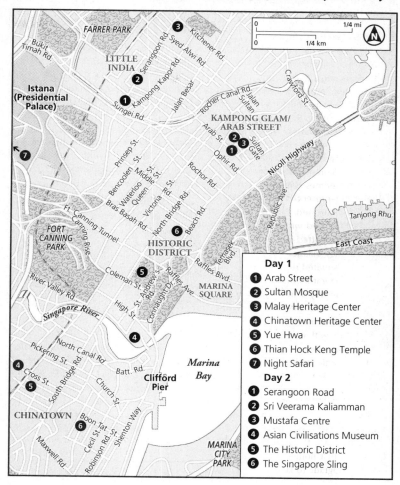

Day 1
1. Arab Street
2. Sultan Mosque
3. Malay Heritage Center
4. Chinatown Heritage Center
5. Yue Hwa
6. Thian Hock Keng Temple
7. Night Safari

Day 2
1. Serangoon Road
2. Sri Veerama Kaliamman
3. Mustafa Centre
4. Asian Civilisations Museum
5. The Historic District
6. The Singapore Sling

SUGGESTED ITINERARIES SINGAPORE

THE BEST OF SINGAPORE

THE BEST OF SINGAPORE IN 1 DAY

Centre to pick up copies of their walking tour pamphlets, one for each of Singapore's ethnic neighborhoods. The brochures identify points of interest and bits of local color as you walk along neighborhood streets. They're very well done. I recommend you start in Kampong Glam, Singapore's historical home base for Malay heritage (Malays were, after all, the original inhabitants). Chinatown makes an excellent afternoon of strolling, and in the evening, the night safari in Singapore Zoological Gardens is always a good time. **Start:** *Taxi to Arab Street.*

❶ Arab Street

This short street is lined with shops that sell Malaysian and Indonesian batik cloth

and home decor items, baskets, carved wood, objets d'art, and other gifts. Most places will be open by 10am, but if it's a

Sunday, they'll be closed; in that case, head straight to the Sultan Mosque instead. See p. 169.

❷ Sultan Mosque ★

Just off Arab Street, you can't miss the towering onion dome of this mosque. The most historic in Singapore, its grounds are open, so feel free to explore within its walls, including the ablutions area, where worshipers wash up before prayers according to Muslim tradition, and a small grave site with unmarked stones. Inside the front entrance, they can provide robes if you're wearing shorts or a sleeveless top. Come before the noontime prayers, especially on Fridays; otherwise, you may be asked to wait until they're finished. Non-Muslims are not permitted inside the main prayer hall. See p. 137.

❸ Malay Heritage Centre

Just a 2-minute stroll from the mosque, the Malay Heritage Centre is inside the restored palace of the original sultanate. The staff here is really nice and can also chat about the local Malay culture from their personal experiences. See p. 136.

Take a taxi from Arab Street to the Chinatown Heritage Centre.

❹ Chinatown Heritage Centre ★★

Say goodbye to Malay culture and hello to Chinese *and* a welcome respite from the midday heat (it's air-conditioned!). The streets surrounding the center are packed

with souvenir shops with tons of curious finds, plus some beautiful art and antiques galleries, so be sure to wander around a bit. See p. 128.

❺ Yue Hwa ★★

This Chinese emporium is practically a museum of Chinese handicrafts, filled with floor after floor of fabulous shopping. Excellent buys here include ready-made silk clothing, embroidered handbags, carved jade, pottery, and cloisonné. Unusual buys include musical instruments, men's coolie outfits, and plenty of strange Chinese interpretations of Western goods. See p. 168.

Take a taxi from Yue Hwa to Thian Hock Keng Temple.

❻ Thian Hock Keng Temple ★★★

If you see any one Chinese temple in Singapore, this is it. One of the earliest built, it is a meaningful tribute to the Taoist gods and goddesses that have guided the Chinese community here. Try to get here before 5pm so you have time for relaxed exploration. See p. 132.

❼ Night Safari ★★★

If you come from temperate climes, this is a rare chance to see nocturnal animals. This is the one place where all Singaporeans bring their foreign visitors, and I have yet to see anyone walk away unimpressed. Also, an easy dinner can be had from local- and fast-food stalls at the park entrance. See p. 147.

3 THE BEST OF SINGAPORE IN 2 DAYS

On your second day, continue to explore life at ground level with a morning meander through Little India, the heart of Singapore's Indian community. After lunch, escape the afternoon heat at the Asian Civilisations Museum, then finish your day with a Singapore Sling at Raffles Hotel. *Start: Taxi to Serangoon Road or MRT to Little India station.*

❶ Serangoon Road

A long strip where the locals come to buy spices (check out the old grinding mill on Cuff Rd. just off Serangoon), flowers (see the sellers making jasmine garlands by the

roadside), Bollywood DVDs (you can hear the music blaring out into the street), saris (you can have one made for yourself), and all kinds of ceremonial items, many of which make excellent gifts. This is one of the few old neighborhoods in Singapore that hasn't been "Disney-fied" by the government. If you love chaos, come on Sundays, when most workers have their day off. This place is packed like Calcutta!

❷ Sri Veerama Kaliamman ★★

Midway down Serangoon Road you'll find this brightly colored temple humming with devotees all times of the day. Take off your shoes to explore the dioramas inside. If you get here early enough, you can watch as the statues inside are bathed. The water, considered blessed, runs off a small spout behind the left side of the main altar. See p. 135.

❸ Mustafa Centre ★★

Farther along Serangoon Road, Mustafa's is a crazy Indian emporium. While many of the goods are pretty standard, look for all the neat India imports. Explore the basement sari fabric department, one of the largest in Singapore. I love the groceries section with row after row of boxed curry mixes—great to take back home! Or check out Mustafa's three floors of the most elaborate gold jewelry you've ever seen. See p. 169.

Take a taxi from Mustafa's to the Asian Civilisations Museum.

❹ Asian Civilisations Museum ★★★

This is my favorite museum, for its well-planned displays and handsome presenta-

tions of the many cultures that influenced Singapore's heritage. Don't leave without checking out the gift shop, which features exceptional regional handicrafts. They take special care to support crafting communities. See p. 115.

❺ The Historic District

From ACM, take a walk through the downtown civic center, where you'll pass the Old Parliament House, the Padang, the Supreme Court, City Hall, and St. Andrew's Cathedral. The stroll takes only about a half-hour, a bit more if you linger at any of the sights. See p. 114.

❻ The Singapore Sling

Walk past Raffles City Shopping Centre and you'll find Raffles Hotel. Take your time to wander through her public spaces (visitors are not allowed in residents' corridors). There's upscale shopping, pretty courtyards, and lots of dining options. Head for the Long Bar where you can sip a sweet Singapore Sling at the place where the drink was invented. To be honest, this isn't the actual bar; the current Long Bar is a replica built into the Raffles' new wing. But after a couple of these powerful concoctions, you won't care. See p. 179.

4 THE BEST OF SINGAPORE IN 3 DAYS

According to the Singapore Tourism Board, the average visitor stays 3.5 days. If this describes you, there's still plenty of good things to see and do before you depart. An early-morning visit to the Singapore Botanic Gardens is especially recommended for joggers and photographers. Once the sun has burned away the dew, head for the newly renovated National Museum of Singapore to cool off (notice I always recommend the air-conditioned attractions during the hottest time of the day). A late-afternoon visit to the Jurong BirdPark rounds out a relaxing day of sights. *Start: Orchard MRT, then bus no. 7, 105, 106, or 174 from Orchard Blvd.*

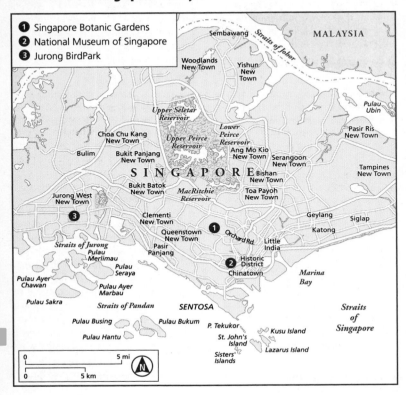

❶ Singapore Botanic Gardens ★★

There's no reason to stop your workout routine just because you're traveling. Start your jog—or walk—early (it opens at 5am!) to beat the heat and so you won't feel rushed through the beautiful displays of tropical plants, shady trees, vivid blooms, and delicate bonsai, and don't forget to visit the National Orchid Garden (open at 8:30am) while you're there. See p. 144.

❷ National Museum of Singapore ★★★

Recently redone, there's nothing musty about this history lesson. An interactive,

multimedia, IMAX-ed good time, it's also highly recommended for children, as the goal of the National Heritage Board was to make history accessible to everyone. They did a great job. See p. 121.

❸ Jurong BirdPark ★

As long as you're in the Tropics, check out the birds in this beautifully executed park. Feeding activities, educational tours, and shows keep it lively. See p. 141.

Where to Stay in Singapore

Competition is fierce among hotels in the Garden City, driven by a steady stream of business and convention travelers, many of whom stay at international hotel chains such as Hyatt, Hilton, Sheraton, and Marriott (all represented here). These companies invest millions in a never-ending cycle of renovations, constantly upgrading their super-royal-regal executive facilities, all in an attempt to lure suits and CEOs and—eventually, it is hoped—land lucrative corporate accounts.

Sadly, this means that good-quality budget accommodations are not a high priority on the island. Between the business community's demand for luxury on the one hand and the inflated Singaporean real estate market on the other, room prices tend to be high. What this means for leisure travelers is that you may end up paying for a business center you'll never use or a 24-hour stress-reliever masseuse you'll never call—and all this without the benefit of a corporate discount rate.

Don't fret, though: I'm here to tell you that there's a range of accommodations out there—you just have to know where to look. In this chapter, I'll help you pick the right accommodations for you, based on your vacation goals and your budget, so you can make the most of your stay.

CHOOSING YOUR NEIGHBORHOOD

In considering where you'll stay, think about what you'll be doing in Singapore—that way, you can choose a hotel that's close to the particular action that suits you. (On the other hand, because Singapore is a small place and public transportation is excellent, really nothing's ever too far away.)

Orchard Road has the largest cluster of hotels in the city and is right in the heart of Singaporean shopping mania—the malls and wide sidewalks where locals and tourists stroll to see and be seen. The **Historic District** has hotels that are near museums and sights, while those in **Marina Bay** center more around the business professionals who come to Singapore for Suntec City, the giant convention and exhibition center located there. These hotels in Marina Bay overlook the bay, the Singapore Flyer, and the Harbor, offering some of the best views in town. **Chinatown** and **Tanjong Pagar** have some lovely boutique hotels in quaint back streets, and **Shenton Way** has a couple of high-rise places for the convenience of people doing business in the downtown business district. On a strict budget, but want to be close to the center of things? Check out my recommendations on and around Bencoolen Street for decent backpacker stops. Many hotels have free morning and evening shuttle buses to Orchard Road, Suntec City, and Shenton Way. I've also listed two hotels on **Sentosa,** an island to the south that's a popular day or weekend trip for many Singaporeans and might be a good choice for families or honeymooners. (It's connected to Singapore by a causeway, cable cars, and a light-rail system.) Remember, Singapore isn't huge and has myriad transport options, so nothing's ever really far away.

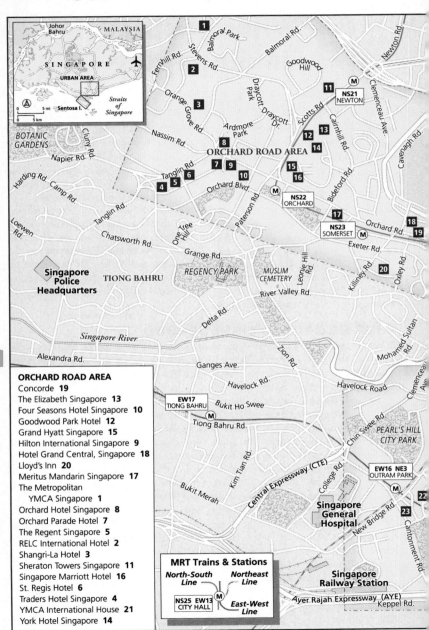

ORCHARD ROAD AREA

Concorde **19**
The Elizabeth Singapore **13**
Four Seasons Hotel Singapore **10**
Goodwood Park Hotel **12**
Grand Hyatt Singapore **15**
Hilton International Singapore **9**
Hotel Grand Central, Singapore **18**
Lloyd's Inn **20**
Meritus Mandarin Singapore **17**
The Metropolitan
    YMCA Singapore **1**
Orchard Hotel Singapore **8**
Orchard Parade Hotel **7**
The Regent Singapore **5**
RELC International Hotel **2**
Shangri-La Hotel **3**
Sheraton Towers Singapore **11**
Singapore Marriott Hotel **16**
St. Regis Hotel **6**
Traders Hotel Singapore **4**
YMCA International House **21**
York Hotel Singapore **14**

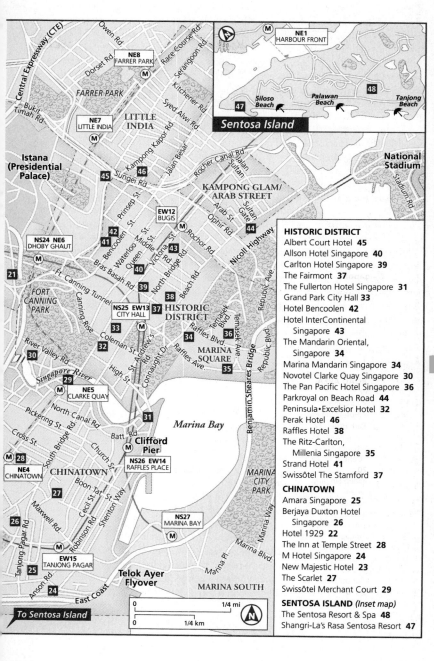

NE8 FARRER PARK

NE7 LITTLE INDIA

LITTLE INDIA

Istana (Presidential Palace)

45

46

KAMPONG GLAM/ ARAB STREET

National Stadium

EW12 BUGIS

42
41

NS24 NE6 DHOBY GHAUT

43

44

21

40

FORT CANNING PARK

39

38

NS25 EW13 CITY HALL

37 HISTORIC DISTRICT

33

32

34

36

MARINA SQUARE

30

35

29 NE5 CLARKE QUAY

Singapore River

31

Marina Bay

Clifford Pier

NS26 EW14 RAFFLES PLACE

28 NE4 CHINATOWN

27

MARINA CITY PARK

26

NS27 MARINA BAY

EW15 TANJONG PAGAR

25

24

Telok Ayer Flyover

MARINA SOUTH

0 ——— 1/4 mi
0 ——— 1/4 km

To Sentosa Island

NE1 HARBOUR FRONT

48

Siloso Beach

Palawan Beach

Tanjong Beach

47

Sentosa Island

HISTORIC DISTRICT
Albert Court Hotel **45**
Allson Hotel Singapore **40**
Carlton Hotel Singapore **39**
The Fairmont **37**
The Fullerton Hotel Singapore **31**
Grand Park City Hall **33**
Hotel Bencoolen **42**
Hotel InterContinental
  Singapore **43**
The Mandarin Oriental,
  Singapore **34**
Marina Mandarin Singapore **34**
Novotel Clarke Quay Singapore **30**
The Pan Pacific Hotel Singapore **36**
Parkroyal on Beach Road **44**
Peninsula•Excelsior Hotel **32**
Perak Hotel **46**
Raffles Hotel **38**
The Ritz-Carlton,
  Millenia Singapore **35**
Strand Hotel **41**
Swissôtel The Stamford **37**

CHINATOWN
Amara Singapore **25**
Berjaya Duxton Hotel
  Singapore **26**
Hotel 1929 **22**
The Inn at Temple Street **28**
M Hotel Singapore **24**
New Majestic Hotel **23**
The Scarlet **27**
Swissôtel Merchant Court **29**

SENTOSA ISLAND (Inset map)
The Sentosa Resort & Spa **48**
Shangri-La's Rasa Sentosa Resort **47**

What appeals to you? A big, flashy, internationalist palace or a small, homier place? Hyatt, Sheraton, Hilton, and InterContinental are just a few of the international chain hotels you will find in Singapore. For the most part, these city hotels are nondescript towers—though Swissôtel The Stamford has the distinction of being the tallest hotel in Southeast Asia, with 71 floors. A few exceptions stand out. The Shangri-La, operating a highly reputable luxury hotel chain in Asia, has a property near Orchard Road with gorgeous landscaped grounds and a pool area, making it truly a resort inside the city. Meanwhile, Shangri-La's Rasa Sentosa Resort and the Sentosa Resort & Spa on Sentosa Island are out-of-the-way but have a real "get-away-from-it-all" ambience. In addition, a few hotels offer charming accommodations in historical premises. The most notable is Raffles, a Southeast Asian classic, and the Fullerton Hotel Singapore, converted from the old general post office building. But you need not pay a fortune for quaint digs. Budget places like Albert Court Hotel and the SHA Villa offer budget rooms with old-world charm in great locations.

A newer trend is the boutique hotel. Conceived as part of the Urban Restoration Authority's renewal plans, rows of old shophouses and historic buildings in ethnic areas like Chinatown and Tanjong Pagar have been restored and transformed into small, lovely hotels. Places like the Scarlet Hotel and the Inn at Temple Street are beautiful examples of local flavor turned into quaint accommodations. Others, like the trendy New Majestic, focus on art and design, with rooms dramatically different from each other and from the usual corporate tones of tan and beige that predominate in the city's high-rises. Although these places can put you closer to the heart of Singapore, they do have their drawbacks—for one, both the hotels and their rooms tend to be smaller than their modern counterparts, and due to building codes and a lack of space, most are unable to provide facilities like swimming pools, Jacuzzis, or fitness centers.

Although budget hotels have very limited facilities and simpler interior style, you can always expect a clean room. What's more, service can sometimes be more personal in smaller hotels, where front desk staff has fewer faces to recognize and is accustomed to helping guests with the sorts of things a business center or concierge would handle in a larger hotel. Par for the course, many of the guests in these places are backpackers, and mostly Western backpackers, at that. However, you will see some regional folks staying in these places. *Note:* The budget accommodations listed here are places decent enough for any standards. While cheaper digs are available, the rooms can be dreary and depressing, musty and old, or downright sleazy.

Unless you choose one of the extreme budget hotels, there are some standard features you can expect to find everywhere. Although no hotels offer a courtesy car or limousine, many have courtesy shuttles to popular parts of town. Security key cards are catching on, and while in-room safes are standard, many are shifting to safes that incorporate a plug so you can charge electronics gadgets while they're locked away. You'll also see in-house movies and, many times, CNN, ESPN, and HBO on your TV. Voice mail is gaining popularity, and fax services can always be provided upon request. You'll find most places have adequate fitness center facilities, almost all of which offer a range of massage treatments—hotels generally do not offer in-room massage treatments. Pools tend to be on the small side, and Jacuzzis are often placed in men's and women's locker rooms, making

Tips **Making Hotel Reservations Online**

The website **www.asiarooms.com** offers the best rates I've seen for Internet bookings, particularly for hotels in the Very Expensive and Expensive categories; however, they don't have deals for every hotel property. It's worth it to browse and compare.

it impossible for couples to use them together. Although tour desks can be found in some lobbies, car-rental desks are nonexistent.

Many of the finest restaurants in Singapore are located in hotels, either operated by the hotel directly or just inhabiting rented space. Some hotels host five or six restaurants, each serving a different cuisine. Generally, you can expect these restaurants to be more expensive than places located outside hotels. In each hotel review, the distinguished restaurants have been noted; these restaurants are also fully reviewed in chapter 6.

RATES

For a "Little Red Dot," Singapore gets big visitor numbers. Hotel prices—already comparatively expensive for Asia—continued to set records in 2007, when occupancy rates hit an all-time high of 87%. With room rates rising more than 20% year-on-year and an average room now breaking the S$200 ($134/£90) barrier for the first time, this can be a tough destination for travelers on a budget. As more and more hotels move away from the rack rate system of published room prices, it can be difficult to compare value, so although some rack rates are included here, there are plenty of promotional rates on offer. A little research can really pay off, leaving your expensive hotel costing less on a particular date than a so-called moderate hotel. If you've decided where you want to stay, make sure you call in advance and ask what special deals are available. Also check out hotel discount websites on the Internet (such as www.asiarooms.com, above), though they don't list every hotel. Places that have just completed renovation programs tend to offer good discounts, and many business-orientated hotels have special rates for weekends and longer stays.

Rates shown here represent the price of a standard double room in high season, booked via the Internet. For the purposes of this guide, I've divided hotels into these categories: very expensive, S$450 (US$302/£203) and up; expensive, S$300 to S$450 (US$201–US$302/£135–£203); moderate, S$200 to S$300 (US$134–US$201/£90–£135); and inexpensive, under S$200 (US$134/£90).

TAXES & SERVICE CHARGES

All rates listed are in Singapore dollars, with U.S. dollar and British pound equivalents provided as well (remember to check the exchange rate when you're planning, though, because rates fluctuate). Most rates do not include the so-called "++" taxes and charges: the 10% service charge and 7% goods and services tax (GST). Keep these in mind when figuring your budget. Some budget hotels will quote discount rates inclusive of all taxes, and Internet sites normally include taxes.

THE BUSY SEASON

Busy season? It's all busy season in Singapore, with month-by-month occupancy rates holding steady over 80%. Visitors are advised to book rooms well in advance, and check with the Singapore Tourism Board to make sure there are no huge conventions in town during your dates. That said, probably the worst time to find a last-minute room or to negotiate a favorable rate will be between Christmas and the Chinese New Year, when folks travel on vacation and to see their families.

MAKING RESERVATIONS ON THE GROUND

If you are not able to make a reservation before your trip, a reservation service is available at Changi International Airport. The Singapore Hotel Association operates desks in all three main terminals, with reservation services based upon room availability for many hotels. Reservation lines are open 24 hours: Terminal 1 ℭ 65/6542-6966; Terminal 2 ℭ 65/6545-0318; Terminal 3 ℭ 65/6542-0442.

1 THE HISTORIC DISTRICT

VERY EXPENSIVE

The Fairmont ★★★   The Fairmont is designed to make life easy for the weary traveler. Close to the sights of the historic district, it's also directly above an MRT hub and next to the enormous Raffles City shopping center replete with restaurants, supermarkets, and swish stores. Rooms in the North Tower have an attractive and contemporary Asian flavor, while South Tower rooms have polished wooden floors, Bose sound systems, and Heavenly Beds with 10 layers of goose feathers. Ask for a harbor view in the South Tower to enjoy the best views of the financial district skyscrapers overlooking Marina Bay. The Amrita Spa is Singapore's largest spa, with plunge pools, a huge range of Asian and European treatments, and a state-of-the-art fitness center that's open around the clock. Business facilities are outstanding, with a dedicated executive floor with its own lounge, complimentary use of meeting rooms, in-room espresso machines, and a private gym.

2 Stamford Rd., Singapore 178882. ℭ **65/6339-7777.** Fax 65/6337-1554. www.fairmont.com/singapore. 769 units. S$484 (US$324/£218) double; from S$1,177 (US$789/£530) suite. AE, DC, MC, V. City Hall MRT. **Amenities:** 12 restaurants; martini bar, lobby lounge, and a live jazz venue; outdoor pool; spa w/gym, Jacuzzi, sauna, steam, and massage; concierge; airport transfers; room service; babysitting; smoke-free rooms; executive-level rooms. *In room:* A/C, TV w/satellite programming and in-house movies, minibar, hair dryer.

The Fullerton Hotel Singapore ★★   The historic Fullerton, which rivals Raffles in luxury and architecture, is regularly voted one of Asia's top hotels. Superb views in almost every direction include the Singapore River and historic district, the city skyline, and the harbor. Built in 1928 as the General Post Office, its location, immense size, and classical Doric columns are testament to its vital role in the colonial government. The restoration and hotel conversion have been done beautifully, with lofty, elegant public spaces and guest rooms cleverly arranged to fit the original structure. Rooms are oases of comfort, stylish and contemporary with flatscreen TVs, PlayStations, large desks, and Philippe Starck fittings in the enormous bathrooms. Facilities are excellent, too, with a state-of-the-art gym and spa and an infinity pool that overlooks the river. Standards of

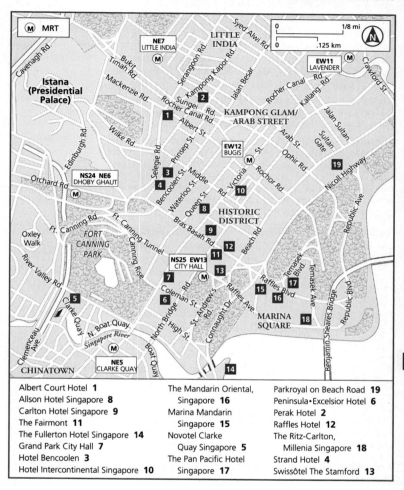

Albert Court Hotel **1**
Allson Hotel Singapore **8**
Carlton Hotel Singapore **9**
The Fairmont **11**
The Fullerton Hotel Singapore **14**
Grand Park City Hall **7**
Hotel Bencoolen **3**
Hotel Intercontinental Singapore **10**

The Mandarin Oriental,
 Singapore **16**
Marina Mandarin
 Singapore **15**
Novotel Clarke
 Quay Singapore **5**
The Pan Pacific Hotel
 Singapore **17**

Parkroyal on Beach Road **19**
Peninsula•Excelsior Hotel **6**
Perak Hotel **2**
Raffles Hotel **12**
The Ritz-Carlton,
 Millenia Singapore **18**
Strand Hotel **4**
Swissôtel The Stamford **13**

WHERE TO STAY IN SINGAPORE

5

THE HISTORIC DISTRICT

service are second to none. A range of restaurants offer fine dining, sophisticated bars, and a location that's perfect for business and pleasure.

1 Fullerton Sq., Singapore 049178. Ⓒ **800/44-UTELL** (448-8355) in the U.S. and Canada, 800/221-176 in Australia, 800/933-123 in New Zealand, or 65/6733-8388. Fax 65/6735-8388. www.fullertonhotel.com. 400 units. S$507 (US$340/£228) double; S$900 (US$603/£405) suite. AE, DC, MC, V. 5-min. walk to Raffles Place MRT. **Amenities:** 3 restaurants; bar and lobby lounge; outdoor infinity pool w/view of the Singapore River; health club w/Jacuzzi, sauna, and steam; spa w/massage and beauty treatments; concierge; airport transfers; room service; babysitting; smoke-free rooms; executive-level rooms. *In room:* A/C, TV w/ satellite programming and in-house movies, high-speed Internet, minibar, hair dryer.

The Mandarin Oriental Singapore ★★★   The Mandarin Oriental is the most elegant of the Marina Bay atrium-style hotels, with its subdued lobby of dark polished marble, rich fabrics, and stunning orchid arrangements. Even the central elevator lobby is surrounded by softly trickling limpid pools. The king- and queen-size bedrooms have a sophisticated contemporary Asian look and beautiful silk prints and upholstered wicker chairs. Bathrooms have a separate bath and shower, separated from the bedroom by a glass wall (with wooden blinds, for modesty). Oceanview rooms overlook the Singapore Flyer and the bay, though only suites have balconies with a seating area. The newly refurbished city-facing rooms have attractive modern oak partitions and marble bathrooms. The Mandarin Oriental's restaurants and bars are excellent, though expensive, and its hushed, exotic spa is to die for. Service is superb.

5 Raffles Ave., Marina Square, Singapore 039797. ℂ **800/526-6566** in the U.S. and Canada, 800/123-693 in Australia, 800/2828-3838 in New Zealand or the U.K., or 65/6338-0066. Fax 65/6339-9537. www. mandarinoriental.com/singapore. 524 units. S$458 (US$307/£206) double; from S$786 (US$527/£354) suite. AE, DC, MC, V. 10-min. walk to City Hall MRT. **Amenities:** 4 restaurants; bar and lobby lounge; outdoor pool; health club; spa w/Jacuzzi, sauna, and steam; concierge; airport transfers; room service; babysitting; smoke-free rooms; executive-level rooms. *In room:* A/C, TV w/satellite programming and in-house movies, minibar, hair dryer.

Raffles Hotel ★★   Walking into Raffles has a palpable sense of event. Liveried Sikh doormen usher you through the ornate wrought-iron portico into a lobby that seems faithfully unaltered from the hotel's 1930s heyday. If price is no object, then Raffles will deliver a blend of luxury, history, and colonial ambiance no other hotel can match. Only residents are allowed into the private inner lobby, or to stroll across the polished teak verandas overlooking tropical courtyards to suites decorated with a small elegant lounge, period furnishings, and a lovely four-poster bed. Although suites are on the small side, every detail is true to the hotel's heritage, making a stay here the ultimate in romance. Butlers provide customized service for each suite. There is a small landscaped rooftop pool and a spa that can arrange individualized treatments with the utmost discretion. Residents also have the benefit of eight exceptional dining choices in house. A stay at Raffles is an event in itself.

1 Beach Rd., Singapore 189673. ℂ **800/232-1886** in the U.S. and Canada, or 65/6337-1886. Fax 65/6339-7650. www.raffleshotel.com. 103 suites. From S$907 (US$608/£408) suite. AE, DC, MC, V. Next to City Hall MRT. **Amenities:** 8 restaurants; 2 bars and a billiards room; outdoor pool; health club w/Jacuzzi, sauna, steam, and spa; concierge; free airport transfers; room service; babysitting; personal butler service. *In room:* A/C, TV w/satellite programming and in-room VCR, fax, high-speed Internet, minibar, hair dryer.

The Ritz-Carlton, Millenia Singapore ★★★   No one could accuse the Ritz-Carlton of looking like just another international hotel. A little less than 3 hectares (7 acres) of landscaped grounds give a sense of peace, despite its busy Marina Bay location. Inside the award-winning Kevin Roche's building, the lobby and public areas showcase extraordinary art: Hockney and Warhol brush shoulders with more than 4,000 works by international artists. You can't miss Dale Chihuly's vivid glass tendrils, which exude from the walls of the lounge and restaurant areas on either side of the lobby. Guest rooms are quiet and larger than most in Singapore, and each has stunning views of either the Kallang or Marina bays. Decor and furnishings are sumptuous and comfortable, from big wood-posted beds dressed in crisp white linens, to lounges, walk-in closets, and, for Club rooms, even Bulgari toiletries. Best of all are the huge octagonal picture windows placed next to the bathtub in every room, surely the most luxurious way possible to unwind after a long day's business or sightseeing.

7 Raffles Ave., Singapore 039799. ℭ **800/241-3333** in the U.S. and Canada, 800/241-33333 in Australia, 800/241-33333 in New Zealand, 800/234-000 in the U.K., or 65/6337-8888. Fax 65/6338-0001. www. ritzcarlton.com. 610 units. S$475 (US$318/£214) double; from S$681 (US$456/£306) suite. AE, DC, MC, V. 10-min. walk to City Hall MRT. **Amenities:** 3 restaurants; lobby lounge; outdoor pool; health club w/ sauna, steam, and massage; outdoor Jacuzzi; concierge; airport transfers; room service; babysitting; smoke-free rooms; executive level rooms; outdoor lighted tennis court. *In room:* A/C, TV w/satellite programming and in-house movies, high-speed Internet, minibar, hair dryer.

EXPENSIVE

Carlton Hotel Singapore ★★ This Carlton property comprises two buildings, the 26-story Main Wing and the 19-story Annex Wing. Leisure travelers will be most interested in the lower-priced superior and deluxe rooms in the Main Wing. While rooms in both categories are the same size, deluxe rooms have broadband Internet access in-room, a flatscreen TV, plus marble bathroom decor (superiors are humble ceramic tile). The Annex houses premier deluxe rooms, which, for a premium, feature larger bathrooms with separate bath and shower stall, an in-room safe to fit your laptop, and access to a coin-operated launderette. All public spaces have been upgraded as well, including the lobby entrance, alfresco coffee shop, and tiny wine and cigar room. The location, in the center of the historic district, is great. Ask for a room with a view of the city, but try to avoid the building noise from the Carlton's new Executive Wing, due to be completed in 2009.

76 Bras Basah Rd., Singapore 189558. ℭ **65/6338-8333.** Fax 65/6339-6866. www.carltonhotel.sg. 627 units. S$315 (US$211/£142) double; from S$500 (US$3350/£225) suite. AE, DC, MC, V. 5-min. walk to City Hall MRT. **Amenities:** 2 restaurants; lobby lounge; outdoor pool; health club w/sauna, steam, and massage; concierge; airport transfers; room service; babysitting; smoke-free rooms; executive-level rooms. *In room:* A/C, TV w/satellite programming and in-house movies, minibar.

Grand Park City Hall ★ Formerly the Grand Plaza Parkroyal and the Parkroyal on Coleman Street, this property changed hands in 2007. Built on top of (and incorporating) 2 blocks of prewar shophouses, there are still hints of shophouse detail throughout the lobby. Renovation of the public areas, including the lobby, restaurants, and spa, are newly completed, and executive rooms are due to be refurbished by the end of 2009. The hotel is located at the corner of Coleman and Hill streets, close to the Armenian Church, the Asian Civilisations Museum, and Fort Canning Park—plus there's a shuttle to Orchard Road. Guest rooms are of smaller size than average, have decent closet space, and sport sharp Italian contemporary furniture in natural tones, with homey touches like snuggly comforters on all the beds.

10 Coleman St., Singapore 179809. ℭ **65/6336-3456.** Fax 65/6339-9311. www.parkhotelgroup.com/ gpch. 326 units. S$336 (US$225/£151) double; from S$500 (US$335/£225) suite. AE, DC, MC, V. 5-min. walk to City Hall MRT. **Amenities:** 3 restaurants; lobby lounge; outdoor pool w/view of Armenian Church across the street; health club; spa w/Jacuzzi, sauna, steam, and massage; concierge; airport transfers; room service; babysitting; executive-level rooms. *In room:* A/C, TV w/satellite programming, minibar.

Hotel InterContinental Singapore ★ InterContinental has brilliantly incorporated a block of prewar shophouses into its design. While the hotel remains unmistakably modern and efficient, it's been admirably successful in infusing signatures of the local Peranakan style, evident in the carved panels dotted around the hotel, and the use of ornate fabrics and porcelain in the vivid Peranakan palette. Deluxe rooms on the upper floors are large, pleasant, and well equipped, but in my view, it's worth paying extra to get one of the Shophouse rooms or suites in the original part of the building. Although they are slightly smaller, they have been beautifully and atmospherically renovated, with wooden floors, oriental rugs, and good reproduction antiques. The Club Lounge has recently been relocated to the second floor of the old building. For an additional charge, guests can enjoy complimentary breakfast, afternoon tea, and cocktails here.

80 Middle Rd., Singapore 188966 (near Bugis Junction). ☎ **800/327-0200** in the U.S. and Canada, 800/221-335 in Australia, 800/442-215 in New Zealand, 800/0289-387 in the U.K., or 65/6338-7600. Fax 65/6338-7366. www.intercontinental.com. 406 units. S$429 (US$287/£193) double; from S$513 (US$344/£231) suite. AE, DC, MC, V. Bugis MRT. **Amenities:** 3 restaurants; bar and lobby lounge; outdoor pool; health club w/Jacuzzi, sauna, and massage; concierge; airport transfers; room service; babysitting; executive-level rooms. *In room:* A/C, TV w/satellite programming and in-house movies, hair dryer, minibar, hair dryer.

Marina Mandarin Singapore ★★

The atrium of the Marina Mandarin is a colossal 21-story space, but it is peaceful and serene for its size and busy location due to the natural light that streams through skylights and birdsong from caged Chinese nightingales. The recently renovated rooms are spacious and attractive, with crisp white bed linen offset by dark wood furniture, Asian fabrics, and frosted glass walls around the well-equipped bathrooms. Premier Suites are more Western in flavor, using light wood and gold and white fabrics. Venus rooms offer women travelers comforts and conveniences, including bath oils, custom pillows, and hair tongs. Each room has a balcony—ask for a harborview room. The Marina Mandarin has the Marina Square and Millennium Walk shopping malls on its doorstep. Though it's a fair walk from this area to the MRT (subway), it's possible to do most of the journey via air-conditioned malls, and taxis are plentiful here.

6 Raffles Blvd., Marina Square, Singapore 039594. ☎ **65/6845-1000.** Fax 65/6845-1001. www.marina-mandarin.com.sg. 575 units. S$395 (US$265/£178) double; from S$506 (US$339/£228) suite. AE, DC, MC, V. 10-min. walk to City Hall MRT. **Amenities:** 3 restaurants; English pub and lobby lounge; outdoor pool; outdoor lighted tennis courts and squash courts; health club; spa w/Jacuzzi, sauna, steam, and massage; concierge; airport transfers; room service; babysitting; smoke-free rooms; executive-level rooms. *In room:* A/C, TV w/satellite programming and in-house movies, minibar, hair dryer.

Novotel Clarke Quay Singapore ★

This hotel towers over the Singapore River just next to Clarke Quay (a popular spot for nightlife, dining, and shopping) and is a stroll away from the Historic District. The rooms and pool area were refreshed in 2008. Guest rooms are a good size, some with space for four single beds. All have small balconies with good views of the river, the financial district, Fort Canning Park, or Chinatown, and even standard rooms have large bathrooms like those you typically see in more deluxe accommodations. Decor is Western contemporary in shades of brown, green, and tan, with small desks next to floor-to-ceiling picture windows. The main lobby is an elevator ride up from the ground level. A recently renovated adjacent shopping mall has groceries in the basement and a few handy shops.

177A River Valley Rd., Singapore 179031. ☎ **800/515-5679** in the U.S. and Canada, or 65/6338-3333. Fax 65/6339-2854. www.novotel.com. 398 units. S$325 (US$218/£146) double; from S$470 (US$315/£212) suite. AE, DC, MC, V. 5-min. walk to Clarke Quay MRT. **Amenities:** Restaurant; lobby lounge; outdoor pool; health club; Jacuzzi; concierge; airport transfers; room service; babysitting; executive-level rooms. *In room:* A/C, TV w/satellite programming, minibar.

The Pan Pacific Hotel Singapore ★★

A recent face-lift has given the Pan Pacific a new look. Public spaces are awash with color; the lobby has a checkerboard-inlay reception counter, vibrant carpeting, and a lobby lounge with walls of lights that change colors. Guest rooms are large, with wood paneling in geometric panels, Asian-inspired fabrics, and large oval desktops with Herman Miller chairs. New entertainment centers allow you to hook up your laptop to the TV and iPod to the stereo. Hands down, Pan Pac has Singapore's best business center—a full floor designated for private offices, with full secretarial services, every piece of office equipment you'd need, plus meeting rooms and even snacks and cocktail lounges. The hotel's restaurants include top choices in Singapore, like the highly regarded Rang Mahal Indian restaurant and the Chinese restaurant Hai Tien Lo. The rooftop pool has a huge open sun deck area and a spa and fitness center with pool view.

7 Raffles Blvd., Marina Square, Singapore 039595 (near Suntec City). © 800/327-8585 in the U.S. and Canada, 800/525-900 in Australia, 800/969-496 in the U.K., or 65/6336-8111. Fax 65/6339-1861. www. singapore.panpacific.com. 784 units. S$454 (US$304/£204) double; from S$645 (US$432/£290) suite. AE, DC, MC, V. 10-min. walk to City Hall MRT. **Amenities:** 6 restaurants; lobby lounge; outdoor pool; 2 outdoor lighted tennis courts; health club w/Jacuzzi, sauna, steam, massage, and spa treatments; concierge; airport transfers; room service; babysitting; smoke-free rooms; executive-level rooms. In room: A/C, TV w/ satellite programming and in-house movies, high-speed Internet, minibar, hair dryer.

Swissôtel The Stamford ★ (Value) With more than a thousand rooms and 73 floors, this immense tower is the tallest hotel in Southeast Asia. The Stamford is now getting a much-needed face-lift, with a refurbishment program that was launched in 2008, working its way down from the 27th floor. Even if you can't manage to get a renovated room, you'll be rewarded with a great bird's-eye view of Singapore island, from the historic Padang beneath to the business district and the iconic harbor. If that's not enough, just head upstairs to the Equinox bar. At 226m (741 feet), you can see almost the entire island and beyond. This hotel is in a great location, over the City Hall MRT and Raffles City Mall, and it also shares many of its facilities—including swimming pools and restaurants—with its sister hotel, the Fairmont.

2 Stamford Rd., Singapore 178882. © 800/637-9477 in the U.S. and Canada, 800/121-043 in Australia, or 65/6338-8585. Fax 65/6338-2862. www.swissotel-thestamford.com. 1,200 units. S$436 (US$292/£196) double; S$1,054 (US$706/£474) suite. AE, DC, MC, V. City Hall MRT. **Amenities:** 12 restaurants; martini bar, lobby lounge, and a live jazz venue; outdoor pool; spa w/gym, Jacuzzi, sauna, steam, and massage; concierge; airport transfers; room service; babysitting; smoke-free rooms; executive-level rooms. In room: A/C, TV w/satellite programming and in-house movies, minibar, hair dryer.

MODERATE

Albert Court Hotel ★ (Value) This eight-story boutique hotel has revitalized a block of charming prewar shophouses and given it Western-style comforts. Decorators placed local Peranakan touches everywhere, from the carved teak furnishings in traditional floral design to the antique china cups used for tea service in the rooms. (*Guaranteed:* The sight of these cups brings misty-eyed nostalgia to the hearts of Singaporeans.) Like most heritage hotels in Singapore, guest rooms aren't large, but details like the teak molding, bathroom tiles in bright Peranakan colors, and old-time brass electrical switches give this place real charm. Albert Court offers new courtyard rooms in the renovated houses that front the hotel's courtyard; these rooms contain all the local touches that make this hotel stand out from the rest. This hotel is especially attractive if you wish to spend a lot of time shopping and eating in Little India, which is just across the street.

180 Albert St., Singapore 189971. © 65/6339-3939. Fax 65/6339-3252. www.albertcourt.com.sg. 210 units. S$218 (US$146/£98) double. AE, DC, MC, V. 5-min. walk to either Bugis or Little India MRT. **Amenities:** 3 restaurants; small lobby lounge; limited room service; babysitting. In room: A/C, TV w/satellite programming, minibar, hair dryer.

Allson Hotel Singapore ★ (Value) Allson continues to be a strong tourist-class hotel in the city's historic district. Five floors have been renovated so far, with an ongoing program scheduled for 2009, which will increase the number of premium rooms. Standard deluxe guest rooms are a good size and simply but pleasantly decorated. Carved rosewood furniture—headboards, side tables, and armchairs in quaint Ming-style carvings—are an elegant touch for such moderately priced accommodations. Premium rooms are more European in flavor, with free Internet and soft drinks. They're certainly attractive but, sadly, lacking the carved furniture that gives standard rooms their charm. Bathrooms are very small but clean, with combined tub/shower. The small pool area and even smaller gym have received some maintenance touch-ups. There are no views here, but with a good location and modest prices, Allson remains a great choice for value-conscious leisure travelers.

101 Victoria St., Singapore 188018. ℂ **65/6336-0811.** Fax 65/6339-7019. www.allsonhotels.com. 450 units. S$218 (US$146/£98) deluxe double; from S$339 (US$227/£153) premium. AE, DC, MC, V. 5-min. walk from Bugis Junction MRT. **Amenities:** 3 restaurants; lounge; small outdoor pool; health club w/ Jacuzzi, sauna, steam, and massage; room service; babysitting; smoke-free rooms; executive-level rooms. *In room:* A/C, TV w/satellite programming and in-house movies, minibar.

Parkroyal on Beach Road Formerly known as The Plaza, the Parkroyal is just across from the color and great restaurants of Arab Street and Kampong Glam. It's 15 minutes' walk to the MRT (subway), so you'll need to take buses or taxis just about everywhere else—but the trade-off is that if you stick around, you can take advantage of the attractive recreation and relaxation facilities, which include a huge swimming pool and a lovely sun deck decorated in a lazy-days Balinese-style tropical motif, and a Bali-themed poolside cafe, cooled by ceiling fans. Two gyms to the side have plenty of space and new equipment, but the most exquisite facility of all is the exotic Bali-inspired spa. Other hotel facilities include outdoor and indoor Jacuzzis, a sauna, and a steam room. Guest rooms were renovated in 2007 and are simple but clean and comfortable.

7500A Beach Rd., Singapore 199591. ℂ **65/6298-0011.** Fax 65/6296-3600. www.parkroyalhotels.com. 350 units. S$230 (US$154/£104) double; from S$500 (US$335/£225) suite. AE, DC, MC, V. 15-min. walk to Bugis MRT. **Amenities:** 2 restaurants; lounge; outdoor pool; health club; spa w/Jacuzzi, sauna, steam, and massage; concierge; airport transfers; room service; babysitting; executive-level rooms. *In room:* A/C, TV w/satellite programming and in-house movies, high-speed Internet, minibar, hair dryer.

Peninsula • Excelsior Hotel ★★ (Value) As its rather uninspiring name suggests, this huge hotel was created when two of the city's busiest tourist-class hotels merged, combining their lobby and pools and other facilities into one giant value-for-money property popular with tour groups. The location really is excellent, in the Historic District within walking distance to Chinatown and Boat Quay, with some fantastic views over the city, the Singapore River, and the marina. A long-overdue renovation is finally taking place, and tired rooms are being freshened up. All the rooms in the Excelsior tower have now been renovated, and the Peninsula revamp is continuing into 2009. If you can bag a refurbished room overlooking Marina Bay, you'll be getting a great deal.

5 Coleman St., Singapore 179805. ℂ **65/6337-2200.** Fax 65/6336-3847. www.ytchotels.com.sg. 600 units. S$190 (US$127/£86) double; from S$295 (US$198/£133) club rooms, suites. AE, DC, MC, V. 5-min. walk to City Hall MRT. **Amenities:** Restaurant; bar and lobby lounge; 2 outdoor pools; health club w/ Jacuzzi; concierge; room service; babysitting. *In room:* A/C, TV, minibar, hair dryer.

INEXPENSIVE

Hotel Bencoolen Bencoolen is the signature backpacker hotel on a block that's best known for budget accommodations. A tiny lobby has a reception desk, bellhop, and one computer for Internet access. Upstairs, the rooms are equally small, with barely room to move around a queen-size bed, only a narrow closet for clothes, and a tiny TV hanging from the ceiling. King-size rooms have space for a small desk, while family rooms have one queen and one slightly oversize single bed squeezed in. Many of the rooms had a basic refurbishment in 2008, with new carpets and more modern decor. Small bathrooms are newly tiled as well but are already beginning to show some age. Don't expect views or creature comforts—the Bencoolen is a good, clean place to sleep before hitting the city again. The hotel has a rooftop restaurant.

47 Bencoolen St., Singapore 189626. ✆ **65/6336-0822.** Fax 65/6336-2250. www.hotelbencoolen.com. 74 units. S$178 double (US$119/£80); S$228 (US$153/£103) family. MC, V. 10-min. walk to City Hall or Dhoby Ghaut MRT. **Amenities:** Restaurant; sauna; smoke-free rooms. *In room:* A/C, TV.

Perak Hotel ★ This pretty budget hotel on the edge of Little India has real character. Its location in a row of white and blue shophouses gives it charm, and there are nice decorative touches, with local fabrics and simple wooden furniture. As with most conversions, guests need to accept a few quirks as well: The atmospheric wooden floorways can be noisy, and the guest rooms, though clean and tidy, are small, with tiny and basic bathrooms. Superior rooms are pleasant, with shuttered windows, but many standard rooms rely on skylights instead. It's popular with the friendly backpacking crowd who gather in the lobby and cafe to chat and make use of the free Internet.

12 Perak Rd., Singapore 208133. ✆ **65/6299-7733.** Fax 65/6392-0919. www.peraklodge.com. 34 units. S$148 (US$99/£67) double; S$228 (US$153/£103) triple. Rates include breakfast. AE, DC, MC, V. 5-min. walk to Bugis or Little India MRT. **Amenities:** Cafe; high-speed Internet. *In room:* A/C, TV.

Strand Hotel ★ The Strand is definitely one of the better backpacker places in Singapore. The lobby doesn't look or feel like a budget hotel, with marble floors, a smart bellhop, and a long reception desk. There's also an inviting cafe to one side, plus a small gift shop. Guest rooms are the largest I've seen in a budget hotel in Singapore—in fact, they are larger than a lot of more expensive rooms as well. Rooms are simply furnished, but decoration is exuberant (the rooms with purple walls and leopard-skin headboards may not be to everyone's taste). Unless you're a bona fide exhibitionist, don't go for the "special room," with the bathtub/shower separated from the main room by only a thin glass wall. Anybody for a free show?

25 Bencoolen St., Singapore 189619. ✆ **65/6338-1866.** Fax 65/6338-1330. 130 units. S$100 (US$67/£45) double; S$120 (US$80/£54) 3-person sharing. AE, DC, MC, V. 10-min. walk to City Hall or Dhoby Ghaut MRT. **Amenities:** Restaurant; room service. *In room:* A/C, TV.

2 CHINATOWN

EXPENSIVE

Amara Singapore Amara, located in the Shenton Way financial district, attracts primarily business travelers, so if your vacation includes a little business, too, this hotel puts you closer to the action. If you're simply in town for a vacation, Amara doesn't offer the best location or environment, but the focus on business travelers means there are some excellent value weekend rates available and a two-room suite that's useful for families. The top eight floors of this hotel are reserved for the corporate set; not only do they have better views, but also modern decor and services attractive to business visitors.

Tropical 6 rooms aimed at the leisure traveler are spacious and closer to the pleasant pool area, but offer little in terms of views.

165 Tanjong Pagar Rd., Singapore 088539. *©* **65/6879-2555.** Fax 65/6224-3910. www.amarahotels.com. 338 units. S$380 (US$254/£171) double; from S$700 (US$469/£315) suite. AE, DC, MC, V. 5-min. walk to Tanjong Pagar MRT. **Amenities:** 2 restaurants; lounge; outdoor pool; outdoor lighted tennis courts; health club w/Jacuzzi, jogging track, sauna, steam, and massage; concierge; airport transfers; room service; babysitting; smoke-free rooms. *In room:* A/C, TV w/satellite programming and in-house movies, high-speed Internet, minibar, hair dryer.

M Hotel Singapore ★★   If work brings you to the Shenton Way downtown business district, then M Hotel is your best bet. Cornering the international business travel market, everything here is designed to make life easier for those with places to go and people to see. Rooms feature large, comfortable workspaces in clutter-free tones (blond wood furnishings, bone upholstery, tan carpeting), with some splashes of darker textiles for variety. Broadband Internet access and laptop safes make for extra convenience. The 11th floor is reserved for unwinding, with pool, spa, and fitness center all in sanitary contemporary white with glass-and-chrome accents everywhere. Good weekend deals are available, but leisure travelers won't find much to inspire in the financial district evenings or weekends. Operated by local firm Haatch, the spa has an excellent menu and reputation for quality. M Hotel's restaurants are packed for power lunches, so book in advance.

81 Anson Rd., Singapore 079908. *©* **866/866-8086** in the U.S. and Canada, 800/147-803 in Australia, 800/782-542 in New Zealand, 800/8686-8086 in the U.K., or 65/6224-1133. Fax 65/6222-0749. www.millennium hotels.com. 413 units. S$378 (US$253/£170) double; S$700 (US$469/£315) suite. AE, DC, MC, V. 10-min. walk to Tanjong Pagar MRT. **Amenities:** 3 restaurants; bar; outdoor pool w/2 Jacuzzis; health club w/rock-climbing wall; spa; room service; babysitting; executive-level rooms. *In room:* A/C, TV w/satellite programming, high-speed Internet, minibar, hair dryer.

New Majestic Hotel ★★   The Art Deco New Majestic Hotel is achingly stylish, with a shining white lobby dotted with a collection of classic chairs that represent the best of 20th-century design. The guest rooms are large, each designed by a Singaporean artist with an unlimited budget. The popular Wayang room, named after traditional Chinese opera, is scarlet and black, with walls entirely covered in fine red silk. Fashion designer Daniel Boey's Pussy Parlour is a confection of fuchsia and electric blue, with silk crepe sheets and a Champagne bar in red lacquer. There are also more understated and practical rooms, though they're no less creative. High-quality amenities include Kiehl's toiletries, Bose systems, espresso machines, and iPod docking stations. The New Majestic proudly boasts "Singapore's smallest pool." The only pool permitted in a conservation building, this compact rectangle of mosaic tiling is placed above the restaurant and features glass portholes in its floor.

31–37 Bukit Pasoh Rd., Singapore 089845. *©* **65/6511-4700.** Fax 65/6227-3301. www.newmajestic hotel.com. 30 units. S$400 (US$268/£180) double; from S$750 (US$503/£338) suite. AE, MC, V. 1-min. walk to Outram Park MRT. **Amenities:** Restaurant; outdoor pool; health club; concierge. *In room:* A/C, TV w/satellite programming, minibar, hair dryer.

Swissôtel Merchant Court ★   Merchant Court is beautifully located in the city center, within easy walking distance of Chinatown and the historic and financial districts. Colorful Clarke Quay opposite offers a superb range of restaurants, cafes, and nightlife, and Robertson and Boat Quays are a short, pleasant stroll along the river. A mall and the MRT are right on the doorstep. All that convenience means it's a busy, buzzing part of town, particularly at night, but the large attractive pool and terrace area gives some room to relax and the Amrita spa is excellent. Standard (Classic) rooms are

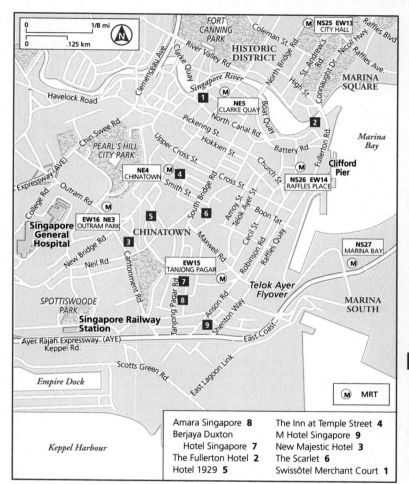

Amara Singapore **8**
Berjaya Duxton
Hotel Singapore **7**
The Fullerton Hotel **2**
Hotel 1929 **5**

The Inn at Temple Street **4**
M Hotel Singapore **9**
New Majestic Hotel **3**
The Scarlet **6**
Swissôtel Merchant Court **1**

simple and pleasant—not large, but with good-sized bathrooms. Renovated business rooms are larger and more stylish, with striking geometric carpets and wall panels, and there's an Executive Lounge on the top floor. Although the hotel is largely geared toward business travelers, if you give advance notice, staff can create a special Kids Room, accessorized with bright rugs, age-appropriate toys, and DVDs.

20 Merchant Rd., Singapore 058281. ✆ **800/637-9477** in the U.S. and Canada, 800/121-043 in Australia, 800/637-94771 in the U.K., or 65/6337-2288. Fax 65/6334-0606. www.swissotel-merchantcourt.com. 476 units. S$330 (US$221/£149) double; from S$750 (US$503/£338) suite. AE, DC, MC, V. Clarke Quay MRT. **Amenities:** Restaurant; bar; outdoor pool; health club and spa w/Jacuzzi, sauna, steam, massage, and beauty treatments; room service; babysitting; smoke-free rooms; executive-level rooms. *In room:* A/C, TV w/satellite programming and in-house movies, high-speed Internet, hair dryer.

MODERATE

Berjaya Duxton Hotel Singapore   The Duxton was one of Singapore's first boutique hotels, transforming shophouses into a small hotel that earned international acclaim. Following a takeover by the Malaysian Berjaya Group, a 2008 refurbishment program has freshened up carpets and upholstery, and the garden suites are pleasant and private, but the building's age means the Berjaya Duxton would really reap rewards from a major investment program, which is not currently scheduled. The Victorian antique–looking decor is pretty and a welcome change from the usual corporate chains, but there's little sense of local Chinatown character in the rooms or the modern new Italian restaurant. However, the Duxton has character and a good location at a good price. The area is great for bars and restaurants, though steer clear of some of the karaoke bars on Duxton Road. Service is friendly and personal.

83 Duxton Rd., Singapore 089540. © **65/6227-7678.** Fax 65/6227-1232. www.berjayaresorts.com. 50 units. S$210 (US$141/£95) double; S$380 (US$255/£171) suite. AE, DC, MC, V. 5-min. walk to Tanjong Pagar MRT. **Amenities:** Restaurant; lobby bar; airport transfers; room service; babysitting. *In room:* A/C, TV w/satellite programming and in-house movies, minibar, hair dryer.

The Inn at Temple Street ★★   They've done a lovely job with this modest boutique hotel. In the heart of Chinatown's tourism hustle and bustle, step into the small lobby to be greeted by pretty antiques and Chinese porcelain. To the side of the lobby, a popular cafe serves Western and local meals three times a day. The friendly front desk handles everything from business center services to arranging laundry, tours, and postal services, but never seems frazzled. Naturally, there's no elevator and rooms can fairly be described as tiny, but they are quite modern for this type of hotel, with keycard locks, in-room safe, tea and coffee, minibar, TV, and room service. Decor is atmospheric, too, with carved wooden bedsteads and pretty fabrics. I like the black-and-white-tiled bathrooms, though you'll need to opt for a deluxe room if you want a bathtub rather than a shower. Attractive, affordable, and friendly.

36 Temple St., Singapore 058581. © **65/6221-5333.** Fax 65/6225-5391. www.theinn.com.sg. 42 units. S$228 (US$153/£103) double; S$328 (US$220/£148) family. AE, DC, MC, V. 5-min. walk to Chinatown MRT. **Amenities:** Restaurant; lounge; room service. *In room:* A/C, TV, minibar.

The Scarlet   Glamour drips from every chandelier onto the polished black marble floors of this groovy little boutique hotel. Swirling patterns of gold and blood red velvet compete for attention in the lobby and its equally stylish lounge. The location, in a row of original shophouses, means that guest rooms are very small and skylights are the only source of daylight in first-floor deluxe rooms. Unless you're in a premium deluxe or a suite, you'll have a shower rather than a bath, but rooms are well designed and comfortably decorated in sophisticated muted color schemes and equipped with flatscreen TVs, DVD, and broadband. Suites are opulent, with swaths of silk drapery, funky lounge areas, and ornate gilt frames. There's not much in the way of facilities (a Jacuzzi and a tiny gym, "Flaunt," and a pleasant rooftop bar and restaurant), but Chinatown and the fashionable haunts of Club Street are just around the corner.

33 Erskine Rd., Singapore 069333. © **65/6511-3333.** Fax 65/6511-3303. www.thescarlethotel.com. 84 units. S$247 (US$165/[bp111) double; from S$485 (US$325/£218) suite. AE, DC, MC, V. 10-min. walk from Chinatown MRT. **Amenities:** 2 restaurants; lounge; health club; outdoor Jacuzzi; concierge; executive-level rooms. *In room:* A/C, TV w/satellite programming, high speed Internet, minibar.

INEXPENSIVE

Hotel 1929 ★ (Finds)   This trendy, inexpensive little place is a real gem in Chinatown, operated by the same people behind the swish New Majestic. Though its target market is very different, there are some clues to the shared parentage in its love of vintage chairs and retro design. The hotel's shophouse location means that rooms are small and quirkily shaped—many of the toilets are extremely close to the shower, but clever design and an eye for detail makes for pleasant, well-organized spaces with real personality. Some of the cheapest rooms have no windows, and facilities are limited to a Jacuzzi and sun deck—though its busy and sometimes noisy location doesn't really lend itself to sunbathing. Staff is friendly and helpful, and the Ember restaurant is popular.

50 Keong Saik Rd., Singapore 089154. © **65/6347-1929.** Fax 65/6327-1929. S$200 (US$134/£90) double; from S$350(US$235/£158) suite. AE, DC, MC, V. 5-min. walk to Outram Park MRT. **Amenities:** Restaurant; Jacuzzi. *In room:* A/C, TV, minibar, hair dryer.

---

3 ORCHARD ROAD AREA

VERY EXPENSIVE

Four Seasons Hotel Singapore ★★★   The Four Seasons has a residential atmosphere, and there's a sense of intimacy and peace that's unusual among international hotels. The hotel is smaller than many of its competitors, and the personable staff delivers ultraefficient service. Located just off Orchard Road, extensive gardens block out much of the sights and sounds of the city center. As well as the elegant pools, there are indoor and outdoor tennis courts (with a resident professional), a spa, and fully staffed fitness area. A 2008 refurbishment has added state-of-the-art entertainment systems and plasma TVs. Premier rooms and suites are huge, with antiques and artworks selected from the Four Season's large collection. Superior rooms are also unusually large and comfortable, decorated in tasteful ivory and chestnut with high ceilings and the kind of comforts that come at a premium elsewhere. Consider a standard room here before a suite in a less expensive hotel.

190 Orchard Blvd., Singapore 248646. © **800/332-3442** in the U.S., 800/268-6282 in Canada, or 65/6734-1110. Fax 65/6733-0682. www.fourseasons.com. 254 units. S$550 (US$369/£248) double; from S$720 (US$482/£324) suite. AE, DC, MC, V. 10-min. walk to Orchard MRT. **Amenities:** 2 restaurants; bar; 2 outdoor pools w/adjacent Jacuzzis; 2 outdoor lighted tennis courts and 2 indoor air-conditioned tennis courts; Singapore's best equipped fitness center; spa w/sauna, steam, massage, and full menu of beauty and relaxation treatments; concierge; airport transfers; room service; babysitting; smoke-free rooms; executive-level rooms; billiards room. *In room:* A/C, TV w/satellite programming and in-room laserdisc player w/complimentary disks available, Wi-Fi, minibar, hair dryer.

Shangri-La Hotel ★★★   On 6 hectares (15 acres) of tropical gardens, the Shang's 750 rooms are spread across three wings, each tailored to meet the needs of different travelers. The vast lobby features columns that rise up from the marble floor, and a series of sparkling chandeliers overhead. The Tower Wing rooms are aimed at the business traveler, with modern blond wood, uncluttered appearance, and large work areas. Bay windows offer floor-to-ceiling views over the city. Leisure travelers prefer the tropical feel of the Garden Wing, where large rooms have balconies that overlook the gardens. Celebrities, government leaders, and high rollers favor the ultraexclusive Valley Wing, which has a separate private driveway and entrance, butler service, complimentary champagne bar and personalized stationery. Its rooms and suites are some of the largest in Singapore, elegant and supremely comfortable with luxurious bathrooms and separate dressing rooms. The hotel's Limousine airport transfer is free to Tower Wing guests.

22 Orange Grove Rd., Singapore 258350. ✆ **800/942-5050** in the U.S., 866/344-5050 in Canada, 800/222-448 in Australia, 800/442-179 in New Zealand, or 65/6737-3644. Fax 65/6737-3257. www.shangri-la.com. 750 units. S$530 (US$355/£239) Tower double; S$740 (US$496/£333) Garden double; S$901 (US$604/£405) Valley double; from S$1,000 (US$670/£450) suite. AE, DC, MC, V. 10-min. walk to Orchard MRT. **Amenities:** 5 restaurants; lobby lounge; resort-style outdoor landscaped pool; 4 outdoor lighted tennis courts; health club looking out into gardens; Spa with Jacuzzi, sauna, steam, and massage; concierge; airport transfers; room service; babysitting; smoke-free rooms; executive-level rooms. *In room:* A/C, TV w/satellite programming and in-house movies, high-speed Internet, minibar, hair dryer.

Sheraton Towers Singapore ★★

Sheraton's lobby is lined with service awards. With the deluxe (standard) room, they'll give you a suit pressing on arrival, daily newspaper delivery, shoeshine service, and complimentary movies. These refurbished rooms are handsome, with textured walls, plush carpeting, and a bed luxuriously fitted with down pillows and dreamy 100% Egyptian cotton bedding. Upgrade to a Tower room, and you get a personal butler, complimentary nightly cocktails and morning breakfast, free laundry, free local calls, your own pants press, and free use of the personal trainer in the fitness center. The cabana rooms, off the pool area, have all the services of the Tower Wing in a very private resort room. The 23 one-of-a-kind suites each feature a different theme: Chinese regency, French, Italian, jungle, you name it. Although Sheraton is a luxe choice, you can find better deals, price wise.

39 Scotts Rd., Singapore 228230. ✆ **800/325-3535** in the U.S. and Canada, 800/073-535 in Australia, 800/325-35353 in New Zealand, 800/353535 in the U.K., or 65/6737-6888. Fax 65/6737-1072. www.sheraton.com. 413 units. S$520 (US$348/£234) double; from S$1,200 (US$804/£540) suite. AE, DC, MC, V. 5-min. walk to Newton MRT. **Amenities:** 3 restaurants; lobby lounge; outdoor landscaped pool; health club w/sauna and massage; concierge; airport transfers; room service; babysitting; smoke-free rooms; executive-level rooms. *In room:* A/C, TV w/satellite programming and in-house movies, high-speed Internet, minibar, hair dryer.

St. Regis Hotel ★★★

Singapore's newest luxury hotel opened in early 2008. Touted as a six-star property, it's distinctly palatial and ornate, with patterned fabrics and carpeting, dainty crockery, and huge chandeliers. Guests are chauffeured in Bentleys. Guest rooms feature walnut furniture, Jim Thomson silks, and plush couches, and are full of gadgets, with Bose sound systems, plasma TVs, and lighting panels. Enormous marble-clad bathrooms have flatscreen TVs in the mirror facing the bath. Each floor is serviced by discreet and expert butlers. Grand Deluxe rooms overlook the greenery of the exclusive Tanglin and Nassim areas. Toiletries are from the in-house Remède spa, with a wet lounge, which is complimentary for guests. While you're there, consider the Remède's version of a hot stone massage, which uses huge silken pebbles of pure jade. Facilities are of the high standard that you would expect, though the pool area is overlooked by nearby towers.

29 Tanglin Rd., Singapore 247911. ✆ **877/STREGIS (787-3447)** in the U.S. and Canada; 800/221-637 in Australia; 800/450-561 in New Zealand; 800/325-78734 in the U.K.; or 65/6506-6888. Fax 65/6506-6708. www.starwoodhotels.com. 299 units. S$545 (US$365/£245) double; from S$1,400 (US$938/£630) suite. AE, DC, MC, V. 15-min. walk to Orchard MRT. **Amenities:** 3 restaurants; 2 bars; outdoor pools w/Jacuzzi; 2 indoor air-conditioned tennis courts; health club; spa w/wet room, sauna, steam, massage, and comprehensive menu of beauty and relaxation treatments; concierge; airport transfers; room service; babysitting; smoke-free rooms; executive-level rooms. *In room:* A/C, plasma TVs w/satellite programming and in-room entertainment center, Wi-Fi, minibar, hair dryer.

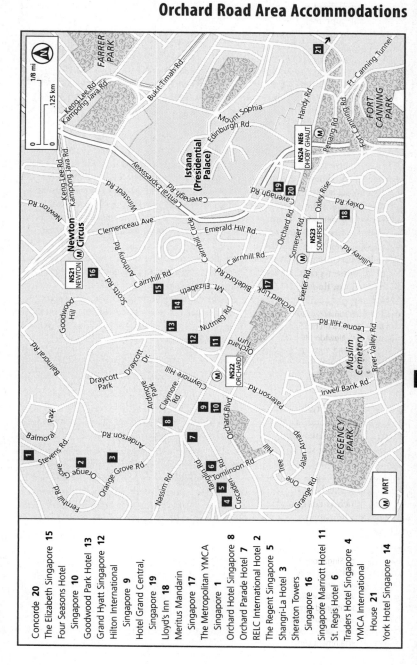

Concorde **20**

The Elizabeth Singapore **15**

Four Seasons Hotel Singapore **10**

Goodwood Park Hotel **13**

Grand Hyatt Singapore **12**

Hilton International Singapore **9**

Hotel Grand Central, Singapore **19**

Lloyd's Inn **18**

Meritus Mandarin Singapore **17**

The Metropolitan YMCA Singapore **1**

Orchard Hotel Singapore **8**

Orchard Parade Hotel **7**

RELC International Hotel **2**

The Regent Singapore **5**

Shangri-La Hotel **3**

Sheraton Towers Singapore **16**

Singapore Marriott Hotel **11**

St. Regis Hotel **6**

Traders Hotel Singapore **4**

YMCA International House **21**

York Hotel Singapore **14**

The Best of Singapore's Spas

In the mid–1990s, spas began making a splash in the Singapore hotel scene. By the millennium, every luxury hotel was either planning a full-blown spa facility or at least offering spa services to its residents. At the same time, day spas sprouted up in shopping centers, and despite the economic downturn, these businesses have stayed afloat. Now the Singapore Tourism Board is positioning Singapore as an urban spa hub in Southeast Asia, luring visitors from the region and beyond with luxurious facilities that go above and beyond the call of relaxation and hedonistic pampering. Here are the best among the many:

Singapore's most celebrated spa, **Amrita** (The Fairmont, Level 6, 2 Stamford Rd.; ✆ **65/6336-4477;** and Swissôtel Merchant Court, Level 2, 20 Merchant Rd.; ✆ **65/6239-1780;** www.amritaspas.com), is operated by Raffles International and has proven so wildly successful that the hotel chain has opened Amritas in Germany, Switzerland, and beyond. This flagship spa at The Fairmont is the largest spa in Singapore, with Southeast Asian–inspired interiors and treatments—over 1,000 to choose from.

Amrita is convenient if you want to stay in the city center; however, if you want more of a retreat spa experience, **Spa Botanica** (2 Bukit Manis Rd., The Sentosa; ✆ **65/6371-1318;** www.spabotanica.com) is a gorgeous pick. It is located at the Sentosa, a scenic resort dripping with laid-back, yet elegant tropical Southeast Asian decor. Spa Botanica has 6,000 sq. m (64,583 sq. ft.) of designated spa space, with pools, mud baths, and treatment pavilions nestled in lush gardens. Treatments center around natural recipes for beauty and relaxation, including spice and floral treatments.

EXPENSIVE

Concorde Formerly Le Meridien, this Orchard Road hotel has been losing its appeal in recent years, but the new management promises a major renovation program will restore its former glory by early 2010. Club rooms and suites have already been refurbished, and the remaining deluxe rooms are scheduled for similar treatment in 2009. Public areas, including the impressive atrium lobby, aren't due to change much, and it's a shame there are no plans yet to overhaul the rather shabby shopping arcade outside. Business facilities have a way to go to make the Concorde a great choice for business travelers, but if you're here to shop, then you can't beat this location; the Concorde's large refurbished rooms makes an enviably convenient place to stash your shopping bags before heading to the Historic District nearby.

100 Orchard Rd., Singapore 238840. ✆ **65/6733-8855.** Fax 65/6732-7886. www.concordehotel.com.sg. 407 units. S$336 (US$225/£151) double; from S$568 (US$381/£256) suite. AE, DC, MC, V. 5-min. walk to Dhoby Ghaut MRT. **Amenities:** 2 restaurants; lobby lounge; outdoor pool; health club w/sauna; concierge; airport transfers; room service; babysitting; executive-level rooms. *In room:* A/C, TV w/satellite programming and in-house movies, minibar, hair dryer.

Goodwood Park Hotel ★ The Goodwood Park is a National Landmark, built in 1900 as the Teutonia Club, and may be Raffles' closest rival for historical significance.

Guestrooms are large and lovely, overlooking the main pool or the Mayfair pool. Spacious Poolside Suites are decorated in a classic European style, and several open directly onto the gardens and main pool terrace. *One caveat:* The main pool is also overlooked by the glass walls of the main lobby, so if you prefer privacy, choose a room beside the Balinese-inspired Mayfair pool. If you're in Singapore for a week or more, the large one-bedroom Parklane Suites, housed in a separate wing, can be a bargain. While Goodwood doesn't come close to matching the business and fitness centers of other hotels in its price range, its four restaurants are highly rated by locals, particularly the dim sum served at the Min Jiang restaurant. The staff at Goodwood Park is particularly friendly and helpful.

22 Scotts Rd., Singapore 228221. © 800/772-3890 in the U.S., 800/665-5919 in Canada, 800/89-95-20 in the U.K., or 65/6737-7411. Fax 65/6732-8558. www.goodwoodparkhotel.com. 235 units. S$389 (US$261/£175) double; from S$648 (US$434/£292) suite. AE, DC, MC, V. 5-min. walk to Orchard MRT. **Amenities:** 6 restaurants; bar and lobby lounge; 2 outdoor pools; tiny health club; spa; concierge; airport transfers; room service; babysitting. *In room:* A/C, TV w/satellite programming and in-house movies, minibar, hair dryer.

Grand Hyatt Singapore ★★

The unusual lobby, with glass windows set at right angles and a reception desk hidden around the corner, brings good feng shui to this excellent hotel. In public spaces, floors of polished cream or black marble are offset by deep wood and streams trickling slowly over hand-chiseled rocks. Guest rooms in the Terrace Wing are decked out in shades of cream and gray with good work desks and big marble bathrooms. Even better are the Grand Wing rooms, which are really suites with separate living areas, small walk-in closets, Bang & Olufsen TVs, and a separate work area. The freeform pool was overhauled in 2008 and is beautifully landscaped with wooden decks and loungers that sit in shallow water. The new Japanese-designed Damai spa and state-of-the-art fitness center overlook the incredible five-story waterfall that sits in the center of the hotel. This is an oasis just steps away from the busiest intersection in the city.

10 Scotts Rd., Singapore 228211. © 800/223-1234 in the U.S. and Canada, or 65/6738-1234. Fax 65/6732-1696. www.singapore.grand.hyatt.com. 663 units. S$442 (US$296/£199) double; from S$565 (US$379/£254) Grand Deluxe. AE, DC, MC, V. Near Orchard MRT. **Amenities:** 5 restaurants; 2 bars; live music bar; landscaped outdoor pool; 2 outdoor lighted tennis courts; squash court and badminton court; excellent health club w/Jacuzzi, sauna, and steam; outstanding spa; concierge; airport transfers; room service; babysitting; executive-level rooms. *In room:* A/C, TV w/satellite programming and in-house movies, high-speed Internet, minibar, hair dryer.

Meritus Mandarin Singapore ★

This tour group favorite is brilliantly located in the center of Orchard Road. A multiphased renovation project launched in 2008 has moved the main lobby around the corner to Orchard Link, and a fifth-floor linkway now connects the hotel's two wings. *A cautionary note:* The Mandarin's first four floors are being converted into a shopping mall—work that has closed the pool and will continue to cause some disruption until fall/winter 2009. Guest rooms are also due for renovations in 2009, so it's worth checking for bargains while the work is ongoing. Try for a Premier room, on higher floors and much quieter, which are more spacious and luxurious. The tower and rooftop revolving restaurant was a landmark when it opened in 1973. Sadly, it no longer revolves, but the Chatterbox restaurant still offers Singaporean specialties such as chicken rice with remarkable 360-degree city views.

333 Orchard Rd., Singapore 238867. © 65/6737-4411. Fax 65/6732-2361. www.asiatravel.com/singapore/mandarin. 1,051 units. S$341 (US$228/£153) double; from S$691 (US$463/£311) suite. AE, DC, MC, V. Near Orchard MRT. **Amenities:** 4 restaurants; revolving observation lounge and lobby lounge; outdoor pool

(closed for renovation, to end 2009); health club w/Jacuzzi, sauna, steam, and massage; concierge; airport transfers; room service; babysitting; smoke-free rooms; executive-level rooms. *In room:* A/C, TV w/satellite programming and in-house movies, minibar.

The Regent Singapore ★

The Regent is tucked between Cuscaden and Tanglin roads, at the northern end of Orchard Road—you'll have to hike about 10 minutes to get to the center of things. But check out the lobby in this place! It's a huge three-level atrium affair with windows on three sides, a skylight, fountains, plenty of small private meeting nooks, and raised walkways straight out of *The Jetsons*. The guest rooms have high ceilings and are decorated with Chinese motifs in refurbished fabrics, but the bathrooms are smaller than at most other comparable hotels and the place is showing its age slightly. You have to request coffee-/tea-making facilities in your room; otherwise, the service is free in the tea lounge, which also serves a high tea the old-fashioned way, with silver tray service.

1 Cuscaden Rd., Singapore 249715. 🄯 **800/545-4000** in the U.S. and Canada, 800/022-800 in Australia, 800/440-800 in New Zealand, 800/917-8795 in the U.K., or 65/6733-8888. Fax 65/6732-8838. www.regenthotels.com. 441 units. S$418 (US$280/£188) double; from S$589 (US$395/£265) suite. AE, DC, MC, V. 15-min. walk to Orchard MRT. **Amenities:** 2 restaurants; very cool bar; lobby tea lounge; outdoor pool; health club w/steam and massage; concierge; airport transfers; room service; babysitting; smoke-free rooms; executive-level rooms. *In room:* A/C, TV w/satellite programming and in-house movies, high-speed Internet, hair dryer.

Singapore Marriott Hotel ★★

The towering green and scarlet–roofed pagoda of the Marriott is a landmark at the corner of Orchard and Scott roads. Geared strongly toward business travelers, its ultracentral location, next to Orchard MRT, makes sightseeing convenient, too. The cosmopolitan lobby is perfect for informal meetings or a comfortable coffee stop. Crossroads Café, which spills from the hotel onto the sidewalk, is one of Singapore's most popular spots to see and be seen. The pagoda tower means that rooms aren't large, though they are cozy and inviting and equipped with all the comforts and conveniences you'd expect for business travel. Leisure travelers may find the pool-terrace rooms and suites more interesting, elegant little cabins that are surprisingly resort-like, considering the Orchard Road location. Each has a poolside veranda, wooden floors with rugs, skylights over the open-plan bath, and walls of carved stone.

320 Orchard Rd., Singapore 238865. 🄯 **800/228-9290** in the U.S. and Canada, 800/251-259 in Australia, 800/22-12-22 in the U.K., or 65/6735-5800. Fax 65/6735-9800. www.singaporemarriott.com. 373 units. S$324 (US$217/£146) double; from S$640 (US$429/£288) suite. AE, DC, MC, V. Orchard MRT. **Amenities:** 4 restaurants; lobby lounge; bar w/live jazz, and dance club w/live bands; outdoor pool w/Jacuzzi; health club w/Jacuzzi, sauna, steam, and massage; concierge; airport transfers; room service; babysitting; smoke-free rooms; executive-level rooms' outdoor basketball court. *In room:* A/C, TV w/satellite programming and in-house movies, high-speed Internet, minibar, hair dryer.

MODERATE

The Elizabeth Singapore

The Elizabeth is European in style, although the lobby has a huge and distinctly Asian waterfall that cascades down to a rock garden below and a gift shop that's good for Asian souvenirs. Executive-floor rooms were refurbished in 2008, as were the four large suites, which are large, if relatively unadventurous, spaces with dark wood furniture. If you need the space, these can be a good deal. Unfortunately, the hotel has no plans yet to invest in the standard (Superior) rooms, which are becoming rather worn and dark since their last refit in 2005. The facilities are nothing to write home about; there are a few workout machines next to the pool area and no business center (although Internet is available and the friendly staff at reception will help with faxes). There is a restaurant, but most would prefer to head to Orchard Road, a short but slightly hilly stroll away.

24 Mount Elizabeth, Singapore 228518. ℂ **65/6738-1188.** Fax 65/6732-3866. www.theelizabeth.com.sg. 256 units. S$220 (US$147/£99) double; S$550 (US$369/£248) suite. AE, DC, MC, V. 10-min. walk to Orchard MRT. **Amenities:** Restaurant; lobby lounge; small outdoor pool; tiny health club; concierge; room service; babysitting; executive-level rooms. *In room:* A/C, TV w/satellite programming, high-speed Internet, minibar, hair dryer.

Hilton International Singapore

This Hilton doesn't measure up with some of their other properties worldwide and definitely can't compete with other hotels in this price category in Singapore. The most famous feature of the Hilton is its glamorous shopping arcade, where you can find your Donna Karan, Louis Vuitton, Gucci—all the greats. With all this, the guest rooms should be pretty sumptuous, no? Well, no. The rooms are simpler than you'd expect, with nothing flashy or overdone. Floor-to-ceiling windows are in each, and although views in the front of the hotel are of Orchard Road and the Thai Embassy property, views in the back are not so hot. In this day and age, when business-class hotels are wrestling to outdo each other, Hilton has a lot of catching up to do.

581 Orchard Rd., Singapore 238883. ℂ **800/445-8667** in the U.S., or 65/6737-2233. Fax 65/6732-2917. www.singapore.hilton.com. 423 units. S$300 (US$201/£135) double; from S$660 (US$442/£297) suite. AE, DC, MC, V. Near Orchard MRT. **Amenities:** 2 restaurants; lobby lounge; outdoor pool; health club w/ sauna and steam; concierge; airport transfers; room service; babysitting; smoke-free rooms; executive-level rooms. *In room:* A/C, TV w/satellite programming and in-house movies, minibar, hair dryer.

Orchard Hotel Singapore ★

There's a pleasant buzz about the Orchard Hotel. Perhaps it's the giant wrought-iron clock in the center of the lobby, ticking away the time in London, Tokyo, Singapore, and New York that gives the Orchard an air of a very plush railway station. The Orchard Wing houses standard (superior) rooms. These aren't huge, but make good use of space with comfortable contemporary furniture and an intriguing round window that lets daylight into the bathrooms. A few Superior rooms have a more Asian feel and local touches like painted wooden furniture. The larger and plusher Executive Deluxe and Club rooms are mostly housed in the Claymore Wing. The hotel's upper Orchard Road location means that views aren't spectacular, but there's a large pool, a fitness center, and a great attached shopping mall that has useful cafes, restaurants, and salons. The staff is friendly and helpful, though at times overworked, so allow plenty of time for checkout.

442 Orchard Rd., Singapore 238879. ℂ **800/637-7200** in the U.S. and Canada, 800/655-147 in Australia, 800/442-519 in New Zealand, or 65/6734-7766. Fax 65/6733-5482. www.orchardhotel.com.sg. 672 units. S$303 (US$203/£136) double; S$697 (US$467/£314) suite. AE, DC, MC, V. 5-min. walk to Orchard MRT. **Amenities:** 2 restaurants; lobby lounge; outdoor pool; health club w/sauna; concierge; room service; babysitting; smoke-free rooms; executive-level rooms. *In room:* A/C, TV w/satellite programming, minibar.

Orchard Parade Hotel ★★ (Value) (Kids)

This Mediterranean-style gem is right at the top of Orchard Road. I recommend its family studios; they are large and comfortable, with a king-size bed and lounge seating area, dining area, and spacious bathroom, plus two extra single beds behind a partition. There's a balcony, too, though the view over the busy junction of Tanglin and Orchard Road isn't exactly peaceful. Deluxe double rooms are also spacious, pleasant, and bright, though the bathrooms are fairly basic. Views are variable, so specify at booking if that's important to you. Standard double and twin rooms tend to face the building at the back of the hotel, so your view's likely to be of concrete. On the sixth-floor roof there's a colorful terracotta-tiled pool area, and the terrace outside is convenient for coffee shops and family restaurants—plus, of course, you have all of Orchard Road to choose from. It's a 10-minute walk to the Botanic Gardens and Orchard MRT.

1 Tanglin Rd., Singapore 247905. ℃ **65/6737-1133.** Fax 65/6733-0242. www.orchardparade.com.sg. 387 units. S$259 (US$174/£117) double; S$550 (US$369/£248) family studio; from S$450 (US$302/£203) suite. AE, DC, MC, V. Orchard MRT. **Amenities:** 5 restaurants; lobby lounge; outdoor pool; health club; concierge; room service; babysitting; executive-level rooms. In room: A/C, TV w/satellite programming, minibar, hair dryer.

Traders Hotel Singapore ★★

Traders doesn't look like a value-for-money hotel, with its smartly designed lobby and restaurants, but that's how it advertises itself—and it's certainly a bargain for leisure travelers in Singapore. Most of the rooms are moderately small, although there are five triple rooms with child-size sofa beds. Superior (standard) rooms are located on the lower floors, with their Deluxe counterparts benefiting from slightly better views. The only major problem with Traders (and its neighbors) is the distance from the main part of Orchard Road and the subway, but they do offer an hourly free shuttle bus to and from Orchard MRT and Ngee Ann/Takashimaya, and weekday shuttles to various business parks. Better still, this value hotel has a cross-signing arrangement with the nearby Shangri-La hotel and the Rasa Sentosa resort on Sentosa Island, giving you access to their awesome pools, spas, and fitness centers, plus the latter's beachfront location.

1A Cuscaden Rd., Singapore 249716. ℃ **800/942-5050** in the U.S. and Canada, 800/222-448 in Australia, 0800/442-179 in New Zealand, or 65/6738-2222. Fax 65/6831-4314. www.shangri-la.com. 547 units. S$272 (US$182/£122) double; from S$518 (US$347/£233) suite. AE, DC, MC, V. 15-min. walk to Orchard MRT. **Amenities:** 2 restaurants; bar and lobby lounge; outdoor pool; health club w/Jacuzzi, sauna, steam, and massage; spa; concierge; airport transfers; room service; babysitting; executive-level rooms. In room: A/C, TV w/satellite programming, high-speed Internet access, minibar, hair dryer.

York Hotel Singapore ★

This charming little hotel has got even better in the past year, thanks to a modernization program that's smartened up the 407 rooms and extended the business and fitness facilities. Pale, contemporary furnishings in neutral colors lend a calming atmosphere to the guest rooms. Superior rooms aren't particularly large, so if you want more space, upgrade to one of the spacious deluxe or colorful cabana rooms that look out over the pool. The York's location, 10 minutes' walk from Orchard Road, offers a good compromise between accessibility and a moderately relaxing environment. Staff here is extremely professional and courteous. All these improvements mean that rates have risen to match and the York isn't the steal it used to be, but it remains a consistently good value option. The buffet breakfast seems to be disproportionately expensive—try to get an inclusive rate or head to Orchard Road instead.

21 Mount Elizabeth, Singapore 228516. ℃ **800/223-5652** in the U.S. and Canada, 800/553-549 in Australia, 800/447-555 in New Zealand, 800/89-88-52 in the U.K., or 65/6732-1217. Fax 65/6732-1217. www. yorkhotel.com.sg. 407 units. S$306 (US$205/£138) double; from S$650 (US$436/£293) suite. AE, DC, MC, V. 10-min. walk to Orchard MRT. **Amenities:** Restaurant; lobby lounge; outdoor pool; health club; Jacuzzi; room service; babysitting. In room: A/C, TV w/satellite programming, minibar.

INEXPENSIVE

Hotel Grand Central, Singapore

The Grand Central certainly ain't grand, but you can't get much more central than smack in the middle of Orchard Road (though, strictly speaking, the lobby is tucked into a lane just around the corner). Permanently busy, its predominantly regional guests throng the small lobby while the staff does its best to keep up. As well as a seafood restaurant, the lobby has a useful tour desk and travel agent, and there's a rooftop pool. Standard guest rooms are backpacker basic, with decent beds, central air-conditioning, and TVs. Not somewhere you'd be tempted to linger, but why would you, with the center of Singapore on the doorstep? Premium rooms have been refurbished with LCD TVs and other standard amenities.

22 Cavenagh Rd./Orchard Rd., Singapore 229617. (C) **65/6737-9944.** Fax 65/6733-3175. www.grand central.com.sg. 390 units. S$237 (US$159/£107) double; S$424 (US$284/£191) family suite. AE, DC, MC, V. 5-min. walk to Somerset or Dhoby Ghaut MRT. **Amenities:** Restaurant; lounge; outdoor pool; health club w/Jacuzzi and steam. *In room:* A/C, TV w/in-house movies, minibar.

Lloyd's Inn   This two-story bungalow is in a quiet residential area just a few blocks from Orchard Road. Lloyd's is a budget motel in every sense, with few facilities. Open-air corridors form a pleasant little courtyard, and standard rooms are small, with a definite budget feeling, though all have en-suite bathrooms, TV, air-conditioning, and phones. Deluxe rooms are a better size and have a small fridge. Published rates include the "++" taxes (see "Taxes & Service Charges," earlier in this chapter), although there's an extra 2% charge for credit cards and rooms are charged in advance. The welcome is friendly and low key. No pool, no fitness center, no nothing—you got your room, that's what you got.

2 Lloyd Rd., Singapore 239091. (C) **65/6737-7309.** Fax 65/6737-7847. www.lloydinn.com. 34 units. S$100–S$120 (US$67–US$80/£45–£54) double. MC, V. 10-min. walk to Somerset MRT. *In room:* A/C, TV.

The Metropolitan YMCA Singapore   This place is a little out-of-the-way in terms of walking distance to the center, but public buses stop right outside the door and there is a shuttle service that operates weekday mornings. Inside there's a wide range of rooms to suit most budget conscious travelers, from dorms to deluxe. Family rooms, including triples and quads, are particularly good, with lots of storage space. None of these is luxurious, but they're clean and stocked with all the basics. ***One caution here:*** The least expensive rooms have no windows; for sunlight, you'll have to pay a little extra. Facilities are good, with a fitness center, a decent in-house restaurant, and a big rooftop pool and children's pool with a lifeguard on duty (unusual in Singapore). However, the pool is also used by the local community, so you can't guarantee access at all times. There's a self-service launderette, a coffee shop, and a tour desk.

60 Stevens Rd., Singapore 257854. (C) **65/6839-8333.** Fax 65/6235-5528. www.mymca.org.sg. 91 units. S$45 (US$30/£20) dorm, S$120 (US$80/£54) inside double; S$225 (US$151/£101) family; S$230 (US$154/ £104) suite. AE, DC, MC, V. Far from MRT. **Amenities:** Restaurant; outdoor pool; health club; concierge; smoke-free rooms; babysitting. *In room:* A/C, TV, minibar.

RELC International Hotel ★★ (Value)   Part of an English language center, this traveler-class hotel offers great value for money and very personable staff. Rooms start at the Standard Budget twin. These resemble a two-bed dorm: very basic, with a shared lobby and bathroom between two rooms. But at just S$150 (US$101/£68), including taxes, these are on a level with standard dorm prices elsewhere, so they're a hit with backpackers. Alcove and Executive rooms offer balconies, minibars, newspapers, and cable TV, and the large Hollywood Queen sleeps four comfortably. There's a small fitness area but no pool, and it's a brisk 10- to 15-minute walk to Orchard Road.

30 Orange Grove Rd., Singapore 258352. (C) **65/6885-7888.** Fax 65/6733-9976. www.relc.org.sg. 128 units. S$150 (US$101/£68) double; from S$190 (US$127/£86) Alcove suite. AE, DC, MC, V. 15-min. walk to Orchard MRT. **Amenities:** Restaurant; smoke-free rooms. *In room:* A/C, TV w/in-house movies, high-speed Internet, minibar, fridge, hair dryer.

YMCA International House Kids With a superb location at the lower end of Orchard Road, this budget gem is very convenient for sightseeing and getting around by mass transit. The guest rooms have been renovated and have private bathrooms that are better than I've seen at some much pricier hotels. All rooms have air-conditioning, a telephone (with free local calls), color television, and a stock-it-yourself refrigerator, but be warned, all standard double-occupancy rooms are twin beds only. The dormitories are small, dark, and quiet, with two bunk beds per room. Across the hall are men's and women's locker rooms for showering. Most of the public areas have no air-conditioning, including the old fitness facility, billiards center, and squash courts—so be warned: They can become unbearably hot. The rooftop pool is nothing to write home about, but a full-time lifeguard is on duty. There's a coffee shop in the lobby. The staff is amazingly friendly.

1 Orchard Rd., Singapore 238824. (©) **65/6336-6000.** Fax 65/6337-3140. www.ymcaih.com.sg. 111 units. S$105 (US$70/£47) double; S$135 (US$90/£61) family room; S$145 (US$97/£65) superior room. AE, DC, MC, V. 5-min. walk to Dhoby Ghaut MRT. **Amenities:** 2 restaurants; outdoor pool; small gym; Internet center; babysitting. *In room:* A/C, TV, fridge.

4 SENTOSA ISLAND

Sentosa's island getaway gets bigger every year, with new attractions, hotels, and facilities being added all the time. Thanks to a huge land reclamation and building project, the island itself is expanding geographically, too. Sentosa's hotels are geared toward couples on romantic breaks and young families, attracted by the beach resort feel and the accessibility of the city.

The Sentosa Resort & Spa ★★ Fashioned after the luxury resorts of Phuket, Thailand, designers have done a great job combining clean, modern lines with tropical touches and courtyard gardens to produce a sophisticated getaway with relaxing charm. Lazy terraces and cozy alcoves tucked all over the grounds invite guests to unwind in privacy—perfect for intimate candlelight dinners that can be requested anywhere you like. The centerpiece is Spa Botanica; its garden massages, treatments, and frangipani baths are repeatedly voted some of the world's best.

The standard guest rooms in the five-story hotel building are small but stunning, featuring camphor burl-wood doors and accents, Thai silk screens in natural browns and greens, and deep tubs and separate showers in the bathrooms, surrounded by thick celadon green tiling and sleek black granite details. Ask for views of the golf course, which are prettier than the views of the hotel courtyards and buildings. The four Garden Villas are supremely romantic and luxurious. Butlers wait 'round-the-clock to serve you—a standard feature for all rooms.

2 Bukit Manis Rd., Sentosa, Singapore 099891. (©) **65/6275-0331.** Fax 65/6275-0228. www.thesentosa. com. 205 units. S$392 (US$263/£176) double; from S$565 (US$379/£254) suite; S$1,500 (US$1,005/£675) villa. AE, DC, MC, V. See "Sentosa Island," in chapter 7, for public transportation. **Amenities:** 3 restaurants; bar; lounge; gorgeous midnight blue-tiled outdoor pool w/views of the harbor; golf at nearby facilities; 2 outdoor lighted tennis courts w/coach; 2 squash courts; health club w/20m (66-ft.) lap pool, Jacuzzi, and sauna; luxury spa w/private pool, mud baths, steam, Jacuzzis, exercise and relaxation classes, salon, beauty treatments, and massage; concierge; airport transfers; room service; babysitting. *In room:* A/C, TV w/satellite programming and in-house movies, high-speed Internet, minibar, hair dryer.

Shangri-La's Rasa Sentosa Resort (Kids)   Set on an immaculate white-sand beach
fringed with coconut palms, this is Singapore's only true beachfront hotel. Great outdoor
activities make the Rasa Sentosa particularly attractive, with a sea-sports center, offering
windsurfing, sailing, and paddle skiing. There's a large free-form swimming pool in the
gardens, a jogging track, aqua bike rentals, an outdoor Jacuzzi, and a fully equipped spa
with gym, sauna, body and facial treatments, hydromassage, and massage therapies. For
children, there is a separate pool with water slides (no lifeguard, though), a playground,
a nursery, and a games room.

Each of the rooms has a balcony with a view over the hillside and the fort or the sea.
Go for the sea view. Though it's slightly more expensive, the view is exceptional, and if
you don't go for it, you'll be missing out on glorious mornings, throwing back the cur-
tains, and taking in the scenery from the balcony. The resort is connected to Singapore's
downtown by frequent and free shuttles.

101 Siloso Rd., Sentosa, Singapore 098970. © **800/942-5050** in the U.S. and Canada, 800/222-448 in
Australia, 800/442-179 in New Zealand, or 65/6275-0900. Fax 65/6275-1055. www.shangri-la.com. 459
units. S$342 (US$229/£154) superior (hill view); from S$750 (US$503/£338) suite. AE, DC, MC, V. See
"Sentosa Island," in chapter 7, for public transportation. **Amenities:** 3 restaurants; poolside bar and lobby
lounge; outdoor lagoon-style pool w/children's pool and Jacuzzi; golf at nearby facilities; health club; spa
w/sauna, steam, and massage; children's center; airport transfers; room service; babysitting; executive-
level rooms. *In room:* A/C, TV w/satellite programming and in-house movies, high-speed Internet, minibar, hair dryer.

Where to Dine in Singapore

Singapore claims an estimated 2,000-plus eating establishments, so you'll never go hungry. But to simply say, "If you like food, you'll love Singapore!" doesn't do justice to the modern concept of eating in this city. Here you'll find a huge selection of local, regional, and international cuisine, served in settings that range from bustling hawker centers to grand and glamorous palaces of gastronomy. The food is authentic, and many times the dining experience is entertainment in its own right. Various ethnic restaurants, with their traditional decor and serving styles, hold their own special sense of theater for foreigners; but Singaporeans don't stop there, dreaming up new concepts in cuisine and ambience to add fresh dimensions to the fine art of dining.

In this chapter, I'll begin by providing an overview of the main types of traditional cuisine to help you decide, and also list those signature dishes that each style has contributed to the "local cuisine," dishes that have crossed cultures to become time-honored favorites—the Singaporean equivalent to bangers and mash or burgers and fries. These suggestions are especially helpful when navigating the endless choices at **hawker centers** (large groupings of informal open-air food stalls).

The restaurants reviewed here offer a crosscut of cuisine and price ranges, and were selected for superb quality or authenticity of dishes. Some were selected for the sheer experience, whether it's a stunning view or just plain old fun. Beyond this list, you're sure to discover favorites of your own without having to look too far.

A good place to start is right in your hotel. Many of Singapore's best restaurants are in its hotels, whether they're run by the hotel itself or operated by outfits just renting the space. Hotels generally offer a wide variety of cuisine, and coffee shops almost always have Western selections. Shopping malls have everything from food courts with local fast food to midpriced and upmarket establishments. Western fast-food outlets are always easy to find— McDonald's burgers or Starbucks coffee—but if you want something a little more local, you'll find coffee shops (called *kopitiam*) and small home-cookin' mom-and-pop joints down every back street. Then there are hawker centers and food courts, where, under one roof, the meal choices go on and on.

1 TIPS ON DINING

In many foreign destinations, the exotic cuisine isn't the only thing that keeps you guessing. Here, I give you the ground rules on Singapore dining.

HOURS Most restaurants are open for lunch as early as 11am but close around 2:30pm or 3pm to give them a chance to set up for dinner, which begins around 6pm. Where closing times are listed, that is the time when the last order is taken. If you need to eat at odd hours, food centers serve all day and some hawker centers are open all night—see the section "Hawker Centers," later in this chapter.

Eating Enclaves

If you're looking for someplace to dine but want to browse around a bit, a few neighborhoods around Singapore host clusters of smaller, and many times quite excellent, restaurants and lounges creating mini-scenes here and there. For example, **CHIJMES,** a charming colonial orphanage located within the Historic District, provides a home for some excellent restaurants, ranging from Cantonese to Mediterranean. In this chapter, I've reviewed Lei Garden, but if you stroll about, you might be tempted by one of the other eateries here.

Boat Quay and **Clarke Quay,** located along the Singapore River, provide boatloads of options. I've reviewed Our Village at Boat Quay, but this is just one of many.

If you want to get away from the tourist traffic, try **Club Street** in Chinatown, a short hilly lane lined with restored shophouses that became a chic after-work place for the nearby ad agencies, graphic designers, and law firms that make their offices in this neighborhood. Stroll past the many quaint bistros that serve everything from Italian to Vietnamese, and you're sure to find something.

Holland Village, located outside the city to the northwest, is the center of Singapore's expatriate community, so you'll find restaurants, bars, and cafes that cater to Western residents living around this neighborhood. Start at the row of restaurants along **Chip Bee Gardens,** and if you still haven't found something (I'd be surprised), then cross Holland Road to Lorong Liput and Lorong Mambong. In this chapter, I've reviewed Original Sin, which is an excellent place to start in this neighborhood.

TIPPING Don't. Restaurants always add a gratuity to the bill. Sometimes I just leave the small change, but it's not expected.

RESERVATIONS Some restaurants, especially the more fashionable or upscale ones, may require that reservations be made up to a couple of days in advance. Reservations are always recommended for Saturday and Sunday lunch and dinner, as eating is a favorite national pastime and a lot of families take meals out for weekend quality time.

ATTIRE Because Singapore is so hot, "smart casual" (a local term, meaning a shirt and slacks for men and a dress or skirt/slacks and blouse for women) is always a safe bet in moderate to expensive restaurants. For the very expensive restaurants, "smart elegant" is required, which in Singapore means jacket and tie for men and a dressier outfit for women. For the cheap places, come as you are, as long as you're decent.

ORDERING WINE WITH DINNER Singaporeans have become more wine savvy in recent years and have begun importing estate-bottled wines from California, Australia, New Zealand, Peru, South Africa, France, and Germany. However, these bottles are heavily taxed. A bottle of wine with dinner starts at around S$50 (US$34/£23), and a single glass runs between S$10 (US$6.70/£4.50) and S$25 (US$17/£11), depending on the wine and the restaurant. Chinese restaurants usually don't charge corkage fees for bringing your own.

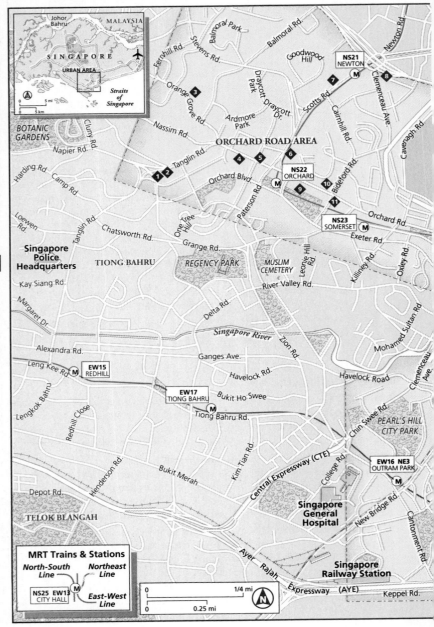

Johor
Bahru
MALAYSIA

SINGAPORE

URBAN AREA

Straits
of
Singapore

0   5 mi
0 5 km

Balmoral Park
Balmoral Rd.
Fernhill Rd.
Stevens Rd.
Goodwood
Hill
NS21
NEWTON
Newton Rd.
Clemenceau Ave.
Cavenagh Rd.
Orange Grove Rd.
Draycott Draycott Dr.
Park
Ardmore
Park
Scotts Rd.
Cairnhill Rd.
7
8

BOTANIC
GARDENS
Cluny Rd.
Napier Rd.
Nassim Rd.
Tanglin Rd.
ORCHARD ROAD AREA

Harding Rd.
Camp Rd.
1   2
Orchard Blvd.
4   5
6
NS22
ORCHARD
Bideford Rd.
10
9
11
NS23
SOMERSET
Orchard Rd.

Loewen
Rd.
Tanglin Rd.
Chatsworth Rd.
One Tree
Hill
Grange Rd.
Paterson Rd.
Exeter Rd.
Killiney Rd.
Oxley Rd.

**Singapore
Police
Headquarters**
TIONG BAHRU
Kay Siang Rd.
REGENCY PARK
MUSLIM
CEMETERY
Leonie Hill
Rd.
River Valley Rd.

Margaret Dr.
Delta Rd.
Singapore River
Zion Rd.
Mohamed Sultan Rd.

Alexandra Rd.
Leng Kee Rd.
EW15
REDHILL
Ganges Ave.
Havelock Rd.
Havelock Road
Clemenceau Ave.

Lengkok Bahru
Redhill Close
EW17
TIONG BAHRU
Bukit Ho Swee
Tiong Bahru Rd.
Bukit Ho Swee
Chin Swee Rd.
PEARL'S HILL
CITY PARK

Henderson Rd.
Bukit Merah
Kim Tian Rd.
Central Expressway (CTE)
College Rd.
EW16 NE3
OUTRAM PARK
New Bridge Rd.

Depot Rd.
TELOK BLANGAH
**Singapore
General
Hospital**
Cantonment Rd.

MRT Trains & Stations
*North-South
Line*
*Northeast
Line*
NS25 EW13
CITY HALL
*East-West
Line*
0   1/4 mi
0   0.25 mi
Ayer Rajah Expressway (AYE)
**Singapore
Railway Station**
Keppel Rd.

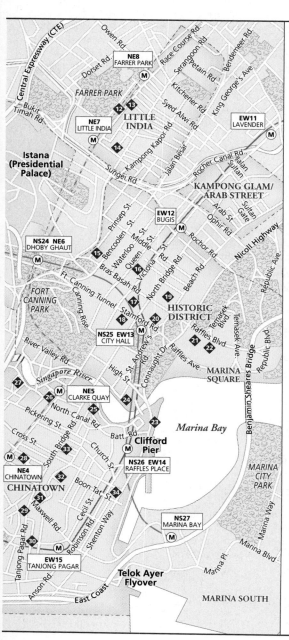

HISTORIC DISTRICT
Doc Cheng's **19**
Equinox **20**
Inagiku **20**
IndoChine Waterfront **24**
Lei Garden **17**
Magic Wok **18**
Morton's of Chicago **22**
Our Village **25**
Pierside Kitchen & Bar **23**
Raffles Grill **19**
Rendezvous **15**
Tiffin Room **19**
Victoria Street
    Hawker Center **16**

CHINATOWN
Blue Ginger **30**
Chen Fu Ji Fried Rice **21, 27**
Da Paolo il Ristorante **32**
Food Alley **28**
Indochine **32**
Lau Pa Sat **34**
Ma Maison **26**
Maxwell Road
    Food Centre **31**
The Tea Chapter **29**
Yixing Xuan **29**
Yum Cha **33**

LITTLE INDIA
Komala Vilas **14**
Muthu's Curry
    Restaurant **13**
Tekka Market **12**

ORCHARD ROAD AREA
Ah Hoi's Kitchen **1**
BLU **3**
Chatterbox **11**
Coca Steamboat **5**
Harbour Grill &
    Oyster Bar **4**
Indochine **9**
Li Bai **7**
Mezza 9 **6**
Newton Circus
    Hawker Center **8**
Patara Fine Thai **2, 20**
Shimbashi Soba **10**
The Rice Table **5**

ORGANIZATION OF RESTAURANT LISTINGS   I've organized the restaurants in this chapter in a few different ways. First, I've grouped them in a simple list by style of cuisine, so if you decide you want a nice Peranakan dinner, for instance, you can scope out your choices all together before referring to the individual restaurant reviews. Second, I've arranged the reviews into four basic neighborhoods: the Historic District, Chinatown, Little India, and the Orchard Road area. Within these divisions, I've arranged them by price. Keep in mind that the divisions by neighborhood are almost as arbitrary as they were when Stamford Raffles created them in 1822. Everything in the city is relatively close and easily accessible, so don't think you should plan your meals by the neighborhood your hotel sits in, when a short taxi ride will take you where you really want to go.

Also, it has become the trend if you've got a terrific restaurant that people love, to open branches in other locations. Some may believe this dilutes the unique appeal of a special restaurant, but in Singapore, generally I find that good restaurateurs retain the consistent quality of food and service for all their outlets. You'll notice many restaurants in the sections that follow have branches in other parts of the city, which I have also listed.

I've selected the restaurants listed here because they have some of the best food and most memorable atmospheres, but there are hundreds of other restaurants serving any kind of food in a variety of price ranges. Many magazines on dining in Singapore are available at newsstands and can help you find other favorite restaurants.

LUNCH COSTS   Lunch at a hawker center can be as cheap as S$4.50 (US$3/£2), truly a bargain. Many places have set-price buffet lunches, but these can be as high as S$48 (US$32/£22). Indian restaurants are great deals for inexpensive buffet lunches, which can be found as reasonably as S$10 (US$6.70/£4.50) per person for all you can eat.

DINNER COSTS   In this chapter, prices for Western restaurants list the range for standard entrees, and prices for Asian restaurants list the range for small dishes intended for two people to share. As a guideline, here are the relative costs for dinner in each category of restaurant, without wine, beer, cocktails, or coffee, and ordered either a la carte or from a set-price menu:

- **Very Expensive ($$$$):** Expect to pay as much as S$160 (US$107/£72) per person. Continental and Japanese cuisines will be the priciest, but a full-course Cantonese dinner, especially if you throw in shark's fin, can be well over S$150 (US$101/£68) per person.
- **Expensive ($$$):** Expect dinner to run between S$50 (US$34/£23) and S$80 (US$54/£36) per person.
- **Moderate ($$):** At a moderate restaurant, dinner for one can be as low as S$25 (US$17/£11) and as high as S$50 (US$34/£23).
- **Inexpensive ($):** Some inexpensive dinners can be under S$5 (US$3.35/£2.25) at hawker stalls and up to around S$15 (US$10/£6.75) for one if you eat at local restaurants. Fortunately, Singapore is not only a haven for cultural gastronomic diversity, but it's also possible to eat exotic foods here to your heart's content, all while maintaining a shoestring budget.

Asian

Doc Cheng's ★★ (Historic District, $$$, p. 100)

Equinox ★ (Historic District, $$$, p. 100)

Ma Maison (Chinatown, $, p. 104)

Chinese

Coca Steamboat (Orchard Road, $$, p. 108)

Imperial Herbal ★★ (Historic District, $$, p. 109)

Lei Garden ★★ (Historic District, $$$, p. 100)

Li Bai ★★★ (Orchard Road, $$$, p. 106)

Yum Cha ★ (Chinatown, $, p. 104)

Contemporary

BLU ★★★ (Orchard Road, $$$, p. 105)

Continental

Equinox ★ (Historic District, $$$, p. 100)

Halia ★ (Singapore Botanic Gardens, $$$, p. 109)

Harbour Grill & Oyster Bar ★★★ (Orchard Road, $$$, p. 105)

Morton's of Chicago ★★★ (Historic District, $$$, p. 98)

Dutch

The Rice Table ★ (Orchard Road, $, p. 108)

French

IndoChine Waterfront ★★★ (Historic District, $$, p. 98)

Raffles Grill ★★★ (Historic District, $$$$, p. 99)

Fusion

Doc Cheng's ★★ (Historic District, $$$, p. 100)

Halia ★ (Singapore Botanic Gardens, $$$, p. 109)

Ma Maison (Chinatown, $, p. 104)

Mezza9 ★★ (Orchard Road, $$$, p. 106)

Indian (Northern)

Our Village ★ (Historic District, $, p. 102)

Tiffin Room ★ (Historic District, $$$, p. 100)

Indian (Southern)

Komala Vilas ★ (Little India, $, p. 104)

Muthu's Curry Restaurant (Little India, $, p. 105)

Samy's Curry Restaurant ★ (Dempsey Road, $, p. 111)

Italian

Da Paolo Ristorante ★★★ (Chinatown, $$, p. 102)

Japanese

Inagiku ★★ (Historic District, $$$$, p. 98)

Shimbashi Soba (Orchard Road, $, p. 109)

Malay/Indonesian

Rendezvous (Historic District, $, p. 102)

The Rice Table ★ (Orchard Road, $, p. 108)

Mediterranean

Original Sin ★ (Holland Village, $$, p. 110)

Peranakan

Blue Ginger ★ (Chinatown, $, p. 102)

Seafood

Long Beach Seafood Restaurant (East Coast Parkway, $$, p. 110)

WHERE TO DINE IN SINGAPORE

6

RESTAURANTS BY CUISINE

Key to Abbreviations: $$$$ = Very Expensive $$$ = Expensive $$ = Moderate $ = Inexpensive

Pierside Kitchen & Bar ★ (Historic
District, $$, p. 101)
UDMC Seafood Centre ★★ (East
Coast Parkway, $$, p. 110)

Singaporean

Ah Hoi's Kitchen (Orchard Road, $,
p. 108)
Chatterbox (Orchard Road, $$,
p. 106)
Chen Fu Ji Fried Rice (Chinatown, $,
p. 104)
Coca Steamboat (Orchard Road, $$,
p. 108)

Southeast Asian

IndoChine Waterfront ★★★ (His-
toric District, $$, p. 97)

Thai

Magic Wok (Historic District, $,
p. 101)
Patara Fine Thai (Orchard Road, $$,
p. 108)

Vegetarian

Original Sin ★ (Holland Village, $$,
p. 110)

Vietnamese

IndoChine Waterfront ★★★ (His-
toric District, $$, p. 101)

3 HISTORIC DISTRICT

VERY EXPENSIVE

Inagiku ★★ JAPANESE   Inagiku serves Japanese food that rivals some of Tokyo's
best restaurants. The dining room is subdued and artistic, with recessed spotlights
designed to illuminate the dish in front of you to maximum effect. It's all very cultured,
despite some unfortunately chosen elevator music. Inagiku's kitchen is separated into
teams, one specializing in sushi and sashimi that's outstandingly fresh and expertly prepared. The *tokusen sashimi moriawase* is a stunning assortment of fresh seafood presented
in an ice-filled shell. The tempura—firm, fresh seafood and vegetables fried in batter that
is incredibly light—is excellent. Lunchtime set menus offer a more affordable way to dine
here, and the quality remains just as high. If sashimi isn't your thing, try the tenderloin
and lobster. Separate dishes of succulent beef, followed by meaty shelled lobster smothered in a rich cheese sauce, make it the ultimate surf 'n' turf. In addition to sake, there is
a good selection of wines.

Raffles The Plaza, Level 3, 80 Bras Basah Rd. ℂ **65/6431-6156.** Reservations recommended. Set lunch
S$40–S$120 (US$27–US$80/£18–£54); set dinner S$180–S$220 (US$121–US$147/£81–£99). AE, MC, V.
Daily noon–2:30pm and 6:30–10:30pm.

Morton's of Chicago ★★★ CONTINENTAL   This is the first Morton's restaurant
outside the U.S. and for the uninitiated, to call Morton's a steakhouse seems a disservice
to the incredibly high quality of the food on offer. But what steaks they are; to guide you
in your choice, the waiter will heave an enormous platter over to your table, laden with
sample cuts of American and Australian prime beef. The seafood is equally superb, with
large and fresh lobsters, oysters, and shrimp vying for your attention. Even the vegetables
are brought by the personable and knowledgeable waitstaff for inspection. Whatever cut
you prefer, it will be flavorsome, succulent, and cooked to absolute perfection. I challenge
you to leave room for the signature melting chocolate cake.

Mandarin Oriental Hotel, 5 Raffles Avenue. ℂ **65/6339-3740.** www.mortons.com. Reservations recommended. Main courses S$79–S$184 (US$53–US$123/£36–£83). AE, DC, MC, V. Mon–Sat 5.30–11pm; Sun
5–10pm.

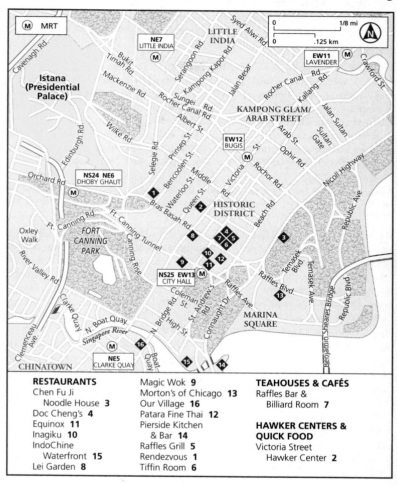

RESTAURANTS

Chen Fu Ji
  Noodle House **3**
Doc Cheng's **4**
Equinox **11**
Inagiku **10**
IndoChine
  Waterfront **15**
Lei Garden **8**

Magic Wok **9**
Morton's of Chicago **13**
Our Village **16**
Patara Fine Thai **12**
Pierside Kitchen
  & Bar **14**
Raffles Grill **5**
Rendezvous **1**
Tiffin Room **6**

TEAHOUSES & CAFÉS

Raffles Bar &
  Billiard Room **7**

**HAWKER CENTERS &
QUICK FOOD**

Victoria Street
  Hawker Center **2**

Raffles Grill ★★★ FRENCH   Dining in the grande dame of Singapore achieves a level of sophistication unmatched by any other five-star restaurant. The architectural charm and historic significance of the old hotel will transform dinner into a cultural event, but don't come here just for the ambience; the food is outstanding as well. Chef Jean-Charles changes the menu every season, but I assure you, anything you order will still be divine. The dégustation menu, seven courses at S$220 (US$147/£99), is the best way to explore their finest dishes if you have trouble choosing from an a la carte menu that features pigeon, lamb, suckling pig, veal, and a carving trolley of amazing cuts of beef prepared to perfection. The 1,200-label wine list (going back to 1900 vintages) could be a history lesson, and if you'd like, you can request the cellar master to select a wine to match each course. The fabulously attentive service will make you feel like you own the place. Formal dress is required.

Raffles Hotel, 1 Beach Rd. © **65/6412-1816.** www.raffles.com. Reservations required. Main courses S$68–S$108 (US$46–US$72/£31–£49). AE, DC, MC, V. Mon–Fri noon–2pm and 7–10pm; Sat 7–10pm.

EXPENSIVE

Doc Cheng's ★★ ASIAN/FUSION   The witty menu here tells the story of Doc Cheng, a mythological colonial figure who was a sought-after physician, local celebrity, and notorious drunk. His concept of "restorative foods" is, therefore, rather decadent; on the menu you'll find fabulous pan-Asian dishes that are more flavorful than medicinal. The menu changes regularly, but you won't go far wrong with perennial favorites like the mouthwatering Sichuan rack of lamb and miso cod with bonito emulsion. The house wine is a Riesling (sweet wines are more popular with Singaporeans) from Raffles's own vineyard. Two dining areas allow you to dine alfresco under the veranda or in cool air-conditioning inside.

1 Beach Rd., Raffles Hotel Arcade #02-20, Level 2. © **65/6412-1816.** www.raffles.com. Reservations recommended. Main courses S$44–S$56 (US$29–US$38/£20–£25). AE, DC, MC, V. Mon–Fri noon–2pm; daily 7–10pm.

Equinox ★ CONTINENTAL/ASIAN   What a view! From the top of the tallest hotel in Southeast Asia, you can see out past the marina to Malaysia and Indonesia—and the restaurant's three-tier design and floor-to-ceiling windows mean every table has a view. It's decorated in contemporary style with nice Chinese accents. Lunch is an extensive display of seafood served in a host of international recipes, with chefs searing scallops to order. Dinner is a la carte, with a menu that's divided between Eastern and Western cuisine, plus some dishes that combine Eastern and Western ingredients and cooking styles such as charred tuna steak with anchovy and chili sauce, coriander chimichurri and sweet potato, and hot smoked chicken on a spicy papaya and green mango salad. For dessert, order the Manjari chocolate pudding with sabayon, morello sorbet, and chili compote.

Raffles City, 2 Stamford Rd., Level 70. © **65/6431-6156.** www.equinoxcomplex.com. Reservations required. Daily buffet lunch S$56 (US$38/£25); dinner main courses S$40–S$68 (US$27–US$46/£18–£31). AE, DC, MC, V. Mon–Sat noon–2:30pm, 3:30–5pm, and 6:30–11pm; Sun 11am–2:30pm and 7–11pm.

Lei Garden ★★ CHINESE/CANTONESE   Lei Garden lives up to a great reputation for the highest-quality Cantonese cuisine in one of the most elegant settings, nestled within the unique ambience of CHIJMES just outside its towering picture windows. Highly recommended dishes are the fried shrimp with tangerine peel and black bean sauce, and crispy roasted kurobuta pork. If you reserve 24 hours in advance, try the beggar's chicken, a whole stuffed chicken wrapped and baked in a lotus leaf covered in yam, which makes the chicken moist with a delicate flavor you won't forget. Also try the barbecued Beijing duck, which is exquisite. Dim sum here is excellent. A small selection of French and Chinese wines is available.

30 Victoria St., CHIJMES #01-24. © **65/6339-3822.** Reservations required. Small dishes S$22–S$68 (US$15–US$46/£9.90–£31). AE, DC, MC, V. Daily 11:30am–2:30pm and 6–10:30pm.

Tiffin Room ★ NORTHERN INDIAN   Tiffin curry came from India and is named after the three-tiered containers that Indian workers would use to carry their lunch. The tiffin box idea was adopted by the British colonists, who changed around the recipes a bit so they weren't as spicy. The cuisine that evolved is pretty much what you'll find served at Raffles's Tiffin Room, where a buffet spread lets you select from a variety of curries, chutneys, rice, and Indian breads. Highlights include the red snapper with almond and cashew nut sauce, and south Indian spring chicken cooked with coconut, but there's a vast array of vegetarian dishes to choose from, too. The restaurant is just inside the lobby entrance of Raffles Hotel and carries the trademark Raffles elegance throughout its decor. Very British Raj.

Raffles Hotel, 1 Beach Rd. ✆ **65/6412-1816.** www.raffles.com. Reservations recommended. All meals served buffet style. Breakfast S$45 (US$30/£20); lunch S$48 (US$32/£22); high tea S$39 (US$26/£18); dinner S$52 (US$35/£23). AE, DC, MC, V. Daily 7–10am, noon–2:30pm, 3:30–5:30pm (high tea), and 7–10pm.

MODERATE

IndoChine Waterfront ★★★ VIETNAMESE/LAO/CAMBODIAN/FRENCH IndoChine Waterfront shares the stately Empress Place Building with the Asian Civilisations Museum, enhancing the sophistication of its chic oriental decor. The views over the water make for true romance. The menu combines the best dishes from the Indochinese region, many with hints of the French cuisine that was added into regional palates during colonial days. Their two most popular dishes are the house specialty beef stew ragout and the pepper beef with sweet-and-sour sauce. More traditional Vietnamese favorites, like spring rolls and prawns grilled on sugar cane, are fresh starters. After dinner, don't miss the Vietnamese coffee; it's mind-blowingly delicious. The only weakness here is the slightly lackluster service, but the concept and food have proved so popular that Indo-Chine now has several bars and restaurants around the city. After Waterfront, the best are in a quaint Chinatown shophouse (49B Club St.; ✆ **65/6323-0503**) and Wisma Atria (Orchard Rd. #01–18/23; ✆ **65/6238-3470**).

1 Empress Place, Asian Civilisations Museum. ✆ **65/6339-1720.** www.indochine.com.sg. Reservations required. Main dishes S$24–S$46 (US$16–US$31/£11–£21). AE, DC, MC, V. Sun–Fri noon–2:30pm and 6:30–11:30pm; Fri–Sat noon–2:30pm and 6:30pm–12:30am.

Pierside Kitchen & Bar ★ SEAFOOD A light and healthy menu centers on seafood prepared with fresh flavors in a wide variety of international recipes, like the house specialty cumin-spiced crab cakes with marinated cucumber and chili or the lobster linguini. A new menu has added some new favorites, including Maine lobsters with sweet basil and chili and chargrilled octopus. Nothing can compete with the view, really—the panoramic view of the Esplanade Theatres and the marina is lovely. After sundown, the alfresco dining area cools off with breezes from the water, and the stars make for some romantic dining. Relax, enjoy the scenery, and linger over raspberry and lychee soufflé or the divine seven textures of dark chocolate.

Unit 01–01, One Fullerton, 1 Fullerton Rd. ✆ **65/6438-0400.** Reservations recommended. Main courses S$32–S$45 (US$21–US$30/£14–£20). AE, DC, MC, V. Mon–Thurs 11:30am–2:30pm and 7–10:30pm; Fri–Sat 7–11pm.

INEXPENSIVE

Magic Wok Value THAI Here's an excellent value-for-money restaurant in town. The decor doesn't do much, it's usually crowded, and staff doesn't pamper, but food is reliably good and cheap. Thai favorites include a spicy tom yam seafood soup that doesn't skimp on the seafood, a mild green curry with chicken, and sweet pineapple rice. If you come too late, the yummy fried chicken chunks wrapped in pandan leaf will be sold out. If you're adventurous, the fried baby squid are crunchy and sweet. During busy times, you'll have to line up, but it moves fast. Other outlets are located at #03-23/25 Novena

Square, 238 Thomson Road (© **65/6352-9077**) and #01-17/18 Ten Mile Junction, 1 Woodlands Road (© **65/6766 9813**).

#01–20 Capitol Building, 11 Stamford Rd. © **65/6338-1882.** Reservations not accepted. Small dishes S$5–S$18 (US$3.35–US$12/£2.25–£8.10). MC, V. Daily 11am–10pm.

Our Village ★ NORTHERN INDIAN   With its antique white walls stuccoed in delicate and exotic patterns and glistening with tiny silver mirrors, you'll feel like you're in an Indian fairyland here. Even the ceiling twinkles with silver stars, and hanging lanterns provide a subtle glow for the heavenly atmosphere—it's a perfect setting for a delicate dinner. Every dish here is made fresh from hand-selected imported ingredients, some of them coming from secret sources. In fact, the staff is so protective of its recipes, you'd almost think their secret ingredient was opium—and you'll be floating so high after tasting the food that it might as well be. There are vegetarian selections as well as meats (no beef or pork) prepared in luscious gravies or in the tandoor oven. The dishes are light and healthy, with all-natural ingredients and not too much salt.

46 Boat Quay (take elevator to 5th floor). © **65/6538-3058.** Reservations recommended on weekends. Small dishes S$9–S$24 (US$6.05–US$16/£4.05–£11). AE, MC, V. Mon–Fri noon–1:45pm and 6–11:30pm; Sat–Sun 6–11:30pm.

Rendezvous MALAY/INDONESIAN   Line up to select from a large number of Malay dishes, cafeteria style, like sambal squid in a spicy sauce of chili and shrimp paste, and beef *rendang,* in a dark spicy curry gravy. The waitstaff will bring your order to your table. The old-style coffee shop setting instills a sense of nostalgia for locals. On the wall, black-and-white photos trace the restaurant's history back to its opening in the early 1950s. It's a great place to experiment with a new cuisine.

#02–02/03 Hotel Rendezvous, 9 Bras Basah Rd. © **65/6339-7508.** Reservations not necessary. Meat dishes sold per piece S$4–S$7 (US$2.70–US$4.70/£1.80–£3.15). AE, DC, MC, V. Daily 11am–9pm. Closed on public holidays.

4 CHINATOWN

MODERATE
Da Paolo il Ristorante ★★★ ITALIAN   This Italian-owned place in trendy Club Street is coolly elegant, with whitewashed walls and starched linens, but has a casual, comfortable feel. The pasta is made fresh every morning and often served with fresh seafood in classic and modern Italian style. The house specialty of fresh squid ink spaghetti, lightly dressed with olive oil and garlic, is divine and the home-made tiramisu shouldn't be missed. The owners have other branches that are equally satisfying: **Da Paolo il Giardino** (501 Bukit Timah Rd., #01–05 Cluny Court, beside the Singapore Botanic Gardens; © **65/6463-9628**) and **Da Paolo la Terrazza** (44 Jalan Merah Saga, #01–56, at Chip Bee Gardens in Holland Village; © **65/6476-1332**).

80 Club St. © **65/6224-7081.** Reservations recommended. Main courses S$22–S$38 (US$15–US$25/£9.90–£17). AE, DC, MC, V. Mon–Sat 11:30am–2:30pm and 6:30–10:30pm.

INEXPENSIVE
Blue Ginger ★ PERANAKAN   The standard belief is that Peranakan cooking is reserved for home-cooked meals, and therefore restaurants are not as plentiful—and where they do exist, are very informal. Not so at Blue Ginger, where traditional and

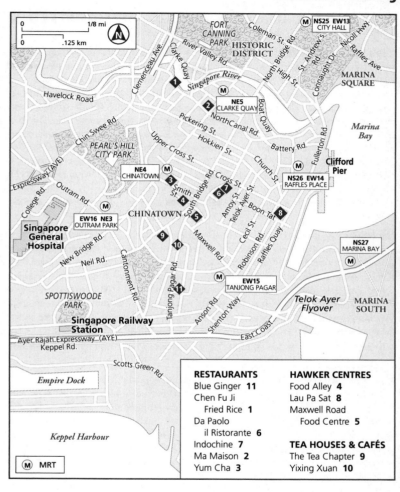

RESTAURANTS

Blue Ginger **11**

Chen Fu Ji
  Fried Rice **1**

Da Paolo
  il Ristorante **6**

Indochine **7**

Ma Maison **2**

Yum Cha **3**

HAWKER CENTRES

Food Alley **4**

Lau Pa Sat **8**

Maxwell Road
  Food Centre **5**

TEA HOUSES & CAFÉS

The Tea Chapter **9**

Yixing Xuan **10**

modern mix beautifully in a style fitting for Singapore. Snuggled in a shophouse, the decor combines clean and neat lines of contemporary styling with paintings by local artists and touches of Peranakan flair like carved wooden screens. The cuisine is Peranakan from traditional recipes, making for some very authentic food—definitely something you can't get back home. A good appetizer is the *kueh pie tee:* bite-size "top hats" filled with turnip, egg, and prawn with sweet chili sauce. A wonderful entree is the *ayam panggang* "Blue Ginger," really tender grilled, boneless chicken thigh and drumstick with a mild coconut-milk sauce. One of the most popular dishes is the *ayam buah keluak* (my favorite), a traditional chicken dish made with a hard black Indonesian nut with sweetmeat inside. The favorite dessert here is *durian chendol,* red beans and *pandan* jelly in coconut milk with *durian* purée. Served with shaved ice on top, it smells strong—though they can make a durian-free version for guests who aren't fans of the pungent fruit.

97 Tanjong Pagar Rd. ✆ **65/6222-3928.** Reservations recommended. Small dishes S$6.50–S$35 (US$4.35–US$23/£2.90–£16). AE, DC, MC, V. Daily noon–2:30pm and 6:30–9:45pm.

Chen Fu Ji Fried Rice SINGAPOREAN   With bright fluorescent lighting, the fast-food ambience is nothing to write home about, but the riverside views are pleasant and after you try the fried rice here, you'll never be able to eat it anywhere else again, ever. These people take loving care of each fluffy grain, frying the egg evenly throughout. The other ingredients are added abundantly, and there's no hint of oil. On the top is a crown of shredded crabmeat. If you've never been an aficionado, you'll be one now. The spicy chicken with cashew nuts and spring onions is delicious, and their soups are also very good. There is an additional branch, the **Chen Fu Ji Noodle House,** at Suntec City Mall, 3 Temasek Blvd. #03–020 Sky Garden (✆ **65/6334-2966**), and the true devotee can grab a bowl before boarding a plane at Changi's Terminal 2 transit lounge (✆ **65/6542-8097**).

#02–31 Riverside Point, 30 Merchant Rd. ✆ **65/6533-0166.** Reservations not accepted. Small dishes S$10–S$20 (US$6.70–US$13/£4.50–£9) AE, DC, MC, V. Daily noon–2:30pm and 6–9:45pm.

Ma Maison ASIAN/FUSION   This cozy little timber-paneled place is tucked away in a mall between the Historic District and Chinatown. Try to get a window seat for views over the river and Clarke Quay, while you browse an eclectic menu that ranges from hamburgers and pasta to *tonkatsu,* a pork cutlet in light Japanese breadcrumbs, fried and served with rice, pickles, and shredded cabbage. Most of the Western dishes have an Asian twist to them and are often served with rich Japanese-style tomato or brown sauce. The house special is a comforting, rich beef stew. The predominantly Japanese staff is friendly and attentive.

6 Eu Tong St., The Central #03-96 ✆ **65/6327-8122.** Reservations recommended on weekends. Main courses S$13–S$22 (US$8.70–US$15/£5.85–£9.90). AE, DC, MC, V. Daily 11:30am–3pm and 6–10pm.

Yum Cha ★ CHINESE   Dim sum aficionados swear by Yum Cha's crystal chive dumplings, tiny translucent parcels of chunky fresh prawns and herbs, as well as the soft-shell crabs and delicious steamed dumplings filled with meat and clear broth called *xiao long bao.* The main attraction certainly isn't the service, which tends to be a little brusque at the best of times, even more so on weekends, when the place is packed with families and groups of friends. Get there early to compete for the attention of the trolley-wielding waitresses (especially if you want help with ordering) and try to leave room for the gorgeous miniature baked egg tarts.

20 Trengganu St. ✆ **65/6372-1717.** Reservations recommended. Small dishes S$2.50–S$8 (US$1.65–US$5.35/£1.10–£3.60). AE, DC, MC, V. Daily 8am–10:30pm.

5 LITTLE INDIA

INEXPENSIVE

Komala Vilas ★ SOUTHERN INDIAN   Komala Vilas is famous with Singaporeans of every race. Don't expect the height of ambience—it's pure fast food, local style—but to sit here during a packed and noisy lunch hour is to see all walks of life come through the doors. Komala serves vegetarian dishes in southern Indian style, so there's nothing fancy about the food; it's just plain good. Order the *dosai,* a huge, thin pancake used to scoop up luscious and hearty gravies and curries. Even for carnivores, it's very satisfying. What's more, it's cheap: Two samosas, *dosai,* and an assortment of stew-style gravies *(dhal)* for two are under S$10 (US$6.70/£4.50) with tea. For a quick fast-food meal, this place is second to none.

76–78 Serangoon Rd. ✆ **65/6293-6980.** Reservations not accepted. Dosai S$2.20 (US$1.45/£1); lunch for 2 S$10 (US$6.70/£4.50). No credit cards. Daily 7am–10:30pm.

Muthu's Curry Restaurant SOUTHERN INDIAN   Muthu's is a local institution that is synonymous with one local delicacy, fish head curry, a giant fish head floating in a huge portion of delicious curry soup, its eye staring and teeth grinning. The cheek meat is the best part of the fish, but to be truly polite, let your friend eat the eye. The list of accompanying dishes is long and includes crab *masala,* chicken *biryani,* and mutton curry, with fish cutlet and fried chicken sold by the piece. We're not talking the height of dining elegance here, but Muthu's really has come a long way since its simple coffee shop opening, with its recent shift to newer, larger digs, with matching tables and chairs and waitstaff taking orders on PDAs! I miss the old grotty ambience, but still it's a good place to try this dish. Go either at the start or toward the end of mealtime so you don't get lost in the rush and can find staff with more time to help you. There's another branch in town at 3 Temasek Blvd., #B1–056, Suntec City Mall (✆ **65/6835-7707**).

138 Race Course Rd. ✆ **65/6392-1722.** Reservations recommended. Small dishes S$4–S$13 (US$2.70–US$8.70/£1.80–£5.85); fish head curry from S$21 (US$14/£9.45). AE, DC, MC, V. Daily 10am–10pm.

6 ORCHARD ROAD AREA

EXPENSIVE

BLU ★★★ CONTEMPORARY   Molecular gastronomy comes to town under BLU's new chef de cuisine, Kevin Cherkas. Drawing on his work at Michelin-starred restaurants El Bulli in Spain and New York's Daniel, the Canadian has created an a la carte menu, from which guests can choose individually or select six dishes for a set price. Thought-provoking creations include foie gras with savory caramel, and the Egg Came First (a boiled egg served with onion broth, crumbs, and black truffle). The decor is stylish and European, with modern glass sculptures by Danny Lane and fiber optics glowing through the glass bar and floor. Try to get a window table, since it commands an awe-inspiring view of Orchard Road from its 24th-floor perch.

Shangri-La Hotel, 22 Orange Grove Rd., 24th floor. ✆ **65/6213-4598.** Reservations recommended. Six courses for S$139 (US$93/£63). AE, DC, MC, V. Daily 6:30–11pm.

Harbour Grill & Oyster Bar ★★★ CONTINENTAL   Grilled seafood and U.S. prime rib are perfectly prepared and served with attentive style in this award-winning restaurant. The Continental cuisine is lighter than most, with recipes that focus on the natural freshness of their ingredients rather than on creams and fat. Caesar salad is made at your table so you can request your preferred blend of ingredients, and the oyster bar serves juicy fresh oysters from around the world. For the main course, the prime rib is the best and most-requested entree, but the rack of lamb is another option worth considering—it melts in your mouth. Resident chef Alexandre Lozachmeur's specialty is a meltingly tender lamb shoulder braised with fennel and semolina cake. Guest chefs from international culinary capitals are flown in for monthly specials. The place is small and cozy, with nautical-inspired murals and a finishing kitchen in the dining room.

Hilton Singapore, Level 3, 581 Orchard Rd. © 65/6730-3393. Reservations recommended. Main courses S$40–S$60 (US$27–US$40/£18–£27). AE, DC, MC, V. Mon–Fri noon–2:30pm; Mon–Sat 7–10:30pm.

Li Bai ★★★ CHINESE/CANTONESE   Chinese restaurants are typically unimaginative in the decor department—slapping up a landscape brush painting or two here and there is sometimes about as far as they go. Not at Li Bai, which is very sleekly decorated in contemporary black and red lacquer, with comfortable black leather seating. Creative chefs and guest chefs turn out a constantly evolving menu, refining specialties, and jade-and-silver chopsticks and white bone china add opulent touches to their flawless meals. Shark's fin soup and abalone creations are a requirement for any self-respecting Cantonese restaurant, and although Li Bai's preparation of these delicacies is tops, I recommend you bypass them—too much hype and expense. Go for the chef's special creations, which are always imaginative. Or try the pan-fried lamb chop with black pepper sauce, or goose liver with honeyed chicken. The crab fried rice is fabulous, with generous chunks of fresh meat. Li Bai's signature XO chili sauce adds delicious spice to almost any dish. The wine list is international, with many vintages.

Sheraton Towers, Lower lobby level, 39 Scotts Rd. © 65/6839-5623. Reservations required. Small dishes S$18–S$60 (US$12–US$40/£8.10–£27) and up. AE, DC, MC, V. Daily 11:30am–2:30pm and 6:30–10:30pm.

Mezza9 ★★ FUSION   This is your best bet if your party can't agree on what to eat because Mezza9 offers an extensive menu that includes Chinese steamed treats, Japanese, Thai, deli selections, Italian, fresh seafood, and Continental grilled specialties. Start with big and juicy raw oysters on the half-shell. If you want to consider more raw seafood, the combination sashimi platter is also very fresh. Grilled meats include various cuts of beef, rack of lamb, and chicken dishes, with a host of delicious sides to choose from. The enormous 400-seat restaurant has a warm atmosphere, with glowing wood and contemporary Zen accents, but service can be harried. Before you head in for dinner, grab a martini in their très chic martini bar.

Grand Hyatt, 10 Scotts Rd. © 65/6732-1234. www.singapore.grand.hyatt.com. Reservations recommended. Main courses S$28–S$53 (US$19–US$36/£13–£24). AE, DC, MC, V. Daily noon–3pm and 6–11:30pm.

MODERATE

Chatterbox SINGAPOREAN   If you'd like to try the local favorites but don't want to deal with hawker food, then Chatterbox is the place for you. This restaurant is located in the Meritus Mandarin Hotel, and while the hotel is undergoing renovations, Chatterbox has a prime spot on the 39th floor, so get here during 2009 to enjoy the 360° views of the city, before it's relocated back down to the 5th floor. Their Hainanese chicken rice is highly acclaimed, and the other dishes—like *nasi lemak, laksa,* and carrot cake—are as close to the street as you can get. For a quick and tasty snack, order *tahu goreng,* deep-fried tofu in peanut chili sauce. This is also a good place to experiment with some of those really weird local drinks. *Chin chow* is the dark brown grass jelly drink; *chendol* is green jelly, red beans, palm sugar, and coconut milk; and *bandung* is pink rose syrup milk with jelly. For dessert, order the ever-favorite sago pudding, made from the hearts of the sago palm.

Mandarin Hotel, 333 Orchard Rd. © 65/6831-6291. Reservations recommended for lunch and dinner. Main courses S$20–S$36 (US$13–US$24/£9–£16). AE, DC, MC, V. Sun–Thurs 5pm–1am; Fri–Sat 24 hr.

WHERE TO DINE IN SINGAPORE

6 ORCHARD ROAD AREA

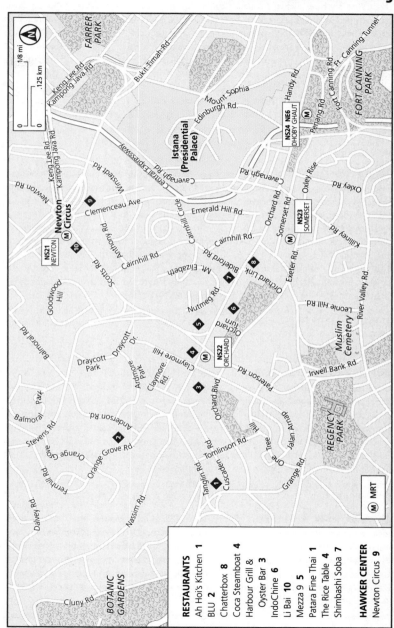

RESTAURANTS

Ah Hoi's Kitchen **1**
BLU **2**
Chatterbox **8**
Coca Steamboat **4**
Harbour Grill &
 Oyster Bar **3**
IndoChine **6**
Li Bai **10**
Mezza 9 **5**
Patara Fine Thai **1**
The Rice Table **4**
Shimbashi Soba **7**

HAWKER CENTER

Newton Circus **9**

Coca Steamboat ★ CHINESE/SINGAPOREAN Beloved by Singaporeans, a steamboat is a tureen of stock that's kept simmering at the table. Diners choose a flavor of stock and add side vegetables, fish, and meats, which are dipped into the broth to cook, then eaten. The best part of the meal is at the end, when the flavored stock is enjoyed as a soup on its own or with rice. Coco has a huge range of side dishes and consistently good, fresh ingredients, from simple cuts of meat to authentic Singaporean staples like fish balls. I particularly like the duck breast and the wontons, and there's a good selection of unusual mushrooms. Throw caution to the winds and pick some old favorites and new flavors, dipped in the signature chili sauce if you like it spicy. Not a place to choose if you're in a hurry, but great fun for families and groups.

International Bldg., 360 Orchard Rd., #02–05. © **65/6738-2588.** Reservations recommended. Lunch buffet S$20–S$25 (US$13–US$17/£9–£11), dinner buffet S$39–S$45 (US$26–US$30/£18–£20). AE, DC, MC, V. Daily 11am–3:45pm and 4–10pm.

Patara Fine Thai THAI Patara may say "fine" dining in its name, but the food here is home cooking: not too haute, not too traditional. Seafood and vegetables are the stars here. Deep-fried *garoupa* (grouper) is served in a sweet sauce with chili that can be added sparingly upon request. Curries are popular, too. The roast duck curry in red curry paste with seasonal fruits is juicy and hot. For something really different, Patara's own invention, the Thai taco, isn't exactly traditional, but it is good, filled with chicken, shrimp, and sprouts. Their green curry, one of my favorites, is perhaps the best in town. Their Thai-style iced tea (which isn't on the menu, so you'll have to ask for it) is fragrant and flowery. A small selection of wines is also available. Patara has another outlet at Swissôtel The Stamford, Level 3, Stamford Road (© **65/6339-1488**).

#03–14 Tanglin Mall, 163 Tanglin Rd. © **65/6737-0818.** Reservations recommended for lunch, required for dinner. Small dishes S$22–S$30 (US$15–US$20/£9.90–£14). AE, DC, MC, V. Daily noon–2:30pm and 6–10pm.

INEXPENSIVE

Ah Hoi's Kitchen SINGAPOREAN I like Ah Hoi's for its casual charm and its selection of authentic local cuisine. The menu is extensive, specializing in local favorites like fried black pepper *kuay teow* (noodles), *sambal kang kong* (a spinach-like vegetable fried with chili), and fabulous grilled seafood. The alfresco poolside pavilion location gives it a real "vacation in the Tropics" sort of relaxed feel—think of a hawker center without the dingy florescent bulbs, greasy tables, and sludgy floor. Also good here is the chili crab—if you can't make it out to the seafood places on the east coast of the island, it's the best alternative for tasting this local treat. Make sure you order the fresh lime juice. It's very cooling.

Traders Hotel, 1A Cuscaden Rd., 4th level. © **65/6831-4373.** Reservations recommended. Small dishes S$14–S$26 (US$9–US$17/£6–£12). AE, DC, MC, V. Daily noon–2:30pm and 6:30–10:30pm.

The Rice Table ★ MALAY/INDONESIAN/DUTCH Indonesian Dutch *rijsttafel,* meaning "rice table," is a service of many small dishes (up to almost 20) with rice. Traditionally, each dish would be brought to diners by beautiful ladies in pompous style. Here, busy waitstaff brings all the dishes out and places them in front of you—feast on favorite Indo-Malay wonders like beef *rendang,* chicken *satay, otak otak,* and *sotong assam* (squid) for a very reasonable price. It's an enormous amount of food and everything is terrific. You will pay extra for your drinks and desserts.

International Bldg., 360 Orchard Rd., #02–09/10. © **65/6835-3783.** Reservations not necessary. Set lunch S$15 (US$10/£6.75); set dinner S$24 (US$16/£11). AE, DC, MC, V. Daily noon–2:15pm and 6–9:15pm.

Shimbashi Soba (Value) (Kids) JAPANESE   It's easy to identify Shimbashi's specialty from the chef who works behind a glass wall, preparing fresh soba noodles at every stage from the grindstone that mills the wheat into flour to the table where he kneads and rolls the dough before slicing each noodle by hand. Glance at the walls, and you'll see photos of the fields in Hokkaido and Tasmania where the buckwheat grew. Whether you slurp them hot in a clear, tasty broth or munch them cold and dipped in sauce, these are the best in town. Reservations aren't accepted, and if you hit the lunchtime or evening rush you might have to wait, but the line moves quickly. The busy wait staff are really friendly and pleasant with kids.

#B1-41 Paragon, 290 Orchard Rd. (C) **65/6735-9882.** Reservations not accepted. Set meals S$13–S$37 (US$8.70–US$25/£5.85–£17). AE, DC, MC, V. Daily 11:30am–9:30pm.

7 RESTAURANTS A LITTLE FARTHER OUT

Many travelers will choose to eat in town for convenience, and although there's plenty of great dining in the more central areas, there are some other really fantastic dining finds if you're willing to hop in a cab for 10 or 15 minutes. These places are worth the trip— for a chance to dine along the water at UDMC or go for superior seafood at Long Beach Seafood Restaurant. And don't worry about finding your way back: Most places always have cabs milling about. If not, restaurant staff will always help you call a taxi.

EXPENSIVE

Halia ★ CONTINENTAL/FUSION   You really need to come to Halia, most notable for its location within the aromatic ginger garden of the Singapore Botanic Gardens, for a daytime meal—either a weekend breakfast buffet, relaxing lunch, or weekday high tea, if you want to enjoy the lush greenery of the surroundings. Cuisine is contemporary fare, with ginger permeating quite a few of the recipes—*halia* being "ginger" in Malay. The specialty of the house is the chunks of seafood stewed in Asian flavors of chili and lemon grass served over a bed of *papardelle* pasta. To get there, ask the taxi driver to take you along Tyersall Avenue, and look for the HALIA signboard at the Tyersall Gate near the Ginger Garden.

1 Cluny Rd., in the Singapore Botanic Gardens, Tyersall Gate. (C) **65/6476-6711.** Reservations recommended. Main courses S$26–S$43 (US$17–US$29/£12–£19); breakfast buffet S$18 (US$12/£8.10). AE, DC, MC, V. Daily noon–3pm; high tea 3pm–5pm; dinner 6:30–10:15pm; breakfast/brunch Sat–Sun 9am–3:30pm.

MODERATE

Imperial Herbal ★★ CHINESE   After 20 years at the Metropole Hotel, Imperial Herbal has moved to a bigger site at the VivoCity shopping center. However, loyal regulars are still coming for the healing powers of the food served here, enriched with herbs and other secret ingredients prescribed by a resident Chinese herbalist. Upon entering, you'll be ushered to the herb counter. The herbalist, Dr. Foo, who is also trained in Western medicine, will ask for the symptoms of what ails you and take your pulse. While you sit and order (from a range of set menus or an extensive a la carte menu of meats, seafood, and vegetable dishes), he'll prepare a packet of ingredients and ship them off to the kitchen, where they'll be added to the food in preparation. Surprisingly, dishes turn out tasty, without the anticipated medicinal aftertaste.

Dr. Foo is in house for dinner every night except Sunday. It's always good to call ahead, though, as he's the main attraction. When you leave, present him with a small *ang pau*—a gift of cash in a red envelope—maybe S$5 (US$3.35/£2.25) or S$10 (US$6.70/£4.50). Red envelopes are available in any card or gift shop.

VivoCity, Lobby G #03-08. © **65/6337-0491.** Reservations recommended for lunch, necessary for dinner. Small dishes S$18–S$32 (US$12–US$21/£8.10–£14). AE, DC, MC, V. Daily 11:30am–2:30pm and 6:15–10:30pm.

Long Beach Seafood Restaurant SEAFOOD   They really pack 'em in at this place. Tables are crammed together in what resembles a big indoor pavilion, complete with festive lights and the sounds of mighty feasting. This is one of the best places for fresh seafood of all kinds: fish like *garoupa* (grouper), sea bass, marble goby, and kingfish, and other creatures of the sea, from prawns to crayfish. The chili crab here is good, but the house specialty is really the pepper crab, chopped and deliciously smothered in a thick concoction of black pepper and soy. Huge chunks of crayfish are also tasty in the black pepper sauce and can be served in variations like barbecue, sambal, steamed with garlic, or in a bean sauce. Don't forget to order buns so you can sop up the sauce. You can also get vegetable, chicken, beef, or venison dishes to complement, or choose from their menu selection of local favorites. Long Beach now has several branches, including at Dempsey Hill, 25 Dempsey Rd. opposite the Botanic Gardens (© **65/6323-2222**).

1018 East Coast Pkwy. © **65/6445-8833.** Reservations recommended. Seafood is sold by weight according to seasonal prices. Most nonseafood dishes S$11–S$22 (US$7.35–US$15/£4.95–£9.90). AE, DC, MC, V. Daily 11am–3pm; Sun–Fri 5pm–12:15am; Sat 5pm–1:15am.

Original Sin ★ MEDITERRANEAN/VEGETARIAN   This cozy place is a perennial favorite with Singapore's expatriate population. Located in Holland Village, Singapore's expat enclave, the restaurant is close to shopping, pubs, and numerous other dining choices that cater to this international group. This particular restaurant is a favorite, with generous portions of favorites like baba ghanouj, *tzatziki,* and hummus served with olives, feta, and pita bread. And although the menu features standard Mediterranean fare like moussaka and risotto dishes, people always seem to go for the pizzas, which are loaded with interesting Middle Eastern toppings. The owners also run two other properties of equal quality and popularity in Chip Bee Gardens, Italian restaurants **Michelangelo's,** Block 44, Jalan Merah Saga #01–60 (© **65/6475-9069**); and **Sistina,** Block 44, Jalan Merah Saga #01–58 (© **65/6476-7782**). All of these restaurants have a casual bistro-style atmosphere inside and sidewalk dining outside.

Block 43 Jalan Merah Saga, #01–62, Chip Bee Gardens, Holland Village. © **65/6475-5605.** Reservations recommended. Main courses S$22–S$28 (US$15–US$19/£9.90–£13). AE, DC, MC, V. Tues–Sun 11:30am–2:30pm and 6–10:30pm; Mon 6–10:30pm.

UDMC Seafood Centre ★★ SEAFOOD   Eight seafood restaurants are lined side by side in 2 blocks, their fronts open to the view of the sea outside. UDMC is a fantastic way to eat seafood Singapore style, in the open air, in restaurants that are more like grand stalls than anything else. Eat the famous local chili crab and pepper crab here, along with all sorts of squid, fish, and scallop dishes. Noodle dishes are also available, as are vegetable dishes and other meats. But the seafood is the thing to come for. Of the eight restaurants, there's no saying which is the best, as everyone seems to have his own opinions about this one or that one (I like Jumbo at the far eastern end of the row; call © **65/6442-3435** for reservations, which are recommended for weekends). Have a nice stroll along the walkway and gaze out to the water while you decide which one to go for.

INEXPENSIVE

Samy's Curry Restaurant ★ SOUTHERN INDIAN   There are many places in Singapore to get good southern Indian banana leaf, but none quite so unique as Samy's out on Dempsey Road. Samy's is situated in a huge, high-ceilinged, open-air hall, with shutters thrown back and fans whirring above. Wash your hands at the back and have a seat, and soon someone will slap a banana-leaf place mat in front of you. A blob of white rice will be placed in the center, and then buckets of vegetables, chicken, mutton, fish, prawn, and you-name-it will be brought out, swimming in the richest and spiciest curries to ever pass your lips. Take a peek in each bucket, nod your head yes when you see one you like, and a scoop will be dumped on your banana leaf. Eat with your right hand or with a fork and spoon. When you're done, wipe the sweat from your brow, fold the banana leaf away from you, and place your tableware on top. Samy's serves no alcohol, but the fresh lime juice is nice and cooling, and lassi, the flavored yogurt drink, helps to counteract the spiciness.

Block 25 Dempsey Rd., Civil Service Club. Ⓒ **65/6472-2080.** Reservations not accepted. Sold by the scoop or piece, S80¢–S$4 (US55¢–US$2.70/35p–£1.80). V. Daily 11am–3pm and 6–10pm. No alcohol served.

---

8 HAWKER CENTERS

Hawker centers—large groupings of informal open-air food stalls—were Singapore's answer to fast and cheap food in the days before McDonald's and are still the best way to sample every kind of Singaporean cuisine. The traditional hawker center is an outdoor venue, usually under cover with fans whirring above, and individual stalls each specializing in different dishes. In between rows of cooking stalls, tables and stools offer open seating for diners.

Each center has an array of food offerings, with most dishes costing between S$3.50 and S$7 (US$2.35–US$4.70/£1.55–£3.15). You'll find traditional dishes like *char kway teow*, flat rice noodles fried with seafood; **fishball noodle soup,** with balls made from pounded fish and rice flour; **claypot chicken rice,** chicken and mushrooms baked with rice and fragrant soy sauce; *bak kut teh*, pork ribs stewed with Chinese herbs; **Hainanese chicken rice,** soft chicken over rice prepared in rich chicken stock; *laksa*, seafood and rice noodles in a spicy coconut chili soup; *popiah*, turnip, egg, pork, prawn, and sweet chili sauce wrapped in a thin skin; *rojak*, fried dough, tofu, cucumber, pineapple, and whatever the chef has handy, mixed with a sauce made from peanuts and fermented shrimp paste; plus many, many more Chinese, Malay, and Indian specialties. You'll also find hot and cold drink stalls and usually a stall selling fresh fruits and fruit juices.

If you want to become a real Singapore Foodie, buy a copy of *Makansutra*, by K. F. Seetoh (Makansutra Publishing) at any bookstore. Seetoh is the local guru of hawker foods and has sniffed out the tastiest, most authentic local delicacies you can imagine.

Within the city limits, most traditional-style hawker centers have been closed down, but you can still find a few. Singapore's most famous, or notorious, hawker center is **Newton Circus Hawker Center,** a 24-hour center near the Newton MRT stop and a tour-bus darling; beware of gouging, especially when ordering seafood dishes, which are sold by the kilo.

For local-style hawker centers, in Chinatown you can find stalls at the **Maxwell Road Food Centre** at the corner of Maxwell and South Bridge roads, or you can try **Lau Pa Sat** at the corner of Raffles Way and Boon Tat Street. A new food attraction, a row of stalls along Smith Street called **Food Alley** was conceived by the STB. Rumor has it, these guys are having a hard time making a living selling local food to the very touristy crowd that passes down this street in the evenings. In the Historic District, try the **small center next to Allson Hotel** on Victoria Street, or Makansutra, next to the Esplanade–Theatres on the Bay. In Little India, **Tekka Market** is under construction, but nearby on Race Course Road the hawkers have set up under a temporary structure.

When you eat at a hawker center, the first thing to do is claim a seat at a table. (*Local trick:* If you put a tissue packet down on the table in front of your seat, people will understand it's reserved.) Remember the number on your table so that when you order from each stall, you can let them know where you're seated. They will deliver your food to the table, and you must pay upon delivery. Change will be provided. When you are finished, there's no need to clear your dishes; it will be taken care of for you.

The modern version of the hawker center is the **food court.** Similar to hawker centers, food courts are air-conditioned spaces inside shopping malls and public buildings. They also have individual stalls offering a variety of foods and tables with free seating. Generally, food courts offer a more "fast-food," less authentic version of local cuisine, but you also get greater variety—many food courts have a stall that sells Western burgers and fish and chips, and stalls with Japanese *udon* or Korean barbecue. Food courts also differ in that they're self-service. When you approach the stall, you take a tray, pay when you order, then carry the food yourself to a table, similar to cafeteria style. When you finish, you are not expected to clear your tray.

Food courts are everywhere within the city, most of them operated by popular chains like **Food Junction, Kopitiam,** and **Banquet.** You'll find them in shopping malls and public buildings, most likely on the top floor or in the basement. Your hotel's concierge will be able to point you to the nearest food court, no problem.

9 CAFE SOCIETY

In Singapore, traditions such as British high tea and the Chinese tea ceremony live side by side with a growing coffee culture. These popular hangouts are all over the city. Here are a few places to try.

BRITISH HIGH TEA

Two fabulous places to take high tea in style are at **Raffles Bar & Billiard Room** at Raffles Hotel, 1 Beach Rd. (© **65/6412-1816**), and **Equinox** at Swissôtel The Stamford, 2 Stamford Rd. (© **65/6431-6156**). Both places are lovely, if pricey. The buffet will cost anywhere from S$33 to S$38 (US$22–US$25/£15–£17), more at peak seasons. High tea is served in the afternoons from 3 until 5 or 5:30pm.

CHINESE TEA

There are a few places in Chinatown where tea is still as important today as it has always been in Chinese culture. **The Tea Chapter,** 9-11A Neil Rd. (© **65/6226-1175**), and **Yixing Xuan,** 30–32 Tanjong Pagar Rd. (© **65/6224-6961**), offer tranquil respites from the day and cultural insight into Chinese tea appreciation.

CAFES

Western-style coffee joints have been popping up left and right all over the island, so coffee-addicted travelers can rest assured that in the morning their favorite blends are brewing close by—as long as you don't mind spending up to S$7 (US$4.70/£3.15) for a cup of brew. **Starbucks,** the **Coffee Bean & Tea Leaf,** the **Coffee Club, Spinelli,** and many more international chain cafes have outlets in just about every shopping mall in the city.

Singapore Attractions

Of Singapore's many sights and attractions, I enjoy the historical and cultural sights the most. The city's many old buildings and well-presented museum displays bring history to life. Chinese and Hindu temples and Muslim mosques welcome curious observers to discover their culture as they play out their daily activities, and the country's natural parks make the great outdoors easily accessible from even the most urban neighborhood. That's the best benefit of traveling in Singapore: Most attractions are situated within the heart of the city, and those that lie outside the urban center still can be easily reached.

Singapore also has a multitude of planned attractions for visitors and locals alike. Theme parks devoted to cultural heritage, sporting fun, and even kitsch amusement pop up all over the place. In this chapter, I've outlined the many attractions here and provided historical and cultural information to help you appreciate each sight in its local context. To help you plan your activities, I've put stars next to those attractions I've enjoyed the most—either for significance, excellent planning, or just plain curiosity.

I've divided this chapter into the main sections of the urban center—the Historic District, Chinatown, Little India, Kampong Glam, and Orchard Road, where you'll find the more historical sights of the city—and those outside the city, to the west, north, and east, where you'll find large areas dedicated to nature reserves, a zoo, other wildlife attractions, theme parks, and sprawling temple complexes, all easily accessible by public transportation or a cab ride. As a kicker, I'll take you to Sentosa (a small island to the south with amusements, historical exhibits, nature displays, and outdoor activities for families) and to some of the smaller outlying islands, and will fill you in on sports and recreation options.

When you're traveling to attractions outside the urban area, I recommend keeping this book handy—taxis are not always easy to find, so you may need to refer to the guide to call for a pickup or use the bus and MRT system, route numbers for which I've included with listings of most noncentral attractions.

A note: Many of the sights to see in Singapore are not of the "pay your fee and see the show" variety, but rather historic buildings, monuments, and places of religious worship. Monuments and statues tell the stories of events and heroes important to Singapore in both the past and the present. The places of worship listed in this chapter are open to the public and free of entrance charge. Expect temples to be open from sunup to sundown. Visiting hours are not specific to the hour, but unless it's a holiday (when hours may be extended), you can expect these places to be open during daylight hours.

1 THE HISTORIC DISTRICT

When Sir Stamford Raffles first sailed up the Singapore River, he saw a small fishing and trading village along the banks and a thick overgrowth of jungle and mangrove forest creeping up a gentle hill that overlooked the harbor. Over the years to follow, the left bank of the river would become the nerve center for sea trade, and the right bank, at the foot of the hill, would be cleared for the center of government activity.

Raffles's Town Plan of 1822 had special plans for this district, referred to in this book as the Historic District but also called the City Centre. The center point was the **Padang,** a large field for sports and ceremonies. Around the field, government buildings were erected, each reflecting preferred British tastes of the day. European hotels popped up, as well as cultural centers, and the park along the marina became a lively focal point for the European social scene.

The oldest part of the city is Fort Canning Park, the hill where Raffles built his home. Its history predates Raffles, with excavation sites unearthing artifacts and small treasures from earlier trading settlements, and a sacred shrine that's believed to be the final resting place of Iskander Shah, founder of the Sultanate of Melaka.

Armenian Church ★   Of all colonial buildings, the Armenian Church (more formally called the Church of St. Gregory the Illuminator) is one of the most beautiful examples of early architectural style here. Designed by George Coleman, one of Singapore's most prolific and talented architects, it is his finest work. Although there were many alterations in the last century, the main style of the structure still dominates. The round congregation hall is powerful in its simplicity, its long louvered windows letting in cooling breezes while keeping out the imposing sunlight. Roman Doric columns support symmetrical porticos that protect the structure from rain. All in all, it's a wonderful achievement of combined European eclectic tastes and tropical necessity.

The first permanent Christian church in Singapore, it was funded primarily by the Armenian community, which was at one time quite powerful. Today few Singaporeans can trace their heritage back to this influential group of immigrants. The church was consecrated in 1836, and the last appointed priest serving the parish retired in 1936. Although regular Armenian services are no longer held, other religious organizations make use of the church from time to time. The cemetery in the back of the church is the burial site of many prominent Armenians, including Ashgen Agnes Joachim, discoverer of the Vanda Miss Joachim, Singapore's national flower.

60 Hill St., across from the Grand Plaza Park Hotel. 🄯 **65/6334-0141.** Free admission. 15-min. walk from City Hall MRT.

Asian Civilisations Museum ★★★   If you have time for only one museum, this is the one I recommend. This fantastic and well-executed exhibit of Southeast Asian culture highlights the history of the region and explores the Chinese, South Indian, and Islamic heritage that helped to shape regional cultures here. Well-planned galleries showcase fine arts, furniture, porcelain, jade, and other relics with excellent descriptions.

The Empress Place Building that houses the museum stood as a symbol of British colonial authority as sea travelers entered the Singapore River. The stately building housed almost the entire government bureaucracy around the year 1905 and was a government office until the 1980s, housing the Registry of Births and Deaths and the Citizenship Registry.

Don't forget to stop at the Museum Shop (🄯 **65/6336-9050**) to browse exquisite ethnic crafts of the region. Also, check out the museum's website to find out more about their free lecture series.

1 Empress Place. 🄯 **65/6332-7798.** www.acm.org.sg. Adults S$5 (US$3.35/£2.25), children and seniors S$2.50 (US$1.65/£1.10); free on Fri 7–9pm. Mon 1–7pm; Tues–Sun 9am–7pm (extended hours Fri 9am–9pm). Free guided tours in English Mon 2pm, Tues–Fri 11am and 2pm, with an extra tour on weekends at 3:30pm. 15-min. walk from City Hall MRT.

HISTORIC DISTRICT
Armenian Church **19**
Asian Civilisations Museum **29**
Boat Quay **30**
Cathedral of the Good Shepherd **13**
CHIJMES (Convent of the
    Holy Infant Jesus) **14**
City Hall (Municipal Building) **23**
Clarke Quay **20**
Esplanade Park **25**
Fort Canning Park **17**
Hill Street Building **21**
Kuan Yin Thong
    Hood Cho Temple **11**
Merlion Park **26**
National Museum of Singapore **12**
Old Parliament House **27**
The Padang **24**
Peranakan Museum **16**
Raffles Hotel **15**
Raffles Landing Site **28**
Singapore Art Museum **12**
Singapore Flyer **40**
Singapore Philatelic Museum **18**
Sri Thandayuthapani Temple **3**
St. Andrew's Cathedral **22**
Statue of Raffles **29**
Supreme Court **23**
Victoria Theatre and
    Concert Hall **29**

CHINATOWN
Al-Abrar Mosque **37**
Chinatown Heritage Centre **32**
Jamae Mosque **33**
Lau Pa Sat Festival Pavilion **39**
Nagore Durgha Shrine **38**
Sacred Buddha Tooth Temple **35**
Singapore City Gallery **36**
Sri Mariamman Hindu Temple **34**
Thian Hock Keng Temple **38**
Wak Hai Cheng Bio Temple **31**

LITTLE INDIA
Abdul Gafoor Mosque **7**
Sakya Muni Buddha Gaya
    Temple of a Thousand Lights) **4**
Sri Perumal Temple **5**
Sri Veerama Kaliamman Temple **6**

ARAB STREET &
    KAMPONG GLAM
Alsagoff Arab School **8**
Hajjah Fatimah Mosque **9**
Malay Heritage Centre
    (Istana Kampong Glam) **10**
Sultan Mosque **10**

ORCHARD ROAD AREA
The Istana and Sri Temasek **1**
Peranakan Place **2**

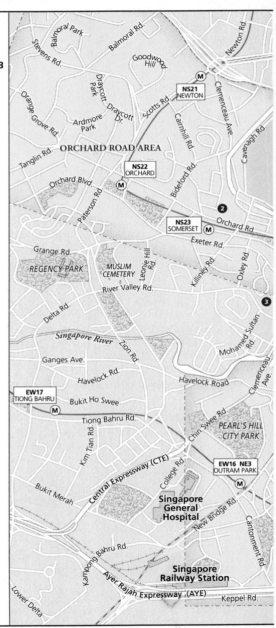

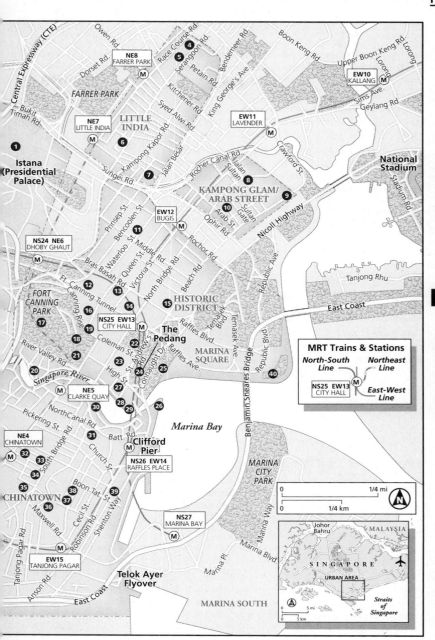

Cathedral of the Good Shepherd   This cathedral was Singapore's first permanent Catholic church. Built in the 1840s, it unified many elements of a fractured parish. In the early days of the colony, the Portuguese Mission thought itself the fount of the Holy Roman Empire's presence on the island, and so the French bishop was reduced to holding services at the home of a Mr. McSwiney on Bras Basah Road, a dissenting Portuguese priest held services at a certain Dr. d'Ameida's residence, and the Spanish priest was so reduced that we don't even know where he held his services. These folks were none too pleased with their makeshift houses of worship and so banded together to establish their own cathedral—the Cathedral of the Good Shepherd. Designed in a Latin cross pattern, much of its architecture is reminiscent of St. Martin-in-the-Fields and St. Paul's in Covent Garden. The archbishop's residence, in contrast, is a simple two-story bungalow with enclosed verandas and a portico. Also on the grounds are the residents' quarters and the priests' residence, the latter more ornate in design, with elaborate plasterwork.

4 Queen St. (at the corner of Queen St. and Bras Basah Rd.). (*C*) **65/6337-2036.** Free admission. Open to the public during the day. 5-min. walk from City Hall MRT.

CHIJMES (Convent of the Holy Infant Jesus)   As you enter this bustling enclave of retail shops, restaurants, and nightspots, it's difficult to imagine this was once a convent which, at its founding in 1854, consisted of a lone, simply constructed bungalow. After decades of buildings and add-ons, this collection of unique yet perfectly blended structures—a school, a private residence, an orphanage, a stunning Gothic chapel, and many others—was enclosed within walls, forming peaceful courtyards and open spaces encompassing an entire city block. Legend has it the small door on the corner of Bras Basah and Victoria streets welcomed hundreds of orphan babies, girl children who just appeared on the stoop each morning, either born during inauspicious years or to poor families. In late 1983, the convent relocated to the suburbs, and some of the block was leveled to make way for the MRT Headquarters. Thankfully, most of the block survived and the Singapore government, in planning the renovation of this desirable piece of real estate, wisely kept the integrity of the architecture. For an evening out, the atmosphere at CHIJMES is exquisitely romantic.

A note on the name: CHIJMES is pronounced "Chimes"; the "Chij," as noted, stands for Convent of the Holy Infant Jesus, and the "mes" was just added on so they could pronounce it "Chimes."

30 Victoria St. (*C*) **65/6336-1818.** Free admission. 5-min. walk from City Hall MRT.

City Hall (Municipal Building)   During the Japanese Occupation, City Hall was a major headquarters, and it was here in 1945 that Adm. Lord Louis Mountbatten accepted the Japanese surrender. In 1951, the Royal Proclamation from King George VI was read here declaring that Singapore would henceforth be known as a city. Fourteen years later, Prime Minister Lee Kuan Yew announced to its citizens that Singapore would henceforth be called an independent republic.

City Hall, along with the Supreme Court, was judiciously sited to take full advantage of its prime location. Magnificent Corinthian columns march across the front of the symmetrically designed building, while inside, two courtyards lend an ambience of informality to otherwise officious surroundings. For all its magnificence and historical fame, however, its architect, F. D. Meadows, relied too heavily on European influence. The many windows afford no protection from the sun, and the entrance leaves pedestrians unsheltered from the elements. In defining the very nobility of the Singapore government, it appears the Singaporean climate wasn't taken into consideration.

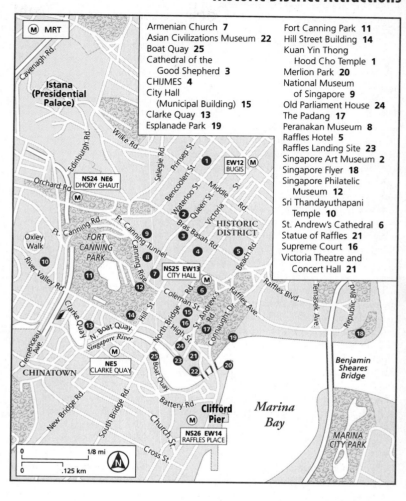

(M) MRT	
Istana (Presidential Palace)	
Armenian Church **7**	Fort Canning Park **11**
Asian Civilizations Museum **22**	Hill Street Building **14**
Boat Quay **25**	Kuan Yin Thong Hood Cho Temple **1**
Cathedral of the Good Shepherd **3**	Merlion Park **20**
CHIJMES **4**	National Museum of Singapore **9**
City Hall (Municipal Building) **15**	Old Parliament House **24**
Clarke Quay **13**	The Padang **17**
Esplanade Park **19**	Peranakan Museum **8**
	Raffles Hotel **5**
	Raffles Landing Site **23**
	Singapore Art Museum **2**
	Singapore Flyer **18**
	Singapore Philatelic Museum **12**
	Sri Thandayuthapani Temple **10**
	St. Andrew's Cathedral **6**
	Statue of Raffles **21**
	Supreme Court **16**
	Victoria Theatre and Concert Hall **21**

From 2013, City Hall and the Supreme Court are slated to become the new National Art Gallery, giving much-needed space to display the nation's collection of Southeast Asian art and providing a platform for major international exhibitions. Though not open to the public, the buildings will continue to be used occasionally for special events until conversion work begins in 2010.

3 St. Andrew's Rd., across from the Padang. Entrance is not permitted. 5-min. walk from City Hall MRT.

Fort Canning Park These days, Fort Canning Park is known for great views over Singapore, but in days past it served as the site of Raffles's home and the island's first botanic garden. Its history goes back even farther, though: Excavations have unearthed ancient brick foundations and artifacts that give credence to the island natives' belief that their royal ancestors lived and were buried on the site. Atop the hill, a mysterious *keramat*, or sacred grave, marks what is believed to be the burial site of Iskander Shah (also known as Parameswara), the Palembang ruler who came to Singapore in the late 1300s before settling in Melaka.

From the start, Raffles chose this hill to build his home (at the site of the present-day lookout point), which later became a residence for Singapore's diplomats and governors. In 1860, the house was torn down to make way for Fort Canning, which was built to quell British fears of invasion but instead quickly became the laughingstock of the island. The location was ideal for spotting invaders from the sea, but defending Singapore? Not likely. The cannons' range was such that their shells couldn't possibly have made it all the way out to an attacking ship—instead, most of the town below would have been destroyed. In 1907, the fort was demolished for a reservoir. Today the only reminders of the old fort are some of the walls and the Fort Gate, a deep stone structure. Behind its huge wooden door you'll find a narrow staircase that leads to the roof.

Raffles also chose this as the location for the first botanic garden on the island, with ambitious plans to develop commercial crops, particularly spices. The garden was short-lived due to lack of funding; however, the park still has a pretty interesting selection of plants and trees, like the cannonball tree with its large round seed pods, and the cotton tree, whose pods open to reveal fluffy white "cotton" that was commonly used for stuffing pillows and mattresses. In many parts, these plants are well marked along the pathways. Also look for the ASEAN sculpture garden; five members of the Association of Southeast Asian Nations each donated a work for the park in 1982 to represent the region's unity.

Fort Canning was also the site of a **European cemetery.** To make improvements in the park, the graves were exhumed and the stones placed within the walls surrounding the outdoor performance field that slopes from the Music and Drama Society building. A large Gothic monument was erected in memory of James Napier Brooke, infant son of William Napier, Singapore's first law agent, and his wife, Maria Frances, the widow of prolific architect George Coleman. Although no records exist, Coleman probably designed the cupolas as well as two small monuments over unknown graves. The Music and Drama Society building itself was built in 1938. Close by, in the wall, are the tombstones of Coleman and of Jose D'Almeida, a wealthy Portuguese merchant.

Inside the park, the **Battle Box** is an old World War II bunker that displays in wax dioramas and a multimedia show the surrender of Singapore. It's open daily from 10am to 6pm; adults S$8 (US$5.35/£3.60), children S$5 (US$3.35/£2.25); ✆ **65/6333-0510.**

The National Parks Board gives free guided tours of the park, but not the Battle Box, every last Saturday of the month at 4pm; call ✆ **65/6332-1302** to register.

51 Canning Rise. ✆ **65/6332-1302.** www.nparks.gov.sg. Free admission. Major entrances are from behind the Hill Street Building, Percival Rd. (Drama Centre), National Library Carpark, and Canning Walk (behind Park Mall). Dhoby Ghaut or City Hall MRT.

Hill Street Building   Originally built to house the British Police Force, the building was sited directly across from Chinatown for easy access to quell the frequent gang fights. Later it became home to the National Archives, and it is believed that inquisitions and torture were carried out in the basement during the Japanese occupation. Former National Archives employees have claimed to have seen ghosts of tortured souls sitting at their desks.

Today this colorful building houses the Ministry of Information, Communications and the Arts (MICA), and the National Arts Council. Inside the courtyard, check out

ARTrium@MICA, with galleries displaying Singaporean, Southeast Asian, and European fine arts. It's air-conditioned!

140 Hill St. at the corner of River Valley Rd., on Fort Canning Park. ✆ **65/6837-9527.** www.artriumatmica. com. Free admission. 5-min. walk from Clarke Quay MRT.

Kuan Yin Thong Hood Cho Temple   It's said that whatever you wish for within the walls of Kuan Yin Temple comes true, so get in line and have your wish ready. It must work, as there's a steady stream of people on auspicious days of the Chinese calendar. The procedure is simple (watch others to catch on): Wear shoes easily slipped off before entering the temple and join the queue. When it is your turn, light several joss sticks, bow with them, and make a wish before placing them in the urn provided. Pick up the cylindrical container filled with wooden sticks and shake it until one stick falls out—each stick has a number. Give this number to the interpretation office and they will hand you a piece of paper with verses in Mandarin and English. This will tell you your general fortune, plus a clue as to whether your wish will come true. (For a small fee, interpreters outside can help with the translation.) Now for the payback: If your wish comes true, you're supposed to return to the temple and offer fruits and flowers to say thanks (oranges, pears, and apples are a thoughtful choice, and jasmine petals are especially nice). So be careful what you wish for. After you're back home and that job promotion comes through, your new manager might nix a trip back to Singapore so you can bring fruits to this little temple! To be on the safe side, bring the goods with you when you make your wish.

Waterloo St., about 1½ blocks from Bras Basah Rd. Free admission. Open to the public during the day. 15-min. walk from Bugis MRT.

National Museum of Singapore ★★★   The once-little history museum, the former Singapore History Museum, has recently undergone a massive renovation. This beautiful 120-year-old building has not only been restored, but has been expanded to more than twice its original size by adding a striking modernist wing to the rear of the building. Cleverly, the new wing is invisible from the front. An ingenious glass-ceilinged walkway connects the old and new wings and provides a perfect point to view the magnificent Victorian dome with its stained-glass panels and zinc fishtail tiles. The large History Gallery, based in the new wing, tells the story of Singapore from two points of view: from a historian's perspective and from the "man on the street," accompanied by state-of-the-art multimedia exhibits designed to bring history to life and make it accessible for all visitors. You decide which story you'd like to hear, then choose the corresponding audio headset that will guide you through the exhibit. The four Living Galleries are on the second floor of the old wing and show objects and elements of everyday Singaporean life: food, fashion, film, and photography. The museum conducts free guided tours in English Monday through Friday at 11am and 2pm, and on Saturday and Sunday at 11:30am and 3:30pm; the tour takes 1 to 1½ hours. The building itself is a mix of colonial and contemporary architecture; a free tour that focuses just on the architecture is offered Friday through Sunday at 3:30pm.

93 Stamford Rd. ✆ **65/6332-3659.** www.nationalmuseum.sg. Adults S$10 (US$6.70/£4.50), children and seniors S$5 (US$3.35/£2.25); free admission to the Living Galleries daily 6–8pm. History Gallery daily 10am–6pm; Living Galleries daily 10am–8pm. 5-min. walk from Dhoby Ghaut or City Hall MRT.

Old Parliament House   The Old Parliament House is probably Singapore's oldest surviving structure, even though it has been renovated so many times it no longer looks the way it was originally constructed. It was designed as a home for John Argyle Maxwell, a Scottish merchant, but he never moved in. In 1822, Raffles returned to Singapore and was furious to find a residence being built on ground he'd allocated for government use. So the government took over Maxwell's house for its court and other offices. In 1939, when the new Supreme Court was completed, the judiciary moved into Maxwell's House (as it became officially known); then, in 1953, following a major renovation, the small structure was renamed Parliament House and was turned over to the legislature.

The original house was designed by architect George D. Coleman, who had helped Raffles with his Town Plan of 1822. Coleman's design was in the English neo-Palladian style. Simple and well suited to the Tropics, this style was popular at the time with Calcutta merchants. Major alterations have left very little behind of Coleman's design, replacing it with an eclectic French classical style, but some of his work survives.

Today the building has been transformed once again—The Arts House at the Old Parliament has been lovingly restored, with spaces for visual and performance arts, plus special cultural events. A small gallery retells the story of the building. A couple of highbrow eateries offer a variety of Thai, Vietnamese, and Western cuisine. Singapore's parliament now operates out of the new Parliament Building just next door.

The bronze elephant in front of the Old Parliament House was a gift to Singapore in 1872 from His Majesty Somdeth Phra Paraminda Maha Chulalongkorn (Rama V), supreme king of Siam, as a token of gratitude following his stay the previous year.

1 Old Parliament Lane, at the south end of the Padang, next to the Supreme Court. ℂ 65/6332-6900. www.theartshouse.com.sg. Mon–Fri 10am–8pm; Sat 11am–8pm. Free admission, guided tour S$8 (US$5.35/£3.60); extra charge for tickets to events. 15-min. walk from City Hall MRT.

The Padang   This large field has witnessed its share of historical events. Bordered on one end by the Singapore Recreation Club and on the other end by the Singapore Cricket Club, and flanked by City Hall, the area was once known as Raffles Plain. Upon Raffles's return to the island in 1822, he was angry that resident Farquhar had allowed merchants to move private residences into the prime area he had originally intended for government buildings. All building permits were rescinded, and the Padang became the official center point for the government quarters, around which the Esplanade and City Hall were built.

Today the Padang is mainly used for public and sporting events—pleasant activities—but in the 1940s, it felt more forlorn footsteps when the invading Japanese forced the entire European community onto the field. There they waited while the occupation officers dickered over a suitable location for the "conquered." They ordered all British, Australian, and Allied troops, as well as European prisoners, on the 22km (14-mile) march to Changi.

An interesting side note: Frank Ward, designer of the Supreme Court, had big plans for the Padang and surrounding buildings. He would have demolished the Cricket Club, Parliament House, and Victoria Hall & Theatre to erect an enormous government block if World War II hadn't arrived, ruining his chances.

St. Andrew's Rd. and Connaught Dr. Free admission. 5-min. walk from City Hall MRT.

Peranakan Museum   This small branch of the Asian Civilisations Museum (see above) illuminates the fascinating culture of the Peranakans, people born of intermarriages between Chinese immigrants and locally born Malays. The result is a rich and fascinating blend of traditions, cuisine, and decorative influences. Look out for the incredibly beautiful carved teak wedding furniture and the distinctive porcelain decorated in typical Peranakan colors of pink, blue, green, and yellow. The clothing is vivid yet delicate, featuring intricate embroidery and beading. It's a great insight into a culture that appeared and flourished for a brief period of time in a tiny part of the world. The collection is nicely laid out in a lovely building that was the former Tao Nan School, which dates from 1910.

39 Armenian St. Ⓒ **65/6332-7591.** www.peranakanmuseum.sg. Adults S$6 (US$4/£2.70), children and seniors S$3 (US$2/£1.35); free Fri 7–9pm. Mon 1–7pm; Tues–Sun 9:30am–7pm (extended hours Fri 9:30am–9pm). 15-min. walk from City Hall MRT.

Raffles Hotel ★★ Built in 1887 to accommodate the increasing upper-class trade, Raffles Hotel was originally only a couple of bungalows with 10 rooms, but, oh, the view of the sea was perfection. The owners, Armenian brothers named Sarkies, already had a couple of prosperous hotels in Southeast Asia (the Eastern & Oriental in Penang and the Strand in Rangoon) and were well versed in the business. It wasn't long before they added a pair of wings and completed the main building—and reading rooms, verandas, dining rooms, a grand lobby, the Bar and Billiards Room, a ballroom, and a string of shops. By 1899, electricity was turning the cooling fans and providing the pleasing glow of comfort.

As it made its madcap dash through the 1920s, the hotel was the place to see and be seen. Vacancies were unheard of. Hungry Singaporeans and guests from other hotels, eager for a glimpse of the fabulous dining room, were turned away for lack of reservations. The crowded ballroom was jumping every night of the week. During this time Raffles's guest book included famous authors like Somerset Maugham, Rudyard Kipling, Joseph Conrad, and Noël Coward. These were indeed the glory years, but the lovely glimmer from the chandeliers soon faded with the stark arrival of the Great Depression. Raffles managed to limp through that dark time—and, darker still, through the Japanese Occupation—and later pull back from the brink of bankruptcy to undergo modernization in the '50s. But fresher, brighter, more opulent hotels were taking root on Orchard Road, pushing the "grand old lady" to the back seat.

In the 1990s, Raffles was brought back to its former glory, restored and sensitively expanded over the course of a 3-year, multimillion-dollar project. History-minded renovators selected 1915 as a benchmark and, with a few changes here and there, faithfully restored the hotel to that era's magnificence and splendor. Today the hotel's restaurants and nightlife draw thousands of visitors daily to its open lobby, its theater playhouse, the Raffles Hotel Museum, and exclusive boutiques. Its 15 restaurants and bars—especially the Tiffin Room, Raffles Grill, and Doc Cheng's—are a wonder, as is its famous Bar and Billiards Room and Long Bar. If you're arriving by taxi, ask the driver to take you to the front door of the hotel, where you'll be met by Raffles's fabulous sikh doormen.

1 Beach Rd. Ⓒ **65/6337-1886.** City Hall MRT.

Raffles Landing Site The polymarble statue at this site was unveiled in 1972. It was made from plaster casts of the original 1887 figure located in front of the Victoria Theatre and Concert Hall (see below) and stands on what is believed to be the site where Sir Stamford Raffles landed on January 29, 1819.

North Boat Quay. Free admission. 15-min. walk from City Hall MRT.

St. Andrew's Cathedral Designed by George Coleman; erected on a site selected by Sir Stamford Raffles himself; named for the patron saint of Scotland, St. Andrew; and primarily funded by Singapore's Scottish community, the first St. Andrew's was the colonials' Anglican Church. Completed toward the end of the 1830s, its tower and spire were added several years later to accord the edifice more stature. By 1852, because of massive damage sustained from lightning strikes, the cathedral was deemed unsafe and torn down. The cathedral that now stands on the site was completed in 1860. Of English Gothic Revival design, the cathedral is one of the few standing churches of this style in the region. The spire resembles the steeple of Salisbury Cathedral—another tribute from the colonials to Mother England. Not only English residents, but Christian Chinese, Indians, Continental Europeans, and Malays consider this to be their center of worship.

The plasterwork of St. Andrew's inside walls used a material called Madras *chunam,* which, though peculiar, was a common building material here in the 1880s. A combination of shell lime (without the sand) was mixed with egg whites and coarse sugar or jaggery until it took on the consistency of a stiff paste. The mixture was thinned to a workable consistency with water in which coconut husks had steeped and was then applied to the surface, allowed to dry, and polished with rock crystal or smooth stones to a most lustrous patina. Who would've thought?

The original church bell was presented to the cathedral by Maria Revere Balestier, the daughter of famed American patriot Paul Revere. The bell is now on display in the National Museum of Singapore.

11 St. Andrew's Rd., across from the Padang. (© **65/6337-6104.** Free admission. Open during daylight hours. City Hall MRT.

Singapore Art Museum ★ The Singapore Art Museum (SAM) opened in 1996 to house an impressive collection of over 6,500 pieces of art and sculpture, most of it by Singaporean and Malay artists. Limited space requires the curators to display only a small number at a time, but these are incorporated in interesting exhibits to illustrate particular artistic styles, social themes, or historical concepts. A large collection of Southeast Asian pieces rotates regularly, as well as visiting international exhibits. Besides the main halls, the museum offers up a gift shop with fine souvenir ideas, a cafe, a conservation laboratory, an auditorium, and the E-mage Gallery, where multimedia presentations include not only the museum's own acquisitions, but other works from public and private collections in the region as well. A new wing, 8Q, in neighboring Queen Street, opened in 2008 to highlight the work of living Asian artists and experimental art forms. It also contains a Children's Gallery with a hands-on approach. Once a Catholic boys' school established in 1852, SAM has retained some visible reminders of its former occupants: Above the front door of the main building, you can still see inscribed "St. Joseph's Institution," and a bronze-toned, cast-iron statue of St. John Baptist de la Salle with two children stands in its original place.

71 Bras Basah Rd. (© **65/6332-3222.** www.singart.com. Adults S$5 (US$3.35/£2.25), children and seniors S$2.50 (US$1.65/£1.10); free admission Fri 6–9pm. Sat–Thurs 10am–7pm; Fri 10am–9pm. Free guided tours in English Mon 2pm, Tues–Thurs 11am and 2pm, with additional tours Fri at 7pm and Sat–Sun at 3:30pm. 10-min. walk from City Hall and Dhoby Ghaut MRT.

Singapore Flyer ★★★ The new must-have accessory for the world's most ambitious cities is a giant observation wheel, and Singapore's just built itself the world's largest, standing proudly at Marina Bay. But in a typically Singaporean cultural twist, just 6 months after the multimillion-dollar wheel started to revolve in 2008, it was stopped and yet more millions spent on reversing the turning direction. Why? Because feng shui masters observed that the Flyer was turning away from the financial center and taking Singapore's riches with it. The U-turn was a good move; the geomancers are happy and passengers now get to appreciate views that stretch up to 45km (28 miles) to Malaysia and Indonesia before enjoying breathtaking views of the city skyline and the harbor on the way back down—definitely the highlight of the trip. If you need a reminder of Singapore's enduring importance as a trading center, just try to count the number of giant container ships waiting off the east coast to berth at the docks. It takes about 30 minutes to complete the circle, and the glass cabins are large enough to stroll around in while the world moves leisurely past.

30 Raffles Ave. ℂ **65/6333-3311**. www.singaporeflyer.com. Adults S$30 (US$20/£14), children S$21 (US$14/£9.45). Daily 8:30am–10:30pm. Bus 111, 106, or 133 from Raffles Hotel to Temasek Ave. Free shuttle buses every half-hour from St Andrew's Cathedral 10am to 11pm. MRT.

Singapore Philatelic Museum   This building, constructed in 1895 to house the Methodist Book Room, underwent a S$7-million (US$4.7-million/£3.2-million) restoration to become the Philatelic Museum in 1995. Exhibits include a fine collection of old stamps issued to commemorate historically important events, first-day covers, antique printing plates, postal service memorabilia, and private collections. Visitors can trace the development of a stamp from idea to the finished sheet, and you can even add your own picture to your holiday postcards and mail them from the last operational colonial postbox in Singapore. Special-edition folios featuring indigenous trees, flowers, and wildlife make pretty and compact souvenirs. Free guided tours are available upon request.

23B Coleman St. ℂ **65/6337-3888**. www.spm.org.sg. Adults S$5 (US$3.35/£2.25), children and seniors S$4 (US$2.70/£1.80). Mon 1–7pm; Tues–Sun 9am–7pm. 10-min. walk from Clarke Quay MRT.

Statue of Raffles   This sculpture of Sir Stamford Raffles was erected on the Padang in 1887 and moved to its present position after getting in the way of one too many cricket matches. During the Japanese Occupation, the statue was placed in the Singapore History Museum (then the Raffles Museum) and was replaced here in 1945. The local joke is that Raffles's arm is outstretched to the Bank of China building, and his pockets are empty. (*Translation:* In terms of wealth in Singapore, it's Chinese 1, Brits 0.)

Behind the Victoria Theatre and Concert Hall, 9 Empress Place. Free admission. 10-min. walk from City Hall, Clarke Quay and Raffles Place MRT.

Supreme Court   The Supreme Court stands on the site of the old Hotel de L'Europe, a rival of Raffles Hotel until it went bankrupt in the 1930s. The court's structure, a classical style favored for official buildings the world over, was completed in 1939. With its spare adornment and architectural simplicity, the edifice has a no-nonsense, utilitarian attitude, and the sculptures across the front, executed by the Italian sculptor Cavaliere Rodolpho Nolli, echo what transpires within. Justice is the most breathtaking, standing 2.7m (8.9 ft.) high and weighing almost 4 tons. Kneeling on either side of her are representations of Supplication and Thankfulness. To the far left are Deceit and Violence. To the far right, a bull represents Prosperity, and two children hold wheat, to depict Abundance.

Two and a half million bricks were used in building this structure, but take a moment to note the stonework: It's fake! Really a gypsum type of plaster, it was applied by Chinese plasterers who molded it to give the appearance of granite. A dome, a copy of the one at St. Paul's Cathedral in London, covers an interior courtyard, which is surrounded by the four major portions of the Supreme Court building.

There is currently no public access to the Old Supreme Court building, but visitors are permitted to attend court hearings, which are held in the modern court building, provided appropriate dress and etiquette codes are observed.

1 St. Andrew's Rd., across from the Padang. ✆ **65/6336-0644.** Free admission. Mon–Fri 8:30am–5pm; Sat 8:30am–1pm. 10-min. walk from City Hall MRT.

Victoria Theatre and Concert Hall   Designed by colonial engineer John Bennett in a Victorian Revival style that was fashionable in Britain at the time, the theater portion was built in 1862 as the Town Hall. Victoria Memorial Hall was built in 1905 as a memorial to Queen Victoria, retaining the same style of the old building. The clock tower was added a year later. In 1909, with its name changed to Victoria Theatre, the hall opened with an amateur production of the *Pirates of Penzance.* Another notable performance occurred when Noël Coward passed through Singapore and stepped in at the last moment to help out a traveling English theatrical company that had lost a leading man. The building looks much the same as it did then, though of course the interiors have been modernized. It was completely renovated in 1979, conserving all the original details, and was renamed Victoria Concert Hall. It housed the Singapore Symphony Orchestra until the opening of the Esplanade–Theatres on the Bay, when they shifted to the larger digs.

9 Empress Place, at the southern end of the Padang. ✆ **65/6339-6120.** www.vch.org.sg. Free admission to lobby areas. Concert tickets priced depending on performance and seat location. 15-min. walk from City Hall MRT.

ALONG THE RIVER

The Singapore River had always been the heart of life in Singapore even before Raffles landed, but for many years during the 20th century, life here was dead—quite literally. Rapid urban development that began in the 1950s turned the river into a giant sewer, killing all plant and animal life in it. In the mid-1980s, though, the government began a large and very successful cleanup project; shortly thereafter, the buildings at Boat Quay and Clarke Quay, and later Robertson Quay, were restored. A display on the second floor of the Asian Civilisation Museum relates the story of the river and its cleanup. Now the areas on both banks of the river offer entertainment, food, and pubs day and night, and the river bank is dotted with life-size bronze sculptures of the "people of the river."

Boat Quay ★   Known as "the belly of the carp" by the local Chinese because of its shape, this area was once notorious for its opium dens and coolie shops. Nowadays, thriving restaurants boast every cuisine imaginable and the rocking nightlife offers up a variety of sounds—jazz, rock, blues, Indian, and Caribe—that are lively enough to get any couch potato tapping his feet. See chapters 6 and 9 for dining and nightlife suggestions. *Note:* Pronounce *quay* like *key.*

Located on the south bank of the Singapore River between Cavenagh Bridge and Elgin Bridge. Free admission. 5-min. walk from Clarke Quay MRT.

Clarke Quay   The largest of the waterfront developments, Clarke Quay was named for the second governor of Singapore, Sir Andrew Clarke. In the 1880s, a pineapple cannery, iron foundry, and numerous warehouses made this area bustle. Today, with 60 restored warehouses hosting restaurants, bars, and nightclubs, the Quay still hops. **River House,** formerly the home of a *towkay* (company president), occupies the oldest building, a beautiful building that's become a popular bar and restaurant run by the Indochine group. During the day, children love to play in the water jets that shoot up from the floor in Clarke Quay's central hub, but when the fountains are switched off, the area is used for special events and occasional markets.

Also here, **G-Max Reverse Bungy** (3E River Valley Rd.; ☎ **65/6338-1146;** www. gmax.co.nz) will strap you and two buddies into a cage and fling you around at the end of giant bungee cords for only S$45 (US$30/£20) each. You'll go up 60m (197 ft.) high at 200kmph (124 mph). Woo! Despite its name, the next-door **Xtreme Swing** is slightly less extreme, propelling five people above the river and back for $40 (US$27/£18) a time, though it's still not for the fainthearted. Stop by during weekdays from 1pm to 1am, and on weekends from noon until late.

River Valley Rd. west of Coleman Bridge. ☎ **65/6337-3292.** www.clarkequay.com.sg. Free admission. Clarke Quay MRT.

Esplanade Park   Esplanade Park and Queen Elizabeth Walk, two of the most famous parks in Singapore, were established in 1943 on land reclaimed from the sea. Several memorials are located here. The first is a fountain built in 1857 to honor **Tan Kim Seng,** who gave a great sum of money toward the building of a waterworks. Another monument, **the Cenotaph,** commemorates the 124 Singaporeans who died in World War I; it was dedicated by the Prince of Wales. On the reverse side, the names of those who died in World War II have been inscribed. The third prominent memorial is dedicated to **Maj. Gen. Lim Bo Seng,** a member of the Singaporean underground resistance in World War II who was captured and killed by the Japanese. His memorial was unveiled in 1954 on the 10th anniversary of his death. At the far end of the park, the Esplanade–Theatres on the Bay opened in October 2002. Fashioned after the Sydney Opera House, the unique double-domed structure is known locally as the Durians, because their spiky domes resemble halves of durian shells (the building itself is actually smooth—the "spikes" are sun shields).

Connaught Dr., on the marina, running from the mouth of the Singapore River along the Padang to the Esplanade–Theatres on the Bay. Daily until midnight. Free admission. 10-min. walk from City Hall MRT.

Merlion Park   The Merlion is Singapore's half-lion, half-fish national symbol, the lion representing Singapore's roots as the "Lion City" and the fish representing the nation's close ties to the sea. Bet you think a magical and awe-inspiring beast like this has been around in tales for hundreds of years, right? No such luck. Rather, he was the creation of some scheming marketers at the Singapore Tourism Board in the early 1970s. Despite the Merlion's commercial beginnings, he's been adopted as the national symbol and spouts continuously every day at the mouth of the Singapore River.

South bank, at the mouth of the Singapore River, adjacent to One Fullerton. Free admission. Daily 7am–10pm. 15-min. walk from either City Hall or Raffles Place MRT.

Sri Thandayuthapani Temple   One of the richest and grandest of its kind in Southeast Asia, the Sri Thandayuthapani Temple is most famous for a *thoonganai maa-dam,* a statue of an elephant's backside in a seated position. It's said that there are only four others of the kind, located in four temples in India.

The original temple was completed in 1860, restored in 1962, and practically rebuilt in 1984. The many sculptures of Hindu deities and the carved Kamalam-patterned rosewood doors, arches, and columns were executed by architect-sculptors imported from Madras, India, specifically for the job. The Hindu child god, Lord Muruga, rules over the temple and is visible in one form or another wherever you look. Also notice the statues of the god Shiva and his wife, Kali, captured in their lively dance competition. The story goes that Kali was winning the competition, so Shiva lifted his leg above his head, something a woman wasn't thought capable of doing. He won and quit dancing— good thing, too, because every time Shiva did a little jig, he destroyed part of the world.

Outside in the courtyard are statues of the wedding of Lord Muruga; his brother, Ganesh; another brother, Vishnu; and their father, Shiva; along with Brahma, the creator of all.

Used daily for worship, the temple is also the culmination point of Thaipusam, a celebration of thanks (see chapter 3). You may also hear this temple called Chettiar's Hindu Temple or the Tank Road Temple.

15 Tank Rd., close to the intersection of Clemenceau Ave. and River Valley Rd. ℂ **65/6737-9393.** Daily 8am–noon and 5:30–8pm. Free admission. 20-min. walk from Clarke Quay MRT.

2 CHINATOWN & TANJONG PAGAR

When the first Chinese junk landed in Singapore sometime around 1821, the sailors aboard rushed to the shore and prayed to Ma Cho Po, the Goddess of Heavenly Sages, for bringing them safely to their destination. Small shrines were built on the shore, which became the first stops for all Chinese sailors as they landed—many of these shrines still exist today.

The Chinese and other merchants set up warehouses along the western bank of the Singapore River, and business offices, residences, clan associations, and coolie houses filled the area behind Boat Quay. In 1822, when Raffles developed his Town Plan, he reserved this area for the Chinese to live.

As you tour Chinatown, you may be surprised to see a Hindu Temple and even a couple of Indian mosques. Although the area was predominantly Chinese, many Hindus and Muslims settled here, drawn by commerce.

For a long time, Chinatown remained basically as it always had, but the past 15 years have seen major changes by the Urban Redevelopment Authority, with schemes to renovate and preserve historic buildings and to clean up the streets. Unfortunately after shophouses were lovingly restored, the old calligraphers, cobblers, kite-makers, fortune-tellers, and other craftspeople who'd inhabited them could no longer afford the rents. Sadly, many of these beautiful streets are now lined with souvenir shops.

Al-Abrar Mosque This mosque, also called Masjid Chulia after the Chulias, the group of Indian moneylender immigrants who funded its construction (*masjid* is Malay for mosque), was originally erected as a thatched building in 1827, thus its Tamil name Kuchu Palli, which means "hut mosque." The building that stands today was built in the 1850s, and even though it faces Mecca, the complex conforms with the grid of the neighborhood's city streets. It was designated a national monument in 1974, and in the late 1980s, the mosque underwent major renovations that enlarged the mihrab and stripped away some of the ornamental qualities of the columns in the building. The one-story prayer hall was extended upward into a two-story gallery. Little touches like the timber window panels and fanlight windows have been carried over into the new renovations.

192 Telok Ayer St., near the corner of Telok Ayer St. and Amoy St., near Thian Hock Keng Temple. ℂ **65/6220-6306.** Free admission. 15-min. walk from either Raffles Place or Tanjong Pagar MRT.

Chinatown Heritage Centre ★★ This block of three old shophouses in the center of the Chinatown heritage district has been converted into a display that tells the story of the Chinese immigrants who came to Singapore to find work in the early days of the colony. Walk through rooms filled with period antiques replicating coolie living quarters, shops, clan association houses, and other places that were prominent in daily life. It

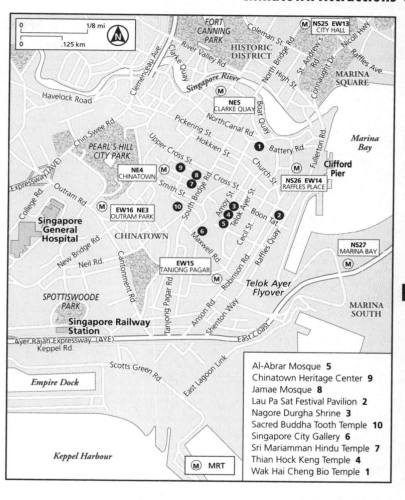

SINGAPORE ATTRACTIONS

7

CHINATOWN & TANJONG PAGAR

Al-Abrar Mosque **5**
Chinatown Heritage Center **9**
Jamae Mosque **8**
Lau Pa Sat Festival Pavilion **2**
Nagore Durgha Shrine **3**
Sacred Buddha Tooth Temple **10**
Singapore City Gallery **6**
Sri Mariamman Hindu Temple **7**
Thian Hock Keng Temple **4**
Wak Hai Cheng Bio Temple **1**

MRT

reminded me of the museum on Ellis Island in New York City that walks visitors through the immigrant experience of the early 1900s. Like Ellis Island, this display also has detailed descriptions to explain each element of the immigrant experience. The tiny cubicles where large families and groups scratched out a meager existence are an affecting picture of the hardships they faced.

48 Pagoda St. ✆ **65/6325-2878.** www.chinatownheritage.com.sg. Adults S$9.80 (US$6.50/£4.40), children S$6.30 (US$4.20/£2.85). Daily 9am–8pm. English-language tour every hr. 5-min. walk from Chinatown MRT.

Jamae Mosque Jamae Mosque was built by the Chulias, Tamil Muslims who were some of the earlier immigrants to Singapore and who had a very influential hold over

Indian Muslim life centered in the Chinatown area. The Chulias built not only this mosque, but the Al-Abrar Mosque and the Nagore Durgha Shrine as well. Jamae Mosque dates from 1827 but wasn't completed until the early 1830s. The mosque stands today almost exactly as it did then.

Although the front gate is typical of mosques you'd see in southern India, inside, most of the buildings reflect the neoclassical style of architecture introduced in administrative buildings and homes designed by George Coleman and favored by the Europeans. There are also some Malay touches in the timber work. A small shrine inside, which may be the oldest part of the mosque, was erected to memorialize a local religious leader, Muhammad Salih Valinva.

218 South Bridge Rd., at the corner of South Bridge Rd. and Mosque St. ⓒ 65/6221-4165. Free admission. Chinatown MRT. 10-min. walk from Chinatown MRT.

Lau Pa Sat Festival Pavilion Though it used to be well beloved, the locals think this place has become quite touristy—though lunchtime finds it still packed with financial district workers. Once the happy little hawker center known as Telok Ayer Market, it began life as a wet market, selling fruits, vegetables, and other foodstuffs. Now it's part hawker center, part Western fast-food outlets.

It all began on Market Street in 1823, in a structure that was later torn down, redesigned, and rebuilt by G. D. Coleman. Close to the water, seafood could be unloaded fresh off the pier. After the land in Telok Ayer Basin was reclaimed in 1879, the market was moved to its present home. A new design by James MacRitchie kept the original octagonal shape and was constructed of 3,000 prefab cast-iron elements brought in from Europe.

In the 1970s, as the financial district began to develop, the pavilion was dominated by hawkers who fed the lunchtime business crowd. In the mid-1980s, the structure was torn down to make way for the MRT construction and then meticulously put back together, puzzle piece by puzzle piece. By 1989, the market was once again an urban landmark, but it sat vacant until Scotts Holdings successfully tendered to convert it into a festival market. At this time, numerous changes were made to the building, which was renamed Lau Pa Sat (Old Market) in acknowledgment of the name by which the market had been known by generations of Singaporeans. Lau Pa Sat is one of the few hawker centers that's open 24 hours, in case you need a coffee or snack before retiring.

18 Raffles Quay, located in the entire block flanked by Robinson Rd., Cross St., Shenton Way, and Boon Tat St. Free admission. Daily 24 hr. 10-min. walk from Raffles Place MRT.

Nagore Durgha Shrine Although this is a Muslim place of worship, it is not a mosque, but a shrine, built to commemorate a visit to the island by a Muslim holy man of the Chulia people (Muslim merchants and moneylenders from India's Coromandel Coast) who was traveling around Southeast Asia spreading the word of Indian Islam. The most interesting visual feature is its facade: Two arched windows flank an arched doorway, with columns in between. Above these is a "miniature palace"—a massive replica of the facade of a palace, with tiny cutout windows and a small arched doorway in the middle. The cutouts in white plaster make it look like lace. From the corners of the facade, two 14-level minarets rise, with three little domed cutouts on each level and onion domes on top. Inside, the prayer halls and two shrines are painted and decorated in shockingly tacky colors.

Controversy surrounds the dates that the shrine was built. The government, upon naming the Nagore Durgha a national monument, claimed it was built sometime in the

1820s; however, Nagoreallauddeen, who is the 15th descendant of the holy man for **131** whom the shrine is named, claims it was built many years before. According to Nagore-allauddeen, the shrine was first built out of wood and *attap* (a thatch roof made from a type of palm), and later, in 1815, was rebuilt from limestone, 4 years before the arrival of Sir Stamford Raffles. In 1818, rebuilding materials were imported from India to construct the present shrine. *Note:* The shrine has been closed for renovation but is due to reopen in summer 2009.

140 Telok Ayer St., at the corner of Telok Ayer St. and Boon Tat St. 15-min. walk from either Raffles Place or Tanjong Pagar MRT.

Sacred Buddha Tooth Temple ★★

Allow at least an hour and a half to appreciate this huge temple, which was founded in 2002. Built in the Tang Dynasty style, this is actually a Chinese cultural center, encompassing, among other things, a temple, a museum and reference library, a theater, a dining hall providing free meals, and, of course, the magnificent reliquary that gives the temple its name. The best place to start is in the huge 100 Dragons Hall on the first floor, where services dedicated to the Maitreya Buddha take place, with a further hall behind celebrating the Avalokitesvara Bodhisattva. I'd then take the elevator (lined with gold-embroidered fabric) to the third story, where a nicely laid-out museum examines the life of the Buddha and explains the role of the future Maitreya Buddha and the Bodhisattva Avalokitesvara, the representation of Kindness and Compassion. The sacred tooth itself is on the fourth floor, encased in a magnificent golden stupa, which itself sits on a (presumably reinforced) floor of pure gold tiles. The stupa depicts the 35 Buddhas who have achieved enlightenment and nirvana, surrounding the serene figure of the Maitreya Buddha who is guarded by four lions. The stupa is unveiled from 9am to noon and 3 to 6pm daily. A staircase leads to the lovely roof garden (there is a stairlift, if required) where the world's largest enameled prayer wheel turns slowly in the Ten Thousand Buddhas Pavilion. Still not enough Buddhas for you? There are another 12,000 in the galleries outside the pavilion. These are dedicated to the Buddha of Longevity. For S$68 (US$46/£31) a year, you can light up one of these tiny figures and help to negate all the bad karma created since the beginning of time. Or you could spend S$2 (US$1.35/90p) to sponsor a very tangible vegetarian meal, distributed from the basement dining hall.

288 South Bridge Rd. 🕐 **65/6220-0220.** www.btrts.org.sg. Free admission. Daily 4:30am–9pm. 5-min. walk from Chinatown MRT.

Singapore City Gallery

This enormous exhibit is perhaps of real interest only to Singaporeans and civil planners, but if you're in the neighborhood, it's worth a pop inside to see the giant wooden plan of the city in miniature that sits on the right side of the lobby. If you have time, sift through 48 permanent exhibits and 25 interactive displays that paint a historical picture of the development of urban Singapore.

URA Centre, 45 Maxwell Rd. 🕐 **65/6321-8321.** www.ura.gov.sg. Free admission. Mon–Fri 9am–5pm; Sat 9am–1pm. 10-min. walk from Tanjong Pagar MRT.

Sri Mariamman Hindu Temple

As the oldest Hindu temple in Singapore, Sri Mariamman has been the central point of Hindu tradition and culture. In its early years, the temple housed new immigrants while they established themselves and also served as social center for the community. Today the main celebration here is the Thimithi Festival in October or November (see chapter 3). The shrine is dedicated to the goddess Sri Mariamman, who is known for curing disease (a very important goddess to have around in those days), but as is the case at all other Hindu temples, the entire pantheon of Hindu gods are present to be worshipped as well. On either side of the *gopuram* are statues of Shiva and Vishnu, while inside are two smaller shrines to Vinayagar and Sri Ararvan. Also note the sacred cows that lounge along the top of the temple walls.

The temple originated as a small wood-and-thatch shrine founded by Naraina Pillai, an Indian merchant who came to Singapore with Raffles's first expedition and found his fortune in trade. In the main hall of the temple is the small god that Pillai originally placed here.

244 South Bridge Rd., at the corner of South Bridge Rd. and Pagoda St. ℂ 65/6223-4064. Free admission. 10-min. walk from Chinatown MRT.

Thian Hock Keng Temple ★★★
Thian Hock Keng, the "Temple of Heavenly Bliss," is one of the oldest Chinese temples in Singapore. Before land reclamation, when the shoreline came right up to Telok Ayer Road, the first Chinese sailors landed here and immediately built a shrine, a small wood-and-thatch structure, to pray to the goddess Ma Cho Po for allowing their voyage to be safely completed. For each subsequent boatload of Chinese sailors, the shrine was always the first stop upon landing. Ma Cho Po, the Mother of the Heavenly Sages, was the patron goddess of sailors, and every Chinese junk of the day had an altar dedicated to her.

The temple that stands today was built in 1841 over the shrine with funds from the Hokkien community, led by the efforts of two Melaka-born philanthropists, Tan Tock Seng and Tan Kim Seng. All of the building materials were imported from China, except for the gates, which came from Glasgow, Scotland, and the tiles on the facade, which are from Holland. The doorway is flanked by two lions, a male with a ball to symbolize strength and a female with a lion cub to symbolize fertility. On the door are door gods, mythical beasts made from the combined body parts of many animals. Note the wooden bar that sits at the foot of the temple entrance (as do similar bars in so many Chinese temples). This serves a couple of purposes: First, it keeps out wandering ghosts, who cannot cross over the barrier. Second, it forces anyone entering the temple to look down as they cross, bowing their head in humility. Just inside the door are granite tablets that record the temple's history.

Ahead at the main altar is Ma Cho Po, and on either side are statues of the Protector of Life and the God of War. To the side of the main hall is a Gambler Brother statue, prayed to for luck and riches. From here you can see the temple's construction of brackets and beams, fitting snugly together and carved with war heroes, saints, flowers, and animals, all in red and black lacquer and gilded in gold. Behind the main hall is an altar to Kuan Yin, the Goddess of Mercy. Beside her are the sun and moon gods.

To the left of the courtyard are the ancestral tablets. In keeping with Confucian filial piety, each represents a soul. The tablets with red paper are for souls still alive. Also in the temple complex are a pagoda and a number of outer buildings that at one time housed a school and community associations. The right wing of the temple is shared with The Faculty, a center for creative arts, holding classes for dance, acting, and vocals. Even if you don't have a burning desire to learn to tango, the elaborate pagoda is an incredible spot for a cool drink, tucked away behind the ornate temple gate.

158 Telok Ayer St., ¹/₂ block beyond Nagore Durgha Shrine. ℂ 65/6423-4616. Free admission. 15-min. walk from Tanjong Pagar MRT.

Wak Hai Cheng Bio Temple ★★
One of the oldest Taoist temples in Singapore, this is also known as Yueh Hai Ching Temple. Like most of Singapore's Chinese temples, Wak Hai Cheng Bio had its start as a simple wood-and-thatch shrine where sailors, when they got off their ships, would go to express their gratitude for sailing safely to their

destination. Before the major land-reclamation projects shifted the shoreline outward, the temple was close to the water's edge, and so it was named "Temple of the Calm Sea Built by the Guangzhou People." It's a Teochew temple, located in a part of Chinatown originally populated by this dialect group.

Inside the Taoist temple walls are two blocks, the one on the left devoted to Ma Cho Po, the Mother of Heavenly Sages, who protects travelers and ensures a safe journey. The one on the right is devoted to Siong Tek Kong, the god of business. Both are as important to the Chinese community today as they were way back when. Look for the statue of the Gambler Brother, with coins around his neck. The Chinese pray to him for wealth and luck; in olden days, they would put opium on his lips. This custom is still practiced today, only now they use a black herbal paste called *koyo,* which is conveniently legal.

Inside the temple, you can buy joss sticks and paper for S$2.50 (US$1.65/£1.10). Three joss sticks are for heaven, your parents, and yourself, to be burned before the altar. Three corresponding packets of elaborately decorated paper and gold leaf are to be burned outside in the gourd-shaped kilns (gourd being a symbol of health). The joss or "wishing paper," four thin sheets stamped with black and red characters, has many meanings. The red sheet is for luck (red being particularly auspicious), and the other three are to wash away your sins, for a long life, and for your wishes to be carried to heaven. Even if you are not Taoist, you're more than welcome to burn the joss.

The temple itself is quite a visual treat, with ceramic figurines and pagodas adorning the roof, and every nook and cranny of the structure adorned with tiny three-dimensional reliefs that depict scenes from Chinese operas. The spiral joss hanging in the courtyard adds an additional picturesque effect.

30-B Phillip St., at the corner of Phillip St. and Church St. Free admission. 5-min. walk from Raffles Place MRT.

3 LITTLE INDIA

Little India did not develop as a community planned by the colonial authorities like Kampong Glam or Chinatown, but came into being because immigrants to India were drawn to business developments here. In the late 1920s, the government established a brick kiln and lime pits here that attracted Indian workers, and the abundance of grass and water made the area attractive to Indian cattle traders.

A word of advice: If you visit Little India on a Sunday, be prepared for a mob scene the likes of Calcutta! Sunday is the only day off for Singapore's many immigrant Indian and Bangladeshi laborers, so Serangoon Road gets a little crazy.

Abdul Gafoor Mosque This charming little mosque is resplendent, thanks to a loving restoration completed in 2008. Nestled behind a row of shophouses, you really can't see it until you arrive at the gate. Inside the compound, the bright yellow and green facade and minarets reflect an Indian Muslim architectural preference, most likely imported with the mosque's builder Sheik Abdul Gafoor. The original mosque on this site, called Al-Abrar Mosque, was constructed of wood in 1859 and is commemorated on a granite plaque within the compound above what could have been either an entrance gate or part of the mosque itself. The newer mosque on the site was built in 1907 and includes some unusual features, including ornate European-style columns and the sunburst above the main entrance. This "sundial" has 25 rays in Arabic calligraphy relief said to represent the 25 prophets in the Koran.

An Introduction to Hindu Temples

The *gopuram* is the giveaway—the tiered roof piled high with brightly colored statues of gods and goddesses. Definitely a Hindu temple. So what are they all doing up there? It's because in India, what with the caste system and all, the lower classes were at one time not permitted inside the temple, so having these statues on the outside meant they could still pray without actually entering. Furthermore, although each temple is dedicated to a particular deity, all the gods are represented, in keeping with the Hindu belief that although there are many gods, they are all one god. So everyone is up there, in poses or scenes that depict stories from Hindu religious lore. Sometimes there are brightly colored flowers, birds, and animals as well—especially sacred cows. So why are some of them blue? It's because blue is the color of the sky, and to paint the gods blue meant that they, like the sky, are far reaching and ever present.

There's no special way to pray in these temples, but by custom, most will pray first to Ganesh, the god with the elephant head, who is the remover of obstacles, especially those that can hinder one's closeness to God. Another interesting prayer ritual happens in the temple's main hall around a small dais that holds nine gods, one for each planet. Devotees who need a particular wish fulfilled will circle the dais, praying to their astrological planet god for their wish to come true.

The location of Hindu temples is neither by accident nor by Raffles's Town Plan. By tradition, they must always be built near a source of fresh water so that every morning, before prayer, all of the statues can be bathed. The water runs off a spout somewhere outside the main hall, from which devotees take the water and touch their heads.

Non-Hindus are welcome in the temples to walk around and explore. **Temple etiquette** asks that you first remove your shoes, and if you need to point to something, out of respect, please use your right hand, and don't point with your index finger (use your knuckle instead).

Inside the courtyard, an information office provides robes for those in shorts and sleeveless tops. As in every mosque, the main prayer hall is off-limits to non-Muslims.

41 Dunlop St., btw. Perak Rd. and Jalan Besar. © **65/6295-4209.** Free admission. 15-min. walk from Little India MRT.

Sakya Muni Buddha Gaya (Temple of a Thousand Lights) Thai elements influence this temple, from the *chedi* (stupa) roofline to the huge Thai-style Buddha image inside. Often this temple is brushed off as strange and tacky, but all sorts of surprises are inside, making the place a veritable Buddha theme park. On the right side of the altar, statues of baby bodhisattvas receive toys and sweets from devotees. Around the base of the altar, murals depict scenes from the life of Prince Siddhartha (the Buddha) as he searches for enlightenment. Follow them around to the back of the hall, and you'll find a small doorway to a chamber under the altar. Another Buddha image reclines inside, this one shown at the end of his life, beneath the Yellow Seraka tree. On the left side of the main part of the hall is a replica of a footprint left by the Buddha in Ceylon. Next to that is a wheel of fortune; for S50¢ (US35¢/20p), you get one spin.

336 Race Course Rd., 1 block past Perumal Rd. (*C*) **65/6294-0714.** Free admission, 8am–4pm. 5-min. walk from Farrer Park MRT.

Sri Perumal Temple   Sri Perumal Temple, built in 1855, is devoted to the worship of Vishnu. As part of the Hindu trinity, Vishnu is the sustainer, balancing out Brahma the creator and Shiva the destroyer. When the world is out of whack, he rushes to its aid, reincarnating himself to show mankind that there are always new directions for development.

On the first tier to the left of the front entrance on the *gopuram,* statues depict Vishnu's nine reincarnations. Rama, the sixth incarnation, is with Hanuman, the monkey god, who helped him in the fierce battle to free his wife from kidnapping. Krishna, shown reclining amid devotees, is the eighth incarnation and a hero of many Hindu legends, most notably the Bhagavad-Gita. Also up there is the half-human and half-bird Garuda, Vishnu's steed. Inside the temple are altars to Vishnu, his two wives, and Garuda.

During Thaipusam, the main festival celebrated here (see chapter 3), male devotees who have made vows over the year carry *kavadi*—huge steel racks decorated with flowers and fruits and held onto their bodies by skewers and hooks—to show their thanks and devotion, while women carry milk pots in a parade from Sri Perumal Temple to Chettiar's Temple on Tank Road.

397 Serangoon Rd., 1/2 block past Perumal Rd. Free admission. Best times to visit are daily 7–11am or 5–7:30pm. 5-min. walk from Farrer Park MRT.

Sri Veerama Kaliamman Temple ★★   This Hindu temple is primarily for the worship of Shiva's wife, Kali, who destroys ignorance, maintains world order, and blesses those who strive for knowledge of God. The box on the walkway to the front entrance is for smashing coconuts, a symbolic smashing of the ego, asking God to show "the humble way." The coconuts have two small "eyes" at one end so they can "see" the personal obstacles to humility they are being asked to smash.

Inside the temple in the main hall are three altars, the center one for Kali (depicted with 16 arms and wearing a necklace of human skulls) and two altars on either side for her two sons—Ganesh, the elephant god, and Murugan, the four-headed child god. To the right is an altar with nine statues representing the nine planets. Circle the altar and pray to your planet for help with a specific trouble.

Around the left side of the main hall, the first tier of the *gopuram* tells the story of how Ganesh got his elephant head. A small dais in the rear-left corner of the temple compound is an altar to Sri Periyachi, a very mean-looking woman with a heart of gold. She punishes women who say and do things to make others feel bad. She also punishes men—under her feet is an exploiter of ladies.

Here's a bit of trivia: Red ash, as opposed to white, is applied to the forehead after prayers are offered in a temple devoted to a female god.

141 Serangoon Rd. at Veerasamy Rd. Free admission. Daily 8am–noon and 5:30–8:30pm. 10-min. walk from Little India MRT.

4 ARAB STREET & KAMPONG GLAM

Kampong Glam is the traditional heart of Singaporean Muslim life. Since early colonial days, the area has attracted Muslims from diverse ethnic backgrounds, fusing them into one community by their common faith and lifestyle. The name Kampong Glam comes from the Malay word *kampong*, meaning "village," and *gelam*, a particular kind of tree that at one time grew abundantly in the area.

In 1819, the British made a treaty with Sultan Hussein Shah, then sultan of Singapore, to cede the island to the British East India Trading Company. As part of the agreement, the sultan was offered a stipend and given Kampong Glam as settlement for his palace and subjects. Sultan Hussein built his palace, Istana Kampong Glam, and sold off parcels of land for burial grounds, schools, mosques, and farms. Trade grew in the area, as a wave of merchants and tradesmen moved in to serve the large numbers of pilgrims who debarked from here on their journey to Mecca each year.

Although the ethnic Arab population in Singapore has never reached large proportions, their influence is immediately obvious through such street names as Bussorah, Muscat, Baghdad, and, of course, Arab Street, the center of modern Kampong Glam—a neat little shopping enclave for textiles and regional handicrafts. Note that the shops along Arab Street close on Sunday.

Alsagoff Arab School   Built in 1912, the school was named for Syed Ahmad Alsagoff, a wealthy Arab merchant and philanthropist who was very influential in Singapore's early colonial days and who died in 1906. It is the oldest girls' school in Singapore and was the island's first Muslim school.

121 Jalan Sultan, across from Sultan Plaza. 15-min. walk from Bugis MRT.

Hajjah Fatimah Mosque ★★   Hajjah Fatimah was a wealthy businesswoman from Melaka and something of a local socialite. She married a Bugis prince from Celebes, and their only child, a daughter, married Syed Ahmed Alsagoff, son of Arab trader and philanthropist Syed Abdul Rahman Alsagoff. Hajjah Fatimah had originally built a home on this site, but after it had been robbed a couple of times and later set fire to, she decided to find a safer home and built a mosque here instead.

Inside the high walls of the compound are the prayer hall, an ablution area, gardens and mausoleums, and a few other buildings. You can walk around the main prayer halls to the garden cemeteries, where flat square headstones mark the graves of women and round ones mark the graves of men. Hajjah Fatimah is buried in a private room to the side of the main prayer hall, along with her daughter and son-in-law.

The minaret tower in the front was designed by an unknown European architect and could be a copy of the original spire of St. Andrew's Cathedral. The tower leans a little, a fact that's much more noticeable from the inside. On the outside of the tower is a bleeding heart—an unexpected place to find such a downright Christian symbol. It's a great example of what makes this mosque so charming—all the combined influences of Moorish, Chinese, and European architectural styles.

4001 Beach Rd., past Jalan Sultan. 𝄞 **65/6297-2774.** Free admission. 20-min. walk from Bugis MRT.

Malay Heritage Centre (Istana Kampong Glam) ★★   When the Malay Heritage Centre opened its doors in 2004, it became the first museum dedicated to the history, culture, and arts of this often-marginalized ethnic group. The Centre has lovingly displayed exhibits that offer a glimpse into Singapore's early Malay settlements, the sultan's royal family, Malay arts, and 20th-century Malay life.

There's a bit of irony here. The museum is housed in the Istana Kampong Glam, the former royal palace that housed the descendants of the original sultan that oversaw Singapore. In 1819, Sultan Hussein signed away his rights over the island in exchange for the land at Kampong Glam plus an annual stipend for his family. After the Sultan's death, the family fortunes began to dwindle and disputes broke out among his descendants. In the late 1890s, they went to court, where it was decided that because no one in the family had the rights as the successor to the sultanate, the land should be reverted to the state. The family was allowed to remain in the house, but because they didn't own the property, they lost the authority to improve the buildings. Over the years, the compound fell into a very sad state of dilapidation. Eventually, Sultan Hussein's family was given the boot by the government to make way for this museum heralding the value of the Malay, and the Sultan's, cultural contribution to Singapore. Hmm.

Galleries on the first floor relate the story of the immigration of Muslim Malays to Singapore and their central role in the island's trading culture. Upstairs there are displays that deal with the modern history of the Malay community and a recreation of a traditional kampong (village) house and an early HDB apartment.

The house to the left before the main gate of the Istana compound is called **Gedong Kuning,** or Yellow Mansion. It was the home of Tenkgu Mahmoud, the heir to Kampong Glam. When he died, it was purchased by local Javanese businessman Haji Yusof, the belt merchant. Today it houses a Malay restaurant, **Tepak Sireh** (✆ **65/6393-4373;** daily 11:30am–2:30pm and 6:30–10pm).

85 Sultan Gate. ✆ **65/6391-0450.** Adults S$4 (US$2.68/£1.80), children S$3 (US$2/£1.35); free admission to Istana compound. Mon 1–6pm; Tues–Sun 10am–6pm. 15-min. walk from Bugis MRT.

Sultan Mosque ★ Though more than 80 mosques exist on the island of Singapore, Sultan Mosque is the real center of the Muslim community. The mosque that stands today is the second Sultan Mosque to be built on this site. The first was built in 1826, partially funded by the East India Company as part of their agreement to leave Kampong Glam to Sultan Hussein and his family in return for sovereign rights to Singapore. The present mosque was built in 1928 and was funded by donations from the Muslim community. The Saracenic flavor of the onion domes, topped with crescent moons and stars, is complemented by Mogul cupolas. Funny thing, though: The mosque was designed by an Irish guy named Denis Santry, who was working for the architectural firm Swan and McLaren.

Other interesting facts about the mosque: Its dome base is a ring of black bottles; the carpeting was donated by a prince of Saudi Arabia and bears his emblem; and at the back of the compound, North Bridge Road has a kink in it, showing where the mosque invaded the nicely planned urban grid pattern. Also, if you make your way through the chink where the back of the building almost touches the compound wall, peer inside the *makam* to see the royal graves. Sultan Mosque, like all the others, does not permit shorts, miniskirts, low necklines, or other revealing clothing to be worn inside. However, they do realize that non-Muslim travelers like to be comfortable as they tour around and provide cloaks free of charge. They hang just to the right as you walk up the stairs.

3 Muscat St. ✆ **65/6293-4405.** Free admission. Daily 9am–1pm and 2–4pm. No visiting is allowed during Mass congregation Fri 11:30am–2:30pm. 15-min. walk from Bugis MRT.

An Introduction to Mosques

To appreciate what's going on in the mosques in Singapore, here's a little background on some of the styles and symbols behind these exotic buildings. I have also included some tips that will help non-Muslims feel right at home.

The rule of thumb for mosques is that they all face Mecca. Lucky for these buildings (and for Singaporean urban planners), most of the major mosques in Singapore have managed to fit within the grid of city streets quite nicely, with few major angles or corners jutting into the surrounding streets. One fine example of a mosque that obeys the Mecca rule but disregards zoning orders is Sultan Mosque in Kampong Glam. A peek around the back will reveal how the road is crooked to make way for the building.

The mosques in Singapore are a wonderful blend of Muslim influences from around the world. The grand Sultan Mosque has the familiar onion dome and Moorish styling of the Arabic Muslim influence. The smaller but fascinating Hajjah Fatimah Mosque is a blend of cultures, from Muslim to Chinese to even Christian—testimony to Islam's tolerance of other cultural symbols. On the other hand, the mosques in Chinatown, such as Jamae Mosque and the Nagore Durgha Shrine, are Saracenic in flavor, a style that originated in India in the late 19th century, mixing traditional styles of Indian and Muslim architecture with British conventionality.

Each mosque has typical features such as a **minaret,** a narrow tower from which the call to prayer was sounded (before recorded broadcasts), and a

5 ORCHARD ROAD AREA

In the beginning, Orchard Road was just that, orchards and plantations. But as Singapore began to attract international settlers, this area transformed into an enclave where wealthy Europeans built their homes. Today Orchard Road still represents affluence and luxury even though colonial homesteads have been replaced with glitzy malls and high-rise hotels. And true to its roots, the Orchard Road area still has one of the highest concentrations of Western expatriate residences on the island.

The Istana and Sri Temasek   In 1859, the construction of Fort Canning necessitated the demolition of the original governors' residence, and the autocratic and unpopular governor-general Sir Harry St. George Ord proposed this structure be built as the new residence. Though the construction of such a large and expensive edifice was unpopular, Ord had his way, and design and construction went through, with the building mainly performed by convicts under the supervision of Maj. J. F. A. McNair, the colonial engineer and superintendent of convicts.

In its picturesque landscaped setting, Government House echoed Anglo-Indian architecture, but its symmetrical and cross-shaped plan also echoed the form of the traditional Malay *istana* (palace). During the occupation, the house was occupied by Field Marshal Count Terauchi, commander of the Japanese Southern Army, and Major General Kawamura, commander of the Singapore Defense Forces. With independence, the building

mihrab, a niche in the main hall which indicates the direction of Mecca and in front of which the imam prays, his voice bouncing from inside and resonating throughout the mosque during prayers. You will also notice that there are no statues to speak of, in accordance with Muslim laws, which forbid images of Allah and the Prophet Mohammed. Some mosques will have a **makam,** a burial site within the building for royalty and esteemed benefactors. This room is usually locked but sometimes can be opened upon request. To the side of the main prayer hall there's always an **ablution area,** a place for worshipers to wash the exposed parts of their bodies before prayers, to show their respect. This is a custom for all Muslims, whether they pray in the mosque or at home.

When visiting the mosques in Singapore—and anywhere else, for that matter—there are some important rules of **etiquette** to follow. Appropriate dress is required. For both men and women, shorts are prohibited, and you must remove your shoes before you enter. For women, please do not wear short skirts or sleeveless, backless, or low-cut tops (although modern Singaporean Muslims do not require women to cover their heads before entering). **Also remember:** Never enter the main prayer hall. This area is reserved for Muslims only. Women should also tread lightly around this area, as it's forbidden for women to enter. No cameras or video cameras are allowed, and remember to turn off cellular phones and pagers. Friday is the Sabbath day, and you should not plan on going to the mosques between 11am and 2pm on this day.

was renamed the Istana and today serves as the official residence of the president of the Republic of Singapore. Used mainly for state and ceremonial occasions, the grounds are open to every citizen on selected public holidays, though they're not generally open for visits. The house's domain includes several other houses of senior colonial civil servants. The colonial secretary's residence, a typical 19th-century bungalow, is also gazetted a monument and is now called Sri Temasek.

Orchard Rd., btw. Claymore and Scotts rds. Free admission. 5-min. walk from Dhoby Ghaut MRT.

Peranakan Place ★   Emerald Hill was once nothing more than a wide treeless street along whose sides quiet families lived in typical terrace houses²residential units similar to shophouses, with a walled courtyard in the front instead of the usual "five-foot way." Toward Orchard Road, the terrace houses turned into shophouses, with their first floors occupied by small provisioners, seamstresses, and dry-goods stores.

As Orchard Road developed, so did Emerald Hill—the buildings were all renovated. The shophouses close to Orchard Road became restaurants and bars, and the street was closed off to vehicular traffic. Now it's an alfresco cafe, landscaped with a veritable jungle of potted foliage and peopled by colorful tourists—much different from its humble beginnings.

But as you pass Emerald Hill, don't just blow it off as a tourist trap. Walk through the cafe area and out the back onto Emerald Hill. All of the terrace houses have been redone, and magnificently. The facades have been freshly painted and the tiles polished, and the dark-wood details add a contrast that is truly elegant. When these places were renovated, they could be purchased for a song, but as Singaporeans began grasping at their heritage in recent years, their value shot up, and now these homes fetch huge sums.

For a peek inside some of these wonderful places (and who doesn't like to see how the rich live?), go to a bookstore and look at *Living Legacy: Singapore's Architectural Heritage Renewed,* by Robert Powell. Gorgeous photographs take you inside a few of these homes and some other terrace houses and bungalows around the island, showing off the traditional interior details of these buildings and bringing their heritage to life.

Intersection of Emerald Hill and Orchard Rd. Free admission. 5-min. walk from Somerset MRT.

6 ATTRACTIONS OUTSIDE THE URBAN AREA

The famous image of Singapore, promulgated by the tourism board and recognizable to business travelers everywhere, is of the towering cityscape along the water's edge—but there's a reason they call this place the Garden City. Not only are there picturesque gardens and parks nestled within the urban jungle, but the urban jungle is nestled within real jungle. While it's true that most of the wooded areas have been replaced by suburban housing, it's also true that thousands of acres of secondary rainforest have survived the migration of Singaporeans to the suburbs. Better yet, there are still some areas with primary rainforest, some of which are accessible by paths.

Singapore has spectacular **gardens,** from the well-groomed Botanic Gardens to **nature preserves** like Bukit Timah and Sungei Buloh, where tropical rainforest and mangrove swamps are close enough to the city that you can visit them on a morning or afternoon visit. Outside the city center you'll also find **historic sites and temples** like the edifying Changi Prison Museum and the Siong Lim Temple, as well as **museums** and **science centers.**

WESTERN SINGAPORE ATTRACTIONS

The attractions grouped in this section are on the west side of Singapore, beginning from the Singapore Botanic Gardens at the edge of the urban area all the way out to the Singapore Discovery Centre past Jurong. Transportation can be problematic in this part of the island; as the MRT system rarely goes directly to any of the main sights, taxis can be hard to find, and bus routes get more complex. Keep the telephone number for taxi booking handy. Sometimes ticket salespeople at each attraction can help and make the call for you.

Bukit Timah Nature Reserve ★★   Bukit Timah Nature Reserve is pure primary rainforest. Believed to be as old as 1 million years, it's the only place on the island with vegetation that exists exactly as it was before the British settled here. The park is more than 160 hectares (405 acres) of soaring canopy teeming with mammals and birds and a lush undergrowth with more bugs, butterflies, and reptiles than you can shake a vine at. Here you can see more than 700 plant species, many of which are exotic ferns, plus mammals like long-tailed macaques, squirrels, and lemurs. There's a visitor center and four well-marked paths, one of which leads to Singapore's highest point. At 163m (535 ft.) above sea level, don't expect a nosebleed, but some of the scenic views of the island are really nice. Also at Bukit Timah is Hindhede Quarry, which filled up with water at some point, so you can take a dip and cool off during your hike. The National Parks Board gives free guided tours on the first Sunday of the month at around 4pm; call © 65/6554-5127 to register.

Chinese and Japanese Gardens   Situated on two islands in Jurong Lake, the gardens are reached by an overpass and joined by the Bridge of Double Beauty. The **Chinese Garden** dedicates most of its area to "northern style" landscape architecture, the style of Imperial gardens, integrating brightly colored buildings with the surroundings. The Stoneboat is a replica of the stone boat at the Summer Palace in Beijing. Inside the Pure Air of the Universe building are courtyards and a pond, and there is a seven-story pagoda, the odd number of floors symbolizing continuity.

I like the Garden of Beauty, in Suzhou style, representing the southern style of landscape architecture. Southern gardens were built predominantly by scholars, poets, and men of wealth. Sometimes called Black-and-White gardens, these smaller gardens had more fine detail, featuring subdued colors, as the plants and elements of the rich natural landscape gave them plenty to work with. Inside the Suzhou garden are 2,000 pots of *penjiang* (bonsai) and displays of small rocks.

While the Chinese garden is more visually stimulating, the **Japanese Garden** is intended to evoke feeling. And though it can't compete with the attention with which its native counterparts are lavished, it is successful in capturing the themes at the heart of Japanese garden design. Marble-chip paths let you hear your own footsteps and meditate on the sound. They also serve to slow the journey for better gazing. The Keisein, or "Dry Garden," uses white pebbles to create images of streams. Ten stone lanterns, a small traditional house, and a rest house are nestled between two ponds with smaller islands joined by bridges. The pond area is regularly patrolled by huge monitor lizards! There is also a live turtle and tortoise museum, with a famous two-headed specimen; adults S$5 (US$3.35/£2.25), children S$3 (US$2/£1.35).

Toilets are situated at stops along the way, as well as benches to have a rest or to just take in the sights. Paddle boats can be rented for S$5 (US$3.35/£2.25) per hour just outside the main entrance.

1 Chinese Garden Rd. ℂ **65/6261-3632.** Free admission; admission to garden of abundance: adults S$2 (US$1.35/90p), children S$1 (US65¢/45p). Daily 6am–11pm. Chinese Garden MRT.

Haw Par Villa (Tiger Balm Gardens) ★   In 1935, brothers Haw Boon Haw and Haw Boon Par—creators of Tiger Balm, the camphor and menthol rub that comes in those cool little pots—took their fortune and opened Tiger Balm Gardens as a venue for teaching traditional Chinese values. They made more than 1,000 statues and life-size dioramas depicting Chinese legends and historical tales, and illustrating morality and Confucian beliefs. Many of these were gruesome and bloody, and some of them were really entertaining. But Tiger Balm Gardens suffered a horrible fate. In 1985, it was converted into an amusement park and reopened as Haw Par Villa. Most of the statues and scenes were taken away and replaced with rides. Well, business did not exactly boom. In fact, the park lost money fast. But recently, in an attempt to regain some of the original Tiger Balm Garden edge, they replaced many of the old statues, some of which are a great backdrop for really kitschy vacation photos, and ditched the rides. They also decided to open the gates free of charge.

262 Pasir Panjang Rd. ℂ **65/6872-2780.** Free admission. Daily 9am–7pm. Buona Vista MRT and transfer to bus no. 200.

Jurong BirdPark ★ **Kids**   Jurong BirdPark, with a collection of 9,000 birds from more than 600 species, showcases Southeast Asian breeds plus other colorful tropical

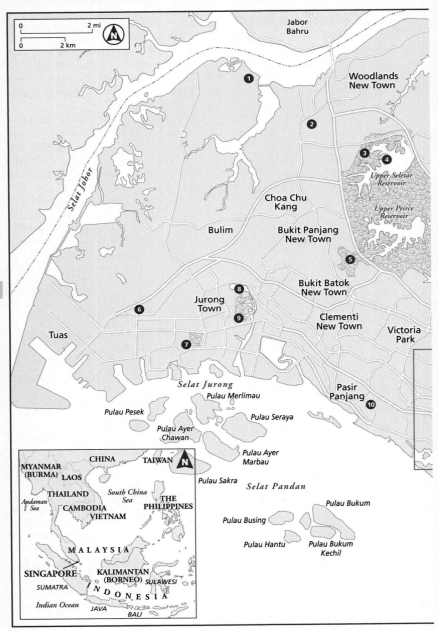

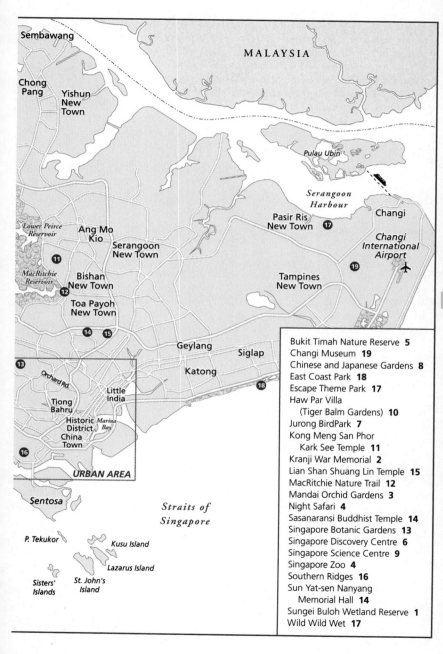

MALAYSIA

Sembawang

Chong Pang

Yishun New Town

Pulau Ubin

Serangoon Harbour

Changi

Pasir Ris New Town **17**

Changi International Airport

Lower Peirce Reservoir

Ang Mo Kio

Serangoon New Town

11

MacRitchie Reservoir

Bishan New Town

12

Toa Payoh New Town

14 **15**

Tampines New Town

19

Geylang

Siglap

Katong

13

Orchard Rd

Little India

Tiong Bahru

Historic District *Marina Bay*

China Town

16

18

URBAN AREA

Sentosa

Straits of Singapore

P. Tekukor

Kusu Island

Lazarus Island

Sisters' Islands

St. John's Island

Bukit Timah Nature Reserve	**5**
Changi Museum	**19**
Chinese and Japanese Gardens	**8**
East Coast Park	**18**
Escape Theme Park	**17**
Haw Par Villa (Tiger Balm Gardens)	**10**
Jurong BirdPark	**7**
Kong Meng San Phor Kark See Temple	**11**
Kranji War Memorial	**2**
Lian Shan Shuang Lin Temple	**15**
MacRitchie Nature Trail	**12**
Mandai Orchid Gardens	**3**
Night Safari	**4**
Sasanaransi Buddhist Temple	**14**
Singapore Botanic Gardens	**13**
Singapore Discovery Centre	**6**
Singapore Science Centre	**9**
Singapore Zoo	**4**
Southern Ridges	**16**
Sun Yat-sen Nanyang Memorial Hall	**14**
Sungei Buloh Wetland Reserve	**1**
Wild Wild Wet	**17**

beauties, some of which are endangered. The more than 20 hectares (49 acres) can be easily walked or, for five Singapore dollars ($3.35/£2.25) extra, you can ride the panorail for a bird's-eye view (so to speak) of the grounds. I enjoy the Waterfall Aviary, the world's largest walk-in aviary. It's an up-close-and-personal experience with African and South American birds, plus a pretty stroll through landscaped tropical forest. This is where you'll also see the world's tallest man-made waterfall, but the true feat of engineering here is the panorail station, built inside the aviary. Another smaller walk-in aviary is for Southeast Asian endangered bird species; at noon every day, this aviary experiences a man-made thunderstorm, and in the Lory Loft, a couple of dollars on bird feed buys you a swooping entourage of colorful friends. The daily guided tours and regularly scheduled feeding times are enlightening. Other bird exhibits are the flamingo pools, the World of Darkness (featuring nocturnal birds), and the penguin parade, a favorite for Singaporeans, who adore all things arctic.

The **World of Hawks** show at 10am and **Kings of the Skies** at 4pm feature birds of prey either acting out their natural instincts or performing falconry tricks. The **Birds n' Buddies** show takes place at 11am and 3pm, with trained parrots that race bikes and birds that perform all sorts of silliness, including staged birdie misbehaviors.

2 Jurong Hill. ℂ 65/6265-0022. www.birdpark.com.sg. Adults S$18 (US$12/£8.10), children 3–12 S$9 (US$6.05/£4.05). Park Hopper Ticket for Zoo, Night Safari, and BirdPark: adults S$40 (US$27/£18), children S$20 (US$13/£9). Daily 9am–6pm. Boon Lay MRT and transfer to bus no. 194 or 251.

Singapore Botanic Gardens ★★ In 1822, Singapore's first botanic garden was started at Fort Canning by Sir Stamford Raffles. After it lost funding, the present Botanic Garden came into being in 1859, thanks to the efforts of a horticulture society; it was later turned over to the government for upkeep. More than just a garden, this space occupied an important place in the region's economic development when "Mad" Henry Ridley, one of the garden's directors, imported Brazilian rubber tree seedlings from Great Britain. He devised improved latex-trapping methods and led the campaign to convince reluctant coffee growers to switch plantation crops. The garden also pioneered orchid hybridization, breeding a number of internationally acclaimed varieties.

Carved out within the tropical setting lies a marshgarden awash with water lilies and papyrus plants, the sundial garden with pruned hedges, a ginger garden filled with 300 related specimens of a family that includes lilies, turmeric, and even bananas. Who knew? Sculptures by international artists dot throughout. As you wander, look for the Cannonball tree (named for its cannonball-shaped fruit), Para rubber trees, teak trees, bamboos, and a huge array of palms, including the sealing wax palm—distinguished by its bright scarlet stalks—and the rumbia palm, which bears the pearl sago. The fruit of the silk-cotton tree is a pod filled with silky stuffing that was once used for stuffing pillows. Flowers like bougainvilleas and heliconias add beautiful color.

The **National Orchid Garden** is 3 hectares (7¹⁄₂ acres) of gorgeous orchids growing along landscaped walks. The English Garden features hybrids developed here and named after famous visitors to the garden—there's the beautifully twisted Margaret Thatcher, the Benazir Bhutto, the Vaclav Havel, and more. The gift shops sell live hydroponic orchids in test tubes for unique souvenirs.

At the Bukit Timah edge of the Botanic Gardens is Asia's first dedicated children's garden. The **Jacob Ballas Children's Garden** is a lovely place for under-12s to play and explore, while developing an appreciation for plants and nature. Children can do outdoor puzzles, learn about food and drinks that comes from plants, explore the maze or become happily soaked pumping water in the potting garden (swimming gear or a change of clothing is recommended here). Admission is free and it's open Tuesday to Sunday from 8am to 7pm (© **65/6465-0196**).

The gardens have three lakes. Symphony Lake surrounds an island band shell for "Concert in the Park" performances by the local symphony and international entertainers. Call visitor services at the number below for performance schedules.

Volunteers run free guided tours of different areas of the park every Saturday at 9am and 10am, often with additional tours at 11am and 4pm. Register 15 minutes before the walk at the Visitor Centre near Nassim Gate.

Main entrance at corner of Cluny Rd. and Holland Rd. © **65/6471-7361**. www.nparks.gov.sg. Free admission. Daily 5am–midnight. The National Orchid Garden adults S$5 (US$3.35/£2.25), children under 12 and seniors S$1 (US65¢/45p). Daily 8:30am–7pm. Orchard MRT, then bus no. 7, 105, 106, or 174 from Orchard Blvd.

Singapore Discovery Centre (Kids)

Billing itself as an "edutainment" center, the SDC uses a phenomenal array of multimedia exhibits to encourage young Singaporeans to reflect on the culture of modern Singapore and its global ambitions. One offers visitors a chance to be an on-the-spot TV reporter, another lets you build a virtual community, measuring your success in providing basic infrastructure and meeting cultural needs along the way. Though the SDC is more focused on civilian life than it used to be, national defense is still the underlying focus of many exhibits—National Service remains mandatory for Singaporean men. That means there are plenty of military-style exhibits and games, including the Shooting Gallery, a computer-simulated combat firing range using real but decommissioned M16 rifles. IMAX features roll at the five-story iWERKS Theatre regularly, in two and three dimensions. When you get hungry, there's a fast-food court. You can also have a 30-minute bus tour of the neighboring Singapore Air Force Training Institute free with SDC admission. Inquire about tour times at the front counter.

510 Upper Jurong Rd. © **65/6792-6188**. www.sdc.com.sg. Adults S$10 (US$6.70/£4.50), children 11 and unde S$6 (US$4/£2.70). Tues–Sun 9am–6pm. MRT to Boon Lay; transfer to SBS no. 182 or 193.

Singapore Science Centre (Kids)

The center features hands-on exhibits in true science-center spirit. Interestingly, the 7,500 sq. m (80,729 sq. ft.) of exhibits directly relate to the science syllabus of the local school system, from primary school level all the way through junior college. The galleries are all clearly marked to explain their interactive use, and study sheets are also available. The free Water Works gallery outside is fantastic fun for kids (*warning:* they'll be soaked in moments). The Technology Gallery is one of the more interesting exhibits, if you can wrestle the kids away from the machines. The Discovery Zone's insectarium is fascinating for anyone who isn't horrified by bugs. In the main atrium, there's a Tesla coil that generates electrical sparks 5m (16 ft.) long. There's a Virtual Voyages simulation theater plus the Omni Theatre planetarium, which has a projection booth encased in glass so you can check out how it works and an IMAX dome theatre. Best to avoid visits during weekends and school holiday times in June and December.

15 Science Centre Rd., off Jurong Town Hall Rd. © **65/6425-2500**. www.science.edu.sg. Adults S$6 (US$4/£2.70), children 15 and under S$3 (US$2/£1.35). Tues–Sun and public holidays 10am–6pm. Jurong East MRT to bus no. 66 or 335.

Southern Ridges ★★

This 9km (5¹/₂-mile) chain of park area starts at Mount Faber Park (where you can catch the cable car to Harbourfront and Sentosa island) and ends at the West Coast Park. It incorporates two new pedestrian bridges, the Alexandra Arch and, my favorite, The Henderson Waves bridge, which connects Mount Faber Park to

Telok Blangah Hill; this is the highest pedestrian bridge in Singapore, offering great views over the city. It's also a beautiful piece of design in its own right, weaving like a ribbon over the treetops and featuring a curved wooden deck that rises in places to resemble a breaking wave, creating sheltered areas with seating. The Henderson Waves lead to a forest walk with an elevated pedestrian walkway and cycling trails through the Telok Blangah Hill Park. You can take bus numbers 131, 145, 176, or 648 to Henderson Road and walk up the hill, but it's more fun to take the MRT to Harbourfront and then the cable car to Mount Faber, and walk from there.

Mount Faber Park entrance is from Telok Blangah Rd. or Henderson Rd., or via Harbourfront MRT/cable car. (℃ **800/471-7300.** www.nparks.gov.sg. Free admission. Daily 24 hr. Bus no. 131, 145, 176, or 648 to Henderson Rd., or MRT to Harbourfront and then cable car to Mount Faber.

CENTRAL & NORTHERN SINGAPORE ATTRACTIONS

The northern part of Singapore contains most of the island's nature reserves and parks. Here's where you'll find the Singapore Zoo, in addition to some sights with historical and religious significance. Despite the presence of the **MRT** in the area, there is not any simple way to get from attraction to attraction with ease. Bus transfers to and from MRT stops are the way to go—or you could stick to taxicabs.

Kong Meng San Phor Kark See Temple The largest religious complex on the island, this place, called Phor Kark See for short, is comprised of prayer and meditation halls, a hospice, gardens, and a vegetarian restaurant. The largest building is the Chinese-style Hall of Great Compassion. There is also the octagonal Hall of Great Virtue and a towering pagoda. For S50¢ (US35¢/20p), you can buy flower petals to place in a dish at the Buddha's feet. Compared to other temples on the island, Phor Kark See seems shiny, having only been built in 1981. As a result, the religious images inside carry a strange, almost artificial, cartoonlike air about them.

88 Bright Hill Dr., located in the center of the island to the east of Bukit Panjang Nature Preserve (Bright Hill Dr. is off Ang Mo Kio Ave.). (℃ **65/6453-4046.** Take MRT to Bishan, then take bus no. 410.

Kranji War Memorial Kranji Cemetery commemorates the Allied men and women who fought and died in World War II. Prisoners of war in a camp nearby began a burial ground here, and after the war it was enlarged to provide space for all the casualties. The Kranji War Cemetery is the site of 4,000 graves of servicemen, while the Singapore State Cemetery memorializes the names of over 20,000 who died and have no known graves. Stones are laid geometrically on a slope with a view of the Strait of Johor. The memorial itself is designed to represent the three arms of the services.

Woodlands Rd., located in the very northern part of the island. Daily 7am–6pm. Kranji MRT.

Lian Shan Shuang Lin Temple This temple, in English "the Twin Groves of the Lotus Mountain Temple," has a great story behind its founding. One night in 1898, Hokkien businessman Low Kim Pong and his son had the same dream[2] of a golden light shining from the west. The following day, the two went to the western shore and waited until, moments before sundown, a ship appeared carrying a group of Hokkien Buddhist monks and nuns on their way to China after a pilgrimage to India. Low Kim Pong vowed to build a monastery if they would stay in Singapore. They did.

Laid out according to feng shui principles, the buildings include the Dharma Hall, a main prayer hall, and drum and bell towers. They are arranged in *cong lin* style, a rare type of monastery design with a universal layout so that no matter how vast the grounds are, any monk can find his way around. The entrance hall has granite wall panels carved with scenes from Chinese history. The main prayer hall has fantastic details in the ceiling, wood panels, and other woodcarvings. In the back is a shrine to Kuan Yin, goddess of mercy.

Originally built amid farmland, the temple became surrounded by suburban high-rise apartments in the 1950s and 1960s, with the Toa Payoh Housing Development Board New Town project and the Pan-Island Expressway creeping close by.

184-E Jalan Toa Payoh. (C) **65/6259-6924.** Free admission. Daily 8:30am–5pm. Located in Toa Payoh New Town. Toa Payoh MRT to bus no. 232, 237, or 238.

MacRitchie Nature Trail   Of all the nature reserves in Singapore, the Central Catchment Nature Reserve is the largest, at 2,000 hectares (4,940 acres). Located in the center of the island, it's home to four of Singapore's reservoirs: MacRitchie, Seletar, Pierce, and Upper Pierce. The rainforest here is secondary forest, but the animals don't care; they're just as happy with the place. There's one path for walking and jogging (no bicycles allowed) that stretches 3km (1³/₄ miles) from its start in the southeast corner of the reserve, turning to the edge of MacRitchie Reservoir, then letting you out at the Singapore Island Country Club. The TreeTop Walk is a 250m-long (820-ft.) suspension walkway that rises 25m (82 ft.) from the forest floor. The views are great, but it is a hike from the parking lots. The National Parks Board gives free guided tours on the second Sunday of the month at 9:30am ((C) **65/6554-5127**).

Central Catchment Nature Reserve. (C) **65/6468-5736.** www.nparks.gov.sg. Free admission. From Orchard Rd., take bus no. 132 from the Orchard Parade Hotel. From Raffles City, take bus no. 130. Get off at the bus stop near Little Sisters of the Poor. Next to Little Sisters of the Poor, follow the paved walkway, which turns into the trail.

Mandai Orchid Gardens   John Laycock, the British founder of the Orchid Society of Southeast Asia, began the Mandai garden in 1951 to house his own collection. Now owned and operated by Singapore Orchids Pte. Ltd, Mandai breeds and cultivates hybrids for international export, and the gardens double as an STB tourist attraction. Some of Mr. Laycock's original collection survives, though many were lost in World War II. Arranged in English garden style, orchid varieties are separated in beds that are surrounded by grassy lawn. Tree-growing varieties prefer the shade of the covered canopy. On display is Singapore's national flower, the Vanda Miss Joaquim, a natural hybrid in shades of light purple. Behind the gift shop is the Water Garden, where a stroll will reveal many houseplants common to the West, as you would find them in the wild.

The Vanilla Pod restaurant gets many of its ingredients from its own herb and spice gardens, and the specialty crabmeat salad uses the garden's orchid as an ingredient. (Tues–Fri 11:30am–3pm and 6:30–11pm; Sat–Sun 9am–11pm; (C) **65/6368-0672**).

Mandai Lake Rd., on the route to the Singapore Zoo. (C) **65/6269-1036.** Adults S\$3 (US\$2/£1.35), children 11 and under S\$1 (US65¢/45p). Mon 8am–6pm; Tues–Sun 8am–7pm. Ang Mo Kio MRT bus no. 138.

Night Safari ★★★ (Kids)   Singapore takes advantage of its unchanging tropical climate and static ratio of daylight to night to bring you the world's first open-concept zoo for nocturnal animals. Here, as in the zoological gardens, animals live in landscaped areas, their barriers virtually unseen by visitors. These areas are dimly lit to create a moonlit effect, and a guided tram leads you through "regions" designed to resemble the Himalayan foothills, the jungles of Africa, and, naturally, Southeast Asia. Some of the free-range prairie animals come very close to the tram. The 45-minute ride covers almost 3.5km (2¹/₄ miles) and has a stop half-way to get off and have a rest or stroll along trails for closer views of smaller creatures. It costs S$10 ($6.70/£4.50) extra, but it's worth it since it reaches areas of the zoo that don't have paths.

Staff, placed at regular intervals along each of the three trails, help you find your way, though it's almost impossible to get lost along the trails; however, it is nighttime, you are in the forest, and it can be spooky. The guides are there to add peace of mind (and all speak English). Flash photography is strictly prohibited, and be sure to bring plenty of insect repellent. Check out the bathrooms; they're all open-air, Bali style.

Singapore Zoo, 80 Mandai Lake Rd., at the western edge of the Bukit Panjang Nature Reserve, on the Seletar Reservoir. © **65/6269-3411.** www.zoo.com.sg. Adults S$22 (US$15/£9.90), children 11 and under S$11 (US$7.35/£4.95). Combination Zoo and Night Safari ticket (without tram): adults S$30 (US$20/£14), children S$15 (US$10/£6.75). Park Hopper Ticket for Zoo, Night Safari, and BirdPark: adults S$40 (US$27/£18), children S$20 (US$13/£9). Daily 7:30pm–midnight. Ticket sales close at 11pm. Entrance Plaza, restaurant, and fast-food outlet 6:30–11:30pm. Ang Mo Kio MRT to bus no. 138.

Sasanaransi Buddhist Temple

Known simply as the Burmese Buddhist Temple, it was founded by a Burmese expatriate to serve the overseas Burmese Buddhist community. His partner, an herbal doctor also from Burma, traveled home to buy a 10-ton block of marble from which was carved the 3.3m-tall (11-ft.) Buddha image that sits in the main hall, surrounded by an aura of brightly colored lights. The original temple was off Serangoon Road in Little India and was moved here in 1991 at the request of the Housing Development Board. On the third story is a standing Buddha image in gold and murals of events in the Buddha's life.

14 Tai Gin Rd., located next to the Sun Yat-sen Villa near Toa Payoh New Town. Daily 6:30am–9pm. Chanting Sun 9:30am, Wed 8pm, and Sat 7:30pm. Take MRT to Toa Payoh, then take a taxi.

Singapore Zoo ★★ (Kids)

They call themselves the Open Zoo because, rather than coop the animals in jailed enclosures, they let them roam freely in landscaped areas. Beasts of the world are kept where they are supposed to be using psychological restraints and physical barriers that are disguised behind waterfalls, vegetation, and moats. Some animals are grouped with other species to show them coexisting as they would in nature. For instance, the white rhinoceros is neighborly with the wildebeest and ostrich—not that wildebeests and ostriches make the best company, but certainly contempt is better than boredom. Guinea and pea fowl, Emperor tamarinds, and other creatures are free-roaming and not shy; however, if you spot a water monitor or long-tailed macaque, know that they're not zoo residents—just locals looking for a free meal. Major zoo features are the Primate Kingdom, Wild Africa, the Reptile Garden, and underwater views of polar bears, sea lions, and penguins. Daily shows are themed around ecological issues and include "The Rainforest Fights Back," featuring 15 species, including orangutans, lemurs, otters, and birds at 10:30am and 1:30pm; sea lions, penguins, and pelicans at 11:30am, 2:30pm, and 5pm; and the elephants at 11:30am and 3:30pm. You can take your photograph with an orangutan, chimpanzee, or snake, and there are elephant and camel rides, too. The new Rainforest Kidzworld area is phenomenal: part water park, part adventure playground, and part petting zoo.

Zoo literature includes half-day and full-day agendas to help make the most of your visit. The best time to arrive, however, is at 9am, to have breakfast with an orangutan, which feasts on fruits and puts on a hilarious and very memorable show. If you miss that, you can also have tea with it at 4pm. Another good time to go is just after a rain, when the animals cool off and get frisky. See also the Night Safari listing, above.

80 Mandai Lake Rd., at the western edge of the Bukit Panjang Nature Reserve, on the Seletar Reservoir. © **65/6269-3411.** www.zoo.com.sg. Adults S$18 (US$12/£8.10), children 3–12 S$9 (US$6.05/£4.05).

Combination Zoo and Night Safari ticket: adults S$30 (US$20/£14), children S$15 (US$10/£6.75). Park Hopper Ticket for Zoo, Night Safari, and BirdPark: adults S$40 (US$27/£18), children S$20 (US$13/£9). Daily 8:30am–6pm. Ang Mo Kio MRT to bus no. 138.

Sungei Buloh Wetland Reserve ★

Located to the very north of the island and devoted to the wetland habitat and mangrove forests that are so common to the region, 130-hectare (321-acre) Sungei Buloh (pronounced "Soong-eye Bull-low") is out-of-the-way, and not the easiest place to get to; but it's a beautiful park, with constructed paths and boardwalks taking you through tangles of mangroves, soupy marshes, grassy spots, and coconut groves. More than 75% of Singapore's wildlife species are represented here, but of the flora and fauna, the most spectacular sights here are the birds, of which there are somewhere between 140 and 170 species in residence or just passing through for the winter. Of the migratory birds, some have traveled from as far as Siberia to escape the cold months from September to March. Bird observatories are set up at different spots along the paths. Also, even though you're in the middle of nowhere, Sungei Buloh has a visitor center, a cafeteria, and souvenirs. Go early to beat the heat, and douse yourself well in mosquito repellent. The National Parks Board gives free guided tours every Saturday at 9 and 10am, and 3 and 4pm; call for registration.

301 Neo Tiew Crescent. ✆ **65/6794-1401.** Adults S$1 (US65¢/45p), children and seniors S50¢ (US35¢/20p). Daily 7:30am–7pm. Audiovisual show Mon–Sat 9am, 11am, 1pm, 3pm, and 5pm; hourly Sun and public holidays. Kranji MRT to bus no. 925. Stop at Kranji Reservoir Dam and cross causeway to park entrance.

Sun Yat-sen Nanyang Memorial Hall ★

Dr. Sun Yat-sen visited Singapore eight times to raise funds for his revolution in China and made Singapore his headquarters for gaining the support of overseas Chinese in Southeast Asia. A wealthy Chinese merchant built the villa around 1880 for his mistress, and a later owner permitted Dr. Sun Yat-sen to use it. The house reflects the classic bungalow style, which is becoming endangered in modern Singapore. Renovated in 2008, its typical bungalow features include a projecting carport with a sitting room overhead, verandas with striped blinds, second-story cast-iron railings, and first-story masonry balustrades. A covered walkway leads to the kitchen and servants' quarters in the back.

Inside, the life of Dr. Yat-sen is traced in photos and watercolors, from his birth in southern China through his creation of a revolutionary organization.

12 Tai Gin Rd., near Toa Payoh New Town. ✆ **65/6256-7377.** Adults S$4 (US$2.70/£1.80), children and seniors S$3 (US$2/£1.35). Tues–Sun 9am–5pm. Toa Payoh MRT to bus no. 45.

EASTERN SINGAPORE ATTRACTIONS

The east coast leads from the edge of Singapore's urban area to the tip of the eastern part, at Changi Point. Eastern Singapore is home to Changi International Airport, nearby Changi Prison, and the long stretch of East Coast Park along the shoreline. The **MRT** heads east in this region, but swerves northward at the end of the line. A new MRT track, the circle line, will extend the network wider in the east and west from 2010. A popular **bus line** for east-coast attractions not reached by MRT is bus no. 2, which takes you to Changi Prison, Changi Point, and East Coast Park.

Changi Museum ★

Upon successful occupation of Singapore, the Japanese marched all British, Australian, and Allied European prisoners to Changi by foot, where they lived in a prison camp for 3 years, suffering overcrowding, disease, and malnutrition. Prisoners were cut off from the outside world except to leave the camp for labor duties. The hospital conditions were terrible; some prisoners suffered public beatings, and many died. In

The Peranakans of Katong

If you'd like to experience local culture that's a bit off the beaten track, come to Katong. This neighborhood came to prominence before World War II, when Peranakans and Eurasians, families of mixed heritage, populated this area outside of the city center along the east coast of the island. Many Peranakans, because of their mixed Chinese and Malay heritage, rose to financial power and were known to build lavish homes (many of which still line the streets of Katong), furnishing them with ornate, Chinese-inspired interiors, and they dress with opulent flair.

Peranakan antique furniture sports detailed woodcarvings in classic Chinese design, but with unbelievably gaudy mother-of-pearl inlay everywhere. Their pottery also follows Chinese aesthetics, with pretty floral, phoenix, and dragon patterns, but in vivid colors more representative of Malay tastes—bright yellows, pinks, and greens.

Peranakan ladies wore the *sarong kebaya,* a two-piece outfit consisting of a brightly colored cotton sarong topped with a delicately embroidered fitted blouse pinned with silver or gold broaches. Peranakan ladies (called Nonyas) were also known for their dainty beaded slippers. The outfit is really quite elaborate, but if you think it's a thing of the past, you'll be surprised to see how many local women still wear full traditional costume to weddings and other special events.

To visit Katong, start by taking a taxi to the corner of East Coast and Joo Chiat roads (don't worry, there are plenty of taxis here to bring you back to town). This is the epicenter of a boom in Peranakan heritage appreciation that has seen restaurants, a clothier, and an antiques house find cheers from locals who are keen to see this heritage survive. From this junction, you can find **Kim Choo Kueh Chang** (109 and 111 East Coast Rd.; *C* **65/6741-2125**), a place for traditional Nonya glutinous rice dumplings—the tetra-pack-shaped bundles wrapped in *pandan* leaves you may see hanging in bunches in food stalls around the island. Here you can buy and try, and also see how they are made.

an effort to keep hope alive, they built a small chapel from wood and attap. Years later, at the request of former POWs and their families and friends, the government built this replica.

The museum displays sketches by W. R. M. Haxworth, replicas of the murals painted by Bombardier Stanley Warren in St Luke's Chapel and secret photos taken by George Aspinall—all POWs who were imprisoned here. Displayed with descriptions, the pictures, along with writings and other objects from the camp, bring this period to life, depicting the day-to-day horror with a touch of high morale.

1000 Upper Changi Rd., in the same general area as the airport. *C* **65/6214-2451.** www.changimuseum. com. Free admission. Guided tour or audio tour headset rental: adults S$8 (US$5.35/£3.60), children S$4 (US$2.70/£1.80). Daily 9:30am–5pm. Tanah Merah MRT to bus no. 2.

East Coast Park East Coast Park is a narrow strip of reclaimed land, 8.5km (5¼ miles) long, tucked in between the shoreline and East Coast Parkway, and serves as a

Just next door is **Rumah Bebe** (113 East Coast Rd.; © **65/6247-8781**), a boutique that specializes in fantastic quality sarongs and *kebayas* with all the accessories. Proprietress Bebe Seet, a well-known pillar of the Peranakan community, is the local authority on traditional beaded slippers, selling her handmade creations, giving demonstrations, and teaching the art of beading. You can even custom-order a pair.

You'll notice these shops are newly renovated, freshly painted, and quite welcoming. If you prefer your cultural experience a bit more down-and-dirty, backtrack down East Coast Road to the next block. At the junction of East Coast and Ceylon roads is the heart of the *laksa* wars. On two street corners, opposite each other, about four open-air hawker stalls fight over who has the best *laksa* in Singapore. This local specialty, a rich, spicy coconut-based soup with noodles, prawns, fishcake, and cockles, is delicious, and you'll find the best right here. I usually go for the *laksa* at **No. 49** (no phone). Pull up a stool and eat on the sidewalk. (A hidden treasure—if you walk half a block down Ceylon Rd., you'll find an old but recently renovated Sri Lankan Hindu temple dedicated to Ganesh, the elephant-headed god. If you're dressed modestly, they'll welcome you in for a look-see.)

If you follow East Coast Road in the opposite direction, you'll find two older establishments. **The Katong Antique House** (208 East Coast Rd.; © **65/6345-8544**) is operated by Peter Wee, the president of the local Peranakan heritage association. It's a very small display, but everything's authentic and for sale, as opposed to the objects at the museum, in case you wanted to take a bit of Peranakan heritage home.

Next door is my favorite Nonya restaurant, **The Peranakan Inn** (210 East Coast Rd.; © **65/6440-6195**), a simple coffee shop–style restaurant with authentic home-style food at very reasonable prices. What you lack in decor you gain in authenticity.

hangout for Singaporean families on the weekends. Moms and dads barbecue under the trees while the kids swim at the beach, which is nothing more than a narrow lump of grainy sand sloping into yellow-green water that has more seaweed than a sushi bar. Paths for bicycling, in-line skating, walking, or jogging run the length of the park and are crowded on weekends and public and school holidays. On Sundays, you'll find kite flyers in the open grassy parts. The lagoon is the best place to go for bicycle rentals, canoeing, and windsurfing. If you go to the McDonald's Carpark C entrance, you'll find beach cafes, some sea kayak rentals, plus in-line skates and bicycle rentals as well. A couple of outfits, listed in "Sports & Recreation," later in this chapter, offer equipment rentals and instruction. The park is also home to **UDMC Seafood Centre** (reviewed in chapter 6), located not far from the lagoon.

East Coast Pkwy. Free admission. Bus no. 36 or 16 to Marine Parade and use the underpass to cross the highway.

Escape Theme Park (**Kids**)   If you think your kids will pass out at the sight of another museum, Singapore's newest and best amusement park will keep them occupied. There are rides for small kiddies and families, plus exciting ones for big kiddies as well. The go-kart circuit is happening. They also have carnival games with prizes, plus snacks and beverages. If it gets too hot, visit Wild Wild Wet, below. A beach and good seafood hawker fare are also nearby.

Downtown East 1, Pasir Ris Close. ℭ 65/6581-9128. www.escapethemepark.com.sg. Adults S$18 (US$12/£8.10), children S$8.90 (US$5.95/£4). Sat–Sun and public and school holidays 10am–8pm. Pasir Ris MRT.

Wild Wild Wet (**Kids**)   Beat the heat at this water park, with flumes, raft slides, a wave pool, plus lots of water activities for children. Locker rooms and food and beverage facilities are all convenient, plus water safety is provided by trained lifeguards. This park and neighboring Escape Theme Park both opened in 2003, so the facilities still feel relatively new and fresh.

Downtown East 1, Pasir Ris Close. ℭ 65/6581-9128. www.wildwildwet.com. Adults S$16 (US$11/£7.20), children S$11 (US$7.35/£4.95). Mon, Wed, Thurs, Fri 1–7pm; Sat–Sun and public and school holidays 10am–7pm. Pasir Ris MRT.

7 SENTOSA ISLAND

In the 1880s, Sentosa was a hub of British military activity, with hilltop forts built to protect the harbor from sea invasion from all sides. Today it has become a weekend getaway spot and Singapore's answer to Disneyland. Tomorrow it will be the site of one of Singapore's new "integrated resorts"—hotels, resorts, amusement and entertainment parks, plus gambling casinos, slated for opening in 2010. In the meantime, Sentosa is spending gobs of money to upgrade all existing facilities to meet the bar raised by the coming attractions.

If you're spending the day, there are numerous restaurants and a couple of food courts. For a unique dining option, consider **Sky Dining,** aboard a glass-bottomed cable car, where you can spend a couple hours eating a three- or four-course Western meal (set menus S$115/US$77/£52 or S$198/US$133/£89 for two; children's set menu S$24/US$16/£11). It's especially popular on Valentine's Day or for birthdays and wedding proposals. Meals are pretty tasty, provided by the Jewel Box restaurant. For more information, call ℭ 65/6377-9688, or visit www.mountfaber.com.sg.

For overnights, the **Shangri-La's Rasa Sentosa Resort and Spa** and the **Sentosa Resort & Spa** (see chapter 5) are popular hotel options. For general Sentosa inquiries, call ℭ 1800/736-8672 or see www.sentosa.com.sg.

GETTING THERE

Island admission is S$2 (US$1.35/90p) each for adults and children, payable at the causeway upon entry or factored into the cost of transport to the island. Tickets to additional attractions can be bought as a package from the Sentosa Express office at Harbour-Front or purchased separately on the island.

The most entertaining way to get there is to take the cable car. From the Cable Car Towers (ℭ 65/6270-8855), they make the trip daily from 8:30am to 11pm at a cost of S$19 (US$13/£8.55) round-trip adults and S$9.50 (US$6.35/£4.25) children. The one-way ticket is only one Singapore dollar less (67¢/45p). The view is okay (but too far from

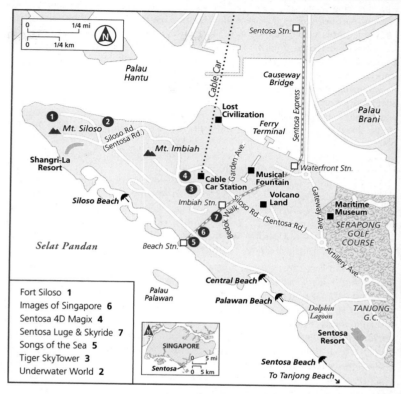

Fort Siloso **1**
Images of Singapore **6**
Sentosa 4D Magix **4**
Sentosa Luge & Skyride **7**
Songs of the Sea **5**
Tiger SkyTower **3**
Underwater World **2**

the city to see skyline) and the ride is especially fun for kids. The cable cars also extend up Mt. Faber on the Singapore side. If you choose to take a cable car up to the top, you can take it back down again. Otherwise, if you choose to alight at this stop, you can take a taxi back to civilization.

The new Sentosa Express opened in January 2007. This light-rail train operates between VivoCity at the HarbourFront MRT station and Sentosa, with stops at the beach, major attractions, and the future site of the integrated resort. Pick up the train to Sentosa at VivoCity, third level, where you can purchase tickets for S$3 (US$2/£1.35), which includes all-day rides, plus Sentosa admission.

A bus operates from the HarbourFront Interchange (near HarbourFront MRT) daily from 7am to 11pm, with extended hours until 12:30am on Friday, Saturday, and the eve of public holidays; it costs S$3 (US$2/£1.35) per person. Or any city taxi can take you there; just pay the entrance fee after you cross the causeway, and the driver can drop you anywhere you'd like to go within the island.

GETTING AROUND

Once on Sentosa, a free bus system with three color-coded routes snakes around the island from 7am to 11pm on weekdays and 12:30pm at weekends.

The most notable attractions that you get free with your Sentosa admission are the Animal and Bird Encounters, a range of displays featuring reptiles, macaques, parrots, and birds of prey that runs from noon to 5:30pm at the amphitheater at Palawan Beach; the Nature Trail that starts from the bottom of the Merlion statue and the **Dragon Trail Nature Walk,** a 1.5km (1-mile) stroll through secondary rainforest to see dragon sculptures and local flora and fauna; and the **beaches.**

Sentosa has three beaches. At **Siloso Beach,** deck chairs, beach umbrellas, and a variety of **watersports equipment** like pedal boats, aqua bikes, fun bugs, canoes, surfboards, and banana boats are available for hire at nominal charges. This is where the beautiful young things hang out and play beach volleyball. Bicycles are also available for hire. Shower and changing facilities, food kiosks, and snack bars are at rest stations. **Palawan Beach** has a greater assortment of beachside bars and restaurants, while **Tanjong Beach** is the quietest and most laid back of the three.

Most attractions on Sentosa charge separate entrance fees; they include the **Songs of the Sea** laser fountain show (S$8/US$5.35/£3.60 per person for 3 and over), **Sentosa Luge & Skyride** (S$10/US$6.70/£4.50 per ride; daily 10am–9:30pm), **Sentosa 4D Magix** motion cinema (adults S$18/US$12/£8.10, children S$11/US$7.35/£4.95; daily 10am–9pm), and the **TigerSky Tower** (adults S$12/US$8.05/£5.40, children S$8/US$5.35/£3.60; daily 9am–9pm). The best attractions, in my opinion, are as follows:

Fort Siloso   Fort Siloso guarded Keppel Harbour from invasion in the 1880s. It's one of three forts built on Sentosa, and it later became a military camp in World War II. The buildings have been outfitted to resemble a barracks, kitchen, laundry, and military offices as they looked back in the day. In places, you can explore the underground tunnels and ammunition holds, but they're not as extensive as you would hope they'd be. The **Surrender Chambers** lead you through authentic footage, photos, maps, and recordings of survivors to chronologically tell the story of the Pacific theater activity of World War II and how the Japanese conquered Singapore. The grand finale is a wax museum depicting, first, a scene of the British surrender and, last, another of the Japanese surrender.

⌁ **65/6275-0388.** Adults S$8 (US$5.35/£3.60), children S$5 (US$3.35/£2.25). Daily 10am–6pm.

Images of Singapore ★★   Images of Singapore is a highlight of a visit to Sentosa. "Pioneers of Singapore" is an exhibit of beautifully constructed life-size dioramas that place figures like Sultan Hussein, Sir Stamford Raffles, Tan Tock Seng, and Naraina Pillai, to name just a few, in the context of Singapore's timeline and note their contributions to its development. Also interesting are the dioramas depicting scenes from the daily routines of the different cultures as they lived during colonial times. It's a great stroll that brings history to life and gives a good introduction to the cultural influences that continue to shape modern Singapore

The newest addition, **Festivals of Singapore,** is another life-size diorama exhibit depicting a few of the major festivals and traditions of the Chinese, Malay, Indian, and Peranakan cultures in Singapore.

⌁ **65/6275-0388.** Adults S$10 (US$6.70/£4.50), children S$7 (US$4.70/£3.15). Daily 9am–7pm.

Underwater World ★ Kids   Underwater World is without a doubt one of the most-visited attractions on Sentosa. Everybody comes for the tunnel: 83m (272 ft.) of transparent acrylic tube through which you glide on a conveyor belt, gaping at sharks, stingrays, eels, and other creatures of the sea drifting by, above and on both sides. If you're lucky, you might see the scuba diver who hops in several times a day and feeds them by hand. In smaller tanks, you can view other unusual sea life, like the puffer fish and the mysteriously weedy and leafy sea dragons. The price also includes admission to the Dolphin Lagoon, with pink dolphin shows daily at 1:30pm, 3:30pm, and 5:30pm, with an additional show at 11am at weekends.

☎ **65/6275-0388.** www.underwaterworld.com.sg. Adults S$23 (US$15/£10), children S$15 (US$10/£6.75). Daily 9am–9pm.

8 ORGANIZED TOURS

Although touring Singapore is simple enough for DIY travelers, visitors with little time or those who want to delve deeper into local sights can take advantage of convenient organized activities.

COACH TOURS

Tour East (*☎* **65/6738-2622**) organizes typical half-day coach tours of the city every day (adults S$30/US$20/£14, children S$15/US$10/£6.75), and full-day coach excursions on Tuesday, Thursday, Friday, and Sunday to some of the main attractions around the island (adults S$73/US$49/£33, children S$36/US$24/£16), some with meals included. The Peranakan Trail (Tues–Sun) takes visitors out to Katong, a suburban neighborhood that is the focal point of Peranakan heritage (adults S$45/US$30/£20, children S$22/US$15/£9.90).

For something different, go for the **DUCKTour** (*☎* **65/6338-6877**; www.ducktours. com.sg), a combined coach and boat tour in an amphibious vehicle, a decommissioned military craft, that circles you around the Historic District for a tour of the harbor. The hour-long tour starts every hour, departing from the Suntec City Mall Galleria, with additional transfers from the DUCKTours office on Orchard Road (at the corner of Cairnhill Rd.). Reservations are highly recommended, and tours cost S$33 (US$22/£15) adults, S$17 (US$11/£7.65) children ages 3 to 12, and $2 (US$1.35/90p) kids 2 and under. DUCKTours also operates the **HiPPO Tour** aboard an open-top double-decker bus, cruising Orchard Road, Little India, Kampong Glam, Chinatown, and the Historic District. Pick it up at the DUCKTours office on Orchard Road or at Suntec City, then get on and off at sights that interest you along the way. The day ticket costs S$33 (US$22/£15) adults, S$13 (US$8.70/£5.85) children 3 to 12, and $2 (US$1.35/90p) for kids 2 and under. Call DUCKTours for information.

WALKING TOURS

Singapore Walks (*☎* **65/6325-1631**; www.singaporewalks.com) is a reputable outfit that organizes guided walking tours of the Historic District, Chinatown, Little India, Kampong Glam, and other neighborhoods Monday through Saturday, except for public holidays. Call them to find out the meeting time and place for the tour you want; for most walks, adults pay S$25 (US$17/£11), children tour for S$15 (US$10/£6.75). Their river walk, at S$28 (US$19/£13), includes a bumboat tour.

RIVER TOURS & CRUISES

Singapore River Cruises (*☎* **65/6339-6833**; www.rivercruise.com.sg) operates boats up and down the Singapore River and into the harbor from 9am to 11pm daily. A bumboat ride with recorded info about the riverside sights costs adults S$18 (US$12/£8.10) and children S$8 (US$5.35/£3.60). You can also use the river cruise boats as a taxi, as it has pick-up points from the Merlion (Fullerton), Boat Quay, Clarke Quay, and Robertson Quay.

The *Imperial Cheng Ho,* operated by **Watertours** (© **65/6533-9811;** www.water tours.com.sg), is a huge boat modeled after the sort of Chinese junk that Admiral Cheng Ho might have sailed when he explored this region in the 15th century. A 2¹/₂-hour cruise takes you from Marina South Pier past the Singapore skyline, the mouth of the Singapore River, then out past Sentosa, with a stop on Kusu Island. I recommend the Morning Glory Cruise at 10:30am (adults S$27/US$18/£12, children S$14/US$9.40/£6.30). There's also a High Tea Cruise at 3pm (adults S$32/US$21/£14, children S$16/US$11/£7.20) and a dinner cruise at 6:30pm (adults S$55/US$37/£25, children S$29/US$19/£13). Watertours can arrange hotel transfer with your booking.

TRISHAW TOUR

These cycle rickshaws were once a staple form of public transportation. Now they're permitted on busy streets only with special permits, and only for guided tours. **Singapore Explorer** (© **65/6339-6833;** www.singaporeexplorer.com.sg) coordinates regular outings through Chinatown from 10am to 7pm daily. You can either call ahead to book a ride or just show up at the corner of Sago and Terrenganu streets; you'll see the collection of trishaws under cover. The half-hour trip takes you through Chinatown's quaint streets for a charge of S$39 (US$26/£18), children S$20 (US$13/£9) per person. Singapore Explorer can arrange pickup from anywhere if you book in advance.

9 THE SURROUNDING ISLANDS

Sixty smaller islands surround Singapore, some of which are open for full- or half-day trips. The ferry rides are cool and breezy, and they provide interesting up-close views of some of the larger ships docked in the harbor. The islands themselves are small and, for the most part, don't have a lot going on. The locals basically see them as little escapes from the everyday grind—peaceful respites for the family.

KUSU & ST. JOHN'S ISLANDS

Kusu Island and St. John's Island are both located to the south of Singapore proper, about a 15- to 20-minute ferry ride to Kusu, 25 to 30 minutes to St. John's.

Its name meaning "Tortoise Island" in Chinese, many popular legends exist about how **Kusu Island** came to be. The most popular ones involve shipwrecked people, either fishermen or monks, who were rescued when a tortoise turned himself into an island. Kusu Island was originally two small islands and a reef, but in 1975, reclaimed land turned it into a (very) small getaway island. There are two places of worship: a Chinese temple and a Malay shrine. The Chinese temple becomes a zoo during "Kusu Season" in October, when thousands of Chinese devotees flock here to pray for health, prosperity, and luck. There are two swimming lagoons (the one to the north has a pretty view of Singapore Island), picnic tables, toilets, and public telephones.

Historically speaking, **St. John's Island** is an unlikely place for a day trip. As far back as 1874, this place was a quarantine for Chinese immigrants sick with cholera; in the 1950s, it became a deportation holding center for Chinese Mafia thugs; and later it was a rehab center for opium addicts. Today you'll find a mosque, holiday camps, three lagoons, bungalows, a cafeteria, a huge playing field, and basketball. It's much larger than

Kusu Island, but not large enough to fill a whole day of sightseeing. Toilets and public phones are available.

Ferries leave at regular intervals from the Marina South Pier (© 65/1800-736-8672); take the MRT to Marina Bay, then bus no. 402 to the pier. The boat makes a circular route, landing on both islands. Adult tickets cost S$15 (US$10/£6.75), and tickets for children under 12 are S$12 (US$8.05/£5.40). *Tip:* Pack a lunch and bring drinks, sunblock, and mosquito repellent.

PULAU UBIN ★

My favorite island getaway has to be Ubin. Located off the northeast tip of Singapore, Pulau Ubin remains the only place in Singapore where you can find life as it used to be before urban development. Lazy kampong villages pop up alongside trails perfect for a little more rugged bicycling. It's truly a great day trip for those who like to explore nature and rural scenery. Rumors have it that during the occupation, the Japanese brought soldiers here to be tortured, and so some believe the place is haunted.

At the eastern tip of the island is the **Chek Jawa** marine reserve with a visitor center and a kilometer-long (½-mile) boardwalk that loops over the seashore and the mangrove. Halfway around there's a 20m-high (66-ft.) viewing tower that overlooks the tree canopy, so look out for bulbul birds, owls, and bats. Come at low tide to get the best view of the crabs, starfish, anemones, and sponges that cling to survival on the beach. Chek Jawa is about 40 minutes walk from the jetty, so rent a bicycle or a van to get there.

To get to Ubin, take bus no. 2 to Changi Village (or just take a cab—the bus ride is long). Walk past the food court down to the water and find the ferry. There's no ticket booth, so you should just approach the captain and buy your ticket from him—it'll cost you about S$2 (US$1.35/90p). The boats leave regularly, but only when they've got enough passengers to justify a trip, with the last one returning from the island as late as 11pm (make sure you double-check with the ferryman so you don't get stranded!). If you want to avoid a long wait for a boat, peak hours are from 7am to 7pm.

Once you're there, bicycle rental places along the jetty can provide you with bikes and island maps at reasonable prices. The new 45-hectare (111-acre) Ketam Mountain Bike Park has trails with three levels of difficulty—one that meets international competition standards. A few coffee shops cook up rudimentary meals, and you'll also find public toilets and coin phones in the more populated areas.

10 SPORTS & RECREATION

BEACHES

Besides the beach at East Coast Park (see "Attractions Outside the Urban Area," earlier in this chapter) and those on Sentosa Island (see earlier), you can try the smaller beach at Changi Village, called Changi Point. From the shore, you have a panoramic view of Malaysia, Indonesia, and several smaller islands that belong to Singapore. The beach is calm and frequented mostly by locals who set up camps and barbecues to hang out all day. There are kayak rentals along the beach, and in Changi Village you'll find, in addition to a huge hawker center, quite a few international restaurants and pubs to hang out in and have a fresh seafood lunch when you get hungry. To get there, take SBS bus no. 2 from either the Tanah Merah or Bedok MRT stations.

On Kusu and St. John's Islands, there are quiet swimming lagoons, a couple of which have quite nice views of the city.

BICYCLE RENTAL

Bicycles are not for rent within the city limits, and traffic does not really allow for cycling on city streets, so sightseeing by bicycle is not recommended for city touring. If you plan a trip out to **Sentosa,** cycling provides a great alternative to that island's tram system and gets you closer to the parks and nature there. For a little light cycling, most people head out to **East Coast Park,** where rentals are inexpensive, the scenery is nice on cooler days, and there are plenty of great stops for eating along the way. One favorite place where the locals go for mountain-biking sorts of adventures (and to cycle amid the old kampong villages) is **Pulau Ubin,** off the northeast coast of Singapore.

AT EAST COAST PARK There are several rental shops for bicycles and inline skates along the East Coast Park; couples and families often hire tandems, too. Try **SDK Recreation** (✆ **65/6445-2969**), near McDonald's at Carpark C; open 7 days from about 11am to 8 or 9pm. Rentals are S$4 to S$8 (US$2.70–US$5.35/£1.80–£3.60) per hour, depending on the type and quality bike you're looking for. Identification may be requested, or leave a S$50 (US$34/£23) deposit.

ON SENTOSA ISLAND There are several rental places near Siloso Beach off Siloso Road, a short walk from Underwater World (see "Sentosa Island," earlier in this chapter). There's a kiosk at Sakae Sushi (✆ **65/6271-6385**) and another at Costa Sands (✆ **65/6275-2471**). Both are open 7 days from around 10am to 6:30 or 7pm. Rental for a standard bicycle is S$5 (US$3.35/£2.25) per hour. A mountain bike goes for S$8 (US$5.35/£3.60) per hour. Identification is required.

IN PULAU UBIN When you get off the ferry, there are a number of places to rent bikes. The shops are generally open between 8am and 6pm and will charge between S$8 and S$14 (US$5.35–US$9.40/£3.60–£6.30) per day, depending on which bike you choose. Most rental agents will have a map of the island for you—take it. Even though it doesn't look too impressive, it'll be a great help.

GOLF

Golf is big in Singapore, and although there are quite a few clubs, many are exclusively for members only. However, many places are open for limited play by nonmembers. All will require you bring an international par certificate. Most hotel concierges will be glad to make arrangements for you, and this may be the best way to go. Also, it's really popular for Singaporeans to go on day trips to Malaysia for the best courses.

Changi Golf Club This 9-hole walking course is par 34, and nonmembers may play at this private club only on weekdays (walk-ins okay, but advance booking recommended). They may even be able to set you up with other players. The course opens at 7:30am. Last tee is 4:30pm.

20 Netheravon Rd. ✆ **65/6545-5133.** Greens fees S$45 (US$30/£20); caddy fees S$10 (US$6.70/£4.50). Mon–Fri 7:30am–4:30pm. Closed for maintenance Mon mornings.

Marina Bay Golf Course This 18-hole golf course opened in 2006 and comes with a great view of the city skyline. It's designed to resemble a Scottish links-style course, with 91 challenging pot bunkers. Marina Bay even offers night golfing from Wednesday to Friday, with the course entirely floodlit. The attached driving range is open daily from 7am to 10:15pm.

80 Rhu Cross, #01-01 ✆ **65/6345-7788.** Greens fees Mon–Fri S$80 or S$110 (9 or 18 holes; US$54 or US$74/£36 or £50), Sat–Sun S$100 or S$195 (US$67 or S$131/£45 or £88). Sat–Tues 7am–5pm; Wed–Fri 7am–8:20pm.

159

Sentosa Golf Club   The best idea if you're traveling with your family and want to get in a game, Sentosa's many activities will keep the kids happy while you practice your swing guilt-free at one of the club's two 18-hole 72-par courses, the Tanjong and the Serapong (the home of the Singapore Open). This private club charges much more for nonmembers than other courses (and weekend play for nonmembers is restricted to Sun afternoon), but both are beautiful championship courses and a relaxing time away from the city. Advance phone bookings are required.

27 Bukit Manis Rd., Sentosa Island. ✆ **65/6275-0022.** Greens fees Mon–Fri S$305–S$355 (US$204–US$238/£137–£160); Sun S$425–S$475 (US$285–US$318/£191–£214). Daily 7am–7pm.

SCUBA DIVING

The locals are crazy about scuba diving but are more likely to travel to Malaysia and other Southeast Asian destinations for good underwater adventures. The most common complaint is that the water surrounding Singapore is really silty—sometimes to the point where you can barely see your hand before your face. See chapters 13 through 15 for scuba activities in Malaysia.

SEA CANOEING

Rubber sea canoes and one- or two-person kayaks can be rented at Siloso Beach on Sentosa, the beach at East Coast Park (near McDonald's Carpark C), and the beach at Changi Point. Prices range from S$14 to S$35 (US$9.40–US$23/£6.30–£16) per hour, depending on the type of craft you rent. Life jackets are provided. These places don't have phones, so just go to the beach and scout out the rental places on the sand.

TENNIS

Quite a few hotels in the city provide tennis courts for guests, many floodlit for night play (which allows you to avoid the daytime heat), and even a few that can arrange lessons, so be sure to check out the hotel listings in chapter 5. If your hotel doesn't have tennis facilities, ask your concierge for help to arrange a game at a facility outside the hotel. Many hotels have signing agreements with sister hotel properties or special rates with independent fitness centers within the city.

WATER-SKIING & WAKEBOARDING

The new hot spot for waterskiing and wakeboarding is **Ski 360°** at the East Coast Park (✆ **65/6442-7318;** www.ski360degree.com). Rather than a boat, skiers are pulled by an overhead cable like a snow ski lift around the perimeter of the lake. Ski passes range from S$32 (US$21/£14) per hour on weekdays to S$42 (US$28/£19) on weekends and public holidays. Boat-based skiing is run by various clubs on Seletar Island—contact the Singapore Waterski and Wakeboard Federation (✆ **65/6348-9943;** www.swwf.org.sg) for information on courses and contacts.

WINDSURFING & SAILING

You'll find both windsurfing boards and sailboats for rent at the lagoon in East Coast Park, which is where these activities primarily take place. Many require membership, but the Mana Mana Beach Club rents out to visitors at 1212 East Coast Pkwy. (✆ **65/6339-8878**). For S$55 (US$37/£25) an hour, you can rent a Laser, or for S$45 (US$30/£20) an hour, you can rent windsurf gear.

Singapore Shopping

In Singapore, shopping is a sport, and from the practiced glide through haute couture boutiques to skillful back-alley bargaining, it's always exciting, with something to satiate every pro shopper's appetite.

The focal point of shopping in Singapore is **Orchard Road,** a very long stretch of glitzy shopping malls packed with Western clothing stores, from designer apparel to cheap chic, and many other mostly imported finds. Singaporeans have a love-hate relationship with Orchard Road. As the shopping malls developed, they brought hip styles into the reach of everyday Singaporeans, adding a cosmopolitan sheen to Singapore style. But Orchard Road also ushered in a new culture of obsessive consumerism.

Even to outsiders, Orchard Road is a drug; however, most of the clothing and accessories shops sell Western imports, and the average visitor will find that the prices of Western brand-name fashions are only slightly less expensive than at home, if at all.

Another myth about shopping in Asia is that consumer electronics, cameras, and computer hardware and software are a steal. Although some good bargains can be found if you hunt well, be careful if the offer sounds too good to be true—it usually is. By and large, prices here are comparable to those of the West.

For shopping with an Asian flavor, there are some exciting shopping areas—**Little India, Arab Street,** and **Chinatown**—where shopping for unusual handicrafts is as much a main attraction as the sights. Anybody who's been around Singapore long enough will tell you that most of the really juicy bargains went the way of the dodo when the huge shopping malls came to town, but if you know the value of certain items that you'd like, some comparison shopping may save you a little money. In this chapter, I'll give you some tips on where to find the better merchandise, competitive prices, and memorable shopping experiences.

Take note: I am an *expert* shopper and have shopped just about everywhere in Singapore. The shops that I have singled out for this book are the best of the best; my family and I have purchased goods and services from virtually every one of them.

1 SINGAPORE SHOPPING: THE GROUND RULES

HOURS   Shopping malls are generally open from 10am to 9pm Monday through Saturday, with some stores keeping shorter Sunday hours. The malls sometimes remain open until 10pm on holidays. Smaller shops are open from around 10am to 5pm Monday through Saturday but are almost always closed on Sunday. Hours will vary from shop to shop. Arab Street is closed on Sunday.

PRICES   Almost all of the larger stores in shopping malls have fixed prices. Sometimes these stores will have seasonal sales, especially from June into July, during the month-long **Great Singapore Sale,** when prices are discounted 50% or 70%. In the smaller shops and at street vendors, prices are sometimes not marked, and vendors will quote you higher prices than the going rate in anticipation of the bargaining ritual. These are the places to find good prices, if you negotiate well.

BARGAINING   In Singapore, not all shops fix prices on merchandise, and even many that display price tags are open to negotiation. For outsiders who are unaccustomed to this tradition, bargaining can be embarrassing and frustrating at first—especially for those who are used to accepting fixed prices without an argument. But with a little practice, soon you'll be bargaining with the best of 'em.

The most important tip for successful bargaining is to first have an idea of the value of what you're buying. This can be difficult for unusual items, but a little comparison shopping may help you out. By comparison shopping, I mean look at prices for the same item here in Singapore. Many foreigners overpay because they consider what the same item might cost back home, which naturally will be far more expensive than in Singapore.

When bargaining it's important to keep a friendly, good-natured banter between you and the seller. In local terms, it's called, "showing face." Keep it friendly and respectful.

A simple "How much?" is the place to start, to which they'll reply with their highest price. Tell them you're willing to pay half that amount and go from there. When buying more than one item, ask for a discount. If you've seen it cheaper elsewhere, tell them. Or you can pull the old "But I only have $20" ploy. (Just make sure you don't turn around and ask them to change a $50!) Try anything, even if it's just a wink and a little "Don't you have any special discounts for ladies shopping on Wednesdays?"

Some people have said that once you start the bargaining ritual, it's rude to walk away and not purchase the item. Well, I see it this way: It's my money, and if I still don't feel comfortable shelling it out, then I won't do it under any feeling of obligation. (However, if you've spent hours negotiating over a high-priced item, and the owner agrees to your offer, it will be considered harsh to walk away after going through all that trouble.) Besides, your final bargaining strategy is to just politely say, "No, thank you" and walk away. You'll be surprised at how fast prices can come down as you're walking out the door.

GLOBAL REFUND SCHEME   When you shop in stores that display the blue "Tax Free Shopping" logo, the government will refund the 7% goods and services tax (GST) you pay on purchases totaling S$100 (US$67/£45) or more, if you are leaving Singapore via air travel. At the point of purchase, the sales clerk will fill out a Tax Free Shopping Cheque, which you retain with your receipt.

When you leave Singapore, present your checks at Customs along with your passport and let them see the goods you've purchased to show that you're taking them out of the country with you. Customs will stamp the forms, which you then present at any of the Global Refund Counters in the airport for an on-the-spot cash refund (in Singapore dollars), a check, a direct transfer of the amount to your credit card account, or an airport shopping voucher. For complete details, call the Global Refund Scheme hot line at ✆ **65/6225-6238;** www.globalrefund.com.

Another company, Premier Tax Free (www.premiertaxfree.com), also offers GST refunds with kiosks at the airport.

CLOTHING SIZES   Those of you used to shopping in big-and-tall stores will unfortunately find little ready-to-wear clothing in Singapore that'll fit you—but that doesn't mean you can't take advantage of the many excellent tailors around town. Shopping for ready-made clothing in standard sizes can be confusing, because clothing made in Singapore is generally for export and everything else is imported from outside. This means that

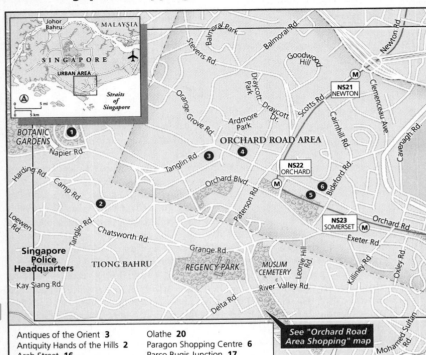

See "Orchard Road Area Shopping" map

Antiques of the Orient **3**
Antiquity Hands of the Hills **2**
Arab Street **16**
Artrium@MICA **26**
Aspara **3**
Basharahil Brothers **16**
Cathay Photo **24**
CHIJMES **20**
Chinatown Complex **32**
Eu Yan Sang **31**
Funan Digitalife Mall **25**
Gim Joo Trading **15**
Hadjee Textiles **16**
Hassan's Carpets **3**
Jamal Kazura Aromatics **14**
Justmen's **3**
Kin Lee & Co. **16**
Kuna's **11**
Kwong Chen
 Beverage Trading **31**
Larry Jewelry **6**
Little India Arcade **10**
Marina Square **23**
Maruti Textiles **16**
Melor's Curios **14**
Millenia Walk **19**
Mumbai Sé **4**
Mustafa Centre **7**

Olathe **20**
Paragon Shopping Centre **6**
Parco Bugis Junction **17**
Poppy Fabric **16**
Punjab Bazaar **10**
Raffles City
 Shopping Centre **22**
Raffles Hotel
 Shopping Arcade **21**
Roopalee Fashions **9**
Royal Selangor **27**
RISIS (Singapore Botanic
 Gardens gift shop) **1, 18**
Seiyu **17**
Shanghai Tang **5**
Sim Lim Square **13**
Singapore Handicraft Center **28**
Siong Moh Paper Products **30**
Stylemart **12**
Suntec City Mall **18**
Takashimaya
 Shopping Centre **5**
Tanglin Shopping Centre **3**
Tea Chapter **33**
Tekka Centre **8**
Tudor Court **2**
VivoCity **34**
Yue Hwa **29**

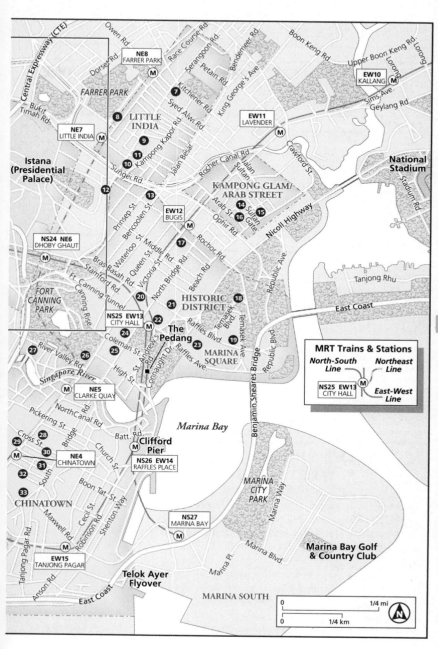

clothing in local shops can reflect American, British, or Continental sizes, depending on which country it came from or was intended for. The chart below may help you figure out your size, but really the only way to be sure it's your size is to try it on.

Ladies' Dress Sizes

U.S.	8	10	12	14	16	18
U.K.	30	32	34	36	38	40
Continental	36	38	40	42	44	46

Ladies' Shoes

U.S.	5	5½	6	6½	7	7½	8	8½	9
U.K.	3½	4	4½	5	5½	6	6½	7	7½
Continental	35	35	36	37	38	38	38	39	40

Men's Suits

U.S. & U.K.	34	36	38	40	42	44	46	48
Continental	44	46	48	50	52	54	56	58

Men's Shirts

U.S. & U.K.	14	14½	15	15½	16	16½	17	17½
Continental	36	37	38	39	40	41	42	43

Men's Shoes

U.S.	7	7½	8	8½	9	9½	10	10½	11	11½
U.K.	6½	7	7½	8	8½	9	9½	10	10½	11
Continental	39	40	41	42	43	43	44	44	45	45

Children's Clothes

U.S.	2	4	6	8	10	13	15
U.K.	1	2	5	7	9	10	12
Continental	1	2	5	7	9	10	12

2 THE SHOPPING SCENE, PART 1: WESTERN-STYLE MALLS

The newest and grandest shopping mall in Singapore is **VivoCity** (1 HarbourFront Walk; © **65/6377-6860**). Opened in November 2006, it's Singapore's biggest shopping mall, with 300 retailers, plus dining, entertainment, and even a rooftop sun deck with a bandshell and kiddie wading pool. It's conveniently built on top of the HarbourFront MRT station.

The excitement over VivoCity will soon be replaced by **ION Orchard,** which is slated to open by 2010. A coveted location at the corner of Orchard and Patterson roads, a central MRT station below, and a tower of super-luxury residences above, this high-end shopping mall is slated to be the be-all and end-all of the Singapore shopping scene. Another hot mall, **313@Somerset,** is also scheduled to open along Orchard Road at the Somerset MRT station around the same time.

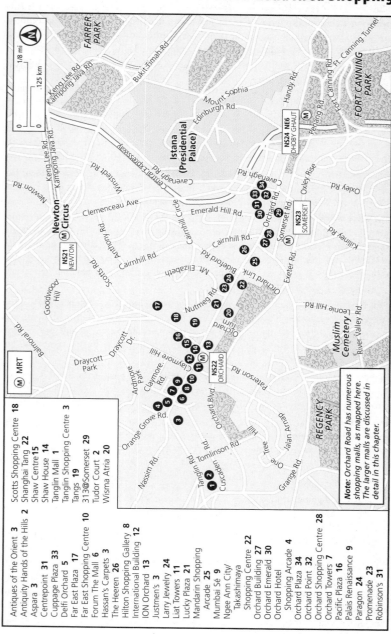

FARRER PARK

FORT CANNING PARK

1/8 mi

.125 km

Keng Lee Rd
Kampong Java Rd.

Bukit Timah Rd.

Handy Rd.

Mount Sophia

Edinburgh Rd.

Penang Rd.

Ft. Canning Tunnel

Fort Canning Rd.

NS24 NE6
DHOBY GHAUT

Newton Rd.

Keng Lee Rd.
Kampong Java Rd.

Istana
(Presidential
Palace)

Cavenagh Rd.

Oxley Rise

Oxley Rd.

Newton
Circus

NS21
NEWTON

Clemenceau Ave.

Winstedt Rd.

Central Expressway

Cairnhill Circle

Emerald Hill Rd.

Cavenagh Rd.

Orchard Rd.

33
32
31
30
29

Somerset
NS23
SOMERSET

Killiney Rd.

Anthony Rd.

Cairnhill Rd.

Cairnhill Rd.

Bideford Rd.

28
27
26

25

Exeter Rd.

Scotts Rd.

Mt. Elizabeth

23
24
22

21

20

Orchard Link

Leonie Hill Rd.

Muslim
Cemetery

Goodwood
Hill

17

18

19

Nutmeg Rd.

River Valley Rd.

Balmoral Rd.

Draycott
Dr.

16
15
14
13

Orchard
Turn

Exeter Rd.

MRT

Draycott
Park

Ardmore
Park

Claymore Hill

Claymore
Rd.

12
11
10
9
8
7
6
5
4

Paterson Rd.

NS22
ORCHARD

Orchard Blvd.

Jalan Arnap

REGENCY
PARK

3

Orange Grove Rd.

Grange Rd.

Nassim Rd.

Tanglin Rd.

Tomlinson Rd.

Cuscaden

One Tree Hill

Grange Rd.

1 2

Note: *Orchard Road has numerous shopping malls, as mapped here. The larger malls are discussed in detail in this chapter.*

Antiques of the Orient **3**
Antiquity Hands of the Hills **2**
Aspara **3**
Centrepoint **31**
Cuppage Plaza **33**
Delfi Orchard **5**
Far East Plaza **17**
Far East Shopping Centre **10**
Forum The Mall **6**
Hassan's Carpets **3**
The Heeren **26**
Hilton Shopping Gallery **8**
International Building **12**
ION Orchard **13**
Justmen's **3**
Larry Jewelry **24**
Liat Towers **11**
Lucky Plaza **21**
Mandarin Shopping
Arcade **25**
Mumbai Sé **9**
Ngee Ann City/
Takashimaya
Shopping Centre **22**
Orchard Building **27**
Orchard Emerald **30**
Orchard Hotel
Shopping Arcade **4**
Orchard Plaza **34**
Orchard Point **32**
Orchard Shopping Centre **28**
Orchard Towers **7**
Pacific Plaza **16**
Palais Renaissance **9**
Paragon **24**
Promenade **23**
Robinson's **31**

Scotts Shopping Centre **18**
Shanghai Tang **22**
Shaw Centre **15**
Shaw House **14**
Tanglin Mall **1**
Tanglin Shopping Centre **3**
Tangs **19**
313@Somerset **29**
Tudor Court **2**
Wisma Atria **20**

The malls on Orchard Road are a tourist attraction in their own right, with smaller boutiques and specialty shops intermingled with huge department stores. Takashimaya and Isetan have been imported from Japan. **John Little** is the oldest department store in Singapore, followed by **Robinson's. Tangs** is significant, having grown from a cartful of merchandise nurtured by the business savvy of local entrepreneur C. K. Tang. Boutiques range from the younger styles of Topshop and Miss Selfridge to the sophisticated fashions of Chanel and Salvatore Ferragamo. You'll also find antiques, oriental carpets, art galleries and curio shops, HMV music stores, Kinokuniya and Borders bookstores, video arcades, and scores of restaurants, local food courts, fast-food joints, and coffeehouses—even a few bars, which open in the evenings (see chapter 9). It's hard to say when Orchard Road is not crowded, but it's definitely a mob scene on weekends, when folks have the free time to come and hang around, looking for fun.

Centrepoint   Centrepoint is home to Robinson's department store, which first opened in Singapore in 1858. Here you'll find about 150 other shops, plus fast-food outlets and a Times bookstore. 176 Orchard Rd. © 65/6235-6629.

Far East Plaza   At this crowded mall, the bustle of little shops will sell everything from CDs to punk fashions, luggage to camera equipment, eyewear to souvenirs. Mind yourself here: Most of these shops do not display prices, but rather gauge the price depending on how wealthy the customer appears. If you must shop here, use your shrewdest bargaining powers. It may pay off to wear an outfit that has seen better days. 14 Scotts Rd. © 65/6235-2411.

The Heeren   Thanks to the opening of a Singapore branch of Britain's HMV music stores, the Heeren is the big hangout for teens. The front entrance of the mall hums with towers of video monitors flashing and blaring the latest in American and British chart toppers. There is also a nice pub on a balcony overlooking the busy intersection. 260 Orchard Rd. © 65/6733-4725.

Hilton Shopping Gallery   The shopping arcade is the most exclusive in Singapore. Gucci, Donna Karan, Missoni, and Louis Vuitton are just a few of the international design houses that have made this their Singapore home. 581 Orchard Rd. © 65/6737-2233.

Lucky Plaza   The map of this place will take hours to decipher, as more than 400 stores are here. It's basically known for sportswear, camera equipment, watches, and luggage. If you buy electronics, please make sure you get an international warranty with your purchase. Also, like Far East Plaza, Lucky Plaza is a notorious rip-off problem for travelers. Make sure you come here prepared to fend off slick sales techniques. It may also help to take the government's advice and avoid touts and offers that sound too good to be true. 304 Orchard Rd. © 65/6235-3294.

Ngee Ann City/Takashimaya Shopping Centre   Takashimaya, a major Japanese department store import, anchors Ngee Ann City's many smaller boutiques. Alfred Dunhill, Chanel, Coach, Tiffany & Co., Royal Copenhagen, Waterford, and Wedgwood boutiques are found here, along with many other local and international fashion shops. 391 Orchard Rd. © 65/6738-2411.

Palais Renaissance   Shops here include upmarket boutiques like Prada, Versus, and DKNY. 390 Orchard Rd. © 65/6737-1520.

Paragon   Another upmarket shopping mall, with tenants including Diesel, Emanuel Ungaro, Escada, and Ferragamo. 290 Orchard Rd. © 65/6737-6993.

Shaw House   The main floors of Shaw House are taken up by Isetan, a large Japanese
department store with designer boutiques for men's and women's fashions, accessories, and cosmetics. On the fifth level, the Lido Theatre screens new releases from Hollywood and around the world. 350 Orchard Rd. ℂ 65/6735-4225.

Tanglin Mall ★   A Mecca for expatriates, this mall has charming boutiques filled with regional handicrafts for the home and interesting Southeast Asian ethnic-inspired fashions. 163 Tanglin Rd. ℂ 65/6736-4922.

Tanglin Shopping Centre ★★   Tanglin Shopping Centre is unique and fun. You won't find many clothing stores here, but you'll find shop after shop selling antiques, art, and collectibles—from curios to carpets. 19 Tanglin Rd. ℂ 65/6373-0849.

Tangs   Once upon a time, C. K. Tang peddled goods from an old cart in the streets of Singapore. An industrious fellow, he parlayed his business into a small department store. A hit from the start, Tangs has grown exponentially over the decades and now competes with the other international megastores that have moved in. But Tang's is truly Singaporean, and its history is a local legend. 320 Orchard Rd. ℂ 65/6737-5500.

Wisma Atria   Wisma Atria caters to the younger set. Here you'll find everything from Gap to Nine West mixed in with numerous eyewear, cosmetics, and high- and low-fashion boutiques. 435 Orchard Rd. ℂ 65/6235-2103.

MARINA BAY

The Marina Bay area arose from a plot of reclaimed land and now boasts the giant Suntec Singapore convention center and all the hotels, restaurants, and shopping malls that support it. Shopping here is convenient, with the major malls and hotels interconnected by covered walkways and pedestrian bridges, making it easy to get around with minimal exposure to the elements. It's also connected to Raffles City Shopping Centre by an underground shopping mall, the **City Link Mall** (ℂ **65/6339-9913**).

Marina Square   Marina Square is a huge complex that, in addition to a wide variety of shops, has a cinema, fast-food outlets and cafes, pharmacies, and convenience stores. 6 Raffles Blvd. ℂ 65/6335-2613.

Millenia Walk   Smaller than Marina Square, Millenia Walk has more upmarket boutiques, like Fendi, Guess?, and Liz Claiborne, to name a few. 9 Raffles Blvd. ℂ 65/6883-1122.

Suntec City Mall   Tons of shops selling fashion, sports equipment, books, CDs, plus restaurants and food courts, and a cinema adjacent to the Suntec convention center. 3 Temasek Blvd. ℂ 65/6825-2667.

AROUND THE CITY CENTER

Although the Historic District doesn't have as many malls as the Orchard Road area, it still has some good shopping. Raffles City Shopping Centre can be overwhelming in its size but is convenient because it sits right atop the City Hall MRT stop. One of my favorite places to go, however, is the very upmarket Raffles Hotel Shopping Arcade, where you can enhance your post-shopping high with a Singapore Sling.

Parco Bugis Junction   Here you'll find a few restaurants—fast food and fine dining—mixed in with clothing retailers, most of which sell fun fashions for younger tastes. 230 Victoria St. ℂ 65/6557-6557.

Raffles City Shopping Centre   Raffles City sits right on top of the City Hall MRT station, which makes it a very well-visited mall. Men's and women's fashions, books, cosmetics, and accessories are sold in shops here, along with gifts. 252 North Bridge Rd. ℂ 65/6338-7766.

Raffles Hotel Shopping Arcade   These shops are mostly haute couture; however, there is the Raffles Hotel gift shop for interesting souvenirs. For golfers, there's a Jack Nicklaus signature store. 328 North Bridge Rd. ℂ 65/6337-1886.

---

3 THE SHOPPING SCENE, PART 2: MULTICULTURAL SHOPPING

The most exciting shopping can be found within the ethnic enclaves throughout the city. Down narrow streets, bargains are to be had on all sorts of unusual items. If you're stuck for a gift idea, read on. Chances are, I'll mention something for even the most difficult person on your list.

CHINATOWN

For Chinese goods, nothing beats **Yue Hwa** ★★, 70 Eu Tong Sen St. (ℂ 65/6538-4222), a five-story Chinese emporium that's an attraction in its own right. The superb inventory includes all manner of silk wear (robes, underwear, blouses), embroidery and house linens, bolt silks, tailoring services (for perfect mandarin dresses), cloisonné (enamel work) jewelry and gifts, pottery, musical instruments, traditional Chinese clothing for men and women (from scholars' robes to coolie duds), jade and gold, cashmere, art supplies, herbs—I could go on and on. Prices are terrific. Plan to spend some time here.

For one-stop souvenir shopping, you can tick off half your list at **Chinatown Point,** aka the **Singapore Handicraft Center,** 133 New Bridge Rd. (ℂ 6534-0112), with dozens of small shops that sell mainly Chinese handicraft items from carved jade to imported Chinese classical instruments and lacquerware. The best gifts there include hand-carved chops (Chinese seals), with a few shops offering good selections of carved stone, wood, bone, glass, and ivory chops ready to be carved to your specifications. Simple designs are affordable, although some of the more elaborate chops and carvings fetch a handsome sum. You can also commission a personalized Chinese scroll painting or calligraphy piece.

In the heart of Chinatown, Pagoda and Trengganu streets are closed to vehicular traffic and host a vibrant **Chinatown Street Market** (open daily about 11am–11pm), where you can find a wide variety of Chinese silk robes, Indonesian batik souvenirs, Vietnamese lacquerware, Thai silk home linens, and Singaporean souvenirs—the list goes on. I've found the prices here to be inflated. If you're on a shoestring budget, find similar items at the market at the corner of Trengganu and Sago Streets, called **Chinatown Complex,** where you may find it easier to bargain.

My all-time favorite gift idea? Spend an afternoon learning the traditional Chinese tea ceremony at the **Tea Chapter,** 9–11 Neil Rd. (ℂ 65/6226-1175), and pick up a tea set—they have a lovely selection of tea pots, cups, and accessories, as well as quality teas for sale. When you return home, you'll be ready to give a fabulous gift—not just a tea set, but your own cultural performance as well. Another neat place to visit is **Kwong**

Chen Beverage Trading, 16 Smith St. (© 65/6223-6927), for some Chinese teas in 9
handsome tins. Although the teas are really inexpensive, they're packed in lovely tins—
great to buy lots to bring back as smaller gifts. For serious tea aficionados or those curious
about Traditional Chinese Medicine (TCM), stop by **Eu Yan Sang,** 269 South Bridge
Rd. (© 65/6223-6333; www.euyansang.com.sg), where they have stocks of very fine
(and expensive) teas, plus herbal remedies for health. For something a little more
unusual, check out **Siong Moh Paper Products,** 39 Mosque St. (© 65/6224-3125),
which carries a full line of ceremonial items. Pick up some joss sticks (temple incense) or
joss paper (books of thin sheets of paper, stamped in reds and yellows with bits of gold
and silver leaf). Definitely a conversation piece, as is the hell money, stacks of false paper
notes that believers burn at the temple for their ancestors to use for cash in the afterlife.
Perfect for that friend who has everything. Also, if you duck over to **Sago Lane** while
you're in the neighborhood, there are a few souvenir shops that sell Chinese kites and
Cantonese Opera masks—cool for kids.

ARAB STREET

On Arab Street, shop for handicrafts from Malaysia and Indonesia. I go for sarongs at
Hadjee Textiles, 75 Arab St. (© 65/6298-1943), for their stacks of folded sarongs in
beautiful colors and traditional patterns. They're perfect for traveling, as they're light-
weight, but can serve you well as a dressy skirt, bed sheet, beach blanket, window shade,
bath towel, or whatever you need—when I'm on the road, I can't live without mine. Buy
a few here and the prices really drop. For modern styles of batik, check out **Basharahil
Brothers,** 101 Arab St. (© 65/6296-0432), for their very interesting designs, but don't
forget to see their collection of fine silk batiks in the back. For batik household linens,
you can't beat **Maruti Textiles,** 93 Arab St. (© 65/6392-0253), where you'll find high-
quality placemats and napkins, tablecloths, pillow covers, and quilts from India. The
buyer for this shop has a good eye for style.

I've also found a few shops in the area that carry **handicrafts** from Southeast Asia. For
antiques and curios, try **Gim Joo Trading,** 16 Baghdad St. (© 65/6293-5638), a jumble
of the unusual, some of it old. A lovely antiques shop, **Melor's Curios,** 39 Bussorah St.
(© 65/6292-3934), is almost a mini-museum of furnishings, home fixtures, and objets
d'art that will fill any Singaporean with nostalgia.

Other unique treasures include the large assortment of fragrance oils at **Jamal Kazura
Aromatics,** 21 Bussorah St. (© 65/6293-3320). Muslims are forbidden from consum-
ing alcohol in any form (a proscription that includes the wearing of alcohol-based perfumes as well), so these oil-based perfumes re-create designer scents plus other floral and
heady creations. Check out their delicate cut-glass bottles and atomizers as well. Finally,
for the crafter in your life, **Kin Lee & Co.,** 109 Arab St. (© 65/6291-1411), carries a
complete line of patterns and accessories to make local Peranakan beaded slippers. In
vivid colors and floral designs, these traditional slippers were always made by hand, to be
attached later to a wooden sole. The finished versions are exquisite, plus they're fun to
make.

LITTLE INDIA

I have a ball shopping the crowded streets of Little India. The best shopping is on Serangoon Road, where Singapore's Indian community heads for Indian imports and cultural
items. The absolute best place to start is **Mustafa Centre** ★★, 320 Serangoon Rd./145
Syed Alwi Rd., at the corner of Serangoon and Syed Alwi roads (© 65/6295-5855), but

be warned, you can spend the whole day there—and night, too, because Mustafa's is open 24 hours every day. This maze of a department store fills 2 city blocks full of imported items from India. Granted, much of it is everyday stuff, but the real finds are rows of saris and silk fabrics; two floors of jaw-dropping gold jewelry in Indian designs; an entire supermarket packed with spices and packets of instant curries; ready-made Indian-style tie-dye and embroidered casual wear; incense and perfume oils; cotton tapestries and textiles for the home—the list goes on. And prices can't be beat, seriously.

Little India offers all sorts of small finds, especially throughout **Little India Arcade** (48 Serangoon Rd.) and just across the street on Campbell Lane at **Kuna's,** 3 Campbell Lane (© **65/6294-2700**). Here you can buy inexpensive Indian costume jewelry like bangles, earrings, and necklaces in exotic designs and a wide assortment of decorative dots (called *pottu* in Tamil) to grace your forehead. Indian handicrafts include brass work, woodcarvings, dyed tapestries, woven cotton household linens, small curio items, very inexpensive incense, colorful pictures of Hindu gods, and other ceremonial items. Look here also for Indian cooking pots and household items.

Across the street from Little India Arcade, **Tekka Centre** is being renovated. This popular market carried stall after stall of inexpensive *salwar kameez,* or Punjabi suits, the three-piece outfits—long tunic over pants, with matching shawl—worn by northern Indian ladies, plus lots of cheap Indian-made prêt-a-port. They've all put up in a temporary location along Race Course Road, not far from Tekka Centre.

Punjab Bazaar, #01–07 Little India Arcade, 48 Serangoon Rd. (© **65/6296-0067**), carries a more upmarket choice of *salwar kameez,* in many styles and fabrics. If nothing strikes your fancy at Punjab Bazaar, try **Roopalee Fashions,** a little farther down at 88 Serangoon Rd. (© **65/6298-0558**). Both shops carry sandals, bags, and other accessories to complement your new outfit.

4 BEST BUYS A TO Z

ANTIQUES A 5-minute walk north of Orchard Road is the mellow **Tanglin Shopping Centre** (Tanglin Rd.), whose quiet halls are just packed with little antiques boutiques. Tanglin is a quiet place, which adds to the museum feel as you stroll past window displays of paintings, tapestries, and curios made of jade or brass—all kinds of quality collectibles and gifts. A couple of good shops to visit are **Antiques of the Orient,** #02–40 Tanglin Shopping Centre (© **65/6734-9351**), selling old prints and maps, and **Aspara,** #02–30 Tanglin Shopping Centre (© **65/6735-5018**), with an interesting collection of Chinese and Burmese antiques. There are many more—this is a place to really explore.

If you continue along Tanglin Road, you'll find **Tudor Court,** with a few more interesting shops inside, including **Antiquity Hands of the Hills** (© **65/6735-5332**), with textiles, jewelry, and curio items from Tibet.

To get an eyeful of some local furnishings in antique Indonesian, Chinese, and Peranakan styles, take a taxi out to **Dempsey Road** and stroll amid the many warehouses. Inside each are dealers like the **Shang Antique,** full of Chinese antiques and Burmese teak, at Blk. 16, #01–04/05 Dempsey Rd. (© **65/6388-8838**); and the **Renaissance Art Gallery,** with displays of Chinese figurines, Southeast Asian Buddha images, and chests, at Blk. 15, #01–06 Dempsey Rd. (© **65/6474-0338**). There are more than a dozen places here, each specializing in different wares. Some have large furniture pieces, from carved teak Indonesian-style reproduction furniture to authentic pieces from mainland

China. Some have smaller collectible items, like carved scale weights from the old opium trade or collections of Buddha images. Oriental carpet shops are also mixed in. The stores on Dempsey Road are all open daily from around 11am to 6:30pm, though they close for a short lunch break at midday. As with all of the antiques shops in Singapore, they'll help you locate a reliable shipper to send your purchases home.

ASIAN FASHION You can find *cheongsam,* those cute little sleeveless shifts with the Mandarin collars and frog closures, in ready-made polyester styles at souvenir shops all over Chinatown. When you're ready to get serious, go to **Yue Hwa,** 70 Eu Tong Sen St. (© **65/6538-4222**), where they hire expert *cheongsam* tailors from Hong Kong who fit the dress perfectly to your body, help you select your fabric from a wide range of pure Chinese silks, and choose your own preferred style. Expect to drop about S$450 (US$302/£203) for a full-length *cheongsam,* a small price to pay for a drop-dead sexy, one-of-a-kind formal dress.

If Bollywood blockbusters make you drool, you'll die for **Stylemart,** 149–151 Selegie Rd. (© **65/6338-2073**). Specializing in tailored Indian formalwear, they have rows of Indian-style brocade silks that are simply edible and an enormous collection of breathtakingly exotic beaded silks to make your eyes twinkle. They will fashion anything you want—traditional or modern dresses, gowns, and pantsuits. A simple formal gown with shawl in silk brocade will start at S$500 (US$335/£225). Pay more for beaded styles. It's worth it.

A couple of boutiques are making modern fashions with quirky traditional twists. **Shanghai Tang,** at Takashimaya Shopping Centre, Ngee Ann City, 391 Orchard Rd., #02-12G (© **65/6737-3537**), sells whimsical interpretations of traditional Chinese clothing, in campy colored luxurious silk. **Mumbai Sé,** Palais Renaissance #01-00, 390 Orchard Rd. (© **65/6733-7188**), carries a wide selection of casual- and formalwear from India's hottest young fashion designers, most of whom use Indian textiles that are to die for.

The true authentic Singaporean style is that of the Nonyas, Peranakan ladies who wear the traditional *sarong kebaya.* These ladies pair fine sarongs with delicate lace blouses *(kebaya)* closed with silver or gold brooches and accessorized with beaded slippers and a bag. Still today you will see Singaporean ladies don *sarong kebaya* for weddings and special parties. If you'd like to outfit yourself in one, the place to go is **Rumah Bebe** (113 East Coast Rd.; © **65/6247-8781**), located in Katong, the heart of Peranakan culture. Proprietress Bebe Seet is a local *sarong kebaya* expert. Her shop sells fine batiks (much nicer than the ordinary ones on Arab St.), and matching blouses. She also specializes in beaded slippers, teaching classes out of the back of her shop.

ELECTRONICS At **Funan Digitalife Mall,** 109 North Bridge Rd. (© **65/6336-8327**), you can find computers and accessories—there are many, many shops, each with special offers and deals, so compare when you shop. At **Sim Lim Square,** 1 Rochor Canal Rd. (© **65/6332-5839**), you can find not only computers, but office and home electronics as well. Bargain hard here—prices are not marked.

If you're in the market for photographic equipment, the best place to go is **Cathay Photo,** #01–05, #01–07/08, #01–11/14 Peninsula Plaza, 111 North Bridge Rd. (© **65/6337-4274**).

FABRICS Exquisite fabrics like Chinese silk, Thai silk, batiks, and inexpensive gingham are very affordable and the selections are extensive. Most fabrics are sold by the meter and there is no standard width, so make sure you inquire when you're purchasing off the bolt. Be sure to check out **Arab Street.** I adore the selection of silks from India, Thailand, Japan, and Europe at **Poppy Fabric,** 111 Arab St. (© **65/6296-6352**). Buy modern batik fabrics at **Basharahil Bros.,** 101 Arab St. (© **65/6296-0432**), and be sure to take a peek at their batik silks in the back—just gorgeous!

For other finds, a few shops along Serangoon Road in Little India have some fine Indian silks. The largest selection is at **Mustafa Centre,** 320 Serangoon Rd. (© **65/6295-5855**).

FINE ART Singaporean interest in art has created a market far beyond its shores. The island is now a center for trading fine pieces between East and West, so you'll find quality contemporary works from the most celebrated new artists from Southeast Asia, South Asia, and East Asia.

Six galleries are packed into the **Artrium@MICA** (The Ministry of Information, Communications, and The Arts), 140 Hill St., including **Gajah Gallery,** with regional fine arts (© **65/6737-4202**), and **Soobin Gallery** (© **65/6837-2777**).

Artfolio's exhibits at #02–12 **Raffles Hotel Arcade,** 328 North Bridge Rd. (© **65/6334-4677**), always make me wish I were rich enough to collect. If you're in the market for fine arts from the mainland (China, that is), this is the place to look.

Tanglin Shopping Centre also has a ton of art galleries. For contemporary Southeast Asian art, visit **Hakaren Art Gallery,** #02–43 Tanglin Shopping Centre (© **65/6733-3382**). **Kwan Hua Art Gallery,** #02–65 Tanglin Shopping Centre (© **65/6735-5663**), carries a collection of Chinese brush paintings and oils.

JEWELRY Jewelry can be a bargain. Gold, which is sold at the day's rate, is fashioned into modern Western styles and into styles that suit Chinese and Indian tastes. *Note:* Chinese and Indian jewelers work with only 18-karat quality and above, usually 22- and 24-karat designs—Chinese gold tends to be bright yellow, while Indian gold has a reddish hue to it. Loose stones, either precious or semiprecious, are abundant in many reputable shops and can be set for you.

For contemporary upmarket jewels and settings, the most trusted dealer in Singapore is **Larry Jewelry,** #01-12 Paragon Shopping Centre, 290 Orchard Rd. (© **65/6732-3222**), but be prepared to drop some serious coin.

Peek in the window displays of the gold shops along Serangoon Road, and you'll see all kinds of Indian-style gold necklaces and bangles. Each Indian ethnic group has its own traditional patterns, all of them featuring intricate filigree. The selection at **Mustafa Centre,** 320 Serangoon Rd. (© **65/6295-5855**), is absolutely mind-blowing. I can't imagine the staggering value of all their merchandise. Don't forget there are two levels here; the best stuff is downstairs.

For Chinese jade, try **Yue Hwa,** 70 Eu Tong Sen St. (© **65/6538-4222**). Jade is tough for Westerners to buy, because it's hard to discern a good piece from a bad one. Yue Hwa has fixed prices, but the quality is always dependable.

A unique gift or souvenir, a gold-plated orchid is something you don't find every day. The process was developed in the 1970s and is exclusive to Singapore. Different orchid species make up brooches, earrings, and pendants at local jewelry designer **RISIS,** Singapore Botanic Gardens, 1 Cluny Rd. (© **65/6475-5014**), with additional outlets at #01-064 Suntec City Mall, 3 Temasek Blvd. (© **65/6338-8250**), and #01-40 Centrepoint Shopping Centre, Orchard Road (© **65/6235-0988**).

MEN'S TAILORING There are some fine men's tailors for suits and slacks made to fit, but beware touts along Orchard Road. If you can get a cheap price, chances are, you're getting a cheap suit. **Justmen's,** 19 Tanglin Rd., #01–36/39 Tanglin Shopping Centre (✆ **65/6737-4800**), is an institution within the expatriate community here. They are well versed in current fashions, carry the best selection of fine fabrics, and can fit your measurements perfectly—this will probably be one of the best suits you've ever had. The prices are a steal, starting from S$700 (US$469/£315) for a two-piece suit.

ORIENTAL CARPETS   Once you've walked on a hand-knotted **Nain** in your bare feet, trailed your fingers along the pile of an antique **Heriz,** or admired the sensuous colors of a **Tabriz,** you'll never look at broadloom again with the same forbearance. If luxury Oriental carpets seem too expensive for your pocketbook, Singapore prices will surprise you.

Hassan's Carpets, #03–01/06 Tanglin Shopping Centre (✆ **65/6737-5626**), has been a fixture in Singapore for generations. Proprietor Suliman Hamid is the local authority on carpets, having advised on and supplied the carpets for the restoration of Raffles Hotel. He and his staff know the background of every rug and have wonderful stories to tell. They forego the hard sales pitch for more civilized discourse on carpet appreciation. It's an afternoon well spent. Carpets can be shipped home for you, with smaller rugs wrapped small enough to hand-carry onboard a plane.

If you still want to see more carpets, you can take a taxi out to Dempsey Road, where you'll find a few warehouses filled with stock.

PEWTER   Royal Selangor, the famous Malaysian pewter manufacturer since 1885, rode high on the Malaysian tin business at the turn of the 20th century, pewter being a tin alloy. This firm is based in Kuala Lumpur and has eight showrooms in Singapore. If you're really into pewter, you can visit the Royal Selangor Pewter Centre, 3A River Valley Rd., 01–01 Clarke Quay (✆ **65/6268-9600;** www.royalselangor.com.sg), where they have an exhibit of the history of pewter works in the region, with pewtersmith demonstrations daily from 9am to 9pm for S$2 (US$1.35/90p) entry. For S$30 (US$20/£14), you can sign up for a half-hour hands-on pewtersmith workshop. If you just want to shop, you can also stop in at their showrooms at #03–24 Raffles City Shopping Centre (✆ **65/6339-3958**); #02–40 Paragon, 290 Orchard Rd. (✆ **65/6235-6633**); and #02–127 Marina Square (✆ **65/6339-3115**).

POTTERY   Antique porcelain items can be found in the many small shops along Pagoda and Trenagganu streets in Chinatown. But the ultimate in pottery shopping is a place the locals refer to as the "pottery jungle." **Thow Kwang Industry Pte. Ltd.** is a taxi ride away at 85 Lorong Tawas off Jalan Bahar (✆ **65/6265-5808**). This backwoods place has row after row of pots, lamps, umbrella stands—you name it. There's even a room with antique pieces.

SHOES   You can seriously go nuts over cheap shoes here. We're talking prices from S$9.90 to S$39 (US$6.65–US$26/£4.45–£18) for cute little sandals, dressy shoes, and work pumps. Granted, they're not Ferragamo, but at these prices, you can literally buy a pair of shoes to match every outfit in your closet. Unfortunately, if you're bigger than a U.S. size 8, finding your size will be tough. Otherwise, my two favorite places for shoes on the cheap-cheap are the shoe departments at **Seiyu,** Parco Bugis Junction (✆ **65/ 6563-1106**), and **OG,** Orchard Point (✆ **65/6317-2222**).

SOUTHEAST ASIAN HANDICRAFTS   At **Lim's,** 211 Holland Ave., #02–01 Holland Road Shopping Centre (✆ **65/6467-1300**), and #02–154/155 VivoCity (✆ **65/6376-9468**), you'll find items for the home from all over Southeast Asia; think Pier One

Imports, only cheaper. Vietnamese lacquerware and handbags, Indonesian teakwood carvings and batik linens, Thai silk pillow covers and tableware, Chinese pottery and arts, the list goes on and on. Prices are very reasonable, and the merchandise is all of good quality.

I'm a big fan of local clothing designer Peter Hoe's boutique, **Olathe,** at 30 Victoria St., #01–05 CHIJMES (© **65/6339-6880**). This Malaysian fabric and clothing designer fashions very handsome individual fabric patterns pieced together in styles to suit Western wardrobes.

9

Singapore After Dark

Cosmopolitan Singapore has a small but well-developed nightlife, with a clubbing scene that has earned international attention and a burgeoning arts scene that delights audiences nightly with world-class music and theater performances, insightful local and cultural productions, and gritty fringe shows. After a full day of sightseeing, make sure you save some energy for nightlife, which is a window into a different side of life in the Lion City.

As you plan your trip, be sure to log onto the **Singapore Tourism Board**'s site, at www.visitsingapore.com, to find out about worthwhile events that may coincide with your visit. A few of the most notable are the **Mosaic Music Festival** (www.mosaicmusicfestival.com), held for 2 weeks every March and featuring international and local musical performers from a range of genres; The **Singapore International Film Festival** (www.filmfest.org.sg), 2 weeks of international arthouse films with an emphasis on the best releases from Asian directors, held every April; The **Singapore Arts Festival** (www.

singaporeartsfest.com), every May into June, a month-long extravaganza of delightful international performances at various venues city wide; **BayBeats** (www.baybeats.com.sg), an outdoor rock festival featuring the best local alternative bands, with international indie rock guests; and the **Singapore Sun Festival** (www.singaporesunfestival.com), held every October, packed with events that pay homage to the finer things in life, from cuisine to lifestyle and culture.

Performances can range from highbrow orchestral productions at the city's exquisite Esplanade-Theatres on the Bay concert hall to informal talks about local arts at home-grown cultural centers. The offerings presented in this guide will give you a terrific starting point to explore those events that interest you most.

If partying is your thing, Singapore's nightclub scene has a diverse range of possibilities, from intimate music bars to seaside chill-out cafes or glamorous clubs. The venues in this guide have been selected to provide something for everyone and every mood.

1 TIPS ON SINGAPORE NIGHTLIFE

INFORMATION   Major cultural festivals are highly publicized by the **Singapore Tourism Board (STB),** who will give you complete details at their Visitors Centres (see p. 60 for locations) or on their website (www.visitsingapore.com). Another good resource is the Life! section of *The Straits Times* newspaper, which lists events for each day, plus theater and cinema listings. *Where Singapore,* a free magazine with local events listings, is available at STB kiosks as well. Another freebie, *I-S Magazine,* promotes Singapore's clubbing lifestyle.

TICKETS   Sistic (*©* 65/6348-5555; www.sistic.com.sg) handles bookings for almost all theater performances, concert dates, and special events. Their website offers a comprehensive events schedule, with online booking and ticket payment. (Tickets can be picked up at the venue prior to the performance.) Visit them online or at one of their

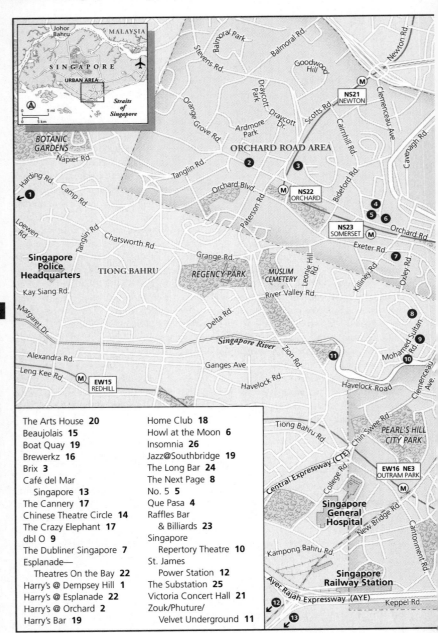

The Arts House **20**
Beaujolais **15**
Boat Quay **19**
Brewerkz **16**
Brix **3**
Café del Mar
  Singapore **13**
The Cannery **17**
Chinese Theatre Circle **14**
The Crazy Elephant **17**
dbl O **9**
The Dubliner Singapore **7**
Esplanade—
  Theatres On the Bay **22**
Harry's @ Dempsey Hill **1**
Harry's @ Esplanade **22**
Harry's @ Orchard **2**
Harry's Bar **19**

Home Club **18**
Howl at the Moon **6**
Insomnia **26**
Jazz@Southbridge **19**
The Long Bar **24**
The Next Page **8**
No. 5 **5**
Que Pasa **4**
Raffles Bar
  & Billiards **23**
Singapore
  Repertory Theatre **10**
St. James
  Power Station **12**
The Substation **25**
Victoria Concert Hall **21**
Zouk/Phuture/
  Velvet Underground **11**

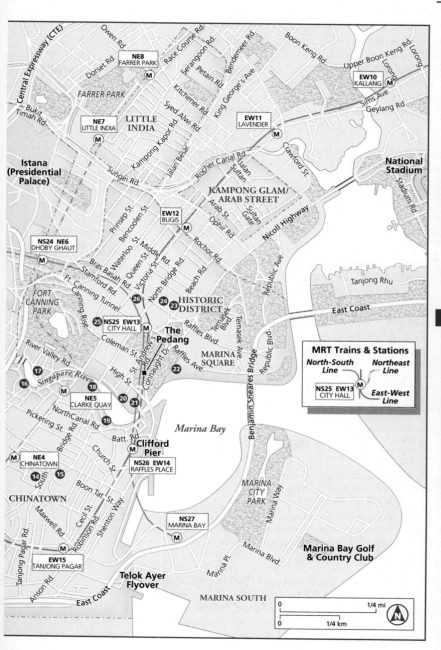

centrally located kiosks at The Centrepoint, Millenia Walk, Plaza Singapura, Raffles City Shopping Centre, VivoCity, or Wisma Atria.

HOURS   Theater and dance performances can begin anywhere between 7:30 and 9pm. Don't be late—at Esplanade, they turn latecomers away. Many bars open in the late afternoon, a few as early as lunchtime. Disco and entertainment clubs usually open around 6pm but generally don't get lively until 10 or 11pm. Closing time for bars and clubs is at 1 or 2am on weekdays, 3 or 4am on weekends. A few have extended hours until 6am.

DRINK PRICES   Because of the government's added tariff, alcoholic beverage prices are high everywhere, whether in a hotel bar or a neighborhood pub. "House pour" drinks (made with inexpensive brands of alcohol) are between S$8 and S$14 (US$5.35–US$9.40/£3.60–£6.30)—this is considered cheap. A glass of house wine will cost between S$10 and S$15 (US$6.70–US$10/£4.50–£6.75), depending on whether it's a red or a white. A pint of local draft beer (Tiger, brewed in Singapore) is around S$10 (US$6.70/£4.50). Hotel establishments are, on average, the most expensive venues, while standalone pubs and cafes are better value. Almost every bar and club has a happy hour in the early evenings, and discounts can be up to 50% off for house pours and drafts. Most of the dance and entertainment clubs charge covers, but they will usually include one or more drinks. Hooray for ladies' nights—usually Wednesdays—when those of the feminine persuasion get in for free and sometimes even drink for free, too.

DRESS CODE   Many clubs will require smart casual attire. Feel free to be trendy, but avoid dressing too casual or you may be turned away. Local clubbers dress up for a night on the town, usually in fashionista threads.

SAFETY   You'll be fairly safe out during the wee hours in most parts of the city, and even a single woman alone has little to worry about. You can always get home safely in a taxi, which, fortunately, isn't too hard to find even late at night, with a couple of exceptions: When clubs close, there's usually a mob of revelers scrambling for cabs. Also, after midnight, a 50% surcharge is added to the fare, so it's become common for drivers to disappear from 11pm until midnight, when they can return to work and earn more in fares.

2 THE BAR & CLUB SCENE

Singaporeans love to go out at night, whether it's to lounge around in a cozy wine bar or to groove on a dance floor until 6am. This city has become pretty eclectic in its entertainment choices, so you'll find everything from live jazz to acid jazz, from polished cover bands to internationally acclaimed guest DJs. The nightlife is happening. Local celebrities and the young, wealthy, and beautiful are the heroes of the scene, and their quest for the "coolest" spot keeps the club scene on its toes.

BARS

Brix   In the basement of the Grand Hyatt Regency, Brix hosts a good house band and international visiting music groups as well. A pickup joint of sorts, it's a bit more sophisticated than others. The Music Bar features live jazz and R&B, while the Wine & Whiskey Bar serves up a fine selection of wine, Scotch, and cognac. Hours are Sunday to Wednesday 9pm to 3am, Thursday to Saturday 9pm to 4am. Happy hour nightly, from

Café del Mar Singapore ★★★   Savor cooling cocktails while you sink your toes in the sand and gaze at the tropical sunset. Café del Mar, based on the successful Ibiza formula, is pure tropical island paradise, with a soundtrack of chill-out grooves, just minutes from Singapore's urban center. The Sentosa island location makes for an all-night beach party—you can even have dinner here from a Mediterranean menu. Singapore's sun sets from about 7 to 7:30pm, so be sure to come early for the Sundowner Special happy hour from 5 to 7pm, with two-for-one cocktails, so you can get lit before it gets dark. Hours are Monday to Thursday 11am to 1am, Friday 11am to 4am, Saturday 10am to 4am, and Sunday 10am to 1am. 40 Siloso Beach Walk, Sentosa Island. ℂ 65/6235-1296. www.cafedelmar.com.sg.

The Crazy Elephant   Crazy Elephant is the city's address for blues-rock. Hang out amid the breezes blowing off the river while listening to classic rock and blues by resident bands. This place has hosted, in addition to some excellent local and regional guitarists, international greats such as Rick Derringer, Eric Burdon, and Walter Trout. It's an unpretentious place to chill out and have a cold one. Beer is reasonably priced as well. Hours are Sunday to Thursday 5pm to 1am, and Friday and Saturday 5pm to 2am, with daily happy hour 5 to 9pm. 3E River Valley Rd., #01–03/04 Traders Market, Clarke Quay. ℂ 65/6337-7859. www.crazyelephant.com.

The Dubliner Singapore   Located in a restored colonial building, Dubliner's got great atmosphere, with vaulted ceilings, tiled floors and pretty plasterwork, and outdoor seating on the veranda. It's also a pretty decent Irish pub, with a friendly staff and a cast of regulars from local and expat drinking crowds. Sports matches are broadcast regularly (mainly soccer), and there's a variety of cold beer on tap. Hours are Sunday to Thursday 11am to 2am, and Friday and Saturday 11am to 3am; daily happy hour runs 5 to 8pm. Winsland Conservation House, 165 Penang Rd. ℂ 65/6735-2220. www.dublinersingapore.com.

Home Club   The "home" of Singapore's arty underground clubbing scene, this small down-to-earth club hosts local DJs that specialize in alternative and retro grooves and indie band parties. True to its name, expect a homey atmosphere, furnished with mismatched cozy chairs and sofas. The crowd is equally funky, with a fun mix of young arty music heads. Open Tuesday to Thursday 9pm to 3am, Friday and Saturday 10pm to 6am. The Riverwalk, #B1-01/06, 20 Upper Circular Rd. ℂ 65/9877-6055. www.homeclub.com.sg. Cover charges are sometimes levied but include a complimentary drink.

Howl at the Moon ★★   Guaranteed laughs, this piano bar features a pair of dueling pianists who play sing-a-long songs all night long, interspersed with impromptu banter. The audience itself becomes part of the performance, and by the end of the night, everyone is guaranteed to have made new friends. This bar also hosts stand-up comedy nights, open-mike sessions, and late-night dancing. Open Tuesday through Sunday from 6pm till late. 2nd floor, Peranakan Place Complex, 180 Orchard Rd. ℂ 65/6838-0281. www.howlatthemoon.com.sg. Cover charges S$20 (US$13/£9) Fri–Sat after 8pm.

The Long Bar ★   Touristy and expensive, the Long Bar is still a cultural institution. With tiled mosaic floors, large shuttered windows, and punkah fans waving above, this Raffles Hotel bar has tried to retain much of the charm of yesteryear so you can enjoy a Singapore Sling in its birthplace. And truly, the thrill at the Long Bar is tossing back one of these sweet, juicy drinks while pondering the Singapore adventures of all the famous actors, writers, and artists who came through here in the first decades of the 20th century.

If you're not inspired by the poetry of the moment, stick around and get juiced for the pop/reggae band at 9pm, which is quite good. Hours are Sunday to Thursday 11am to 12:30am, Friday and Saturday 11am to 1:30am. Happy hour nightly 6 to 9pm, with special deals on pitchers of beer and some mixed drinks. A Singapore Sling is S$26 (US$17/£12), and a Sling with souvenir glass costs S$37 (US$25/£17). Raffles Hotel Arcade, Raffles Hotel, 1 Beach Rd. (℃ 65/6337-1230. www.raffles.com.

The Next Page Mohamed Sultan Road was Singapore's hottest nightspot in the 1990s, but today few bars stand out. This bar started it all but has since changed names, owners, and locations too many times. A freaky Chinese dream in an old Singaporean shophouse, the bar's main room has old walls of crumbling stucco washed in sexy Chinese red and lanterns glowing crimson in the air shaft rising above the island bar. The crowd is mainly young professionals who on the weekends have been known to dance on the bar. The back has a bit more space for seating, darts, and a pool table. A small snack menu is available. Open Sunday to Thursday 5pm to 1am, Friday and Saturday 5pm to 3am. Happy hour daily 5 to 9pm. 17 Mohamed Sultan Rd. (℃ 65/6235-6967.

No. 5 Down Peranakan Place are a few bars, one of which is No. 5, a cool, dark place just dripping with Southeast Asian ambience, from its 1910 shophouse exterior to its partially crumbling interior walls hung with rich woodcarvings. The hardwood floors and beamed ceilings are complemented by seating areas cozied with oriental carpets and kilim throw pillows. Upstairs is more conventional table-and-chair seating. The glow of the skylighted air shaft and the whirring fans above make this an ideal place to stop for a cool drink on a hot afternoon. In the evenings, be prepared for a lively mix of people. Open Monday to Thursday noon to 2am, Friday and Saturday noon to 3am, Sunday 5pm to 2am. Happy hour daily noon to 9pm. 5 Emerald Hill Rd. (℃ 65/6732-0818. www.emeraldhillgroup.com.

MICROBREWERIES

Brewerkz Brewerkz, with outside seating along the river and an airy contemporary style inside—like a giant warehouse built around brewing kettles and copper pipes—brews the best house beer in Singapore. The bar menu features five tasty brew selections from recipes created by their English brew master: Nut Brown Ale, Red Ale, Wiesen, Bitter, and Indian Pale Ale (which, by the way, has the highest alcohol content). Their American-cuisine lunch, dinner, and snack menu is also very good—I recommend planning a meal here as well. Open Monday to Thursday noon to midnight, Friday and Saturday noon to 1am, and Sunday 11am to midnight. Happy hour is held daily noon to 3pm, with two-for-one beers. #01–05 Riverside Point, 30 Merchant Rd. (℃ 65/6438-7438. www.brewerkz.com.

JAZZ BARS

Harry's Bar ★ The official after-work drink stop for finance professionals from nearby Shenton Way, Harry's biggest claim to fame is that it was bank-buster Nick Leeson's favorite bar. But don't let the power ties put you off. Harry's is a cool place, from airy riverside seating to cozy tables next to the stage. Harry's is known for its live jazz and R&B music, which is always good. Of all the choices along Boat Quay, Harry's remains the classiest; even though it's also the most popular, you can usually get a seat. Upstairs, the wine bar is very laid back, with plush sofas and dimly lit seating areas. Recently, Harry's outposts have been opening all over the city: **Harry's @ Dempsey Hill,** Blk. 11 Dempsey Rd., #01-17A (℃ 65/6471-9018); **Harry's @ Esplanade,** Esplanade Mall

#01–05/07, 8 Raffles Ave. (✆ **65/6334-0132**); and **Harry's @ Orchard,** Orchard Towers, #01–05 and #02–08/09, 1 Claymore Dr. (✆ **65/6736-7330**). Open Sunday to Thursday 11am to 1am, Friday and Saturday 11am to 2am. Happy hour daily 11am to 9pm. 28 Boat Quay. ✆ **65/6538-3029.** www.harrys.com.sg.

Jazz@Southbridge (Finds)   While most jazz venues in Singapore adopt a relaxed definition of jazz, incorporating jazzy pop and blues rock into their repertoires, this small and welcoming venue keeps it strictly jazz. Performances change nightly, with excellent regular musicians and fantastic international greats. The place gets crowded, but people are friendly, especially if you want to talk about music. When visiting performers play, a door cover is charged. Open Tuesday to Sunday from 5:30pm until 1am (sometimes later). 82B Boat Quay. ✆ **65/6327-4671.** www.southbridgejazz.com.sg.

Raffles Bar & Billiards   Rich with the kind of elegance only history can provide, Raffles Bar & Billiards began as a bar in 1896 and over the decades has been transformed to perform various functions as the hotel's needs dictated. In its early days, legend has it that a patron shot the last tiger in Singapore under a pool table here. Whether or not the tiger part is true, one of its two billiards tables is an original piece, still in use after 100 years. In fact, many of the fixtures and furniture here are original Raffles antiques, including the lights above the billiards tables and the scoreboards, and are marked with small brass placards. In the evenings, a jazzy little trio shakes the ghosts out of the rafters, while the well-heeled lounge around enjoying single malts, cognacs, coffee, port, champagne, chocolates, and imported cigars. Expect to drop a small fortune. Open daily 11:30am to 12:30am. Raffles Hotel, 1 Beach Rd. ✆ **65/6331-1746.** www.raffles.com.

CLUBS

The Cannery   Clarke Quay houses a number of dining and nightclub venues, many of which are operated under one management: The Cannery. Venues include **Zirca,** a mega dance club with a Cirque du Soleil feel; **Rebel,** a hip-hop club with a street graffiti attitude; and **Yello Jello Retrobar,** spinning nostalgic dance tunes; plus a few more lounges and cafes that serve a variety of styles for discriminating clubbers. Hours vary from club to club. Clarke Quay, 3B River Valley Rd. ✆ **65/6887-3733.** www.the-cannery.com. Cover charges vary from club to club.

dbl O   This cavernous place with a light-up wall and dance floor is very popular with those who want to hang out without the pretenses of some of the newer fashion-victim clubs. Two smaller dance floors within the club play hip-hop and house grooves, and the club has a rooftop terrace garden for alfresco cocktails. Open Tuesday to Friday 8pm to 3am and Saturday 8pm to 4am. 11 Unity St. #01–24 Robertson Walk. ✆ **65/6735-2008.** www. emeraldhillgroup.com. Cover charges vary for men and women, depending on the night.

Insomnia   Modeled after three popular sister clubs in Hong Kong, Insomnia is named for its hours: 24/7. It's one of only a few clubs in Singapore that has a license to operate 24 hours a day every day. A stable of bands revolve from club to club, playing dance rock, Top 40 hits, and pop to a packed dance floor. It has plenty of outside seating and also serves meals. It shares a central location at Chijmes with a number of other bars and restaurants, so you can come here and check out several nightlife options in one place. Open daily 24 hours. 30 Victoria St., Chijmes. ✆ **65/6338-6883.** www.liverockmusic247.com. No cover charge.

St James Power Station   An old 1927 coal-fired power station has been given a new lease on life as a Mecca for clubbing. Its 60,000 square feet of space has been divided between nine independent clubs, each in a different flavor. For a cultural experience, try **Dragonfly,** with nightly Mandarin pop music shows featuring live performers and dancers on stage. Or **Movida,** a dance club that specializes in world beats. Hours vary from club to club. 3 Sentosa Gateway, #01-01. (C) **65/6270-7676.** www.stjamespowerstation.com. Cover charges vary from club to club.

Zouk ★ Singapore's first innovative danceteria, Zouk introduced the city to house music, which throbs nightly in its cavernous disco, comprising three warehouses joined together. They play the best in modern music, so even if you're not much of a groover, you can still have fun watching the party from the many levels that tower above the dance floor. If you need a bit more intimacy in your nightlife, **Velvet Underground (VU),** within the Zouk complex, drips in red velvet and soft lighting—a good complement to the more soulful sounds spinning here. The newer addition to Zouk, **Phuture,** draws a younger, hip-hop-loving crowd than VU. Including the outdoor wine bar, Zouk is your one-stop shop for a party; in Singapore, this place is legendary. All clubs are open daily 6pm to 3am. 17 Jiak Kim St. (C) **65/6738-2988.** www.zoukclub.com. Cover charges vary.

GAY NIGHTSPOTS

Singapore's gay clubbing scene is alive and well but still very underground. Bars come and go, so to get the absolute latest happenings, you'll have to go beyond mainstream media. The Web has listings at **www.utopia-asia.com,** where you'll find the best updated information about the most recent parties and hangouts. For the latest info, I'd recommend one of the chat rooms suggested at the address above, and talk to the experts. **Velvet Underground,** part of the Zouk complex (see above), welcomes a mixed clientele of gays, lesbians, and straight folks.

WINE BARS

Beaujolais (Finds) This little gem, in a shophouse built on a hill, is tiny, but its charm makes it a favorite for loyal regulars. Two tables outside (on the Five-Foot-Way, which serves more as a patio than a sidewalk) and two tables inside don't seem like much room, but there's more seating upstairs. They believe that wine should be affordable, and so their many labels tend to be more moderately priced per glass and bottle. Hours are Monday to Thursday 11am to midnight, Friday 11:30am to 2am, and Saturday 6pm to midnight; happy hours runs from opening until 9pm. 1 Ann Siang Hill. (C) **65/6224-2227.**

Que Pasa One of the more mellow stops along Peranakan Place, this little wine bar serves up a collection of some 70 to 100 labels with plenty of atmosphere and a nice central location. It's another bar in a shophouse, but this one has as its centerpiece a very unusual winding stairway up the air shaft to the level above. Wine bottles and artwork line the walls. In the front, you can order tapas and cigars. The upstairs VIP club looks and feels like a formal living room, complete with wing chairs and board games. Hours are Monday to Thursday noon to 2am, Friday and Saturday noon to 3am, and Sunday 5pm to 2am. 7 Emerald Hill Rd. (C) **65/6235-6626.** www.emeraldhillgroup.com.

3 THE PERFORMING ARTS

Professional and amateur theater companies, dance troupes, opera companies, and musical groups offer a wide variety of not only Asian-focused performances, but Western as well. Broadway road shows don't stop in San Francisco, where the road ends, but continue on to include Singapore in their itineraries, and international stars like Placido Domingo, Yo Yo Ma, Wynton Marsalis, and Michael Jackson have come to town. International stars make up only a small portion of the performance scene, though. Singapore theater comprises four distinct language groups—English, Chinese, Malay, and Tamil—and each maintains its own voice and culture.

CLASSICAL PERFORMANCES

The **Singapore Symphony Orchestra** performs at the Esplanade–Theatres on the Bay, with regular special guest appearances by international celebrities. For information about the orchestra, check out www.sso.org.sg, or for performance dates, see www.esplanade. com. Tickets purchased through **Sistic** (www.sistic.com.sg).

The **Singapore Lyric Opera** collaborates with renowned opera companies from around the world to stage such Western operas as *Turnadot* and *Madame Butterfly* at the Esplanade. Check their website at www.singaporeopera.com.sg for what's on. Sistic handles ticket sales.

The **Singapore Chinese Orchestra,** the only professional Chinese orchestra in Singapore, has won several awards for its classic interpretations. They perform every 2 weeks, mainly at the Singapore Conference Hall, 7 Shenton Way (© **65/6440-3839**). See performance schedules at www.sco.com.sg, and buy tickets through Sistic.

THEATER

Most international companies will perform at the **Esplanade–Theatres on the Bay,** 1 Esplanade Dr., a 10-minute walk from City Hall MRT (© **65/6828-8222;** www. esplanade.com). Smaller shows are sometimes staged at the **Victoria Concert Hall,** 2nd floor Victoria Memorial Hall, 11 Empress Place (© **65/6338-6125**). **Sistic** (© **65/ 6348-5555;** www.sistic.com.sg) handles bookings for both venues.

A few local companies are quite noteworthy and manage their own performance spaces. **The Necessary Stage,** 278 Marine Parade Rd., #B1–02 Marine Parade Community Building (© **65/6440-8115;** www.necessary.org), blazed trails for the local performing arts scene after staging productions that touched tender nerves for the community, including a startlingly frank monologue by the first Singaporean to publicly declare his struggle with AIDS. The **Singapore Repertory Theatre,** DBS Arts Centre, 20 Merbau Rd., Robertson Quay (© **65/6733-0005;** www.srt.com.sg), is another company to watch; in recent years, they've staged local productions of perennial favorites like *The Glass Menagerie* and *Little Shop of Horrors.*

ARTS PROGRAMS

A number of venues have nightly programs of performance art pieces, fringe music productions, art talks, demonstrations, readings, and other specialized arts events.

The **Arts House,** 1 Old Parliament Lane (© **65/6332-6900;** www.theartshouse.com. sg), is housed in the former Parliament House, whose government rooms, in grand colonial style, have been converted into intimate spaces for use as an alternative arts venue. The building also hosts an intimate music club and small cafe.

Also check out the many events at the **Substation,** 45 Armenian St. (© **65/6337-7800;** www.substation.org), which offers its space to smaller theater troupes, cinema groups, fine arts exhibitors and performance artists.

Once upon a time, **Cantonese opera** could be seen under tents on street corners throughout the city. These days, local and visiting companies still perform, but very sporadically. For a performance you can count on, the **Chinese Theatre Circle,** 5 Smith St. (© **65/6323-4862;** www.ctcopera.com.sg), has a show on Fridays and Saturdays, with excerpts from the most famous and beloved tales, with explanations of the craft. Come at 7pm for the preshow "dinner" (chicken nuggets, really; tickets are S$35/US$23/£16), or, better yet, have dinner elsewhere and drop in at 8pm to catch the show with tea and pay only S$20 (US$13/£9).

10

Malaysia in Depth

Malaysia's wow factor is its diversity. Malay Muslims, Chinese Taoists and Buddhists, Indian Hindus, a large number of indigenous people, plus an assortment of Peranakans, Eurasians, and other races and religions all call themselves Malaysian, and each contributes to the fabric of this surprisingly colorful nation. Its long history is the story of how original Malays have accepted newcomers from Arabia, India, China, Thailand, Indonesia, and Europe, and fused their cultures into a hodgepodge of a national identity. Malaysia has survived colonial rule of the Portuguese, Dutch, and English, plus the Japanese Occupation. Today the country manages to hold it together, albeit sometimes by a hair.

Diversity is also present in the landscape of Malaysia's cities and towns, where colonial heritage mixes with modern development and an underlying attitude of *kampung* (village) friendliness. Many visitors delight in the chaos of Kuala Lumpur. Its twisty narrow roads, sweltering traffic jams, haphazard development, and back-alley shops and food stalls represent an Asia that is still a little bit untamed, even as the marvelous futuristic-Moorish Petronas Twin Towers loom overhead. Meanwhile, in places like Georgetown, Melaka, and Kuching, the past is everywhere you turn.

Not far from Malaysia's cities and towns, you'll find rainforests and mountains, beaches and idyllic tropical islands, blue seas and coral reefs, and an abundance of peculiar flora and fauna, all so accessible it's a wonder these places aren't overwhelmed by tourists.

Accessibility is perhaps the best thing about Malaysia. Infrastructure is of good quality, communications are up-to-date, travel operators are very organized, and accommodations and airports are some of the best in Southeast Asia. Better still, many Malaysians are comfortable speaking English, which opens up enormous possibilities for visitors to connect with local people in a very meaningful way.

1 MALAYSIA TODAY

The Malaysia of today is a peaceful nation of many races and ethnicities. Currently, the population is estimated at 27.7 million inhabitants. Of this number, Bumiputeras are the most numerous ethnic group (broadly speaking) and are defined as those with cultural affinities indigenous to the region and to one another. Technically, this group includes people of the aboriginal groups and ethnic Malays. A smaller segment of the population is non-Bumiputera groups such as the Chinese, Indians, Arabs, and Eurasians, most of whom descended from settlers to the region in the past 150 years. It is important to know the difference between the Bumiputera and non-Bumiputera groups to understand Malaysian politics, which favors the first group in every policy. It is equally important to understand that, despite ethnic divisions, each group is considered no less Malaysian.

The state religion is Islam. The Muslim way of life is reflected in almost every element of Malaysian life. The strict adherence to Islam will most likely affect your

The Populace

About 57% of Malaysians are Malay, while the Chinese and Indians make up 25% and 10% of the population, respectively. The remainder includes Eurasians and myriad indigenous groups such as the Orang Asli of Peninsular Malaysia; the Iban, Bidayuh, and Orang Ulu of Sarawak; and the Kadazan Dusun, Bajau, and Murut of Sabah.

vacation plans in some way. If you're traveling to Malaysia for an extended period of time or are planning to work there, I highly recommend *Malaysian Customs & Etiquette: A Practical Handbook,* by Datin Noor Aini Syed Amir (Times Books, 2003), for its great advice on how to negotiate any situation.

As for the non-Muslim, life goes on under the government's very serious policy to protect freedom of religion. *Note:* Despite its "freedom of religion" policy, Malaysia is very anti-Zionist. Almost daily the local papers report anti-Semitic news, and Israel is the only country in the world to which Malaysian citizens may not travel. If you carry an Israeli passport, you will not be granted entry to the country. Jewish people from other countries who still wish to visit are advised to downplay their religion.

THE GOVERNMENT

From 1981 to 2003, the government was led by Dr. Mahathir Mohamad, of the **United Malays National Organisation (UMNO),** the leading government party since Malaysia's independence. He was a popular prime minister who sought to create a competitive economic tiger while maintaining national policies that reflected liberal Islamic values. His outspoken nature created an endless stream of controversies surrounding policies that favored Bumiputeras, protected often shady links between government and industry, and opposed conservative Islamic policies.

In 2003, he stepped down from power so that his successor, Abdullah Badawi, could continue the policies of the UMNO party.

In March 2008, Malaysian politics took an interesting turn when a general election saw the ruling government lose its parliamentary majority as well as control over a number of state legislatures. Even more controversial was the election of Anwar Ibrahim as leader of the Malaysia Opposition. Anwar was Mahathir's former deputy prime minister and was sacked over a sodomy and corruption scandal in 1998—it is generally believed that the charges against Anwar were false and the work of a government who wanted to remove Anwar's dissenting voice.

Malaysians' biggest concerns are the economy, ethnic discord, and rising crime rates.

THE ECONOMY

Until the Asian Economic Crisis that began in July 1997, Malaysia was one of the rising stars of the East Asian Miracle, with an economy built upon the manufacturing sector in electronics and rubber products, as well as on agriculture and mining. Though the crisis hit the country hard, the country bounced back with annual GDP average of 6%.

In January 2009, the government was adamant that the global recession would not seriously affect Malaysia, due to the nation's sound economic fundamentals, predicting a GDP growth estimate for the year at a highly optimistic 3.5%.

Shoe School

In January 2009, luxury shoemaker and Penang native Jimmy Choo announced his plan to create a series of couture shoe academies worldwide. The first is expected to open in his home country, Malaysia.

TOURISM

In 2008, Malaysia attracted a record-breaking 22 million tourists, half of which were Singaporeans. Important inbound tourism markets include Thailand, Indonesia, China, and India. The driving forces behind Malaysia's tourism industry are the Meetings, Incentives, Conventions & Exhibitions (MICE) sector; medical tourism; and educational tourism. The government's main tourism focus is historical site conservation, upgrades to tourism-related infrastructure such as air, land, and sea travel; and the improvement of tourism-related services and products.

In 2008, Melaka and Georgetown were inscribed in the United Nations Educational, Scientific, and Cultural Organization's (UNESCO) World Heritage List for cultural sites. They joined Gunung Mulu National Park and Kinabalu Park, World Heritage List natural sites since 2000.

2 LOOKING BACK AT MALAYSIA

POPULATING THE PENINSULA (PREHISTORY–1ST CENTURY B.C.)

If Malaysia can trace its success to one element, it would be geographic location. Placed strategically at a major crossroads between the Eastern and Western worlds, the result of alternating seasonal northeast and southwest monsoons, Malaysia (formerly known as Malaya) was the ideal center for East–West trade activities. The character of the indigenous Malays is credited to their relationship with the sea, while centuries of outside influences shaped their culture.

The earliest inhabitants of the peninsula were the Orang Asli, who are believed to have migrated from China and Tibet as early as 5,000 years ago. The first Malays were established by 1000 B.C., having migrated not only to Malaya, but throughout the entire Indonesian archipelago as well, including Sumatra and Borneo. They brought with them knowledge of agriculture and metalwork, as well as beliefs in a spirit world (attitudes that are still practiced by many groups today).

Malaysia's earliest trading contacts were established by the 1st century B.C. with China and India. India proved most influential, impacting local culture with Buddhist and Hindu beliefs that are evidenced today in the Malay language, literature, and many customs.

THE INTRODUCTION OF ISLAM (15TH CENTURY)

Recorded history didn't come around until the Malay Annals of the 17th century, which tell the story of Parameswara, also known as Iskander Shah, ruler of Temasek (Singapore), who was forced to flee to Melaka (which was known as Malacca during colonial occupation) around A.D. 1400. He set up a trading port and led it to world-renowned financial glory. Melaka grew in population and prosperity, attracting Chinese, Indian, and Arab traders.

With Arabs and Muslim Indians came Islam, and Iskander Shah's son, who took leadership of Melaka after his father's death, is credited as the first Malay to convert to the new religion. The rule of Melaka was transformed into a sultanate, and the word of Islam won converts not only in Malaya, but throughout Borneo and the Indonesian archipelago.

EUROPEAN INFLUENCES (16TH–19TH CENTURIES)

Melaka's success was not without admirers, and in 1511, the Portuguese decided they wanted a piece of the action. They conquered the city in 30 days, chased the sultanate south to Johor, built a fortress that forestalled any trouble from the populace, and set up Christian missions. The Portuguese stuck around until 1641, when the Dutch came to town, looking to expand their trading power in the region. After Melaka's fall to the Portuguese, its success plummeted and was never regained.

The British came sniffing around in the late 1700s, when Francis Light of the British East India Company landed on the island of Penang and cut a deal with the Sultan of Kedah to cede it to the British. By 1805, Penang had become the seat of British authority in Southeast Asia, but the establishment served less as a trading cash cow and more as political leverage in the race to beat out the Dutch for control of the Southeast Asian trade routes. In 1824, the British and Dutch finally signed a treaty dividing Southeast Asia. The British would have Malaya, and the Dutch, Indonesia. Dutch-ruled Melaka was traded for British-ruled Bencoolen in Sumatra. In 1826, the British East India Company formed the Straits Settlements, uniting Penang, Malacca (Melaka), and Singapore under Penang's control. In 1867, power over the Straits Settlements shifted from the British East India Company to British colonial rule in London.

The Anglo-Dutch treaty never provided for the island of Borneo. The Dutch sort of took over Kalimantan, but the areas to the northwest were generally held under the rule of the Sultan of Brunei. Sabah was ceded for an annual sum to the British North Borneo Company, ruled by London until the Japanese invaded during World War II. In 1839, Englishman James Brooke arrived in Sarawak. The Sultan of Brunei had been having a hard time with warring factions in this territory and was happy to hand control over to Brooke. In 1841, after winning allies and subjugating enemies, Brooke became the Raja of Sarawak, building his capital in Kuching.

Meanwhile, back on the peninsula, Kuala Lumpur sprang to life in 1857 as a settlement at the crook of the Klang and Gombak rivers, about 35km (22 miles) inland from the west coast. Tin miners from India, China, and other parts of Malaya came inland to prospect and set up a trading post, which flourished. In 1896, it became the capital of the British Malayan territory.

WORLD WAR II & MALAYSIAN INDEPENDENCE

In 1941, the Japanese conquered Malaya en route to Singapore. Life for Malayans during the 4-year occupation was a constant and almost unbearable struggle to survive hunger, disease, and separation from the world. After the war, when the British sought to reclaim their colonial sovereignty over Malaya, they found the people thoroughly fed up with foreign rule. The struggle for independence united Malay and non-Malay residents throughout the country. By the time the British agreed to Malayan independence, the states were already united. On August 31, 1957, Malaya was cut loose, and Kuala Lumpur became its official capital. For a brief moment in the early 1960s, the peninsula was united with Singapore and the Borneo states of Sabah and Sarawak. Singapore was ejected from the federation in 1965, and today Malaysia continues on its own path.

POST-INDEPENDENCE (1960S)

As Malaysia was emerging as an independent nation, its growth was stunted by racial tensions that eventually led to race riots. National policies favored ethnic Malays—most of whom were living in rural poverty—in an attempt to level the playing field in terms of access to education, jobs, and business opportunities. The policies were oftentimes at the expense of Chinese and Indian Malaysians, many of whom were business owners, as well as educated and wealthy Malaysians.

In 1969, following a national election, Chinese Malaysians demonstrated in Kuala Lumpur, sparking a backlash from Malays. Riots and violence led to the destruction of almost 6,000 homes and businesses and the deaths of 184 people.

---

3 THE LAY OF THE LAND

Tropical evergreen forests, estimated to be some of the oldest in the world, once covered more than 70% of Malaysia; however, logging and plantation establishment have taken their toll. There are diverse terrains, including mountainous forests, sparsely wooded tangles at higher elevations; lowland forests, dense tropical forests; mangroves along the waters' edge; and peat swamp forests along the waterways. On the peninsula, three national forests—Taman Negara (or "National Forest") and Kenong Rimba Park, both inland, and Endau Rompin National Park, located toward the southeastern end of the peninsula—are the most convenient to visit, especially Taman Negara, a half-day trip from KL. Sabah and Sarawak step up the adventure quotient with countless rainforests, peculiar wildlife, and fascinating indigenous cultures.

Malaysia is surrounded by the South China Sea on the east coast and the Straits of Malacca on the west, and the waters off the peninsula vary in terms of sea life (and beach life). The waters off the east coast house a living coral reef, good waters, and great tropical beaches, while more southerly parts host beach resort areas. By way of contrast, the waters in southern portions of the Straits of Malacca are choppy and cloudy from shipping traffic—hardly ideal for diving. But once you get as far north as Langkawi, the waters become beautiful again. Meanwhile, the sea coast of Sabah and Sarawak includes some resort areas that are ideal for beach vacationing.

Protecting Malaysia's Rare Species

Vast tracks of primary rainforest in Malaysian Borneo are protected and believed to contain such rare species of animals as the Sumatran rhinoceros, the Malaysian sun bear, and the clouded leopard. In forest reserves, visitors can sometimes spot large-nosed proboscis monkeys and hornbills, with their colorful beaks. A number of rehabilitation centers on Borneo protect the orangutan from extinction in the face of their disappearing habitat. On Borneo and Peninsular Malaysia, many species of sea turtles that use Malaysia's beaches for nesting grounds are also protected.

4 MALAYSIA IN POPULAR CULTURE

The mix of cultural influences in Malaysia is the result of centuries of immigration and trade with the outside world, particularly with Arab nations, China, and India. Early groups of incoming foreigners brought wealth from around the world, plus their own unique cultural heritages and religions. Furthermore, once imported, each culture remained largely intact; that is, none have truly been homogenized. Traditional temples and churches exist side by side with mosques.

Likewise, **traditional art forms** of various cultures are still practiced in Malaysia, most notably in the areas of dance and performance art. Chinese opera, Indian dance, and Malay martial arts are all very popular cultural activities. *Silat*, originating from a martial arts form (and still practiced as such by many), is a dance performed by men and women. Religious and cultural festivals are open for everyone to appreciate and enjoy. Unique arts and traditions of indigenous people distinguish Sabah and Sarawak from the rest of the country.

Traditional **Malaysian music** is very similar to Indonesian music. Heavy on rhythms, its constant drum beats underneath the light repetitive melodies of the stringed gamelan (no relation at all to the Indonesian metallophone gamelan, with its gongs and xylophones) will entrance you with its simple beauty.

BOOKS

The Harmony Silk Factory, by Tash Aw (Riverhead Trade). One of Malaysia's most talented novelists, Aw spins a tale about a Chinese businessman in Malaysia at the start of the Japanese Occupation.

A History of Malaysia, by Barbara Watson Andaya (Palgrave Macmillan). This easy-to-read book explores some of the most important themes in Malaysia's history, from prehistory to present day.

Into the Heart of Borneo, by Redmond O'Hanlon (Vintage). This funny travelogue follows two inexperienced travelers as they attempt a rugged trek into the deepest forests of Sarawak.

Kalimantaan, by C. S. Godshalk (Abacus). This is a well-researched fictional account of a colonial adventurer who attempts to rule Borneo, loosely based on the life of Sir James Brooke.

The Long Day Wanes: A Malaysian Trilogy, by Anthony Burgess (W. W. Norton & Co). Written by the author of *A Clockwork Orange,* these three novels mirror the author's experiences as a British civil servant during Malaysia's transition to independence.

Malaysia: A Pictorial History, by Wendy Khadija Moore (Editions Didier Millet). A gorgeous coffee table book, this fantastic collection of illustrations, photographs, and artwork makes reading about history a joy.

Claim to Fame

Famous Malaysians include sexy Bond girl Michelle Yeoh, bestselling feng shui author Lillian Too, and shoe guru Jimmy Choo.

Funky Flowers

Borneo is home to the world's largest flower, the rafflesia, which can grow to over 90 cm (3 ft.) in diameter. The parasitic plant is a rare find, and the smell it gives off is similar to rotting flesh. Another interesting species of Borneo flora is the pitcher plant, which survives in poor soil conditions by drawing nutrients from insects and even small mammals it captures in its pitcher. Both plants are protected species.

FILMS

Anna and the King (1999). A Hollywood blockbuster, this remake starring Chow Yun Fatt and Jodie Foster was filmed on Langkawi, after the Thai government refused to let them film in Thailand. The Thais are not fans of the Western fairytale that claims that one of their most revered monarchs was "civilized" by a simple English teacher.

Entrapment (1999). This thriller starring Sean Connery and Catherine Zeta-Jones has its climax in Kuala Lumpur, with a stunt-filled heist at the top of the Petronas Twin Towers.

Sandokan (1976). Based on the epic novels of Emilio Salgari, this mini-series captured the danger and mystery of colonial Malaya.

South Pacific (1958). Bali Hai is Tioman Island, at least for the cast and crew of South Pacific, who shot parts of the film there in the 1950s, most notably the scenes that accompany the song "Happy Talk."

Zoolander (2001). This low-brow comedy, starring Ben Stiller and Owen Wilson, is banned from Malaysia because of a plot that includes an assassination plan of a so-called prime minister of Malaysia. However, footage of a fictional Malaysia has absolutely no resemblance to the country at all.

5 EATING & DRINKING IN MALAYSIA

Malaysian food seems to get its origins from India's rich curries, influenced by Thailand's herbs and spices. You'll find delicious blends of coconut milk and curry, shrimp paste and chilies, accented by exotic flavors of galangal (similar to turmeric), lime, and lemon grass. Sometimes pungent, a few of the dishes have a deep flavor from fermented shrimp paste that is an acquired taste for Western palates. By and large, Malaysian food is delicious, but in multicultural Malaysia, so is the Chinese food, the Peranakan food, the Indian food—the list goes on (see chapter 2). You'll also find fresh seafood almost everywhere.

I strongly recommend eating in a hawker stall, especially in Penang, which is famous for its local cuisine. Although almost all of the food you encounter in a hawker center will be safe for eating, it is advisable to go for freshly cooked hot or soupy dishes.

(Tips) How to Eat Like a Malaysian

Many Malaysians eat with their right hands and off banana leaves when they are having *nasi padang* or *nasi kandar* (rice with mixed dishes). This is absolutely acceptable. If you choose to follow suit, wash your hands first and try to use your right hand because the left is considered unclean (traditionally, it's the hand used to wash after a visit to the toilet).

Do not drink tap water anywhere in Malaysia. If you ask for water, either make sure it's boiled or buy mineral water. Otherwise, drink refrigerated canned beverages.

TAXES & SERVICE CHARGES A 10% service charge and 5% government tax are levied in large restaurants, but hawkers charge a flat price without tax.

MALAYSIAN CUISINE

A Malay meal always revolves around rice, accompanied with curries, fried chicken or fish, vegetable dishes, and small portions of condiments, called *sambal*. Some of these condiments can be harsh to foreign noses, particularly *sambal belacan,* which is made with extremely pungent fermented shrimp paste. Malays also favor seafood, especially fish, prawns, and squid. As all Malays are Muslim, you won't find pork on the menu and most restaurants are *halal.* Where you see mutton, most times it's goat, which is preferred over lamb for its milder, less musty taste and smell.

A good example of a local favorite is *nasi lemak,* rice cooked in coconut milk and served with fried chicken, prawn crackers, dried anchovies, a bit of egg, and a dark, sweet chili sauce. Other favorites are curry-based dishes like *kari ayam,* a mellow, almost creamy, golden curry with chunks of chicken meat and potatoes; and *rendang,* stewing beef with a dry curry that's as sweet as it is savory.

Probably the most famous Malay dish is *satay,* barbecued skewers of marinated chicken, beef, or mutton that are dipped in a chili peanut sauce. Another great dish is *ikan bakar,* which is fish smothered in chili sauce and grilled in foil over an open flame.

An interesting local variation to try is Malay food influenced by Indian Muslim cooking. *Mamak,* or Indian Muslim, stalls specialize in a dish called *roti canai,* fried bread to be dipped in curry or *dhal cha* (vegetarian curry); as well as *murtabak,* which is bread fried with egg, onion, and meat, which is also dipped in curry. These dishes are best enjoyed with a cup of *teh tarik,* frothy tea made with sweetened condensed milk.

Regional variations are also notable, particularly when it comes to Penang, which is famous for its food. A perfect example of how region affects a dish can be found in *laksa,* a seafood noodle soup created by the Peranakans. In Singapore, *laksa* has a rich, spicy coconut-based broth, almost like gravy. Alternately, Penang *laksa* is not coconut based, but is a fish broth with a tangy and fiery flavor from sour tamarind and spicy bird's-eye chili. Yet another variation, Sarawak *laksa* also forgoes coconut milk and instead focuses on a base of *sambal belacan,* or fermented shrimp paste. There are as many variations of *laksa* as there are towns.

Penang: Malaysia's Food Capital

Penang is world famous for its street food. There is a lot of Chinese food, plus Peranakan favorites, due to the greater proportion of Chinese living on the island. Here you'll find *char kway teow* (fried flat noodles with seafood), *murtabak* (mutton, egg, and onion fried inside Indian bread and dipped in *dhal*), and *rojak* (a spicy fruit and seafood salad), along with classics like fried spring rolls and *satay*.

Sarawak and Sabah also have their own unique cuisines, but mostly visitors will find typical Malay, Chinese, and Indian dishes, but with local twists. One of my favorite purely indigenous dishes is *umai*, raw mackerel seasoned with onion, chili, and salt, "cooked" in lime juice. It can be found primarily in Sarawak, but sometimes also in Sabah.

Planning Your Trip to Malaysia

Compared with spicy Thailand to the north and cosmopolitan Singapore to the south, Malaysia is a relative secret to many from the West, and many travelers to Southeast Asia skip over it, opting for more heavily traversed routes.

Boy, are they missing out. Those who venture here wander through streets awash with international influences from colonial times and trek through mysterious rainforests and caves, sometimes without another tourist in sight. They relax peacefully under palms on lazy white beaches that fade into blue, blue waters. They spy the bright colors of batik *sarongs* hanging to dry in the breeze. They hear the melodic drone of the Muslim call to prayer seeping from exotic mosques. They taste culinary masterpieces served in modest local shops—from Malay with its deep mellow spices to succulent seafood punctuated by brilliant chili sauces. In Malaysia, I'm always thrilled to witness life without the distracting glare of the tourism industry, and I leave impressed by how accessible Malaysia is to outsiders while remaining true to its heritage.

Chapter 13 covers the major destinations of peninsular Malaysia. We begin with the country's capital, Kuala Lumpur (KL), then tour the peninsula's west coast—the cities of Johor Bahru, Melaka (Malacca), the hill resorts at Cameron and Genting Highlands, plus islands like the popular Penang, secluded Pangkor, and luxurious Langkawi. Chapter 14 takes you up the east coast of the peninsula, through resort areas in Kuantan, Cherating, and Terengganu, plus the small and charming Tioman and Redang Islands. My coverage also includes Taman Negara National Park, peninsular Malaysia's largest national forest. Finally, in chapter 15, we cross the South China Sea to the island of Borneo, where the Malaysian states of Sarawak and Sabah feature Malaysia's most impressive forests as well as unique and diverse cultures.

Malaysia is accessible to the rest of the world through its international airport in Kuala Lumpur. Regular flights also connect cities in the region to Malaysia's many smaller international airports. Domestic flights provide access to all parts of the country, and you can also travel by car, bus, or train from Singapore or Thailand.

For additional help in planning your trip and for more on-the-ground resources in Malaysia, please turn to Appendix B on p. 296.

1 VISITOR INFORMATION

Tourism Malaysia (www.tourismmalaysia.gov.my) provides excellent information by way of pamphlets and advice. The information includes websites, brochures, pamphlets, and other information that is regularly updated. Specific destinations like islands, national parks, and cities may also have brochures.

Within Malaysia, each state or tourist destination has its own tourism board that operates a website and local offices for tourist information. These are also good

2 ENTRY REQUIREMENTS

PASSPORTS

To enter Malaysia you must have a valid passport. For information on obtaining a passport, please see "Passports" in Appendix B (p. 296).

VISAS

Citizens of the United States do not need visas for tourism and business visits, and upon entry are granted a Social/Business Visit Pass good for up to 3 months. Citizens of Canada, Australia, New Zealand, and the United Kingdom can also enter the country without a visa and will be granted up to 3 months entry as well. For other countries, please consult the nearest Malaysian consulate before your trip, for visa regulations. *Also note:* Travelers holding Israeli passports are not permitted to travel within Malaysia (likewise, Malaysians are forbidden from traveling to Israel).

MEDICAL REQUIREMENTS

If you are arriving from an area in which yellow fever has been reported, you will be required to show proof of yellow fever vaccination. Contact your nearest Tourism Malaysia office to see which areas fall into this category.

CUSTOMS
What You Can Bring into Malaysia

With regard to currency, you can bring into the country as many foreign currency notes or traveler's checks as you please, but amounts exceeding RM10,000 or its equivalent in foreign currency need to be declared.

Social visitors can enter Malaysia with 1 liter of alcohol and 1 carton of cigarettes without paying duty—anything over that amount is subject to local taxes. Prohibited items include firearms and ammunition, daggers and knives, and pornographic materials. Be advised that, similar to Singapore, Malaysia enforces a very strict drug-abuse policy that includes the death sentence for convicted drug traffickers.

3 WHEN TO GO

There are **two peak seasons** in Malaysia. One peak tourist season falls roughly from the beginning of December to the end of January, covering the major Northern Hemisphere winter holidays—Christmas, New Year's Day, and Chinese New Year. Hari Raya Puasa, celebrating the end of Ramadan, shifts dates from year to year. If you plan to travel to Malaysia around September, I highly recommend calling Tourism Malaysia to find out exactly when this holiday will fall.

The second peak season falls in the months of June, July, and August, and can last into mid-September. During this period, hotels are booked with families from the Middle East, as this is school holiday season for many of the region's countries. After September it's quiet again until December. Both seasons experience approximately equal tourist traffic, but in summer months that traffic may ebb and flow.

Singapore's school holidays occur from mid-May through to the end of June, and again during November and December, when families are likely to flock to Malaysia's seaside resorts, particularly the budget and midpriced properties. Malaysians in general are relaxed about children when on holidays. If you're looking for an intimate couples escape, try to avoid family resorts during this time. Malaysia's school-children are cut loose for about 1 to 2 weeks in March, May, and August, with a longer break from mid-November through December.

CLIMATE

Climate considerations will play a role in your plans. If you want to visit any of the east-coast resort areas, the low season is between November and March, when the monsoon tides make the water a little choppy for watersports and beach activities. During this time, many island resorts may close. On the west coast, the rainy season is from April through May, and again from October through November.

The temperature is basically static year-round. Daily averages range from 67°F to 90°F (21°C–32°C). Temperatures in the hill resorts get a little cooler, averaging 67°F (21°C) during the day, 50°F (10°C) at night.

HOLIDAYS

During Malaysia's official public holidays, expect government offices to be closed, as well as some shops and restaurants, depending on the ethnicity of the shop owner or restaurant owner. During **Hari Raya Puasa** and **Chinese New Year,** you can expect many shop and restaurant closings. However, look out for special sales and celebrations. Also count on public parks, shopping malls, and beaches to be more crowded during public holidays, as locals will be taking advantage of their time off.

Official public holidays fall as follows: New Year's Day (Jan 1), Chinese New Year (Feb 14–15, 2010), Prophet Muhammad's Birthday (Mar), Labor Day (May 1), Wesak Day (May 21, 2010), King's Birthday (Jun 6), National Day (Aug 31), Hari Raya Puasa (also called Eid al-Fitr; Sept 20–21, 2009; Sep 8, 2010), Deepavali (Nov 15, 2009; Nov 5, 2010), Hari Raya Haji (also called Eid al-Adha; Nov 27, 2009; Nov 14, 2010), and Christmas (Dec 25). *Note:* Please confirm all 2010 dates listed above before you plan your trip; some holidays vary, as they are dependent on the phases of the moon. In addition, each state has a public holiday to celebrate the birthday of the state sultan.

For an exhaustive list of events beyond those listed here, check http://events.frommers.com, where you'll find a searchable, up-to-the-minute roster of what's happening in cities all over the world.

4 GETTING THERE AND GETTING AROUND

GETTING TO MALAYSIA
By Plane
Malaysia has five international airports—at Kuala Lumpur, Penang, Langkawi, Kota Kinabalu, and Kuching, although international flights come into some domestic airports—and 15 domestic airports, including Kota Bharu, Kuantan, and Kuala Terengganu. Specific airport information is listed for each city.

A passenger service charge, or **airport departure tax,** is incorporated in all ticket prices: RM5 ($1.45/90p) for domestic flights and RM40 ($12/£7.20) for international flights.

Malaysia Airlines (www.malaysia airlines.com) flies to six continents. I have found Malaysia Airlines service to be of a very good standard, not to mention that they have possibly the lowest rates to Southeast Asia from North American destinations.

AirAsia (www.airasia.com) also flies long-haul flights to Australia and shorter flights throughout the region.

From the United States, Malaysia Airlines (✆ 800/552-9264) flies from Los Angeles and Newark/NYC.

From Canada, North American carriers will have to connect with a Malaysia Airlines flight, in either East Asia, Europe, or the U.S.

From the United Kingdom, Malaysia Airlines (✆ 0870/607-9090) flies from Heathrow Airport to KL.

From Australia, Malaysia Airlines (✆ 132-627) flies directly to KL from Perth, Adelaide, Sydney, and Melbourne, and via Sydney for Brisbane. **AirAsia** flies to Perth, Melbourne, and the Gold Coast.

From New Zealand, Malaysia Airlines (✆ 0800/777-747) flies to KL from Auckland.

By Train

FROM SINGAPORE The **Keretapi Tanah Melayu Berhad (KTM),** Malaysia's rail system, operates trains that connect cities along the west coast of Malaysia with Singapore to the south and Thailand to the north. Trains depart daily from the **Singapore Railway Station** (✆ 65/6222-5165) on Keppel Road in Tanjong Pagar, not far from the city center. Trains to Kuala Lumpur depart daily for fares from S$34 to S$68 (US$23–US$46/£15–£31). The trip takes around 7 hours on an *ekspres* train

(avoid the 10pm mail train if you want to reach there before your next birthday). Kuala Lumpur's KL Sentral railway station (✆ 03/2267-1200) is a 10-minute taxi ride from the center of town and is connected to the Putra LRT, KL Monorail city public transportation trains, and the Express Rail Link (ERL) to Kuala Lumpur International Airport (KLIA).

FROM THAILAND KTM's international service departs from the **Hua Lamphong Railway Station** (✆ 662/223-7010 or 662/223-7020) in Bangkok, with operations to Hua Hin, Surat Thani, Nakhon Si Thammarat, and Hat Yai in Thailand's southern peninsula. The final stop in Malaysia is at Padang Besar, so passage to KL will require you to catch a connecting train onward. The daily service departs at 2:45pm and takes approximately 20 hours from Bangkok to Butterworth. There is no first- or third-class service on this train, only air-conditioned second class; an upper berth goes for about US$20 (S$30/£14), and lower is US$23 (S$34/£16). The latter is roomier.

For a fascinating journey from Thailand, you can catch the **Eastern & Orient Express (E&O)** (www.orient-express. com), which operates a route between Chiang Mai and Bangkok, Kuala Lumpur, or Singapore. Traveling in the luxurious style for which the Orient Express is renowned, you'll finish the journey in about 42 hours. Your entry-level cabin is Pullman, priced at US$3,240(S$4,836/ £2,176) per person double occupancy, with State and Presidential Suites also available. Fares include meals on the train plus accommodation in Bangkok at the Peninsula Hotel. Overseas reservations for the E&O Express can be made through travel agents or by booking online. From Singapore, Malaysia, and Thailand, contact the E&O office in Singapore at ✆ 65/6395-0678.

PLANNING YOUR TRIP TO MALAYSIA

11

GETTING THERE & GETTING AROUND

By Bus

From Singapore, there are many bus routes to Malaysia. If you want to travel on land, I personally prefer the bus over the train from Singapore to Kuala Lumpur. Executive coaches operated by **Aeroline** have huge seats that recline, serve a box lunch on board, and show movies. They also have express buses to various locations in KL and Penang. Call them in Singapore at ℂ **65/6723-7222.** Buses depart from HarbourFront Centre at 1 Maritime Sq. for the 5-hour trip (S$49/US$33/£22 one-way).

Buses to Johor Bahru and Melaka can be picked up at the Ban Sen terminal at the corner of Queen and Arab streets. Call ℂ **65/6292-8149** for buses to Johor Bahru (S$2.40/US$1.60/£1.10) and ℂ**65/ 6293-5915** for buses to Melaka (S$11/ US$7.35/£4.95).

From Thailand, you can grab a bus in either Bangkok or Hat Yai (in the southern part of the country) heading for Malaysia. I don't recommend the bus trip from Bangkok. It's just far too long a journey to be confined to a bus. You're better off taking the train. From Hat Yai, many buses leave regularly to northern Malaysian destinations, particularly Butterworth (Penang). Also be warned, the U.S. Department of State does not recommend U.S. citizens travel in certain parts of southern Thailand due to terrorist violence near Pattani and Narathiwat.

By Taxi (From Singapore)

From the Johor-Singapore bus terminal at Queen and Arab streets, the **Singapore Johor Taxi Operators Association** (ℂ **65/ 6296-7054**) can drive you to Johor Bahru for S$40 (US$27/£18).

By Car

Major international car-rental agencies operating in Singapore will rent cars that you can take over the causeway to Malaysia, but be prepared to pay a small fortune.

They're much cheaper if you rent within the country. At Kuala Lumpur International Airport, find **Avis** at Counter B-16 at the arrival hall in the main terminal (ℂ **03/8776-4540**). There's another branch at the international airport in Penang (**04/643-9633**), or make a booking through www.avis.com.

GETTING AROUND

The modernization of Malaysia has made travel here—whether it's by plane, train, bus, taxi, or self-driven car—easier and more convenient than ever. Malaysia Airlines and AirAsia have service to every major destination within the peninsula and East Malaysia. Berjaya Air and Firefly service some cities and small islands. Buses have a massive web of routes between every city and town. Train service up the western coast and out to the east provides even more options. And a unique travel offering—the outstation taxi—is available to and from most cities on the peninsula. All the options make it convenient enough for you to plan to hop from city to city and not waste too much precious vacation time.

By and large, all the modes of transportation between cities are reasonably comfortable. Air travel can be the most costly of the alternatives, followed by outstation taxis, then buses and trains.

By Plane

Malaysia Airlines (ℂ **1300/883-000;** www.malaysiaairlines.com) links from its hub in Kuala Lumpur to the cities of Johor Bahru, Kota Bharu, Kota Kinabalu, Kuala Terengganu, Kuantan, Kuching, Langkawi, Penang, and other smaller cities not covered in this volume. Malaysia Airline's national hot line (ℂ **1300/883-000**) can be dialed from anywhere in the country. Individual airport information is provided in sections for each city that follows. One-way domestic fares can average RM100 to RM400 ($29–$116/£18–£72).

AirAsia (℃ 03/8775-4000; www.air
asia.com) competes with Malaysia Airlines
with incredibly affordable rates. It links all
the country's major cities with fares that,
on average, run from RM40 and up
($12/£7.20)—seriously.

Berjaya Air (℃ 03/2149-3731; www.
berjaya-air.com) operates a small fleet of
aircraft that services KL to Pangkor, Tioman, and Redang islands.

Firefly (℃ 03/7845-4543; www.fire
flyz.com) has a small fleet that services
some peninsular and East Malaysian destinations.

By Train

The **Keretapi Tanah Melayu Berhad
(KTM)** provides train service throughout
peninsular Malaysia. Trains run from
north to south between the Thai border
and Singapore, with stops including Butterworth (Penang), Kuala Lumpur, and
Johor Bahru. There is a second line that
branches off at Gemas, midway between
Johor Bahru and KL, and heads northeast
to Tempas near Kota Bharu. Fares range
from RM70 ($20/£13) for first-class
between Johor Bahru and KL, to RM95
($28/£17) for first-class passage between
Johor Bahru and Butterworth. Train station information is provided for each city
under individual city headings in the following chapters.

By Bus

Malaysia's intercity coach system is extensive and inexpensive, but I don't really
recommend it. With the exception of
executive coach services between KL, Penang, and Singapore, which are excellent,
standard coaches get dirtier and dirtier
each year, maintenance issues are a question mark, and road safety is a roll of the
dice. Still, if you must, for each city covered, I've listed bus terminal locations, but
scheduling information must be obtained
from the bus company itself.

By Taxi

You can take special hired cars, called **outstation taxis,** between every city and state
on the peninsula. Rates depend on the distance you plan to travel. They are fixed and
stated at the beginning of the trip but many
times can be bargained down. In Kuala
Lumpur, go to the second level of the
Puduraya Bus Terminal to find cabs that
will take you outside the city, or call the
**Kuala Lumpur Outstation Taxi Service
Station** (℃ 03/2078-0213). A taxi from
KL to Melaka will cost you approximately
RM150 ($44/£27), KL to Cameron High-
lands RM240 ($70/£43), KL to Butter-
worth or Johor Bahru RM320 ($93/£58).
Outstation taxi stand locations are included
under each individual city heading in the
following chapters. These cars are usually
basic older-model sedans.

Also, within each of the smaller cities,
feel free to negotiate with unmetered taxis
for hourly, half-day, or daily rates. It's an
excellent way to get around for sightseeing
and shopping without transportation has-
sles. Hourly rates are anywhere from RM30
to RM60 ($8.70–$17/£5.40–£11).

By Car

The cities along the west coast of the peninsula are linked by the North–South
Highway. There are rest areas with toilets,
food outlets, and emergency telephones at
intervals along the way. There is also a toll
that varies depending on the distance
you're traveling.

Driving along the east coast of Malaysia
is actually much more pleasant than driving along the west coast. The highway is
narrower and older, but it takes you
through oil palm and rubber plantations,
and the essence of *kampung* Malaysia permeates throughout. As you near villages,
you'll often have to slow down and swerve
past cows and goats, which are really quite
oblivious to oncoming traffic. You have to

get very close to honk at them before they move.

The speed limit on highways is 110kmph (68 mph). On the minor highways, the limit ranges from 70 to 90kmph (43–56 mph). Do not speed, as there are traffic police strategically situated around certain bends.

Distances between major towns are: from KL to Johor Bahru, 368km (228 miles); from KL to Melaka, 144km (89 miles); from KL to Kuantan, 259km (161 miles); from KL to Butterworth, 369km (229 miles); from Johor Bahru to Melaka,

224km (139 miles); from Johor Bahru to Kuantan, 325km (202 miles); from Johor Bahru to Mersing, 134km (83 miles); from Johor Bahru to Butterworth, 737km (657 miles).

To rent a car in Malaysia, you must produce a driver's license from your home country that shows you have been driving at least 2 years. There are desks for major car-rental services at the international airports in Kuala Lumpur and Penang, and additional outlets throughout the country (see individual city sections in later chapters for this information).

5 MONEY & COSTS

CURRENCY

Malaysia's currency is the **Malaysian ringgit.** Prices are marked as RM (a designation I've used throughout this book). Notes are issued in denominations of RM1, RM2, RM5, RM10, RM20, RM50, and RM100. One ringgit is equal to 100

sen. Coins come in denominations of 5, 10, 20, and 50 sen.

In 2005 Malaysia ended a 7-year peg of the ringgit at RM3.80 to US$1. Now, the country uses a managed float system that measures the currency against a basket of several major currencies. At the time of

Malaysian Ringgit Conversion Chart		
RM	US$	UK£
0.10	0.03	0.02
0.20	0.06	0.04
0.50	0.15	0.09
1.00	0.29	0.18
2.00	0.58	0.36
5.00	1.45	0.90
10.00	2.90	1.80
20.00	5.80	3.60
50.00	14.50	9.00
100.00	29.00	18.00
500.00	145.00	90.00
1,000.00	290.00	180.00

What Things Cost in Kuala Lumpur	RM	US$	UK£
Taxi from the airport to city center	70.00–150.00	20.30–43.50	12.60–27.00
Local telephone call (3 min.)	0.30	0.09	0.05
Double room at an expensive hotel (Hilton)	466.00	135.14	83.88
Double room at a moderate hotel (Meliá Kuala Lumpur)	345.00	100.05	62.10
Double room at an inexpensive hotel (Swiss-Inn)	295.00	85.55	53.10
Dinner for one at an expensive restaurant (Al Nafourah)	100.00	29.00	18.00
Dinner for one at a moderate restaurant (Sao Nam)	50.00–70.00	14.50–20.30	9.00–12.60
Dinner for one at an inexpensive restaurant (hawker stall)	40.00	11.60	7.20
Glass of beer	8.00–25.00	2.32–7.25	1.44–4.50
Coca-Cola	2.00–8.00	0.58–2.32	0.36–1.44
Cup of coffee at common coffee shop	1.50	0.44	0.27
Cup of coffee in a hotel	12.00	3.48	2.16
Roll of 36-exposure color print film	15.00	4.35	2.70
Admission to the National Museum	2.00	0.58	0.36
Movie ticket	10.00	2.90	1.80

writing, 1 ringgit was worth US29¢ and UK18p—this is the conversion rate I've used for this guide.

Currency can be changed at banks and hotels, but you'll get a more favorable rate if you go to one of the moneychangers that seem to be everywhere; in shopping centers, in lanes, and in small stores—just look for signs. They are often men in tiny booths with a display on the wall behind them showing the exchange rate. All major currencies are accepted, and there is never a problem with the U.S. dollar, except for dirty and old notes.

ATMS

Automated teller machines (ATMs) are found throughout the country, especially where tourists frequent. They will be hard to find on smaller islands and remote beach areas. In addition, some ATMs may

not accept credit cards or debit cards from your home bank. I have found that debit cards on the MasterCard/Cirrus or Visa/Plus networks are almost always accepted at **Maybank,** with at least one location in every major town. Cash is dispensed in ringgit deducted from your account at the day's rate.

CREDIT CARDS

Credit cards are widely accepted at hotels and restaurants, and at many shops as well. Most popular are American Express, MasterCard, and Visa. Some banks may also be willing to advance cash against your credit card, but you have to ask around because this service is not available everywhere.

In Malaysia, to report a lost or stolen card, call **American Express** at its head office in Kuala Lumpur (© **03/2161-**

4000); for **MasterCard**, call *C* **800/804-594;** and for **Visa,** call *C* **800/800-159.** Both numbers are toll-free from anywhere in the country. For more on credit cards and what to do if your wallet gets stolen, see Appendix B: Malaysia Fast Facts.

TRAVELER'S CHECKS

American Express and Thomas Cook traveler's checks can be cashed at banks, hotels, and licensed moneychangers. Unfortunately, they are often not accepted at smaller shops. For more on traveler's checks, see chapter 3.

6 HEALTH

STAYING HEALTHY

Whether you are exploring a city, the rainforest, or the beach, you'll need to protect yourself from exposure to sun and heat. Drink plenty of fluids and avoid the outdoors during the middle of the day, if possible. Day or night, mosquito repellent is a must.

COMMON AILMENTS

TROPICAL ILLNESSES **Malaria** has not been a continual threat in most parts of Malaysia, even Malaysian Borneo. **Dengue fever,** on the other hand, which is also carried by mosquitoes, remains a constant threat in most areas, especially rural parts. Dengue, if left untreated, may cause fatal internal hemorrhaging, so if you come down with a sudden fever or skin rash, consult a physician immediately. There are no prophylactic treatments for dengue; the best protection is to wear plenty of insect repellent—the breed of mosquito that carries dengue bites during the day, as opposed to malaria-carrying ones that bite at dusk. Choose a product that contains DEET or is specifically formulated to be effective in the tropics.

In 2003, SARS seemed to skip right over Malaysia, but **Avian Influenza,** or Bird Flu, has found its way here, particularly in the northern state of Kelantan.

The United States Centers for Disease Control (CDC) then advised travelers to Malaysia to avoid contact with live or raw poultry.

DIETARY RED FLAGS The **tap water** in KL is supposedly potable, but I don't recommend drinking it—in fact, I don't recommend drinking tap water anywhere in Malaysia. Bottled water is inexpensive enough and readily available at convenience stores and food stalls. Food prepared in hawker centers is generally safe—I have yet to experience trouble, and I'll eat almost anywhere. If you buy fresh fruit, wash it well with bottled water, and carefully peel the skin if you are really concerned.

WHAT TO DO IF YOU GET SICK AWAY FROM HOME

Consult a physician if you develop a high fever or diarrhea that lasts longer than 24 hours. My recommendation, if you need medical attention, is to consult the manager of your hotel or resort. All hotels and resorts have reputable general practitioners on call who speak English. For extreme emergencies, hotel staff knows the closest hospital and best way to get there.

We list **additional emergency numbers** in Appendix B, p. 297.

Malaysia has been having an unfortunate problem with thievery. "Snatch thieves" are becoming bolder and bolder, riding on motorcycles through heavily populated areas in KL, Johor Bahru, and other cities, snatching handbags from women's shoulders. Some victims have been dragged and seriously injured. When you're out, don't wear your handbag on your side that's facing the street, or better yet, don't carry a handbag at all.

The first thing I do when I check into a hotel is put my passport, international tickets, extra cash, and traveler's checks, plus any credit or ATM card I do not have immediate plans to use, straight into the safe, either in my room or behind the hotel's front desk.

Be careful when traveling on overnight trains and buses where there are opportunities for theft. Keep your valuables close to you as you sleep.

8 SPECIALIZED TRAVEL RESOURCES

TRAVELERS WITH DISABILITIES

Traveling in developing countries is a daunting task for disabled people, and Malaysia is no exception. While airlines and most luxury hotels have facilities for guests in wheelchairs, most every attraction, shopping mall, restaurant, and mode of public transportation provide no accessibility at all. In urban centers, sidewalks are nonexistent, buckled, or cluttered. At the time of writing, there were no inbound tour operators specializing in tours for travelers with disabilities.

Two organizations that can offer assistance are the **Malaysian Association for the Blind** (www.mab.org.my) and the **Society of the Orthopaedically Handicapped Malaysia** (www.pocam.org).

GAY & LESBIAN TRAVELERS

Malaysia is a tolerant society that rarely criticizes others in public, so gay and lesbian travelers tend to be welcomed and treated like other travelers, although public affection for straights or gays and lesbians is usually frowned upon. As in many countries, the rural areas of Malaysia tend to be more conservative than the cities and, therefore, gay and lesbian travelers will have to respect the values and customs of their hosts. The east coast of the peninsula is another conservative area.

In the big cities, there are clubs and bars where visitors of all persuasion are welcome. By asking around, it usually doesn't take long to find out those locations that are most welcoming of gay and lesbian patrons.

SENIOR TRAVELERS

Seniors have few discounts in Malaysia, except at some attractions, where they might pay a bit less—but it's usually such a small discount that it's hardly worth pulling out your passport. However, Malaysia offers great incentives to lure potential retirees to the country under a program called **Malaysia My Second Home;** check out www.mm2h.com for incentives on purchasing a house, car, and education, as well as details on tax breaks.

11

WOMEN TRAVELERS

As a woman who has traveled solo to all corners of Malaysia and back again, I can honestly say I have never once felt threatened. However, my travel philosophy is "When in Rome . . . ." Like Malay women, I wear long skirts or pants, and shirts that cover the tops of my arms. I always carry a scarf in my bag in case etiquette requires I cover my head. I find many doors open to me when the locals feel I am respectful of their ways.

JEWISH TRAVELERS

Travelers with Israeli passports are not permitted to enter Malaysia. If you are of Jewish heritage and carry a passport from a country other than Israel, I recommend you downplay your heritage. Malaysian politicians have been known to make anti-Semitic comments in public, sentiments that, unfortunately, carry over into some sections of the general population.

9 SUSTAINABLE TOURISM

Sustainable tourism is conscientious travel. It means being careful with the environments you explore and respecting the communities you visit. Two overlapping components of sustainable travel are **ecotourism** and **ethical tourism.**

Malaysia naturally lends itself to ecotourism, as many parts of the country are covered in primary vegetation, although logging and agricultural expansion have taken their toll. Malaysia's best natural experiences are found in places like Taman Negara, Endau Rompin, parts of Langkawi, and Sarawak and Sabah on the island of Borneo. Seek out natural eco adventures in Kinabalu Park, Turtle Islands Park, Danum Valley, Tabin Wildlife Reserve, and the Lower Kinabatangan River in Sabah. In Sarawak, similar experiences can be had in national parks like Gunung Mulu, Bako, Batang Ai, and Gunung Gading.

The new travel buzz word is *responsible tourism,* which incorporates the principles of ecotourism, nature-based tourism, and sustainable tourism. Not all operators in Malaysia "walk the talk," so potential participants in certain activities need to read the finer detail or between the lines. **Wild**

Asia (www.wildasia.net), established in 1998 as a grassroots web initiative, provides independent assessments of natural sites, attractions, and Asian ecotourism products.

Some of Malaysia's longest-established and most reputable ecotourism operators include **Asian Overland Services** (head office: © 03/4252-9100; fax 03/4257-1133; www.asianoverland.com.my), with offices in KL, Langkawi, Penang, Kota Kinabalu, and Kuching. They also operate one of the country's leading green hotels, the **Frangipani Langkawi Resort and Spa** (© 04/952-0000; fax 04/952-0001; www.frangipanilangkawi.com). In Sabah, **Wilderness Expeditions** (© 089/219-616; fax 089/214-570; www.wildlife-expeditions.com) offers tours to all the state's leading natural areas. One of Sarawak's most respected eco-touring companies is **Borneo Adventure** (© 082/245-175; fax 082/422-626; www.borneoadventure.com), with offices in Kuching, Miri, and Kota Kinabalu (in neighboring Sabah). They offer tours to Bario, Bintulu, Mulu, and various longhouses.

SPECIAL-INTEREST TOURS

Most of the large inbound tour operators offer special-interest programs and should be contacted directly by those with specific needs and requirements. **Asian Overland Services** (head office: ☏ 03/4252-9100; fax 03/4257-1133; www.asianoverland.com.my), with offices in KL, Langkawi, Penang, Kota Kinabalu, and Kuching, offers programs such as adventures to Belum Valley, Malaysian ancient civilization (visits to Bujang Valley Archaeological Site in Kedah and Ulu Muda Eco Park), Taman Negara home stays, Lemanak longhouse stay (Sarawak), diving off Sipidan Island, and a Malaysia gourmet tour. **Mayflower** (☏ 03/6252-1888; fax 03/6257-0416; www.mayflower.com) is another inbound operator that offers generalist tours as well as specialist golf, rail, and diving packages.

10 PACKAGES FOR THE INDEPENDENT TRAVELER

Award–winning and internationally acclaimed **Asian Overland Services** (head office: ☏ 03/4252-9100; fax 03/4257-1133; www.asianoverland.com.my) has been operating in Malaysia since 1976. They also happen to be one of the country's most sensitive tour operators with regard to the environment and local cultures. They can plan anything from rugged adventure tours to fantasy honeymoons. They have offices in KL, Langkawi, Penang, Kota Kinabalu, and Kuching.

11 SPECIAL-INTEREST TRIPS

MEDICAL TRIPS

Malaysia has been attracting medical tourists who come for quality services in a number of state-of-the-art, internationally accredited hospitals staffed by Western-trained physicians. While cost-cutting is typically the main motivation for such trips, other factors include privacy issues and holiday down-time during recuperation.

Tourism Malaysia recommends two organizations, **Malaysia Healthcare** (www.malaysiahealthcare.com) and **Medi-Travel** (www.meditravel.com.my), both of whom can help travelers plan their medical needs, link them with specialists appropriate to their cases, and help plan all aspects of travel.

FOOD TRIPS

Travelers who are interested in learning more about Malaysian food should contact **Foodies and Friends** (www.foodiesnfriends.com.my) for details on where best to pursue such activities, including cooking classes for children. **Cuisine Studio** (www.cuisine-studio.net) in Kuala Lumpur conducts cooking classes, as well as operates two excellent restaurants in the city. One of the best places to learn about the intricacies of Malay cooking is with Shukri Shafie ("Cook with Shook"), who conducts such classes in a delightful setting on the island of Langkawi. He also operates a beachside restaurant on Langkawi called **The Lighthouse** (www.thelighthouse-langkawi.com).

VOLUNTEER & WORKING TRIPS

The World Wide Fund for Nature (or World Wildlife Fund; ☎ **03/7803-3772;** fax 03/7803-5157; www.wwf.org.my) can provide assistance to those who are seeking to do some nature volunteering in the country, or at least direct potential visitors to those organizations or locations where this could be possible. Resumes should be forwarded directly to careersjob@wwf.org. my.

---

12 STAYING CONNECTED

TELEPHONES

To place a call from your home country to Malaysia: Dial the international access code (011 in the U.S. and Canada; 0011 in Australia; or 00 in the U.K., Ireland, and New Zealand), plus the country code (60), plus the Malaysia area code (Cameron Highlands 5, Desaru 7, Genting Highlands 9, Johor Bahru 7, Kuala Lumpur 3, Kuala Terengganu 9, Kota Bharu 9, Kota Kinabalu 88, Kuantan 9, Kuching 82, Langkawi 4, Melaka 6, Mersing 7, Penang 4, Tioman 9), followed by the six-, seven-, or eight-digit phone number (for example, from the U.S. to Kuala Lumpur, you'd dial 011-60-3/0000-0000).

The nation's fixed telephone provider, Telekom Malaysia, also provides International Direct Dialing (IDD) services from most better hotels.

To place a direct international call from Malaysia: Dial the international access code (00), plus the country code of the place you are dialing (U.S. and Canada 1, Australia 61, Republic of Ireland 353, New Zealand 64, U.K. 44), plus the area/city code and the residential number.

To reach the international operator: Dial ☎ **108.**

Prepaid international calling cards are available from a number of companies and can be purchased at most convenience stores. Be warned that not all phones accept all cards—most likely card-operated phones are located next to the shops that sell corresponding cards.

With widespread mobile phone usage, coin-operated phones are becoming a scarcity. If you find one, local calls are charged at 10 sen for 3 minutes.

To place a call within Malaysia: You must use area codes if calling between states. Note that for calls within the country, area codes are preceded by a zero (Cameron Highlands 05, Desaru 07, Genting Highlands 09, Johor Bahru 07, Kuala Lumpur 03, Kuala Terengganu 09, Kota Bharu 09, Kota Kinabalu 088, Kuantan 09, Kuching 082, Langkawi 04, Melaka 06, Mersing 07, Penang 04, Tioman 09).

For local directory assistance: Dial ☎ **103.**

CELLPHONES

Cellular telephone services are provided by Celcom, DiGi, Maxis, and Telekom Cellular. Celcom sells a Malaysia prepaid SIM card that can be used with an international cellular phone that assigns a local telephone number, allows free incoming calls, and provides a local rate for local calls. It can be obtained before you travel via **Telestial** (☎ **800/707-0031** in the U.S.; 800/795-252 in Australia; www.telestial. com), with courier delivery. Telestial also rents cellphones.

In KL, visit **Celcom** at Levels 1 & 2, Podium Block Menara Naluri, 161B Jalan Ampang (not far from the Malaysia Tourism Centre). Or at KL International Airport in the International Arrival Hall, Level 3, in the Main Terminal Building. Throughout Malaysia, contact Celcom at © **1300/111-000,** www.celcom.com.my. Stored-value cards can be topped up at convenience stores, gas stations, and Celcom outlets throughout the country.

INTERNET & E-MAIL
With Your Own Computer

A growing number of better hotels now include Wi-Fi in guestrooms. If your hotel doesn't have Wi-Fi service, you can surf at a number of centrally located cafes that can be found in the central areas of the country's larger cities. With the exception of budget accommodations, all hotels have broadband internet connection in guestrooms.

Without Your Own Computer

Internet cafes can be found in every corner of the country, particularly in areas frequented by backpackers, near guesthouses, and in major shopping malls. Charges range from as low as RM4 (US$1.15/70p) per hour in cities to RM10 (US$2.90/£1.80) per hour in more remote destinations.

---

13 TIPS ON ACCOMMODATIONS

Peak months of the year for hotels in western peninsular Malaysia are December through February and July through September. For the east coast, the busy times are July through September. You will need to make reservations well in advance to secure your room during these months.

TAXES & SERVICE CHARGES All the nonbudget hotels charge a 10% service charge and 5% government tax. As such, there is no need to tip. But bellhops could be tipped at least RM2 (60¢/35p) per bag.

Suggested Itineraries Malaysia

Most visitors to Malaysia will arrive at Kuala Lumpur's (KL's) international airport, spend a day in the capital, then run around the country trying to see as much as they can in a short span of time. While it's natural to want to maximize your vacation time, I am of the philosophy that to try to pack too much into your holiday will actually detract from your overall travel experience. I've advised countless people on their trips and have been horrified to see some of the itineraries put together by well-meaning but ill-informed travel agents in the West. All are absolutely exhausting, some physically impossible. I recommend that you see no more than three destinations in 1 week, preferably only two. That way you have time not just to see the sights, but to stop and feel the rhythm of local life—to eat the food, smell the smells, speak with the people.

The itineraries I've suggested in this chapter are all based on 1-week stays in Malaysia. Each itinerary differs depending on your point of interest: Do you like historical sights and museums? Do you want to appreciate nature and explore the great outdoors? Or do you just want to relax on the best beaches, scuba, or snorkel?

A major consideration when planning your trip is the heat! Especially if you're not used to it, the heat and humidity can sap the energy from you. By the time you've finished lunch, you'll barely have the stamina to keep up with the rest of your planned activities. Combined with jet lag, you'll be asleep before dinner. Not a swell time. Keep daily itineraries simple, and make time for afternoon coffee or tea!

Also, when flying between cities, budget your time like this: One flight will take about a half-day. So if you're flying from Penang to KL, set aside either a whole morning or a whole afternoon for the flight. That will include airport transfers and whatnot. Along the same lines, all domestic flights either originate or end up in KL. What this means is, if you're flying from Penang to, say, Kota Kinabalu, you'll fly from Penang to KL in the morning, have lunch in the airport, then spend the afternoon flying from KL to Kota Kinabalu. It will take a whole day.

1 MALAYSIA'S REGIONS IN BRIEF

Malaysia's territory covers peninsular Malaysia—bordering Thailand in the north just across from Singapore in the south—and two states on the island of Borneo, Sabah and Sarawak, approximately 240km (149 miles) east across the South China Sea. All 13 of its states total 329,749 sq. km (128,602 sq. miles) of land. Of this area, Peninsular Malaysia makes up about 132,149 sq. km (51,538 sq. miles) and contains 11 of Malaysia's 13 states: Kedah, Perlis, Penang, and Perak

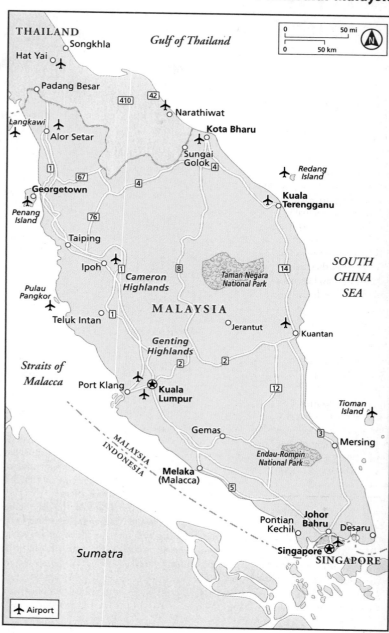

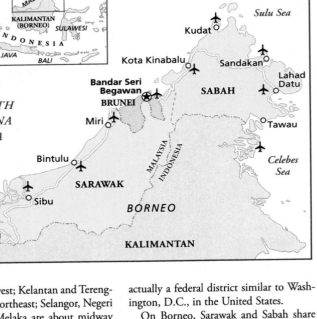

are in the northwest; Kelantan and Terengganu are in the northeast; Selangor, Negeri Sembilan, and Melaka are about midway down the peninsula on the western side; Pahang, along the east coast, sprawls inward to cover most of the central area (which is mostly forest preserve); and Johor covers the entire southern tip from east to west, with two vehicular causeways linking it to Singapore, just over the Strait of Johor. Kuala Lumpur, the nation's capital, appears on a map to be located in the center of the state of Selangor, but it is actually a federal district similar to Washington, D.C., in the United States.

On Borneo, Sarawak and Sabah share the landmass with Indonesia's Kalimantan. Also sharing the island, in a tiny nook on the Sarawak coast, is the tiny oil-rich Sultanate of Brunei Darussalam.

Back on the peninsula, the major cities can be found closer to the coastline, many having built on old trade or mining settlements, usually near one of Malaysia's many rivers.

2 MALAYSIA FOR HISTORY BUFFS & CULTURE VULTURES

This route brings you to Peninsular Malaysia's most historically significant destinations: Kuala Lumpur, Penang, and Malacca. You'll learn about the earliest trading ports and colonial history, and have time to shop and savor local treats.

Days ❶ & ❷: Arrive in Kuala Lumpur

After arriving in Malaysia's capital city, allow yourself a full day to recover and just spend your time wandering through the city's streets. Start at **Merdeka Square,** the focal point of colonial KL. Just behind the Moorish Sultan Abdul Samad Building, in the streets surrounding the Jame Mosque, you'll find KL's Little India of sorts. Continue your walk to the **Central Market ★**, where nearby coffee shops can provide a place to rest. After exploring stall after stall of Malaysian handicrafts at the Central Market, if you still have time and energy, cross the street to **Chinatown,** where you'll find more shopping, a street bazaar, and the **Sri Mahamariaman Hindu Temple.** See p. 227.

Day ❸: Melaka (Malacca) ★★

Take an early-morning bus to Melaka and spend the day exploring the town's historic heart. The most important things to see here are the **Stadthuys ★** (p. 238), the history museum, located in the hard-to-miss red colonial building; the **Cultural Museum ★** (p. 237), in a replica of a Malay-style palace; and the **Baba Nyonya Heritage Museum ★** (p. 237), located inside an old millionaire's mansion. From the Baba Nyonya Museum, head to **Jonker Walk** to wander through temples and antiques shops. See p. 239.

Day ❹: Penang

Take an early-morning bus back to KL, then board a flight to Penang. Allow 1 day for the journey. Check into your resort at **Batu Feringgi** so that when you arrive,

you can unwind with a cocktail as you watch the setting sun from the beach. See p. 245.

Day ❺: Georgetown ★★★

Here's what I have to say about Georgetown: Don't plan your time too closely. Start off at the **Penang Museum and Art Gallery ★★** (p. 249), where you'll get a brilliant overview of the island's history and cultures, then just spend your time walking through the streets. Attractions are all situated within walking distance, but don't rush: Take time to peek in the shop doors and snack on the local treats you'll find along the way. Just make sure you're at the **Cheong Fatt Tze Mansion ★★★** (p. 245) in time for the 11am or 3pm tour—consider it a must! Afterward, mosey over to the **E&O Hotel ★★** (p. 245) for either lunch or high tea in the old colonial dame. See p. 241.

Day ❻: Penang Hill

The funicular train up the side of Penang Hill was built in 1923 to take British colonials up to the cooler climate of the hill, where they built lovely country homes and gardens. Get there before 9am to beat the long queue. At the top of the hill, you'll find restaurants, temples, and trails, one of which will lead you down to the botanical gardens. See p. 250.

Days ❼ & ❽: Back to KL

Hop a flight back to KL to prepare for your return home. If you have time, you can stock up on gifts at **KL Craft Complex** (p. 228)—you'll find something for everyone on your list, in all price ranges, at this handicrafts showroom. See p. 215.

12

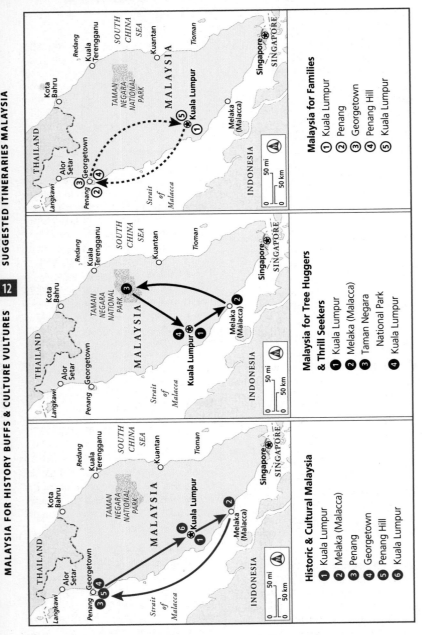

Historic & Cultural Malaysia
1. Kuala Lumpur
2. Melaka (Malacca)
3. Penang
4. Georgetown
5. Penang Hill
6. Kuala Lumpur

Malaysia for Tree Huggers & Thrill Seekers
1. Kuala Lumpur
2. Melaka (Malacca)
3. Taman Negara National Park
4. Kuala Lumpur

Malaysia for Families
1. Kuala Lumpur
2. Penang
3. Georgetown
4. Penang Hill
5. Kuala Lumpur

3 MALAYSIA FOR TREE-HUGGERS & THRILL SEEKERS

This route gives you some choices, depending on your particular interests. Peninsular Malaysia's Taman Negara preserve is hopping distance from KL, so if you want to mix history and nature, it's very easy to combine an overnight trip to Melaka with a 3-night package to the park—I have included this itinerary below. If you want to delve deeper into rainforest habitats, fly to Kota Kinabalu and sign up for a tour of the area's national parks; specialty trips take you into wildlife preserves or trekking up Mt. Kinabalu. If it's indigenous cultures you'd like to visit, fly out to Sarawak, spend a day exploring Kuching, then join a boat trip into the interior to visit longhouse communities. The diverse range of forests in Sabah and Sarawak offers all kinds of adventures, from nature walks to animal sanctuaries, to cave exploring or white-water rafting.

Remember, if you go the outdoor adventure route, be sure to check monsoon seasons with your adventure tour coordinator. You don't want the rains to wash out your trek, or the dry season to take the thrill out of your white-water rapids. Also, for dive tours you'll have to allow extra time between flights and dives, for your body to acclimate to the change in altitudes.

Days ❶–❸: Kuala Lumpur & Melaka

Follow the itinerary in "Malaysia for History Buffs & Culture Vultures," above, for Days 1, 2, and 3.

Days ❹–❼: Taman Negara National Park ★★★

Take an early-morning bus back from Melaka to KL, then board an afternoon bus to Malaysia's premier and most accessible national park. Hop a boat upstream to the resort and check in for a good night's rest. Taman Negara can be done very nicely in a full-board package. You'll have the chance to jungle-trek, traverse a canopy walk, view wildlife from observation stations, go on a night trek, river-raft and fish, and meet Orang Asli communities. See p. 229.

Days ❼ & ❽: Back to KL

See Days 7 and 8 in "Malaysia for History Buffs & Culture Vultures," above.

4 MALAYSIA FOR FAMILIES

Malaysia is a terrific destination for families. It's safe, friendly, and free of some of the seedier trappings of tourism that can be seen in other parts of Asia. For this itinerary, I've included an equal mix of beach and culture—sightseeing in the mornings and fun in the afternoons—at a pace that allows for maximum flexibility.

Days ❶ & ❷: Arrive in Kuala Lumpur

After arriving in Malaysia's capital city, allow yourself a full day to recover and just spend your time wandering through the city's streets. Start in **Chinatown** (p. 269), where you'll find a street bazaar and the Sri Mahamariaman Hindu Temple (p. 227), then cut through the bustling Central Market to **Merdeka Square** (p. 226), the focal point of colonial KL. From the Jame Mosque, hop on the train to Jalan Imbi. Next to the station, you'll find **Berjaya Times Square** (p. 228), KL's largest shopping mall, filled with tons of food and shopping, not to mention **Cosmo's World Theme Park ★★★** (p. 225), the world's largest indoor amusement park.

Day ❸: Penang

Take an early-morning flight to Penang. Check into the **Holiday Inn Resort Penang** (p. 246) at Batu Feringgi, where they have special kids' suites. Have a ball at the beach! Don't forget to book watersports activities for the following days.

Day ❹: Georgetown ★★★

Spend your morning in Georgetown. Hit the **Penang Museum and Art Gallery ★★** (p. 249) at 9am, when it opens. Afterward, head over to the **Cheong Fatt Tze Mansion ★★★** (p. 248) for the 11am tour. Afterward, wander free through

the streets before heading back to your resort for an afternoon of relaxation at the beach. See p. 241.

Day ❺: Penang Hill

The funicular train up the side of Penang Hill was built in 1923 to take British colonials up to the cooler climate of the hill, where they built lovely country homes and gardens. At the top of the hill, you'll find restaurants, temples, and trails, one of which will lead you down to the botanical gardens. The trek lasts only an hour or two, so if your children aren't too young, it should be a nice little adventure. Carry water and snacks! See p. 250.

Days ❻ & ❼: Back to KL

See Days 7 and 8 in "Malaysia for History Buffs & Culture Vultures," above.

13

Peninsular Malaysia: Kuala Lumpur & the West Coast

The more popular destinations in Malaysia dot the west coast of the country's peninsula. If you have little time, you can stick to this central corridor and still experience fascinating Malaysian heritage and gorgeous outdoors without traveling too far.

Kuala Lumpur, the nation's capital, lies about midway between the northern border with Thailand and the tip of the peninsula, before you reach Singapore. For a newcomer, the city's museums, shopping, and delicious dining choices make it a good introduction to Malaysia's culture. Kuala Lumpur is a great jumping-off point for discovering Malaysia's rainforests as well.

The sleepy town of **Melaka (Malacca),** a 2-hour drive south of the capital city, has remarkably retained much of its old-world charm, with evidence of previous Portuguese, Dutch, and British colonists mixed with the cultures of Arabs, Indians, and Chinese who settled and traded here centuries ago.

Pulau Pangkor, or Pangkor Island, is a secluded island hideaway with delicious tropical resorts dripping with Southeast Asian ambience, a mere half-hour's flight from Kuala Lumpur.

Farther north, **Penang** is perhaps Malaysia's most popular destination. Once the seat of British colonial power in the region, Penang still bears signs of its former inhabitants. Georgetown, the main town on the island, bustles with charm—narrow streets, old shophouses, places of worship, and terrific street food. If you stay in Penang's beachfront area, you can enjoy the stimulating culture and a relaxing beach experience.

North of Penang, **Langkawi** has the greatest collection of stunning beach resorts. Situated in the Andaman Sea, it also has the best waters of all the west-coast attractions, and watersports to match.

1 KUALA LUMPUR ★★

Kuala Lumpur (or KL, as it is commonly known) is, more often than not, a traveler's point of entry to Malaysia. As the capital, it is the most modern and developed city in the country, with contemporary high-rises and world-class hotels, glitzy shopping malls, and local and international cuisine.

The city began sometime around 1857 as a small mining boomtown created by the Industrial Revolution's hunger for raw materials. Fueled by tin mining in the nearby Klang River Valley, the town grew under the business interests of three officials: a local Malay ruler, a British resident, and a Chinese headman (Kapitan China). The industry and village attracted Chinese laborers, Malays from nearby villages, and Indian immigrants who followed the British. As the town grew, colonial buildings that housed local administrative offices were erected around Merdeka Square, bounded by Jalan Sultan Hishamuddin and Jalan Kuching. The town, and later the city, spread outward from this center.

Life in 19th-century KL had many difficult starts and stops—tin was subject to price fluctuations, the Chinese were involved in clan "wars," but worst of all, malaria was killing thousands. Still, in the late 1800s, KL overcame its hurdles to become the capital of the state, and eventually of the Federated Malay States. Its development continued to accelerate, with a brief setback during the Japanese World War II occupation, until 1957, when newly independent Malaysia declared Kuala Lumpur its national capital.

Today the original city center at **Merdeka Square** is the core of KL's history. Buildings like the Sultan Abdul Samad Building, the Royal Selangor Club, and the Old Kuala Lumpur Railway Station are stunning examples of British style peppered with Moorish flavor. South of this area is KL's **Chinatown.** Along Jalan Petaling and surrounding areas are markets, shops, food stalls, and the bustling life of the Chinese community. There's also a **Little India** in KL, around the area occupied by Masjid Jame, where you'll find flower stalls, Indian Muslim and Malay costumes, and traditional items. Across the river you'll find **Lake Gardens,** a large sanctuary that houses Kuala Lumpur's bird park, butterfly park, and other attractions and gardens. Modern Kuala Lumpur is rooted in the city's **"Golden Triangle,"** bounded by Jalan Ampang, Jalan Tun Razak, and Jalan Imbi. This section is home to most of KL's hotels, office complexes, shopping malls, and sights like the KL Tower and the Petronas Twin Towers, the tallest buildings in the world from 1998 to 2004, when Taipei 101 stole the title. They are now officially the world's tallest twin towers.

ESSENTIALS
Visitor Information

In Kuala Lumpur, Tourism Malaysia has several offices. The largest is at the **MTC,** the **Malaysia Tourist Centre** (see "Attractions," later in this chapter), located on 109 Jalan Ampang (✆ **03/2164-3929**) and open daily from 8am to 10:30pm. In addition to a tourist information desk, MTC has a moneychanger; ATM; tourist police post; travel agent booking for Taman Negara trips, city tours, and limited hotel bookings; souvenir shops; an amphitheater; and Transnasional bus ticket bookings.

Vision KL Magazine is offered for free in many hotel rooms and has listings for events in KL and Malaysia. At newsstands, it costs RM6.80 ($1.95/£1.25). The monthly *Time Out* is a more comprehensive alternative.

Getting There

BY TRAIN　I love KL's shiny new train station, **KL Sentral.** Not only does it serve as a clean, safe, and orderly base from which to take the train, but it's also a hub for local commuter train services around the city; it's got tons of facilities, moneychangers, ATMs, fast food, and shops; and it's got an easy taxi coupon system (about RM10/$2.90/£1.80 or RM13/$3.75/£2.35 to central parts of the city)—cabs are really easy to find here. For KL Sentral information, call ✆ **03/2267-1200.**

BY BUS　If you're arriving in KL by bus, be warned, different bus companies drop off at different locations around the city. In chapter 11, "Planning Your Trip to Malaysia," I recommended **Aeroline** buses from Singapore (✆ **65/6723-7222**). These buses will drop you off at the Corus Hotel in Kuala Lumpur, which is located in the heart of the city. KL has three official bus terminals that handle intercity bus departures and arrivals

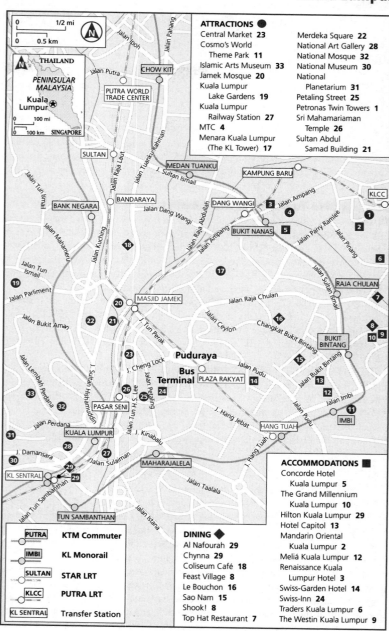

ATTRACTIONS ●

Central Market **23**
Cosmo's World
  Theme Park **11**
Islamic Arts Museum **33**
Jamek Mosque **20**
Kuala Lumpur
  Lake Gardens **19**
Kuala Lumpur
  Railway Station **27**
MTC **4**
Menara Kuala Lumpur
  (The KL Tower) **17**

Merdeka Square **22**
National Art Gallery **28**
National Mosque **32**
National Museum **30**
National
  Planetarium **31**
Petaling Street **25**
Petronas Twin Towers **1**
Sri Mahamariaman
  Temple **26**
Sultan Abdul
  Samad Building **21**

ACCOMMODATIONS ■

Concorde Hotel
  Kuala Lumpur **5**
The Grand Millennium
  Kuala Lumpur **10**
Hilton Kuala Lumpur **29**
Hotel Capitol **13**
Mandarin Oriental
  Kuala Lumpur **2**
Meliá Kuala Lumpur **12**
Renaissance Kuala
  Lumpur Hotel **3**
Swiss-Garden Hotel **14**
Swiss-Inn **24**
Traders Kuala Lumpur **6**
The Westin Kuala Lumpur **9**

DINING ◆

Al Nafourah **29**
Chynna **29**
Coliseum Café **18**
Feast Village **8**
Le Bouchon **16**
Sao Nam **15**
Shook! **8**
Top Hat Restaurant **7**

KTM Commuter PUTRA
KL Monorail IMBI
STAR LRT SULTAN
PUTRA LRT KLCC
Transfer Station KL SENTRAL

to all parts of the country: the Puduraya Terminal on Jalan Pudu, Putra Terminal on Jalan Tun Ismail, and Pekililing Terminal on Jalan Ipoh. If you arrive at Puduraya, the biggest of the three, good luck! It's congested—with both toxic fumes and traffic jams: one of the reasons I avoid standard bus travel in Malaysia. Taxis—another less-than-pleasant mode of transportation (see below) can be found at any of these terminals, but beware of drivers who will try to overcharge you.

BY PLANE   The **Kuala Lumpur International Airport (KLIA)** (© **03/8776-4386**), located in Sepang, 53km (33 miles) outside the city, opened in 1998. KLIA is a huge complex, with business centers, dining facilities, a fitness center, medical services, shopping, post offices, and a nearby luxurious airport hotel operated by **Pan Pacific** (© **03/ 8787-3333;** www.panpacific.com/KLairport). The Low Cost Carrier Terminal (LCCT), which services budget airlines like AirAsia, is 20km (12 miles) away from the KLIA main terminal, so be warned that it is not easy to transfer between the two terminals. Although there are moneychangers, they are few and far between, so hop on the first line you see and don't assume there's another one just around the corner.

Getting into Town from the Airport

BY TAXI   City taxis are not permitted to pick up from the airport (although you will find illegal touts—avoid them!), but special **airport taxis** (© **03/8787-3678**) operate 'round-the-clock, charging RM92 ($27/£17) for premier cars (Mercedes) and RM67 ($19/£12) for standard vehicles (the locally built Proton). Vans with seating capacity up to eight can also be hired for RM180 ($52/£32). Charges may vary depending on your destination. Coupons must be purchased at the arrival concourse.

An **express coach** (© **03/2730-2000**) connects KLIA to KL Sentral train station, where you can catch a cab to the city's major hotels. It costs RM35 ($10/£6.30) for a ticket, so you may as well take the Express Rail Link, listed below. It's faster. There are also express buses from the LCC terminal that connect to KL Sentral; they cost RM9 ($2.60/£1.60).

The **KLIA Ekspres** (© **03/2267-8000**) is an express rail link that runs between KLIA and KL Sentral train station from 5am to 1am daily. Trains depart every 15 minutes and take 28 minutes to complete the journey. Tickets cost RM35 ($10/£6.30) for adults and RM15 ($4.35/£2.70) for children. From KL Sentral, taxis are always on hand and use a coupon system (about RM10/$2.90/£1.80 or RM13/$3.75/£2.35 to central parts of the city), or you can catch one of the city's commuter trains to a station near your hotel.

Getting Around

Kuala Lumpur is a prime example of a city that was not planned, per se, from a master graph of streets. Rather, because of its beginnings as an outpost, it grew as it needed to, expanding outward and swallowing up rural surroundings. The result is a tangled web of streets too narrow to support the traffic of a capital city. Cars and buses weave through one-way lanes, with countless motorbikes sneaking in and out, sometimes in the opposite direction of traffic or up on the sidewalks. Expect traffic jams in the morning rush between 6 and 10am, and again between 5 and 8pm. At other times, taxis are a convenient way of getting around, but the commuter train system, if they're going where you need to, is perhaps the best value and easiest route. City buses are hot and crowded, with some very confusing routes. Walking can also be frustrating. Many sidewalks are in poor condition, with buckled tiles and gaping gutters. The heat can be prohibitive as well. However, areas within the colonial heart of the city, Chinatown, Little India, and some areas in the Golden Triangle are within walking distance of each other.

BY TAXI   If you ask me, KL cabbies should have their tires slashed. If you can get one to stop, the driver will almost always refuse to use the meter (which is against the law), quoting what seems to be the standard—RM10 ($2.90/£1.80), usually for a trip that normally costs RM4 ($1.15/70p). If it's raining, expect that quote to double. I usually don't dicker over the price because it's only a buck and a half. It's just frustrating when cab after cab passes you by. In some places within the city, taxi stands try to solve this problem. Be prepared for taxis to pull over, roll down the window, and hear the pleas from the line before deciding upon which passenger to take, regardless of the order of the line.

Taxis can be booked by phone with an RM1 (29¢/18p) booking charge. Call **Cityline,** ✆ **03/9222-2828; Comfort,** ✆ **03/2692-2525;** or **Sunlight,** ✆ **03/9057-5757.** Sometimes these services are not reliable.

Technically, the metered fare is RM2 (60¢/35p) for the first 2km (1¼ mile) and an additional RM.10 (3¢/2p) for each 200m (656 ft.) after that. Between midnight and 6am, you'll be charged an extra 50% of the total fare.

BY BUS   I don't recommend travel on city buses. They're cheap but not dependable, with city routes that will get newcomers lost for sure. It's not the most relaxing way to get around.

BY RAIL   KL has a network of mass transit trains that snake through the city and out to the suburbs, and it'll be worth your time to become familiar with them, because taxis are sometimes unreliable and traffic jams can be unbearable. Trouble is, there are five train routes and each one is operated by a different company. How confusing! The lines don't seem to connect in any logical way.

The four lines that are most useful to visitors are the **Putra LRT,** the **Star LRT,** the **KL Monorail,** and the **KLIA Ekspres** to the airport. The latter route is explained under "Getting into Town from the Airport," above.

The **Kelana Jaya Line,** formerly called Putra LRT, has stops at Bangsar (featured in the section "Kuala Lumpur After Dark," later in this chapter), KL Sentral (train station), Pasar Seni (Chinatown), Masjid Jamek, Dang Wangi, and KLCC shopping center. The **Ampang & Sri Petaling Line,** formerly called the Star LRT, is convenient if you need to get to the Putra World Trade Centre. It also stops at Masjid Jamek and Plaza Rayat. Average trips on both lines will cost around RM2 (60¢/35p).

The **KL Monorail** provides good access through the main hotel and shopping areas of the city, including stops at KL Sentral, Imbi, Bukit Bintang (the main shopping strip), and Raja Chulan (along Jalan Sultan Ismail, where many hotels are). Fares run between RM1.20 (35¢/20p) and RM2.50 (70¢/45p).

As a rough guide, all lines operate between 5 or 6am until around midnight, with trains coming every 10 minutes or so. Tickets can be purchased at any station either from the stationmaster or from single-fare electronic ticket booths.

ON FOOT   The heat and humidity can make walking between attractions pretty uncomfortable. However, sometimes the traffic is so unbearable that you'll get where you're going much faster by strapping on your tennis shoes and hiking it.

Fast Facts: Kuala Lumpur

The **area code** for Kuala Lumpur is 03, and the city's phone numbers have an eight-digit format. Numbers in the rest of the country have seven digits.

The main office for **American Express** is located in KL at Menara Maybank, Ground Level banking hall, Jalan Perak (✆ **03/2050-0888**). You'll also find headquarters for all

Malaysian and many international banks, most of which have outlets along Jalan Sultan Ismail, plus ATMs at countless locations throughout the city. Look for moneychangers in just about every shopping mall; they're a better bargain than banks or hotel cashiers.

KL's **General Post Office,** on Jalan Sultan Hishamuddin in the enormous Pos Malaysia Komplex Dayabumi (© 03/2274-1122), can be pretty overwhelming. If you can, try to use your hotel's mail service for a much easier time. Internet service in KL will run about RM3 to RM6 (85¢–$1.75/55p–£1.10) per hour for usage. Internet cafes come and go, popping up in backpacker areas like Chinatown and the streets around BB Plaza off Jalan Bukit Bintang.

The emergency number for **police** and **ambulance** is © 999. For **fire** emergencies, call © 994.

WHERE TO STAY

International business-class properties like the Westin, Hilton, Ritz-Carlton, and Mandarin Oriental fill their rooms every night with corporate travelers who are charged corporate rates to their corporate expense accounts. The hotels I've selected here represent only those properties I think are best for leisure travelers. Even the more expensive hotels I've chosen have qualities that extend beyond the business center.

If you plan to travel to KL in July and August and want to stay in an upmarket hotel, you'll need to book your room well in advance. KL's super-peak season falls during these months, when travelers from the Middle East take a break from scorching temperatures back home. Malaysia is the perfect tropical holiday spot for Muslim travelers from around the world, and Tourism Malaysia has done an excellent job of attracting the Middle Eastern market in particular, extending restaurant and cafe hours, and even shopping mall hours into the wee hours of the morning.

Very Expensive

The Grand Millennium Kuala Lumpur ★ One of the best five-star properties in Kuala Lumpur, this landmark along KL's fashionable Jalan Bukit Bintang shopping strip has an ever-bustling lobby to match the excitement along the sidewalks outside—the lobby lounge is busy night and day. Surprisingly, the staff always seems polite and professional, despite the barrage. The guest rooms are spacious, quiet, and cool, with huge plush beds covered in soft cozy cotton sheets and down comforters. Bathrooms are large marble affairs with plenty of counter space. The outdoor pool is a palm-lined free-form escape, and the fitness center is state-of-the-art, with sauna, steam, spa, and Jacuzzi. Pavilion Kuala Lumpur, the city's smart new shopping mall, adjoins the hotel, and while some construction is still ongoing, disturbance to hotel guests is minimized. Night Owls should enjoy the lively entertainment in the hotel's Pulse bar and nightclub.

160 Jalan Bukit Bintang, 55100 Kuala Lumpur. © **866/866-8066** in the U.S. and Canada, 800/124-420 in Australia, 800/808-228 in New Zealand, 800/414-741 in the U.K., or 03/2117-4888. Fax 03/2117-1441. www.millenniumhotels.com. 468 units. RM750 ($218/£135) double; from RM1,450 ($421/£261) suite. AE, DC, MC, V. 5-min. walk to Bukit Bintang Monorail station. **Amenities:** 3 restaurants; bar and lobby lounge; outdoor pool; 2 squash courts; 24-hr. health club w/Jacuzzi, sauna, steam, and massage; concierge; airport transfers; room service; babysitting; smoke-free rooms; executive-level rooms. *In room:* A/C, TV w/ satellite programming and in-house movies, high-speed Internet, minibar, hair dryer.

Mandarin Oriental Kuala Lumpur ★★★ The glistening Petronas Twin Towers are the iconic KL landmarks, and its neighbor, the Mandarin Oriental or "MO," has the best views. The hotel has set the benchmark for hospitality standards in the city and is popular with corporate clients, who receive the finest treatment on club floors and arguably the best club lounge in KL. I love the views from the panoramic windows of the 24th-floor lounge—arrive about 6:45pm when the twin tower lights are turned on. The 10-year-old hotel is due for a renovation, but its service and guest recognition are outstanding. Dine in the new seafood outlet, Pacifica, or in the old Shanghai surroundings of Lai Po Heen. At night, Sultan Lounge turns into the local hot spot.

Kuala Lumpur City Center (KLCC), 50088 Kuala Lumpur, © **866/526-6567** in the U.S. and Canada, 800/123-693 in Australia, 800/2828-3838 in New Zealand, 800/2828-3838 in the U.K., or 03/2380-888, Fax 03/2380-8833. www.mandarinoriental.com. 643 units. RM510 ($148/£92) double; from RM2,173 ($630/£391) suite. AE, DC, MC, V. 2-min walk to KLCC and the Convention Center. **Amenities:** 3 restaurants; lobby lounge; cigar divan; outdoor pool; tennis courts; squash courts; health club w/Jacuzzi, steam room, and sauna; spa; concierge; airport transfers; room service; babysitting. *In room:* A/C, TV w/satellite, high-speed Internet, minibar, hair dryer.

Expensive

Hilton Kuala Lumpur ★★★

Forget anything you've ever experienced in a Hilton—this is the absolute hottest hotel in KL, and probably one of the most innovative hotels in the world. From the airy, art-filled public spaces to the compact rooftop lagoon pool, everything is done with edgy style and sophistication. Large rooms have sleek contemporary decor, with a desk area wired for work, mood lighting, stocked minibar with a coffee plunger and heavy mugs, and a 42-inch plasma TV. A "magic button" handles all service requests, and three "lifestyle boxes" provide little extras like desk accessories, bath treats, and games. Bathrooms are great; they have deep tubs, wide "rain" showerheads, and a mini LCD-screen TV built into the shaving mirror. The hotel's fitness center is operated by the very competent Clarke Hatch company, and the rooftop pool and Balinese-inspired spa are great escapes.

3 Jalan Stesen Sentral, 50470 Kuala Lumpur. © **800/HILTONS** (445-8667) in the U.S. and Canada, 800/445-8667 in Australia, 800/445-866 in New Zealand, 800/448-002 in the U.K., or 03/2264-2264. Fax 03/2264-2266. www.hilton.com. 510 units. RM466 ($135/£84) double; from RM830 ($241/£150) suite. AE, DC, MC, V. Opposite KL Sentral station. **Amenities:** 5 restaurants; 2 bars; outdoor pool; health club; spa; concierge; airport transfers; room service; babysitting; smoke-free rooms; executive-level rooms. *In room:* A/C, TV w/satellite programming and in-house movies, high-speed Internet, minibar, hair dryer.

Renaissance Kuala Lumpur Hotel ★ (Value)

The Renaissance offers terrific value for the money. It has two wings, the posh West Wing and the modern East Wing, and both wings share hotel facilities. Each wing has its own entrance, connected in the middle where the ballroom and banquet rooms are housed. Guest rooms in the West Wing have a European feel to them—very bold and impressive, and typical of a traditional hotel. In fact, you'll never know you're in Malaysia. The East Wing is contemporary, with simpler decor, but is no less comfortable. The enormous outdoor pool, which sits between the two hotel towers, is one of the biggest in the city.

Corner of Jalan Sultan Ismail and Jalan Ampang, 50450 Kuala Lumpur. © **800/HOTELS-1** (468-3571) in the U.S. and Canada, 800/251-259 in Australia, 800/441-035 in New Zealand, or 03/2162-2233. Fax 03/2163-1122. www.marriott.com/hotels/travel/kulrn-renaissance-kuala-lumpur-hotel. 910 units. West Wing: RM695 ($202/£125); from RM1,800 ($522/£324) suite. East Wing: RM645 ($187/£116) double, from RM1,250 ($363/£225) suite. AE, DC, MC, V. 5-min. walk to Bukit Nanas Monorail and Dang Wangi LRT stations. **Amenities:** 9 restaurants and bars; large landscaped outdoor pool; outdoor lighted tennis court; health club w/sauna and massage; concierge; airport transfers; room service; babysitting; smoke-free rooms; executive-level rooms. *In room:* A/C, satellite TV, high-speed Internet, minibar, hair dryer.

Traders Kuala Lumpur ★   Traders is a little deceptive, in that it is supposed to be a four-star Shangri-La, but this centrally located hotel packs a punch bigger than its humble rating. It overlooks the Twin Towers and has magical evening views of floodlight icons and the associated parklands. It adjoins the Convention Center, and golf carts ferry guests to and from the towers and the shopping paradise found at their base. SkyBar, on the hotel's 33rd floor, is my favorite nightspot in KL, with unsurpassed aerial views of the city skyline. Only 2 years old, this hotel has everything business travelers need, and its location makes it popular with conference delegates and leisure travelers.

Kuala Lumpur City Center (KLCC), 50088 Kuala Lumpur. © **866/656-5050** in the U.S. and Canada, 800/222-448 in Australia, 800/442-179 in New Zealand, 800/028-3337 in the U.K., or 03/2332-9888. Fax 03/2332-2667. www.tradershotels.com. 571 units. RM400 ($116/£72) double; from RM725 ($210/£131) suite. AE, DC, MC, V. Brisk 10-min walk to the Twin Towers and 15-min to Bintang Walk. **Amenities:** 2 restaurants; 1 bar; health club; spa; Jacuzzi; sauna; steam bath. *In room:* A/C, satellite TV, high-speed Internet, hair dryer.

The Westin Kuala Lumpur ★★   The Westin is no ordinary hotel. Its sensory approach to hospitality is obvious the minute you enter from busy Bintang Walk and notice the aromatherapy candles, the fruit-flavored welcome drinks, and the mood of the music. The staff looks more like smart shop assistants from the nearby Louis Vuitton store than those of a chain hotel. There is a trendy vibe to everything from restaurants to bars, and the rooms are contemporary, functional, and welcoming. The buffet breakfast is easily the region's best. EEST serves up a wide array of Asian cuisines, and Qba features live salsa bands almost every night.

199 Jalan Bukit Bintang, 55100 Kuala Lumpur. © **800/937-8461** in the U.S. and Canada, 800/656-535 in Australia, 800/490-375 in New Zealand, 800/325-95959 in the U.K., or 03/2731-8333. Fax 03/2773 8087. www.westin.com/kualalumpur. 443 units. RM980 ($284/£176) double; from RM1,530 ($444/£275) suite. AE, DC, MC, V. 5-min walk to monorail station and on the doorstep to the restaurants, bars, and entertainment of Bintang Walk. **Amenities:** 4 restaurants; 2 bars; outdoor pool; health club; airport transfers; room service. *In room:* A/C, satellite TV, high-speed Internet, minibar, hair dryer.

Moderate

Concorde Hotel Kuala Lumpur ★★ (Value)   Concorde is one of my favorites in this price category for its central location and quality accommodations at an incredible price. Although rooms are not as large as those in more expensive hotels, they're well outfitted with desks, side chairs, comfortable beds, and tidy bathrooms. A recent renovation has made them more stylish. Concorde has a small outdoor pool with a charming cafe and small fitness center. The lobby lounge is noisy at night because it's popular. Hard Rock Café is also on the premises.

2 Jalan Sultan Ismail, 50250 Kuala Lumpur. © **03/2144-2200.** Fax 03/2144-1628. www.concorde.net/kl. 570 units. RM330 ($96/£59) double; from RM1,360 ($394/£245) suite. AE, DC, MC, V. 5-min. walk to Bukit Nanas Monorail station and 10-min. walk to Dang Wangi LRT station. **Amenities:** 3 restaurants; lobby lounge and Hard Rock Cafe; small outdoor pool; health club w/sauna, steam room, and massage; concierge; airport transfers; room service; babysitting; executive-level rooms. *In room:* A/C, TV w/satellite programming and in-house movies, high-speed Internet, minibar.

Meliá Kuala Lumpur ★ (Value)   This hotel is located next to a KL Monorail station and across the street from the mind-bogglingly enormous Times Square shopping and entertainment complex, making it an appealing option for visitors. The small lobby is functional, with space for tour groups and a very active and efficient tour desk. Guest rooms have light wood furnishings, contemporary fixtures, wall desks with a swivel arm for extra space, and big-screen TVs. Bathrooms, although small, are well maintained, with good counter space. Mealtimes in the hotel's coffee shop can be a little crowded.

16 Jalan Imbi, 55100 Kuala Lumpur. ☏ **888/33MELIA** (336-3542) in the U.S. and Canada, 800/962-720 in the U.K., or 03/2785-2828. Fax 03/2785-2800. www.solmelia.com. 300 units. RM435 ($126/£78) double; from RM1,200 ($348/£216) suite. AE, DC, MC, V. Imbi Monorail station. **Amenities:** 2 restaurants; bar and karaoke lounge; small outdoor pool; health club w/massage; room service; babysitting; smoke-free rooms; Wi-Fi. *In room:* A/C, TV w/satellite programming and in-house movies, minibar.

Swiss-Garden Hotel For midrange prices, Swiss-Garden offers reliable comfort, okay location, and affordability that attracts many leisure travelers to its doors. It also knows how to make you feel right at home, with a friendly staff (the concierge is on the ball) and a hotel lobby bar that actually gets patronized (by travelers having cool cocktails at the end of a busy day of sightseeing). The guest rooms are decorated in warm earthy tones. Swiss-Garden is within walking distance from KL's lively Chinatown district and close to the Puduraya bus station (which, unfortunately, makes traffic ugly at rush hour). Facilities include an outdoor pool, a small spa, an e-lounge, a new eco-cafe, and a fitness center.

117 Jalan Pudu, 55100 Kuala Lumpur. ☏ 03/2141-3333. Fax 03/2141-5555. www.swissgarden.com. 310 units. RM450 ($131/£81) double; from RM800 ($232/£144) suite. AE, DC, MC, V. **Amenities:** 2 restaurants; lobby lounge; small outdoor pool; small health club; spa w/massage; concierge; airport transfers; room service; babysitting; smoke-free rooms. *In room:* A/C, satellite TV, minibar, hair dryer.

Inexpensive

Hotel Capitol ★ (**Value**) A top pick for a budget hotel, Capitol is located in a lively part of the city's popular Golden Triangle district, close to the junction of Jalan Sultan Ismail and Jalan Bukit Bintang. In the surrounding lanes, you'll find small eateries and shops for necessities, and shopping malls are close by. The place has a minimalist lobby that's function over frills. Inside the guest rooms, the wooden furniture seems like it's been around a while, but the upholstery, bedding, carpeting, and drapes all seem fresh. The big tiled bathroom also has a long bathtub. There are no leisure facilities to speak of, but if you've come to KL to sightsee, you won't miss them.

Jalan Bulan, off Jalan Bukit Bintang, 55100 Kuala Lumpur. ☏ **800/448-8355** in the U.S. and Canada, 800/221-176 in Australia, or 03/2143-7000. Fax 03/2143-0000. www.capitol.com.my/index.html. 225 units. RM250 ($73/£45) double. AE, DC, MC, V. 5-min. walk to Bintang Monorail station. **Amenities:** Restaurant; room service; smoke-free rooms. *In room:* A/C, satellite TV, high-speed Internet access, minibar, hair dryer.

Swiss-Inn This tiny hotel is popular with budget travelers. Tucked away in the heart of Chinatown, Swiss-Inn's best asset is its location, amid the jumble of vibrant night market hawkers. The place is small, but a new contemporary west wing has 41 rooms with 26-inch LCD TVs and smart bathrooms. Higher-priced rooms have a small window, a bit more space (but are still compact), and are somewhat better maintained. Budget rooms, on lower floors, are very small, the cheapest having no windows at all. Room categories are superior, deluxe, and family, and they often have good promotional rates. Make sure you reserve your room early because this place runs at high occupancy year-round. The cafe, hidden behind market stalls, is an interesting place to have a beer and people-watch.

62 Jalan Sultan, 50000 Kuala Lumpur. ☏ 03/2072-3333. Fax 03/2031-6699. www.swissinnkualalumpur. com. 110 units. RM295 ($86/£53) double. AE, DC, MC, V. **Amenities:** 2 restaurants; Internet kiosks (extra charge); smoke-free rooms. *In room:* A/C, TV, hair dryer.

WHERE TO DINE

Kuala Lumpur, like Singapore, is very cosmopolitan. Here you'll not only find delicious and exotic cuisine, but you'll find it served in some pretty trendy settings.

Al Nafourah ★★★ LEBANESE   Dripping with the magical allure of a desert oasis, Al Nafourah is pure Arabian Nights. With Moorish arches, twinkling lanterns, carved screens, silken hangings, mosaic tiles, and woven carpets throughout, the restaurant also has booths in private nooks for extra romance. The Lebanese cuisine is some of the best around, with lamb, chicken, and fish dishes in tangy herbs and warm flatbreads straight from a wood-fire oven. Outside on the terrace, sit back and drink a heady coffee and smoke from a hookah while taking in belly-dance performances. A truly memorable evening.

Le Meridien Kuala Lumpur, 2 Jalan Stesen Sentral. © **03/2263-7888.** Reservations recommended. Main courses RM48–RM128 ($14–$37/£8.65–£23). AE, DC, MC, V. Daily noon–2:30pm and 6:30–10:30pm.

Chynna ★★ CANTONESE   Chynna is pure dinner theater: From the Madam Wong–style red lanterns to the Old China antique replica furnishings, you'll think you're in a highly stylized Shanghai of yesteryear. For fun, there's a show kitchen where you can watch delectable dim sum morsels being prepared, or you can just sit at your table and watch the tea master refill your cup with long-stem tea pourers and acrobatic moves. Pure genius! The delicious lunch dim sum menu is extensive, with most dishes between RM8 and RM12 ($2.30–$3.50/£1.45–£2.15). Dinner is standard Cantonese fare, but expensive, with an extensive menu of soups and rice and noodle dishes.

Hilton Kuala Lumpur, 3 Jalan Stesen Sentral. © **03/2264-2264.** Reservations recommended. Small dishes RM28–RM56 ($8.10–$16/£5.05–£10). AE, DC, MC, V. Daily noon–2:30pm and 6:30–10:30pm.

Coliseum Cafe (Finds) WESTERN/LOCAL   What can I say about Coliseum? Okay, the place is 90 years old, and so is the staff (seriously, some have worked here forever). Located in the grottiest hotel I've ever seen, with stained white walls, worn tile floors, and threadbare linens, this is KL's authentic "greasy spoon." It sounds dreadful, but the place is legendary, and someday it will be gone and there will never be anything else like it. It used to be *the place* for the starched-shirt colonial types to get real Western food back in the day. Now it's a favorite with the locals, who come for enormous sizzling steaks (which fill the place with greasy smoke), baked crabmeat served in the shell, and the house favorite caramel custard pudding. Actually, the food is quite nice, and the prices are terrific for the steaks, which I highly recommend ordering. You either get this place or you don't.

98–100 Jalan Tuanku Abdul Rahman. © **03/2692-6270.** Reservations not accepted. Main courses RM20–RM60 ($5.80–$17/£3.60–£11). MC. Daily 8am–10pm.

Feast Village ★★ INTERNATIONAL   I'm one of those people who can never decide what to eat, so this is the place for me. Located in the basement of Starhill Gallery, an exclusive shopping mall, Feast Village isn't a single restaurant, but a cluster of 13 arranged like a small Malay village. As you stroll along stone and timber pathways, you'll pass cafes that serve seafood, steaks, Malay, Chinese, Thai, Korean, Indian, and more. Within each cafe, the menu is unique and so is the decor. Shook! stands out for its Japanese, Chinese and Western offerings. Wander, smell the smells, read the menus, check out the sights, and find the perfect food for your mood.

Basement, Starhill Gallery, 181 Jalan Bukit Bintang. © **03/2782-3800.** Reservations not required. Main courses vary from outlet to outlet. AE, DC, MC, V. Most outlets daily noon–2:30pm and 6:30–10:30pm.

Le Bouchon ★★ FRENCH   This cozy French provincial restaurant along the bar-and-restaurant street of Changkat Bukit Bintang is a long-time favorite with KL's French community. This place satisfies their discerning palates, so you know it's good. Try the *terrine de fois gras* and ox tongue. The wines are excellent and reasonably priced, considering the quality. The restaurant is French owned and managed, and while the food and wines are first class, there's still a nice unpretentious ambience.

14&16 Changkat Bukit Bintang. ✆ **03/2142-7633.** Reservations recommended. Main courses RM40–RM120 ($12–$35/£7.20–£22). AE, DC, MC, V. Lunch Tues–Fri noon–2pm; dinner daily 7–10:30pm.

Sao Nam ★ VIETNAMESE One of Asia's great restaurants, Sao Nam has colorful decor with revolutionary posters on ochre walls. The power tables are at the courtyard entrance. The food is authentic, fresh, and full of twists and surprises. Try the mangosteen and prawn salad, but order when you book your reservation, as they sell out fast. For starters, try the sample plate and move on to curries, noodle soup, and crispy pancake and duck in orange sauce. Good, reasonably priced wines.

25 Tengkat Tong Shin. ✆ **03/2144-1225.** Reservations essential. Main courses RM22–RM32 ($6.40–$9.30/£3.95–£5.75). AE, MC, V. Tues–Sun noon–2:30pm and 6:30–10:30pm. Closed Mon.

Top Hat Restaurant ★★★ (Finds) ASIAN FUSION Top Hat has a unique atmosphere. In a 1930s bungalow that was once a school, the place winds through room after room, its walls painted in bright hues and furnished with an assortment of mix-and-matched teak tables, chairs, and antiques. The menu is fabulous. While a la carte is available, Top Hat puts together set meals featuring Nyonya, Melaka (Malacca) Portuguese, traditional Malay, Thai, Western, and even vegetarian recipes. They're all brilliant. Desserts are huge and sinful. There's a sampler dish for those who can't decide.

No. 7 Jalan Kia Peng. ✆ **03/2142-8611.** Reservations recommended. Main courses RM30–RM65 ($8.70–$19/£5.40–£12). Set meals RM30–RM100 ($8.70–$29/£5.40–£18). AE, DC, MC, V. Lunch Mon–Fri noon–2:30pm; dinner daily 6–10:30pm.

ATTRACTIONS

Most of Kuala Lumpur's historic sights are located in and around the Merdeka Square/Jalan Hishamuddin area, while many of the gardens, parks, and museums are out at Lake Gardens. Taxi fare between the two locations should run you about RM8 ($2.30/£1.45).

KL Hop-on Hop-off City Tours (✆ **03/2691-1382;** www.myhoponhopoff.com) is the best way to see the city attractions. Double-decker buses circle the inner city daily from 8:30am to 8:30pm at 30-minute intervals; commentaries are in several languages. It costs RM38 ($11/£6.85) adults and RM17 ($4.95/£3.05) children.

Central Market ★ The original Central Market, built in 1936, used to be a wet market, but the place is now a cultural center (air-conditioned!) for local artists and craftspeople selling antiques, crafts, and curios. It's fantastic for buying Malaysian and Asian crafts and souvenirs, with two floors of shops from which to choose.

Jalan Benteng. ✆ **03/2274-6542.** Daily 10am–10pm. Shops open until 8:30 or 9pm.

Cosmo's World Theme Park ★★★ (Kids) I don't care if you have kids or not, Cosmo's rocks. The world's largest indoor amusement park is literally built into the walls of this 900-outlet shopping mall. You don't even need to ride the looping roller coaster to feel that thrill in the pit of your stomach. Just stand and watch it overhead as it flashes by. It really takes your breath away. There are saner rides, too, plus a host of kiddie rides. Highly recommended for families with active kids.

Berjaya Times Square Shopping Mall, No. 1 Jalan Imbi. ✆ **03/2117-3118.** Adults RM32 ($9.30/£5.75), children RM28 ($8.10/£5.05). Daily 10am–10pm.

Islamic Arts Museum ★★   The seat of Islamic learning in Kuala Lumpur, the center has over 7,000 displays of Islamic texts, artifacts, porcelain, and weaponry in local and visiting exhibits. The architecture of blue and white domes is reason enough to visit. There is a fine Middle Eastern restaurant and an excellent book and souvenir shop.

Jalan Lembah Perdana. © 03/2274-2020. www.iamm.org.my. Adults RM12 ($3.50/£2.15), children RM6 ($1.75/£1.10). Daily 10am–6pm.

Jamek Mosque (Masjid Jamek)   The first settlers landed in Kuala Lumpur at the spot where the Gombak and Klang rivers meet, and in 1909 a mosque was built here. Styled after an Indian Muslim design, it is one of the oldest mosques in the city. Interestingly, the mosque was designed by an Englishman, A. B. Hubbock, who was responsible for several other fine buildings in the city. Avoid prayer times, especially on Fridays at midday.

Jalan Tun Perak. Free admission.

Kuala Lumpur Lake Gardens (Taman Tasik Perdana)   Built around an artificial lake, the 92-hectare (227-acre) park has plenty of space for jogging and rowing, and has a playground for the kids. It's the most popular park in Kuala Lumpur. Inside the Lake Gardens, find the **Kuala Lumpur Bird Park** ★ (Jalan Perdana; © 03/2272-1010; www. klbirdpark.com; RM39/$11/£7 adults, RM29/$8.40/£5.20 children; daily 9am–6pm) nestled in beautifully landscaped gardens, with over 3,000 birds within a huge walk-in aviary. Quite impressive. **Kuala Lumpur Orchid Garden** (Jalan Perdana; © 03/2693-5399; weekend and public holiday admission adults RM1/29¢/18p, free for children; free weekday admission for all; daily 9am–6pm) has a collection of over 800 orchid species from Malaysia and thousands of international varieties. The **Kuala Lumpur Butterfly Park** (Jalan Cenderasari; © 03/2693-4799; adults RM15/$4.35/£2.70, children RM8/$2.30/£1.45; daily 9am–6pm) has over 6,000 butterflies belonging to 120 species making their home in this park, which has been landscaped with more than 15,000 plants to simulate the butterflies' natural rainforest environment. There are also other small animals and an insect museum.

Enter through Jalan Parliament. Free admission to the park. Daily 9am–6pm.

Kuala Lumpur Railway Station   Built in 1911, the KL Railway Station is a beautiful example of Moorish architecture. Nearby KL Sentral is now the main rail hub.

Jalan Sultan Hishamuddin.

Malaysia Tourist Centre (MTC)   At MTC you'll find an exhibit hall, tourist information services for Kuala Lumpur and Malaysia, and other travel-planning services. Saloma Café, within the complex, serves Malay food, and in the evening there are cultural dances and performances.

109 Jalan Ampang. © 03/9235-4900. Free admission. Daily 7am–10pm.

Menara Kuala Lumpur   Standing 421m (1,381 ft.) tall, this concrete structure is the third-tallest tower in the world, and the views from the top reach to the far corners of the city and beyond. At the top, the glass windows are fashioned after the Shah Mosque in Isfahan, Iran. Angsana Revolving Restaurant is located near the summit.

Bukit Nanas. © 03/2020-5444. Adults RM20 ($5.80/£3.60), children RM10 ($2.90/£1.80). Daily 9am–10pm.

Merdeka Square   Surrounded by colonial architecture with an exotic local flair, the square was once the site of British social and sporting events. These days, Malaysia holds its spectacular Independence Day celebrations on the field, which is home to the world's tallest flagpole, standing at 100m (328 ft.).

Jalan Sultan. Free admission.

National Art Gallery   In a tranquil complex that combines traditional Malay architectural elements with modern lines, the nation's most prominent art gallery claims a permanent collection of over 2,500 works, most by Malaysia's most celebrated contemporary artists. The museum has six galleries, plus outdoor exhibitions and a cafe.

2 Jalan Temerloh off Jalan Tun Razak. ℭ **03/4025-4990.** www.artgallery.com.my. Free admission. Daily 10am–6pm.

National Mosque (Masjid Negara)   Built in a modern design, the most distinguishing features of the mosque are its 73m (239-ft.) minaret and the umbrella-shaped roof, which is said to symbolize a newly independent Malaysia's aspirations for the future. Could be true, as the place was built in 1965, the year Singapore split from Malaysia. Visitors need to dress respectfully.

Jalan Sultan Hishamuddin (near the KL Railway Station). Free admission. Daily 9am–6pm.

National Museum (Muzim Negara) ★★   Located at Lake Gardens, the museum has many items of historical, cultural, and traditional significance, including art, weapons, musical instruments, and costumes. Most are a little tired.

Jalan Damansara. ℭ **03/2282-6255.** www.museum.gov.my. Adults RM2 (60¢/35p), children under 11 and under free. Daily 9am–6pm.

National Planetarium (Kids)   In 2007, Malaysia's first astronaut went into space. The National Planetarium has a Space Hall with touch-screen interactive computers and hands-on experiments, a Viewing Gallery with binoculars for city views, and an Observatory Park with models of Chinese and Indian astronomy systems. Sadly, the displays are not all functioning properly.

Lake Gardens. ℭ **03/2273-5484.** Admission to exhibition hall adults RM3 (85¢/55p), children RM2 (60¢/35p). Tues–Sun 10am–4pm.

Petaling Street ★   This is the center of KL's Chinatown district. By day, stroll past hawker stalls, dim sum shops, wet markets, and all sorts of shops, from pawnshops to coffin makers. At night, a crazy bazaar (which is terribly crowded) pops up—look for designer knockoffs, fake watches, and pirated CDs and DVDs here.

Petronas Twin Towers ★   Standing at an awesome 452m (1,483 ft.) above street level, with 88 stories, the towers were the tallest buildings in the world from 1998 to 2004 (when Taipei 101 snatched the title). From the outside, the structures are designed with the kind of geometric patterns common to Islamic architecture, and on levels 41 and 42 the two towers are linked by a bridge. Visitors are permitted on the viewing deck on the bridge from 9am to 7pm every day except Mondays and public holidays; otherwise, the building is accessible only if you are conducting business inside. Limited free tickets go fast, so line up early.

Kuala Lumpur City Centre. ℭ **03/2051-7770.** www.petronastwintowers.com.my. Free admission, but tickets are limited.

Sri Mahamariaman Temple   This bright temple livens the gray street scene around it. It's a beautiful temple tucked away in a narrow street in KL's Chinatown area, which was built by Thambusamy Pillai, a pillar of old KL's Indian community.

Jalan Bandar. Free admission.

Sultan Abdul Samad Building   In 1897, this exotic building was designed by two colonial architects, A. C. Norman and A. B. Hubbock, in a style called Muhammadan or neo-Saracenic, which combines Indian Muslim architecture with Gothic and other Western elements. Built to house government administrative offices, today it is the home of Malaysia's Supreme Court and High Court. At night, the building is lit up.

Jalan Raja. Free admission.

GOLF

People from all over Asia flock to Malaysia for its golf courses, many of which are excellent standard courses designed by pros. The **Kuala Lumpur Golf & Country Club,** 10 Jalan 1/70D Off Jalan Bukit Kiara (✆ **03/2093-1111**), has 2 courses, 18 holes each, par 71 and 72, designed by R. Nelson and R. Wright, with greens fees of RM180 ($52/£32) weekdays. The club is closed to nonmembers on weekends and holidays. **Suajana Golf & Country Club,** Km 3, Jalan Lapangan Terbang Sultan Abdul Aziz Shah, 46783 Subang Selangor (✆ **03/7846-1466;** fax 03/7846-7818), has two 18-hole courses, each par 72, designed by Ronald Fream, with greens fees from RM220 ($64/£40) weekdays, RM353 ($102/£64) weekends and holidays.

SHOPPING

Kuala Lumpur is a truly great place to shop. In recent years, mall after mall has risen from city lots, filled with hundreds of retail outlets selling everything from haute couture to cheap chic clothing, electronic goods, jewelry, and arts and crafts. The **major shopping malls** are located in the area around Jalan Bukit Bintang and Jalan Sultan Ismail. Suria KLCC, just beneath the Petronas Twin Towers, is KL's most upmarket mall, while Berjaya Times Square wins the prize for excess, with 900 shops, food and entertainment outlets, plus one of the world's largest indoor amusement parks. Pavilion KL on Jalan Bukit Bintang is the city's latest luxurious mall.

Still the best place for Malaysian handicrafts, the huge **Central Market** on Jalan Benteng (✆ **03/2274-6542**) keeps any shopper occupied for hours. There you'll find local artists and craftspeople selling their wares in the heart of town. It's also a good place to find Malaysian handicrafts from other regions of the country. One specific shop I like to recommend for Malaysian handicrafts is **KL Craft Complex,** Section 3 Jalan Conlay (✆ **03/2162-7533**), with its warehouse selection of assorted goods from around the country, all of it fine quality. Don't forget to walk through the gardens to see the artists' village. In the bungalows toward the side of the building, you'll find some of Malaysia's finest contemporary artists displaying their works for sale. And wear comfy shoes; you may need to walk back to the main road to get a cab.

Another favorite shopping haunt in KL is **Chinatown,** along Petaling Street. Day and night, it's a great place to wander and bargain for knockoff designer clothing and accessories, sunglasses, T-shirts, souvenirs, fake watches, and pirated CDs and DVDs.

Pasar malam **(night markets)** are very popular evening activities in KL. Whole blocks are taken up with these brightly lit and bustling markets packed with stalls selling almost everything you can dream of. Two good bets for catching one: On Saturday nights, head for Jalan Tuanku Abdul Rahman, while the Bangsar Night Market starts at dusk and is popular with trendy residents.

KUALA LUMPUR AFTER DARK

There's nightlife to spare in KL, from fashionable lounges to sprawling discos to pubs perfect for lounging. Basically, you can expect to pay about RM10 to RM25

($2.90–$7.25/£1.80–£4.50) for a pint of beer, depending on what and where you order. Although quite a few pubs are open for lunch, most clubs won't open until about 6 or 7pm. These places must all close by 1 or 2am, so don't plan on staying out too late. Nearly all have a happy hour, usually between 5 and 7pm, when drink discounts apply on draft beers and "house-pour" (lower-shelf) mixed drinks. Generally, you're expected to wear dress-casual clothing for these places, but avoid old jeans, sneakers, and very revealing outfits.

The center of nightlife, if you want to browse, begins at the corner of Jalan Sultan Ismail and Jalan P. Ramlee. Walk along P. Ramlee and you'll find bars of all kinds, plus cafes and coffee shops. Jalan Bukit Bintang is another popular area to visit.

For a little live music with your drinks, the recently renovated **Hard Rock Cafe,** Jalan Sultan Ismail next to Concorde Hotel (© **03/2715-5555**), hosts the best of the regional bands, which play most nights for a crowd of locals, tourists, and expatriates who take their parties very seriously.

The biggest dance club in town is **Zouk,** fashioned after the ultrasuccessful Zouk in Singapore. It's at 113 Jalan Ampang, down the street from MTC (© **03/2171-1997**). There's a cover charge of anywhere between RM25 and RM40 ($7.25–$12/£4.50–£7.20), depending on what's going on inside.

Bangsar, just outside the city limits, is 2 or 3 blocks of bars, cafes, and restaurants that cater to a variety of tastes (in fact, so many expatriates hang out there, they call it Kweiloh Lumpur, "Foreigner Lumpur" in Mandarin). Every taxi driver knows where it is. Get in and ask to go to Jalan Telawi Tiga in Bangsar—fare should be no more than RM7 or RM10 ($2.05 or $2.90/£1.25 or £1.80)—and once there, it's very easy to catch a cab back to town.

SIDE TRIPS FROM KUALA LUMPUR

Batu Caves ★★

Located 13 km (8 miles) north of Kuala Lumpur, **Batu Caves** have become one of the most significant Hindu religious sites outside of India. Built within a series of caves inside a limestone hill, three main caves make up a temple complex devoted to the Lord Murugan. During the Hindu Thaipusam festival, held each year in either January or February, devotees bathe in the nearby Batu River before donning *kevadis,* stainless-steel racks decorated with flowers and fruits and held to the body with pins and skewers. A procession leads from the river to the hill and up the 272 steps to the main cave. The festival draws over 800,000 each year, but the caves are a nice side trip any time. The most convenient way to visit the caves is by taxi, which from KL will take about 25 to 30 minutes and costs approximately RM15 to RM20 ($4.35–$5.80/£2.70–£3.60). During Thaipusam, contact the Tourism Malaysia office for shuttle instructions.

Taman Negara National Park ★★★

Malaysia's most famous national park, **Taman Negara,** covers 434,350 hectares (1.1 million acres) of primary rainforest estimated to be as old as 130 million years, and encompasses within its border **Gunung Tahan,** peninsular Malaysia's highest peak, at 2,187m (7,173 ft.) above sea level.

Prepare to see lush vegetation and rare orchids, some 675 bird species, and maybe, if you're lucky, some barking deer, tapir, elephants, tigers, leopards, and wild cattle or gaur. As for primates, there are long-tailed macaques, leaf monkeys, gibbons, and more. Taman Negara showcases efforts to keep this land in as pristine a state as possible, despite extensive logging in many parts of the country.

There are outdoor activities for any level of adventurer. Short **jungle walks** to observe nature are lovely, but then so are the hard-core 9-day treks or climbs up Gunung Tahan. There are also overnight trips to night hides where you can observe animals up close. The jungle canopy walk is one of the longest in the world, and at 25m (82 ft.) above ground, the view is spectacular. There are also rivers for rafting and swimming, fishing spots, and a couple of caves. Fishing permits must be obtained beforehand from the Ranger Headquarters.

If you plan your trip through one of the main resort operators, they can arrange, in addition to accommodations, all meals, treks, and a coach transfer to and from Kuala Lumpur. Prices vary, depending on the season and your level of comfort desired. The best time to visit is between the months of April and September; other times, it will be a tad wet, and that's why it's called a rainforest.

Mutiara Taman Negara Resort ★, well established in the business of hosting visitors to the park, is the best accommodations in terms of comfort. It organizes trips for 3 days and 2 nights or for 4 days and 3 nights, as well as an a la carte deal where you pay for lodging and activities separately. Accommodations come in many styles: a bungalow suite for families; chalet and chalet suite, both good for couples; standard guesthouse rooms; and dormitory hostels for budget travelers. To get an idea of pricing, a 3-day, 2-night package runs about RM369 ($107/£66) per person, double occupancy in a chalet, with air-conditioning with attached bathroom, plus full board, meals, and activities. What it doesn't include is bus transfer from KL (RM80/$23/£14 per person round-trip) and the boat upriver from the park entrance (RM56/$16/£10 per person round-trip). A la carte activities include a 3-hour jungle trek, a 1¹/₂-hour night jungle walk, the half-day Lata Berkoh river trip with swimming, a 2-hour cave exploration, and a trip down the rapids in a rubber raft (Kuala Tahan, Jerantut, 27000 Pahang; ℂ **09/266-3500,** Kuala Lumpur Sales Office 03/2782-2222, www.mutiarahotels.com).

Genting Highlands

The "City of Entertainment," as Genting is known locally, serves as Malaysia's answer to Las Vegas, complete with bright lights (which can be seen from Kuala Lumpur) and gambling. And although most people come here for the casino, there's a wide range of other activities, although most of them seem to serve the purpose of entertaining the kids while you bet their college funds at the roulette wheel. While it lacks the sophistication of other casino destinations, it is very popular with local punters and families seeking a one-stop destination in the cool mountain air.

Genting has six hotels of varying prices within the resort. Rates vary depending on the season, so be prepared for higher rates during the winter holidays. **Genting Hotel** is the best choice—a newer property that's linked directly to the casino. Weekday rates are from RM245 ($71/£44) for double occupancy, and weekend rates are from RM355 ($103/£64) double occupancy.

Outside of the casino, there's a pond, a bowling alley, and an indoor heated pool. For children, the Genting Theme Park covers 9,300 sq. m (100,104 sq. ft.) of mostly rides, plus many Western fast-food eating outlets, games, and other attractions. The **Awana Golf and Country Club** (ℂ **03/6101-3025**) is the premier golf course in these hills.

For buses from Kuala Lumpur, call **Genting Highlands Transport,** operating buses every half-hour from 6:30am to 9pm daily from KL Sentral train station. The cost one-way is RM7.50 ($2.15/£1.35) and the trip takes 1 hour. The bus lets you off at the foot of the hill, where you take the cable car to the top (price included with bus ticket). For bus information, call ℂ **03/6251-8398.**

You can also get there by hiring an **outstation taxi.** The cost is RM40 ($12/£7.20), and a taxi can be arranged by calling the **Puduraya** outstation taxi stand at ☏ **03/2078-0213.**

The **Genting Highlands Resort** is owned and operated by Resorts World Berhad, who'll be glad to provide you with hotel reservations if you call ☏ **03/2718-1118.**

Cameron Highlands

Located in the hills, this colonial-era resort town has a cool climate, which makes it the perfect place for weekend getaways by Malaysians and Singaporeans who are sick of the heat. If you've been in the region awhile, you might also appreciate the respite.

The climate is also very conducive to agriculture. After the area's discovery by British surveyor William Cameron in 1885, the major crop here became tea, which is still grown today. The area's lovely gardens supply cities throughout the region with vegetables, flowers, and fruit year-round. Among the favorites here are the strawberries, which can be eaten fresh or transformed into yummy desserts in the local restaurants. At the many commercial flower nurseries, you can see chrysanthemums, fuchsias, and roses growing on the terraces. Rose gardens are prominent here.

Temperatures in the highlands average 70°F (21°C) during the day and 50°F (10°C) at night. There are paths for treks though the countryside and to peaks of surrounding mountains. Two waterfalls, the Robinson Falls and Parit Falls, have pools at their feet where you can swim.

There are **no visitor information services** here. They've been closed for a very long time and have no immediate plans for reopening. You'll find banks with ATMs and money-changing services along the main road in Tanah Rata, the main town.

The best accommodation here is the **Smokehouse Hotel.** Situated between Tanah Rata and Brinchang towns, this picturesque Tudor mansion has pretty gardens and a charming old-world ambience. Built in 1937 as a country house in the heyday of colonial British getaways, its conversion into a hotel has kept the place happily in the 1930s. Guest suites have four-poster beds and antique furnishings, with some of the wear that one might expect from an old inn. The hotel encourages guests to play golf at the neighboring course, sit for afternoon tea with strawberry confections, or trek along nearby paths (for which they'll provide a picnic basket). It's all a bizarre escape from Malaysia, but a charming one. (Tanah Rata, Cameron Highlands, Pahang Darul Makmur; ☏ **05/491-1215;** fax 05/491-1214; www.thesmokehouse.com.my, RM440–RM750/$128–$218/£79–£135 suite.)

Most of the sights can be seen in a day, but it's difficult to plan your time well. In Cameron Highlands, I recommend trying one of the sightseeing outfits in either Brinchang or Tanah Rata. **C. S. Travel & Tours,** 47 Main Rd., Tanah Rata (☏ **05/491-1200**), is a highly reputable agency that will plan half-day tours for RM20 ($5.80/£3.60) or full days starting from RM80 ($23/£14). On your average tour, you'll see the Boh tea plantation and factory, flower nurseries, rose gardens, strawberry farms, butterfly farms, and the Sam Poh Buddhist Temple. You're required to pay admission to each attraction yourself (about RM5/$1.45/90p). They also provide trekking and overnight camping tours in the surrounding hills with local trail guides.

If you want to hit around some balls, **Padang Golf,** Main Road between Tanah Rata and Brinchang (☏ **05/491-1126**), has 18 holes at par 71, with greens fees around RM53 ($15/£9.55) on weekdays and RM84 ($24/£15) on weekends. They also provide club rentals, caddies, shoes, and carts.

To get to Cameron Highlands, **Kurnia Bistari Express Bus** (© 05/491-1485) operates between Kuala Lumpur and Tanah Rata daily for around RM20 ($5.80/£3.60) one-way. They don't accept bookings in Kuala Lumpur, asking you to just show up at Puduraya bus terminal to buy your ticket and board the next bus. The bus terminal is in the center of town along the main drag. Just next to it is the taxi stand. It's a two-horse town; you can't miss either of them. Outstation taxis from KL will cost RM240 ($70/£43) for the trip. Call © 03/2078-0213 for booking. Taxis are cheaper on the way back because they don't have to climb the mountains.

2 JOHOR BAHRU

Johor Bahru, the capital of the state of Johor, is at the southern tip of the Malaysian peninsula, where Malaysia's north-south highway comes to its southern terminus. Because it's just over the causeway from Singapore, a very short jump by car, bus, or train, it's a popular point of entry to Malaysia. Johor Bahru, or "JB," is not the most fascinating destination in Malaysia. If you want a good side trip from Singapore, there are more interesting sights in Melaka (see below) or better beaches on Tioman (see chapter 14).

The Malaysia Tourism Board office in Johor Bahru is at the **Johor Tourist Information Centre (JOTIC),** centrally located on Jalan Ayer Molek, on the second floor (© 07/223-4935). You can also find information at www.tourismjohor.com.

The **Sultan Ismail Airport/Senai International Airport,** 30 to 40 minutes outside the city (© 07/599-4737), has regular flights through Malaysia Airlines to and from major cities in Malaysia (© 1300/883-000; www.malaysiaairlines.com). **AirAsia** (© 03/8775-4000; www.airasia.com) also uses JB as a hub to major destinations throughout Malaysia.

Buses to and from other parts of Malaysia are based at the Larkin Bus Terminal off Jalan Garuda in the northern part of the city. Taxis are available at the terminal to take you to the city. If you're coming from Singapore, the **Singapore–Johor Express** (© 65/6292-8149) operates every 10 minutes between 6:30am and midnight from the Ban Sen Terminal at Queen Street near Arab Street, Singapore. The cost for the half-hour trip is S$2.40 ($1.60¢/£1.10). If you take the bus, you can choose to get off at the Malaysian immigration checkpoint, which is more or less in the center of town, instead of going all the way to Larkin.

The **Keretapi Tanah Melayu Berhad (KTM)** trains arrive and depart from the Johor Bahru Railway Station at Jalan Tun Abdul Razak, opposite Merlin Tower (© 07/223-4727). Catch express trains from **KL Sentral** (© 03/2267-1200) twice daily for RM34 to RM68 ($9.85–$20/£6.10–£12), depending on the class you travel. From the **Singapore Railway Station** (© 65/6222-5165), on Keppel Road in Tanjong Pagar, the short trip is S$2.90 (US$1.95/£1.30).

If you find yourself in JB overnight, the **Hyatt Regency** (Jalan Sungai Chat; © 800/233-1234 or 07/222-1234; fax 07/223-2718; http://johorbahru.regency.hyatt.com; RM374/$108/£67 double) is the top pick in terms of quality. JB has some good food, which you can try at the Tepian Tebrau Stalls in Jalan Skudai (along the seafront) and the hawker stalls near the Central Market. The dish that puts Johor Bahru on the map, *ikan bakar* (barbecued fish with chilies), is out of this world at the Tepian Tebrau stalls.

The sights in Johor Bahru are few, but there is an interesting museum inside the old *istana.* The **Royal Abu Bakar Museum,** also called the Istana Bakar, is a gorgeous royal palace built by Sultan Abu Bakar in 1866. Today it houses the royal collection of inter- national treasures, costumes, historical documents, fine art from the family collection, and relics of the sultanate. It's at Jalan Tun Dr Ismail (© **07/223-0555;** adults US$7, children 11 and under US$3; Sat–Thurs 9am–4pm). This museum charges admission in U.S. dollars; when you purchase your ticket, the ticket counter will convert the fee to Malaysian ringgits, according to the day's exchange rate, to be paid in local currency. The saracenic flavor of the **Bangunan Sultan Ibrahim (State Secretariat Building)** on Jalan Abdul Ibrahim makes it feel older than it truly is. Built in 1940, today it houses the State Secretariat.

3 MELAKA (MALACCA) ★

Melaka's attraction is its cultural heritage, around which a substantial tourism industry has grown. If you're visiting, a little knowledge of history will help you appreciate all there is to see.

Melaka was founded around 1400 by Parameswara, called **Iskandar Shah** in the Malay Annals. After he was chased from Palembang in southern Sumatra by invading Javanese, he set up a kingdom in Singapore (Temasek), and after being overthrown by invaders there, ran up the west coast of the Malay peninsula to Melaka, where he settled and established a port city. As the site was in a favorable spot to take advantage of the two monsoons that dominated shipping routes, Melaka soon drew the attention of Arab and Chinese traders, both of whom maintained very close relations for trade and political advantage. It was the early Arab merchants who introduced Islam to Malaysia. After Parameswara's death in 1414, his son, Mahkota Iskandar Shah, converted to Islam and popularized the faith throughout the area.

During the 15th century, Melaka was ruled by a succession of wise sultans who expanded the wealth and stability of the economy; built up the administration's coffers; extended the sultanate to the far reaches of the Malay peninsula, Singapore, and parts of northern Sumatra; and thwarted repeated attacks by the Siamese. The success of the empire drew international attention.

The Portuguese were eyeing the port and formulating plans to dominate the east–west trade route, to establish the naval supremacy of Portugal and promote Christianity in the region. They struck in 1511 and conquered Melaka in a battle that lasted only a month. After the defeat, the sultanate fled to Johor while the Portuguese looted the city and sent its riches off to Lisbon.

The Portuguese were the first of a chain of ruling foreign powers who would struggle in vain to retain the early economic success of the city. The foreign conquerors had a major strike against them: Their staunch Christianity alienated the locals and repelled Arab traders. The city quickly became nothing more than a sleepy outpost.

In 1641, the Dutch, with the help of Johor, conquered Melaka and controlled the city until 1795. Again the Dutch were unsuccessful in rebuilding the glory of past prosperity in Melaka, and the city continued to sleep.

In 1795, the Dutch traded Melaka to the British in return for Bencoolen in Sumatra, being far more concerned with their Indonesian interests anyway. Melaka became a permanent British settlement in 1811, but by this time had become so poor and alienated that it was impossible to bring it back to life.

Today Melaka is a sleepy backwater. The historic heart of town is distinctive, with narrow one-way lanes hugged by old colonial-style shophouses built by the Dutch and British and later inhabited by wealthy Chinese and Peranakan (Straits-born Chinese) families. The buildings that stand out, however, are the bright red structures, a church and administrative buildings built by the Dutch during their rule. Just steps away are the remains of a Portuguese fort and church, and also close by you'll find English churches as well.

ESSENTIALS
Visitor Information
The **Melaka Tourism Information Centre** is on Jalan Kota at the Town Square next to the bridge ((C) **06/281-4803**).

Getting There
BY TRAIN   Melaka doesn't have a proper train station, but the **KTM** stops at Tampin ((C) **06/441-1034**), 38km (24 miles) north of the city. It's not the most convenient way in and out of the city, but if you decide to stop en route between Kuala Lumpur and Johor Bahru, you can easily catch a waiting taxi to your hotel in town for RM40 ($12/£7.20).

BY BUS   From Singapore, contact **Grassland Express** at (C) **65/6293-1166,** www. grassland.com.sg. A bus departs at 8am daily for the 4¹/₂-hour trip (S$27/US$18/£12). From **KL's Puduraya Bus Terminal** on Jalan Pudu, **Transnasional** ((C) **03/6201-3463**) has hourly buses between 8am and 10pm for about RM10 ($2.90/£1.80). The trip takes about 2¹/₂ hours.

The bus station in Melaka is at Jalan Kilang, within the city. Taxis are easy to find from here.

BY TAXI   **Outstation taxis** can bring you here from Kuala Lumpur for RM140 ($41/£25). The outstation taxi stand in Melaka is at the bus terminal on Jalan Kilang.

Getting Around
Most of the historic sights around the town square are well within walking distance. For other trips, **taxis** are the most convenient way around but are at times difficult to find. They're also not as clearly marked as in KL or Johor Bahru. They are not metered, so be prepared to bargain. Basically, no matter what you do, you'll always be charged a higher rate than a local. Tourists are almost always quoted at RM10 ($2.90/£1.80) for local trips. Malaysians pay RM5 ($1.45/90p). If you're feeling sporty, you can bargain for a price somewhere in between.

Trishaws (bicycle rickshaws) are all over the historic areas of town, and in Melaka they're renowned for being very, very garishly decorated (which adds to the fun!). Negotiate for hourly rates of about RM30 ($8.70/£5.40) for two people.

Fast Facts: Melaka
Melaka's **area code** is 06. Major **banks** are located in the historic center of town, with a couple along Jalan Putra. **Internet** places come and go. Your best bet is to ask your hotel's concierge or the Melaka Tourism Information Centre (see above) for the nearest cafes.

WHERE TO STAY
Melaka is not very large, and most of the places to stay are well within walking distance of attractions, shopping, and restaurants.

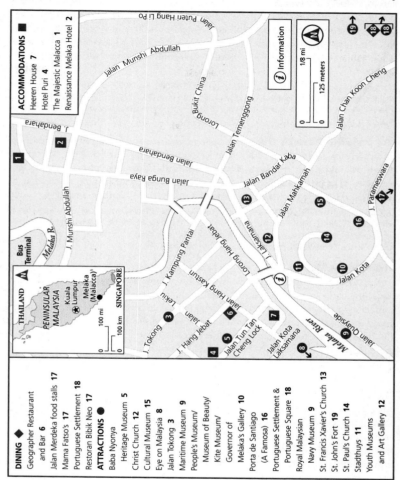

ACCOMMODATIONS ■
Heeren House 7
Hotel Puri 4
The Majestic Malacca 1
Renaissance Melaka Hotel 2

DINING ◆
Geographer Restaurant
and Bar 6
Jalan Merdeka food stalls 17
Mama Fatso's 17
Portuguese Settlement 18
Restoran Bibik Neo 17

ATTRACTIONS ●
Baba Nyonya
Heritage Museum 5
Christ Church 12
Cultural Museum 15
Eye on Malaysia 8
Jalan Tokong 3
Maritime Museum 9
People's Museum/
Museum of Beauty/
Kite Museum/
Governor of
Melaka's Gallery 10
Porta de Santiago
(A Famosa) 16
Portuguese Settlement &
Portuguese Square 18
Royal Malaysian
Navy Museum 9
St. Francis Xavier's Church 13
St. John's Fort 19
St. Paul's Church 14
Stadthuys 11
Youth Museums
and Art Gallery 12

Heeren House ★★   This is the place to stay in Melaka for a taste of the local culture. Started by a local family, the small guesthouse is a renovated 100-year-old building furnished in traditional Peranakan and colonial style and located right in the heart of historical European Melaka. All the bedrooms have views of the Melaka River, and outside the front door of the hotel is a winding stretch of old buildings housing antiques shops. Just walk out and wander. Small rooms have very basic amenities. The rooms on the second floor are somewhat larger. Laundry service is available, and there's a cafe and gift shop on the premises. Very friendly establishment run by a family who is very knowledgeable on local events. Reserve well in advance.

1 Jalan Tun Tan Cheng Lock, 75200 Melaka. ✆ **06/281-4241.** Fax 06/281-4239. 6 units. RM139 ($40/£25) double; RM269 ($78/£48) family room. No credit cards. **Amenities:** Cafe. *In room:* A/C, TV.

Hotel Puri (Value In olden days, Jalan Tun Tan Cheng Lock was known as "Millionaire Row" for all the wealthy families that lived here. This old "mansion" has been converted into a guesthouse, its tiled parlor has become a lobby, and the courtyard is where breakfast is served each morning. Although Hotel Puri isn't big on space, it is big on value (discount rates can be pretty low). Rooms are very clean and, while not overly stylish, are comfortable enough for any weary traveler. A friendly and responsive staff adds to the appeal.

118 Jalan Tun Tan Cheng Lock, 75200 Melaka. © **06/282-5588.** Fax 06/281-5588. www.hotelpuri.com. 50 units. RM138 ($40/£25) double; RM255 ($74/£46) triple; from RM265 ($77/£48) suite. AE, MC, V. **Amenities:** Restaurant; room service; babysitting. *In room:* A/C, TV w/satellite programming, fridge, hair dryer.

The Majestic Malacca ★★ The Majestic Malacca is an integral part of Melaka's history, dating back to the 1800s. The facade is faithfully restored from the original design, but inside, the hotel is stylish and plush, with all the modern conveniences travelers need to enjoy historic Melaka. Those who appreciate heritage properties and grand hotels should choose the Majestic, although it still retains a boutique ambience.

188 Jalan Bunga Raya, 75100 Melaka. © **06/289-8000.** Fax 06/289-8080. www.majesticmalacca.com. 54 units. RM977 ($283/£176) double; from RM2,540 ($737/£457) suite. AE, DC, MC, V. **Amenities:** Restaurant; bar; lounge for afternoon tea; pool; health club; spa; concierge; airport transfers; room service. *In room:* A/C, flatscreen TV w/satellite programming, minibar, hair dryer.

Renaissance Melaka Hotel ★ Renaissance is one of the better hotels in Melaka and, according to business travelers, is the most reliable place for quality accommodations—but aside from the pieces of Peranakan porcelain and art in the public areas, you could almost believe you weren't in Melaka at all. The hotel is, however, situated in a good location, though you'll still need a taxi to most of the sights. Rooms are fairly large and filled with Western comforts. Don't expect much from the views, as the hotel is in the commercial part of the city. No historical landmarks to gaze upon here.

Jalan Bendahara, 75100 Melaka. © **888/236-2427** in the U.S. and Canada, 800/251-259 in Australia, 800/264-333 in New Zealand, 800/221-222 in the U.K., or 06/284-8888. Fax 06/284-9269. www.marriott.com/hotels/travel/mkzrn-renaissance-melaka-hotel. 294 units. RM480 ($139/£86) double; from RM620 ($180/£112) suite. AE, MC, V. **Amenities:** 3 restaurants; bar and lobby lounge; outdoor pool; golf nearby; squash courts; health club w/sauna, steam, and massage; concierge; airport transfers; room service; babysitting; executive-level rooms. *In room:* A/C, TV w/satellite programming and in-house movies, minibar.

WHERE TO DINE

In Melaka you'll find the typical mix of authentic Malay and Chinese food, and as the city was the major settling place for the Peranakans in Malaysia, their unique style of food is featured in many of the local restaurants.

A good recommendation for a quick bite at lunch or dinner if you're strolling in the historic area is the long string of open-air food stalls along Jalan Merdeka, just between Mahkota Plaza Shopping and Warrior Square. **Mama Fatso's** is especially good for Chinese-style seafood and Malay sambal curry. A good meal will run you about RM35 to RM40 ($10–$12/£6.30–£7.20) per person.

Try local Peranakan cuisine at **Restoran Bibik Neo** (No. 6, ground floor, Jalan Merdeka, Taman Melaka Raya; © **06/281-7054**), a small coffee shop that's about as authentic as you can get. *Ikan assam* with eggplant is a tasty mild fish curry that's very rich and tart, and I always go for the *otak-otak* (pounded fish and spices baked in a banana leaf).

For a taste of Portuguese Melaka, the **Portuguese Settlement** has some open-air food stalls by the water, where in the evenings hawkers sell an assortment of dishes inspired by these former colonial rulers, including many fresh seafood offerings. Saturday nights are best, when, at 8pm, there's a cultural show with music and dancing. Other times it may be slow business. (Jalan d'Albuquerque off Jalan Ujon Pasir; dinner from RM20–RM30($5.80–$8.70/£3.60–£5.40) per person; no credit cards.)

Geographer Restaurant and Bar, located along the popular Jalan Hang Jebat (✆ 06/281-6813), is very accommodating to travelers. They know which buttons to push to make travelers happy, so expect icy-cold beer, international comfort food, local dishes, souvenirs, Wi-Fi, and evening entertainment, including bands on some nights. They serve only white meat—the tandoori chicken is recommended. Vegetarians are well catered to. They're open daily from midmorning till late, as the bar and music swings into action. Prices range from RM10 to RM40 ($2.90–$12/£1.80–£7.20).

ATTRACTIONS

To get the most out of Melaka, it's best to have a bit of knowledge about the history of the place, which I've explained briefly in the intro to this section. Most of the preserved historical sites are on both sides of the Melaka River. Start at **Stadthuys** (the old town hall, pronounced "stat-highs"), and you'll see most of Melaka pretty quickly.

Museums

Baba Nyonya Heritage Museum ★ Called "Millionaire's Row," Jalan Tun Tan Cheng Lock is lined with row houses that were built by the Dutch and later bought by wealthy Peranakans; the architectural style reflects their East-meets-West lifestyle. The house dates from 1896, when three houses were combined into one. The entrance fee includes a guided tour.

48⊠50 Jalan Tun Tan Cheng Lock. ✆ **06/283-1273.** Adults RM8 ($2.30/£1.45), children RM4 ($1.15/70p). Daily 10am–12:30pm and 2–4:30pm.

Cultural Museum (Muzium Budaya) ★ A replica of the former palace of Sultan Mansur Syah (1456–77), this museum was rebuilt according to historical descriptions to house a fine collection of cultural artifacts such as clothing, weaponry, and royal items. The gardens are quite nice.

Kota Rd., next to Porta de Santiago. ✆ **06/282-6526.** Adults RM2 (60¢/35p), children RM.50 (15¢/10p). Daily 9am–5:30pm.

Eye on Malaysia This 60m (197 ft.) observation wheel, previously located at Lake Titiwangsa in KL, was moved to its current location, at the mouth of the Melaka River, in November 2008. The 12-minute ride takes you over the oldest parts of Melaka, for bird's-eye views of the town's most historically significant buildings and streets. The Ferris wheel sits atop a 1.6-hectare (4-acre) complex that is being developed in phases through 2009 with a light and sound waterscreen showcase, a Malaysian International Space Adventure (MISA) museum, and food outlets.

Munara Sungai Melaka, Kota Laksamana. ✆ **06/284-1888.** www.eyeonmalaysia.com.my. Adults RM20 ($5.80/£3.60), children RM10 ($2.90/£1.80). Mon–Thurs 10am–11pm; Fri–Sun 10am–midnight.

Maritime Museum and the Royal Malaysian Navy Museum These two museums are located across the street from one another but share admission fees. The Maritime Museum is in a restored 16th-century Portuguese ship, with exhibits dedicated to

Melaka's history with the sea. The Navy Museum is a modern display of Malaysia's less pleasant relationship with the sea.

Quayside Rd. ⓒ **06/282-6526.** Adults RM3 (85¢/55p), children RM1 (30¢/20p). Daily 9am–5:30pm.

The People's Museum, the Museum of Beauty, the Kite Museum, and the Governor of Melaka's Gallery
This strange collection of displays is housed under one roof. The People's Museum is the story of development in Melaka. The Museum of Beauty is a look at cultural differences of beauty throughout time and around the world. The Kite Museum features the traditions of making and flying *wau* (kites) in Malaysia, and the governor's personal collection is on exhibit at the Governor's Gallery.

Kota Rd. ⓒ **06/282-6526.** Adults RM2 (60¢/35p), children RM.50 (15¢/10p). Daily 9am–5:30pm.

Stadthuys—The Museums of History & Ethnography and the Museum of Literature ★
The Stadthuys Town Hall was built by the Dutch in 1650, and it's now home to the Melaka Ethnographical and Historical Museum, which displays customs and traditions of all the peoples of Melaka, and takes you through the rich history of this city. Behind Stadthuys, the Museum of Literature includes old historical accounts and local legends. Admission price is for both exhibits.

Located at the circle intersection of Jalan Quayside, Jalan Laksamana, and Jalan Chan Koon Cheng. ⓒ **06/282-6526.** Adults RM5 ($1.45/90p), children RM2 (60¢/35p). Daily 9am–5:30pm.

Youth Museums and Art Gallery
In the old General Post office are these displays dedicated to Malaysia's youth organizations and to the nation's finest artists. An unusual combination.

Laksamana Rd. ⓒ **06/282-6526.** Adults RM2 (60¢/35p), children RM.50 (15¢/10p). Tues–Sun 9am–5:30pm.

Historical Sites

Christ Church
The Dutch built this place in 1753 as a Dutch Reform Church, and its architectural details include such wonders as ceiling beams cut from a single tree and a Last Supper glazed tile motif above the altar. It was later consecrated as an Anglican church, and mass is still performed today in English, Chinese, and Tamil.

Located on Jalan Laksamana. Free admission.

Jalan Tokong ★
Not far from Jalan Tun Tan Cheng Lock is Jalan Tokong, called the "Street of Harmony" by the locals because it has three coexisting places of worship: the Kampung Kling Mosque, the Cheng Hoon Teng Temple, and the Sri Poyyatha Vinayagar Moorthi Temple.

Melaka River Cruise ★
The Melaka River was once in a pretty nasty state, but the authorities realized its tourism potential and cleaned it up. A flotilla of small boats transports sightseers up and down from the departure and drop-off point on the riverbank in front of Dutch Square. Not only can you see the historic buildings, old warehouses (godowns), interesting mangrove stands, churches, and villages, but you can peer into people's backyards to see the comings and goings of riverside life. The 1998 Sean Connery movie *Entrapment* was partially filmed here. Tours last about 45 minutes in boats ranging from 20- to 40-seaters, and normally a minimum of eight passengers is required before departure.

Departs Taman Rempah near Jalan Mata Kuching. ⓒ **06/281-4322.** Adults RM10 ($2.90/£1.80), children RM5 ($1.45/90p). Daily 9:30am–5pm and 6pm–midnight.

Porta de Santiago (A Famosa) ★   Once the site of a Portuguese fortress called A Famosa, all that remains today of the fortress is the entrance gate, which was saved from demolition by Sir Stamford Raffles. When the British East India Company demolished the place, Raffles realized the arch's historical value and saved it. The fort was built in 1512, but the inscription above the arch, "Anno 1607," marks the date when the Dutch overthrew the Portuguese.

Located on Jalan Kota, at the intersection of Jalan Parameswara. Free admission.

Portuguese Settlement and Portuguese Square   The Portuguese Settlement is an enclave once designated for Portuguese settlers after they conquered Melaka in 1511. Some elements of their presence remain in the Lisbon-style architecture. Later, in 1920, the area was a Eurasian neighborhood. In the center of the settlement, Portuguese Square is a modern attraction with Portuguese restaurants, handicrafts, souvenirs, and cultural shows. It was built in 1985 in an architectural style to reflect the surrounding flavor of Portugal.

Located down Jalan d'Albuquerque off of Jalan Ujon Pasir in the southern part of the city. Free admission.

St. Francis Xavier's Church   This church was built in 1849 and dedicated to St. Francis Xavier, a Jesuit who brought Catholicism to Melaka and other parts of Southeast Asia.

Located on Jalan Laksamana. Free admission.

St. John's Fort   The fort, built by the Dutch in the late 18th century, sits on top of St. John's Hill. Funny how the cannons point inland, huh? At the time, threats to the city came from land. It was named after a Portuguese church to St. John the Baptist, which originally occupied the site.

Located off Lorong Bukit Senjuang. Free admission.

St. Paul's Church   The church was built by the Portuguese in 1521, but when the Dutch came in, they made it part of A Famosa, converting the altar into a cannon mount. The open tomb inside was once the resting place of St. Francis Xavier, a missionary who spread Catholicism throughout Southeast Asia and whose remains were later moved to Goa.

Located behind Porta de Santiago. Free admission.

SHOPPING

Antiques hunting has been a major draw to Melaka for decades. Distinct Peranakan and teak furniture, porcelain, and household items fetch quite a price these days, due to a steady increase in demand for these rare treasures. The area down and around Jalan Hang Jebat and Jalan Tun Tan Cheng Lok called **Jonker Walk** sports many little antiques shops that are filled with as many gorgeous items as any local museum. You'll also find handmade crafts, ready-made *batik* clothing, and other souvenirs. Whether you're buying or just looking, it's a fun way to spend an afternoon.

For crafts and souvenirs, you'll also find a row of shops along the lane beside Stadthuys. Most prices seem fair, but you may need to do a little bargaining.

4 PANGKOR

Pangkor's claim to fame is the spectacular, award-winning Pangkor Laut Resort, nestled on its own private island—without a doubt one of Malaysia's best known. Pangkor's main island supports a wee village and some smaller resorts. For a while, the Pan Pacific group operated a fine resort here, but now the owners operate it themselves as the Pangkor Island Beach Resort. Other than that, there's not much to see.

If the exclusivity of seclusion is exciting for you, then Pangkor is your place. If you feel you need to break up the resort experience with something else, Langkawi (later in this chapter), to the north, has luxury resorts that are all that, plus great restaurants and a range of adventurous natural activities.

The easiest way to get to Pangkor is to hop a flight. **Berjaya Air** (© **03/2149-3731;** www.berjaya-air.com) flies five times a week, and the trip is only 30 minutes. Compared to a 3¹/₂-hour drive from KL, then a ferry ride to the island, it saves a lot of hassle.

Pangkor Laut Resort ★★★   This private island resort comprises private wooden Malay-style chalets perched atop stilts, connected by wooden boardwalks over the green sea. Pangkor Laut creates an effect that is rustic and natural, yet uncompromisingly sophisticated and luxurious. Each roomy villa is adorned with warm wood interiors, uncluttered contemporary wood furnishings, king-size beds, and writing tables with Malaysian arts and textiles throughout. Each has a private sun deck furnished with chaise lounges. Some rooms intentionally have no TV, but some villas come with their own CD or iPod sound system on which you can play CDs from the resort's library. Spa and sea villas sit on stilts, with big picture windows that open out over the water. Lower-priced hill and garden villas are housed in double-story buildings, hill villas commanding the best sea views. Spa villas connect directly to the resort's full-service Spa Village, a seaside collection of landscaped buildings and pavilions where you can select a range of treatments developed from Malay, Chinese, and Indian natural beauty and health secrets. You won't get bored with dining options, either. Pangkor Laut has seven outlets serving either food or beverages. Activities include chartered cruises, sailing, windsurfing, kayaking, and jungle trekking, and golf can be arranged on the mainland. If you take your seclusion seriously, Pangkor Laut has eight full-service private residences on the property as well.

Pangkor Laut Island, 32200 Lumut, Perak. © **05/699-1100.** Fax 05/699-1200. www.pangkorlautresort. com. 142 units. RM1,368–RM2,150 ($397–$624/£246–£387) villa. AE, DC, MC, V. **Amenities:** 4 restaurants; 3 lounges; 2 outdoor pools; 3 outdoor lighted tennis courts; 2 squash courts; health club; spa; Jacuzzi; watersports equipment; concierge; room service; babysitting; TV room. *In room:* A/C, minibar, hair dryer.

5 PENANG ★★★

Penang is unique in Malaysia because it has many things for many people. Tioman Island (see chapter 14) may have beaches and forests, but it has no shopping or historical sights to speak of. And although Melaka has historical sights and museums, it hasn't a grain of decent sand. Penang has all of it: fun beaches, beautiful resorts, rich history, diverse culture, and delicious food. If you have only a short time to visit Malaysia but want to take in as wide an experience as you can, Penang is a good choice.

Penang gets its name from the Malay word *pinang,* in reference to the areca plant, which grew on the island in abundance. The nut of the tree, commonly called *betel,* was

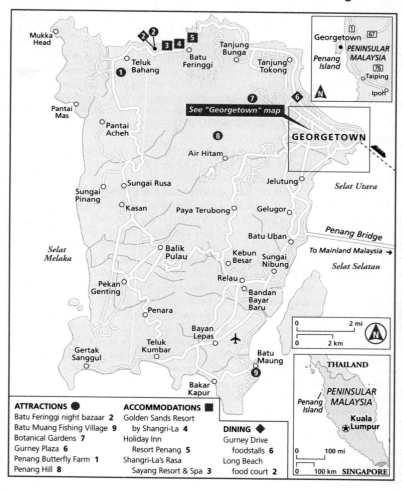

Georgetown
Penang Island
Taiping
Ipoh
PENINSULAR MALAYSIA

Mukka Head
Teluk Bahang
Batu Feringgi
Tanjung Bunga
Tanjung Tokong
Pantai Mas
Pantai Acheh
See "Georgetown" map
GEORGETOWN
Air Hitam
Sungai Rusa
Jelutung
Selat Utara
Sungai Pinang
Kasan
Paya Terubong
Gelugor
Selat Melaka
Balik Pulau
Batu Uban
Kebun Besar
Sungai Nibung
Penang Bridge
To Mainland Malaysia →
Selat Selatan
Pekan Genting
Relau
Penara
Bandan Bayar Baru
Bayan Lepas
0   2 mi
0   2 km
Gertak Sanggul
Teluk Kumbar
Batu Maung
Bakar Kapur
THAILAND
PENINSULAR MALAYSIA
Penang Island
Kuala Lumpur
0   100 mi
0   100 km   SINGAPORE

ATTRACTIONS ●
Batu Feringgi night bazaar **2**
Batu Muang Fishing Village **9**
Botanical Gardens **7**
Gurney Plaza **6**
Penang Butterfly Farm **1**
Penang Hill **8**

ACCOMMODATIONS ■
Golden Sands Resort
by Shangri-La **4**
Holiday Inn
Resort Penang **5**
Shangri-La's Rasa
Sayang Resort & Spa **3**

DINING ◆
Gurney Drive
foodstalls **6**
Long Beach
food court **2**

chewed habitually throughout the East (and in some parts still is). In the 15th century, it was a quiet place populated by small Malay communities, attracting the interest of some southern Indian betel merchants. By the time Francis Light, an agent for the British East India Company, arrived in 1786, the island was already on the maps of European, Indian, and Chinese traders. Light landed on the northeast part of the island, where he began a settlement after an agreement with the sultan of Kedah, on the mainland. He called the town **Georgetown** ★★★, after George III. One story claims that to gain the help of the locals for clearing the site, he shot a cannonload of coins into the jungle.

Georgetown became Britain's principal post in Malaya, attracting Europeans, Arabs, northern and southern Indians, southern Chinese, and Malays from the mainland and Sumatra to trade and settle. But it was never extremely profitable for England, especially when in 1819 Sir Stamford Raffles founded a new trading post in Singapore. Penang couldn't keep up with the new port's success.

In 1826, Penang, along with Melaka and Singapore, formed a unit called the Straits Settlements, over which Penang was voted the seat of government by a narrow margin. Finally, in 1832, Singapore stole its thunder when authority shifted there. In the late 1800s, Penang got a big break. Tin mines and rubber plantations on mainland Malaya were booming, and with the opening of the railway between KL and **Butterworth** (the town on the mainland just opposite the island), Penang once again thrived. Singapore firms scrambled to open offices in Butterworth.

The Great Depression hit Penang hard. So did the Japanese Occupation from 1941 to 1945, when the island was badly bombed. But since Malaysia's independence in 1957, Penang has had relatively good financial success.

Today the state of Penang is made up of the island and a small strip of land on the Malaysian mainland. Georgetown is the seat of government for the state. Penang Island is 285 sq. km (111 sq. miles) and has a population of a little more than one million. Surprisingly, the population is mostly Chinese (59%), followed by Malays (32%) and Indians (7%).

Georgetown reminds me of the way Singapore looked before massive government redevelopment and restoration projects "sanitized" the old neighborhoods. Georgetown's grid of narrow streets are still lined with shophouses that bustle with activity. Historic churches, temples, and mosques mingle with the city's newer architecture.

West of Georgetown, along Penang's northern shore, you'll find a number of popular resorts, sprawling complexes along strips of sandy beaches. Unfortunately, because Penang is located in the Straits of Malacca, the waters are not the idyllic crystal-clear azure you hope for in a tropical vacation. Yes, you've got sun, sand, and seasports, but no snorkeling or scuba. In my opinion, if you really want it all, enjoy the waters and sea life while you stay at one of the luxury resorts on Langkawi to the north (covered later in this chapter), and hop on a ferry to Georgetown for a day trip of sightseeing. There are short flights between the two islands as well.

ESSENTIALS
Visitor Information
The main **Tourism Malaysia** office is located at Level 56, KOMTAR Building (Kompleks Tun Abdul Razak) on Jalan Penang (© 04/264-3494). There's another information center at **Penang International Airport** (© 04/643-0501).

Getting There
BY PLANE   **Penang International Airport** (© 04/643-4411) has flights that connect from all over the world. **Malaysia Airlines** (© 1300/883-000; www.malaysiaairlines. com) has about 20 flights each day from KL, plus connecting flights from all over the country and region. Other airlines that service Penang are **Singapore Airlines, Thai Airways, Cathay Pacific, AirAsia** (© 1300/889-933; www.airasia.com), and **Firefly** (© 03/7845-4543; www.fireflyz.com.my).

The airport is 20km (12 miles) from the city. To get into town, you must purchase fixed-rate coupons for taxis RM38 ($11/£6.85) to Georgetown, RM60 ($17/£11) to Batu Feringgi. There are also car rentals at the airport; choose **Avis** (© 04/643-9633).

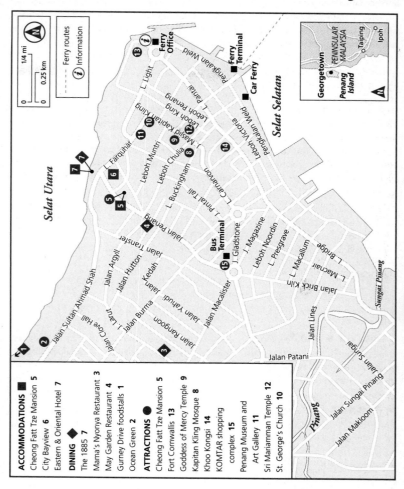

ACCOMMODATIONS ■
Cheong Fatt Tze Mansion **5**
City Bayview **6**
Eastern & Oriental Hotel **7**

DINING ◆
The 1885 **7**
Mama's Nyonya Restaurant **3**
May Garden Restaurant **4**
Gurney Drive foodstalls **1**
Ocean Green **2**

ATTRACTIONS ●
Cheong Fatt Tze Mansion **5**
Fort Cornwallis **13**
Goddess of Mercy Temple **9**
Kapitan Kling Mosque **8**
Khoo Kongsi **14**
KOMTAR shopping
  complex **15**
Penang Museum and
  Art Gallery **11**
Sri Mariamman Temple **12**
St. George's Church **10**

BY TRAIN   By rail, the overnight trip from KL to Butterworth takes 10 hours and costs RM85 ($25/£15) first-class passage, or as low as RM17 ($4.95/£3.05) for economy class. The prices vary greatly depending on whether you choose upper or lower berth and what class of passage you take. Call **KL Sentral** (𝒞 **03/2267-1200**) for schedule information.

The train will let you off at the **Butterworth Railway Station** (𝒞 **04/323-7962**), on Jalan Bagan Dalam (near the ferry terminal) in Butterworth, on the Malaysian mainland. From there, you can take a taxi to the island or head for the ferry close by.

BY BUS   Many buses will bring you to Butterworth or Georgetown, but I really only recommend it if you're not in a hurry. **Aeroline** (𝒞 **03/6258-8800;** www.aeroline.com. my) offers excellent executive coach services from KL to Penang.

BY FERRY   The ferry to Penang is nestled between the Butterworth Railway Station and the Butterworth bus terminal. It operates from 6am to 12:30am daily and takes 20 minutes from pier to pier. Ferries leave every 10 minutes. Purchase your passage by dropping RM1.20 (35¢/20p) exact change in the turnstile (there's a change booth if you don't have it). Fare is paid only on the trip to Penang. The return is free. The ferry lets you off at Weld Quay (© **04/310-2360**).

BY TAXI   The **outstation taxi** stand is in Butterworth next to the bus terminal (© **04/ 323-2045**). Fares to Butterworth from KL will be about RM350 ($102/£63).

Getting Around

BY TAXI   Taxis are abundant, but be warned they do not use meters, so you must agree on the price before you ride. They frequently rip off tourists. Most trips within the city are between RM5 and RM10 ($1.45–$2.90/90p–£1.80). If you're staying out at the Batu Feringgi beach resort area, expect taxis to town to run RM25 to RM40 ($7.25–$12/£4.50–£7.20). The ride is about 15 or 20 minutes but can take 30 minutes during rush hour.

BY BUS   Buses also run all over the island and are well used by tourists who don't want to drop cash every time they want to go to the beach. The dark-blue no. 93 and the white-with-blue no. 202 both operate between KOMTAR in Georgetown and the beach resorts at Batu Feringgi. Fare is anywhere under RM3 (85¢/55p). Get exact change from your hotel's cashier before you set off, and ask the bus driver about the exact fare to your destination.

CAR RENTAL   If you want to drive, call Avis at the Penang International Airport at © **04/643-9633.** They can also provide a car with driver for RM80 ($25/£14) per hour, for a minimum booking of 4 hours. If you plan to visit areas off Penang Island, the rate will increase.

BY BICYCLE & MOTORCYCLE   Along Batu Feringgi, there are bicycles and motorcycles (little 100cc scooters, really) available for rent. I don't recommend renting the scooters. You can never be certain of their maintenance record, and Penang's drivers are careless about watching your back. A sad number of visitors are injured or worse because of scooter accidents.

BY TRISHAW   In Georgetown, it's possible to find some trishaw action for about RM30 ($8.70/£5.40) an hour. It's kitschy and touristy, and I completely recommend it for traveling between in-town sights, at least for an hour or two. Bargain hard; these guys are skilled negotiators, but they do work hard for the money.

ON FOOT   I think everyone should walk at least part of the time to see the sights of Georgetown because in between each landmark and exhibit there's so much to see. A taxi, even a trishaw, will whisk you past back alleys where elderly haircutters set up alfresco shops, bicycle repairmen sit fixing tubes in front of their stores, and Chinese grannies fan themselves in the shade. Georgetown is stimulating, with the sights of old trades still being plied on these living streets, the noise of everyday life, and the exotic smells of an old Southeast Asian port. Give yourself at least a day here. Start wandering early in the morning, by the waterfront, down the back alleys, before the heat of the sun takes hold—the lighting is perfect for photography and you will find fantastic subjects here.

Fast Facts: Penang

Penang's **area code** is 04. The **banking center** of Georgetown is in the downtown area (close to Ft. Cornwallis) on Leboh Pantai, Leboh Union, and Leboh Downing, but you'll

find ATMs in KOMTAR and other smaller shopping plazas as well. **Internet** cafes come
and go, so it's best to ask your hotel's concierge for the closest place to your hotel, or use
the hotel's. If you're in town, Chulia Street, the main drag for backpacker tourists, has
Internet access in a few places.

WHERE TO STAY

Although Georgetown has many hotels right in the city for convenient sightseeing, most
visitors choose to stay at one of the beach resorts 30 minutes away at Batu Feringgi. Trips
back and forth can be a bother (regardless of the resorts' free shuttle services), but if you're
not staying in a resort, most of the finer beaches are off-limits.

Cheong Fatt Tze Mansion ★★ (Finds) This is definitely one of the most unique
and memorable hotel experiences in Malaysia—to sleep inside the walls of one of Asia's
most carefully restored heritage homes, the huge and opulent mansion of 19th-century
millionaire Cheong Fatt Tze. The lobby is a simple desk in the front hall; inside, the only
facilities to speak of are a courtyard breakfast area, a library, and a TV room (guest rooms
do not have TVs). Guest rooms are each distinctive in shape and decor, all with terra
cotta or teak floors, charming architectural detail, and antiques and replicas of the period.
Double rooms have either twin beds or one king-size bed. Suites are also available. All
are air-conditioned and have private bathrooms, though they are pretty small and bare.
The experience is described by the management as an "owner-hosted home-stay," which
is quite accurate. Don't expect the professional polish of the finer hotels, but then, with
so much beauty around you, who cares?

14 Leith St., 10200 Penang. ℰ 04/262-0006. www.cheongfatttzemansion.com. 16 units. RM350 ($102/
£63) double; from RM450 ($131/£81) suite. AE, DC, MC, V. **Amenities:** Breakfast area w/tea and beverage
service; smoke-free rooms; TV room. *In room:* A/C.

The City Bayview Hotel, Penang This city hotel is perfect for those who visit
Penang for its cultural treasures rather than its beaches. A good budget choice, it has a
number of fair dining venues, including a rooftop revolving restaurant with excellent
views of the island. Choose from guest rooms in the newer wing, completed in 1999, or
those in the old wing. Either choice offers cool rooms in neutral tones, not as elegant as
many, but comfortable and definitely offering value for the money.

25-A Farquhar St., Georgetown, 10200 Penang. ℰ 04/263-3161. Fax 04/263-4124. 320 units. RM276
($80/£50) double, from RM828 ($240/£149) suite. AE, DC, MC, V. **Amenities:** 3 restaurants; club w/live
entertainment; lobby lounge; outdoor pool; concierge; airport transfers; room service; babysitting;
smoke-free rooms. *In room:* A/C, TV w/in-house movies, minibar, hair dryer.

Eastern & Oriental Hotel (E&O) ★★ E&O first opened in 1885, established by
the same Sarkies brothers who were behind Raffles Hotel in Singapore. It is without a
doubt the most atmospheric hotel in Penang, with manicured lawns and tropical gardens
flanking a white colonial-style mansion, a lacelike facade, and Moorish minarets. Accommodations are all suites, with cozy sitting nooks and sleeping quarters separated by
pocket sliding doors. You can expect molding details around every door and paned window, oriental carpets over polished teak floorboards, and Egyptian cotton linens dressing
each poster bed. Dining along the hotel's many verandas is gorgeous. *One caveat:* No
beach, but the pool in the seafront garden is very pretty.

10 Farquhar St., 10200 Penang. ℰ 04/222-2000. Fax 04/261-6333. www.e-o-hotel.com. 101 units. RM900–
RM2,050 ($261–$595/£162–£369). AE, DC, MC, V. **Amenities:** 2 restaurants; English-style pub; small
health club w/sauna; concierge; airport transfers; room service. *In room:* A/C, TV w/satellite programming,
minibar.

Golden Sands Resort by Shangri-La ★ (Kids)   Shangri-La has been operating resorts on Penang longer than anyone else, and because it got here first, you can bet it laid claim to the best beach. Shangri-La has two neighboring properties on this site, Golden Sands and its more exclusive sister, Rasa Sayang. A four-star resort, Golden Sands is priced lower than the Rasa Sayang, so it attracts more families. The beach, pool area, and public spaces fill up fast, and folks are occupied all day with beach sports like parasailing and jet-skiing, and pool games. For the younger set, a large indoor playground is popular with kids under 12 while Mom and Dad relax. Rooms are large with full amenities, and the higher-priced categories have views of the pool and sea. A new round of renovations will be completed in mid-2009.

Batu Feringgi Beach, 11100 Penang. (C) **800/942-5050** in the U.S. and Canada, 800/222-448 in Australia, 800/442-179 in New Zealand, or 04/881-1911. Fax 04/881-1880. www.shangri-la.com. 395 units. RM700 ($203/£126) double; RM1,750 ($508/£315) suite. AE, DC, MC, V. **Amenities:** 3 restaurants; lobby lounge; 2 outdoor lagoon-style pools; outdoor lighted tennis courts; watersports equipment and activities; children's center; concierge; airport transfers; room service; babysitting. *In room:* A/C, TV w/satellite programming and in-house movies, Wi-Fi, fridge, hairdryer.

Holiday Inn Resort Penang (Kids)   This is a recommended choice for families, but be warned this resort has little appeal for vacationing couples or singles sans children. For families it has everything—special Kidsuites have a separate room for the wee ones with TV, video, and PlayStation, some with bunk beds—choose from jungle, treasure island, or outer space themes. Holiday Inn also has a Kids Club, fully supervised daycare with activities and games and a lifeguard. Older kids can join in beach volleyball, water polo, bike tours, and an assortment of watersports arranged by the staff. Guest rooms are in two blocks: a low-rise structure near the beach and a high-rise tower along the hillside, connected by a second-story walkway. Naturally, the beachside rooms command the greater rate. Beachside rooms also have better ambience and slightly larger space, with wood floors and details, while tower rooms have less charm. The lack of dining options gets tiring.

72 Batu Feringgi, 11100 Penang. (C) **04/881-1601.** Fax 04/881-1389. www.holidayinnpenang.com. 358 units. RM450–RM550 ($131–$160/£81–£99) hillview double; RM530–RM650 ($154–$189/£95–£117) seaview double; RM800 ($232/£144) Kidsuite; from RM800 ($232/£144) suite. AE, DC, MC, V. **Amenities:** Restaurant; lobby lounge; outdoor pool and children's pool; outdoor lighted tennis courts; health club; watersports equipment rentals; children's club; concierge; airport transfers; room service; babysitting. *In room:* A/C, TV w/satellite programming and in-house movies, miniba, hair dryerr.

Shangri-La's Rasa Sayang Resort & Spa ★★★   Rasa Sayang reopened in 2006 after a RM10.5-million ($3-million/£1.9-million) redevelopment that saw parts of the original buildings gutted to make way for a spa to compete with the deluxe resorts in the region. Rasa Sayang was the first resort to be built along Batu Feringgi, so it commands the best beach of all the resorts, with 12 hectares (30 acres) of grounds—enough for a par-3 executive golf course, two pools, and plenty of gardens, plus two wings of guest rooms, Rasa and Garden. Standard rooms are gorgeous, most with sea views, in contemporary style and natural tones, deep wood built-ins, and big fluffy beds. In the Rasa Wing, guest rooms have private verandas and gardens, or balconies with tubs outside. Rasa Sayang also launched the Shangri-La's new spa brand, CHI, with decor and treatments based on Chinese principles of yin and yang and the five elements: metal, wood, water, fire, and earth.

Batu Feringgi Beach, 11100 Penang. (C) **800/942-5050** in the U.S. and Canada, 800/222-448 in Australia, 800/442-179 in New Zealand, or 04/888-8888. Fax 04/881-1880. www.shangri-la.com. 304 units. RM1,491

($432/£268) double; RM2,266 ($657/£408) Rasa Wing double. AE, DC, MC, V. **Amenities:** 4 restaurants; 2 bars; 2 outdoor lagoon-style pools; outdoor lighted tennis courts; health club; spa; watersports equipment and activities; concierge; airport transfers; room service; babysitting. *In room:* A/C, TV w/satellite programming and in-house movies, fridge, hair dryer.

WHERE TO DINE

The 1885 ★★ CONTINENTAL   If you're celebrating a special occasion while in Penang, The 1885 will make the experience beyond memorable. The nostalgic romance of the E&O Hotel, its colonial architecture, interiors, and manicured lawns evoking times when tigers probably roamed the grounds after dark, provides the most incredible backdrop for a perfect meal. From an ever-changing menu, poultry, special cuts of meats, and fresh seafood are prepared in delicate contemporary Western style. Candlelight, starched linens, silver service, and extremely attentive staff create a magical experience. The wine list is extensive. By Malaysian standards, this is an expensive meal, but if you compare the quality of the service, cuisine, and surroundings, really, you will never find such elegance for this price in Europe or the States. English afternoon teas are also superb. Men are asked to kindly wear a shirt with a collar.

Eastern & Oriental Hotel (E&O), 10 Lebuh Farquhar. ⓒ **04/222-0000.** Reservations recommended. Main courses RM60–RM180 ($17–$52/£11–£32). AE, DC, MC, V. Daily 7–10:30pm.

Mama's Nyonya Restaurant ★ Finds NYONYA   Those who crave Penang's most famous culinary style of Nyonya food (or Peranakan) have to visit this cozy family-run restaurant in Abu Siti Lane. Ruby, one of the four sisters who run the place, learned her cooking from her Mama, hence the name. It's authentic, as Mama keeps a watchful eye on her protégés, although she no longer cooks. You'll see her there every day though lending a helping hand with all the painstaking detail required for this kind of food. You might encounter some of her famous clients, including Malaysia's own international shoemaker, Datuk Jimmy Choo, or Hong Kong director Ang Lee. All the favorite Nyonya dishes are on the menu—try *tau eu bak, purut ikan,* Nyonya fish head curry, and *otak otak.* Look like a tourist, and someone will help you negotiate the menu.

31-D, Abu Siti Lane, Georgetown. ⓒ **04/229-1318.** Main courses RM10–RM25 ($2.90–$7.25/£1.80–£4.50). No credit cards. Tues–Sun 11:30am–2:30pm and 6:30–9:30pm.

May Garden Restaurant CANTONESE   This is a top Cantonese restaurant in Georgetown, and while it's noisy and not too big on ambience, it has excellent food. But how many Chinese do you know who go to places for ambience? It's the food that counts! Outstanding dishes include the tofu and broccoli topped with sea snail slices or the fresh steamed live prawns. They also have suckling pig and Peking duck. Don't agree to all the daily specials, or you'll be paying a fortune.

70 Jalan Penang. ⓒ **04/261-6435.** Reservations recommended. Main courses start at RM15 ($4.35/£2.70). Seafood is priced by weight in kilograms. AE, DC, MC, V. Daily noon–3pm and 6–10:30pm.

Ocean Green ★★ SEAFOOD   I can't rave enough about Ocean Green. If the beautiful sea view and ocean breezes don't fulfill every holiday expectation, the succulent seafood certainly will. A long list of fresh seafood is prepared steamed or fried, with your choice of chili, black-bean, sweet-and-sour, or curry sauces. On the advice of a local food expert, I tried the lobster thermidor, which was expensive but divine, and the chick wings stuffed with minced chicken, prawns, and gravy. Baked crab with cheese i highly recommended.

48F Jalan Sultan Ahmad Shah. © **04/226-2681.** Reservations recommended. Main courses start at RM15 ($4.35/£2.70); seafood priced according to market value. AE, MC, V. Daily 9am–11pm.

Food Stall Dining

No discussion of Penang dining would be complete without coverage of the local food stall scene, which is famous. Penang hawkers can make any dish you've had in Malaysia, Singapore, or even southern Thailand—only better. Penang may be attractive for many things—history, culture, nature—but it is loved for its food.

Gurney Drive Foodstalls, toward the water just down from the intersection with Jalan Kelawai, is the biggest and most popular hawker center. It has all kinds of food, including local dishes with every influence: Chinese, Malay, Indian. Find *char kway teow* (fried flat noodles with seafood), *char bee hoon* (a fried thin rice noodle), *laksa* (noodles and seafood in a tangy and spicy broth), *murtabak* (mutton, egg, and onion fried inside Indian bread and dipped in *dhal*), *oh chien* (oyster omelet with chili dip), and *rojak* (a spicy fruit and seafood salad). After you've eaten your way through Gurney Drive, you can try the stalls on Jalan Burmah near the Lai Lai Supermarket or the stalls at **Long Beach** food court in Batu Ferringi.

ATTRACTIONS

In Georgetown

Cheong Fatt Tze Mansion ★★★
Cheong Fatt Tze (1840–1917), once dubbed "China's Rockefeller" by the *New York Times,* built a vast commercial empire in Southeast Asia, first in Indonesia, then in Singapore. He came to Penang in 1890 and continued his success, giving some of his spoils to build schools throughout the region. His mansion, where he lived with his eight wives, was built between 1896 and 1904.

The mansion is a sight to behold. Cheong spent lavishly for Chinese detail that reflects the spirit of his heritage and the fashion of the day, as well as the rules of traditional feng shui. Every corner is dripping with ambience, outfitted throughout with stained glass, carved moldings, gilded wood-carved doors, ceramic ornaments, lovely courtyard and gardens, plus seven staircases.

In 2000, the mansion won UNESCO's Asia-Pacific Heritage Award for Conservation, so lovingly has this historic treasure been preserved. Guided tours explain the history, personalities, and culture behind the home, plus the details of the conservation efforts. If you're really hooked, accommodation is available.

14 Lebuh Leith. © **04/262-0006.** Admission RM12 ($3.50/£2.15). Daily guided tours at 11am and 3pm.

Fort Cornwallis
Fort Cornwallis is built on the site where Capt. Francis Light, founder of Penang, first landed in 1786. The fort was first built in 1793, but this site was an unlikely spot to defend the city from invasion. In 1810, it was rebuilt in an attempt to make up for initial strategic planning errors. In the shape of a star, the only actual buildings still standing are the outer walls, a gunpowder magazine, and a small Christian chapel. The magazine houses an exhibit of old photos and historical accounts of the old fort.

Lebuh Light. No phone. Adults RM3 (85¢/55p), children RM2 (60¢/35p). Daily 8am–7pm.

Goddess of Mercy Temple
Dedicated jointly to Kuan Yin, the goddess of mercy, and Ma Po Cho, the patron saint of sea travelers, this is the oldest Chinese temple in Penang. On the 19th of each second, sixth, and ninth month of the lunar calendar (the

Leboh Pitt. Free admission.

Kapitan Kling Mosque   Captain Light donated a large parcel of land on this spot for the settlement's sizable Indian Muslim community to build a mosque and graveyard. The leader of the community, known as Kapitan Kling (or Keling, which, ironically, was once a racial slur against Indians in the region), built a brick mosque here. Later, in 1801, he imported builders and materials from India for a new, brilliant mosque. Expansions in the 1900s topped the mosque with stunning domes and turrets, adding extensions and new roofs.

Jalan Masjid Kapitan Kling (Leboh Pitt). Free admission.

Khoo Kongsi ★   The Chinese who migrated to Southeast Asia created clan associations in their new homes. Based on common heritage, these social groups formed the core of Chinese life in the new homelands. The Khoo clan, who immigrated from Hokkien province in China, acquired this spot in 1851 and set to work building row houses, administrative buildings, and a clan temple around a large square. The temple here now was actually built in 1906 after a fire destroyed its predecessor. It was believed the original was too ornate, provoking the wrath of the gods. One look at the current temple, a Chinese baroque masterpiece, and you'll wonder how that could possibly be. Come here in August for Chinese operas.

18 Cannon Sq. *©* **04/261-4609.** Free admission. Daily 9am–5pm.

Penang Museum and Art Gallery ★★   The historical society has put together this marvelous collection of ethnological and historical findings from Penang, tracing the port's history and diverse cultures through time. It's filled with paintings, photos, costumes, and antiques, among much more, all presented with fascinating facts and trivia. Upstairs is an art gallery. Originally the Penang Free School, the building was built in two phases, the first half in 1896 and the second in 1906. Only half of the building remains; the other was bombed to the ground in World War II. Its recent renovation has added life, at least to the exterior. It's a favorite stop on a sightseeing itinerary because it's air-conditioned.

Lebuh Farquhar. *©* **04/261-3144.** Admission RM1 (30¢/20p). Sat–Thurs 9am–5pm.

Sri Mariamman Temple   This Hindu temple was built in 1833 by a Chettiar, a group of southern Indian Muslims, and received a major face-lift in 1978 with the help of Madras sculptors. The Hindu Navarithri festival is held here, whereby devotees parade Sri Mariamman, a Hindu goddess worshiped for her powers to cure disease, through the streets in a night procession. It is also the starting point of the Thaipusam Festival, which leads to a temple on Jalan Waterfall.

Jalan Masjid Kapitan Kling. Free admission.

St. George's Church   Built by Rev. R. S. Hutchins (who was also responsible for the Free School next door, home of the Penang Museum) and Capt. Robert N. Smith, whose paintings hang in the museum, this church was completed in 1818. Although the outside is almost as it was then, the contents were completely looted during World War II. All that remains are the font and the bishop's chair.

Lebuh Farquhar. Free admission.

Batu Muang Fishing Village   If you'd like to see a local fishing village, here's a good one. This village is special for its shrine to Admiral Cheng Ho, the early Chinese sea adventurer.

Southeast tip of Penang. Free admission. From Georgetown, take the Jelutong Expy., then take Teluk Tempoyak into the village.

Botanical Gardens   Covering 30 hectares (74 acres) of landscaped grounds, this botanical garden was established by the British in 1884, with grounds that are perfect for a shady walk and a ton of fun if you love monkeys. They're crawling all over the place and will think nothing of stepping forward for a peanut (which you can buy beneath the DO NOT FEED THE MONKEYS sign). Also in the gardens is a jogging track and kiddie park. The gardens are important for tropical research.

About a 5- or 10-min. drive west of Georgetown. ℂ **04/227-0428.** Free admission. Daily 7am–7pm.

Penang Butterfly Farm   The Penang Butterfly Farm, located toward the northwest corner of the island, is the largest in the world. On its .8-hectare (2-acre) landscaped grounds there are more than 4,000 flying butterflies from 120 species. At 10am and 3pm, there are informative butterfly shows. Don't forget the insect exhibit—there are about 2,000 or so bugs.

Jalan Teluk Bahang. ℂ **04/885-1253.** Adults RM20 ($5.80/£3.60), children RM10 ($2.90/£1.80), free for children 4 and under. Daily 9am–5:30pm.

Penang Hill   Covered with jungle and 20 nature trails, the hill is great for trekking. Or you can go to Ayer Hitam, a town in central Penang, and take the Keretapi Bukit Bendera funicular railway to the top. It sends trains up and down the hill every half-hour from 6am to 9pm, weekends from 6am to 11pm, and costs adults RM4 ($1.15/70p) and children RM2 (60¢/35p), round-trip. In 2008, the train was closed for repairs, so do check with the local Tourism Malaysia office to be sure it has reopened before you head out. If you prefer to make the trek on foot, go to the "Moon Gate" at the entrance to the Botanical Garden for a 5.5km (3½-mile), 3-hour hike to the summit.

A 20- to 30-min. drive southwest from Georgetown. The funicular station is on Jalan Stesen Keretapi Bukit.

SHOPPING

The first place anyone here will recommend you to go for shopping is **KOMTAR.** Short for "Kompleks Tun Abdul Razak," it is the largest shopping complex in Penang, four stories of clothing shops, restaurants, and large department stores. For those staying in Batu Ferringi resorts, **Gurney Plaza** (ℂ **04/228-1111**) is close by.

Good shopping finds in Penang are *batik,* pewter products, locally produced curios, paintings, antiques, pottery, and jewelry. If you care to walk around in search of finds, there are a few streets in Georgetown that are the hub of shopping activity. In the city center, the area around Jalan Penang, Lebuhraya Campbell, Lebuhraya Kapitan Keling, Lebuhraya Chulia, and Lebuhraya Pantai is near the Sri Mariamman Temple, the Penang Museum, the Kapitan Keling Mosque, and other sites of historic interest. Here you'll find everything from local crafts to souvenirs and fashion, and maybe even a bargain or two. Most of these shops are open from 10am to 10pm daily.

Out at Batu Feringgi, the main road turns into a fun **night bazaar** every evening just at dark. During the day, there are also some good shops for *batik* and souvenirs.

Visitors to Penang have to experience the E&O Hotel, even if they're not staying there. **Farquhar's Bar** (*©* **04/222-2000;** daily 11am–11pm) may be as close as many will come to exploring the hotel. Live the life of a colonialist, enjoy pub grub and cool drinks. Possibly the most notorious bar in Penang is the **Hong Kong Bar,** 371 Lebuh Chulia (*©* **04/261-9796),** which opened in 1920 and was a regular hangout for military personnel based in Butterworth. It has an extraordinary archive of photos of the servicemen who have patronized the place throughout the years, plus a collection of medals, plaques, and buoys from ships.

6 LANGKAWI ★★

Where the beautiful Andaman Sea meets the Straits of Malacca, Langkawi Island positions itself as one of the region's best island paradise destinations. Since 1990, Tourism Malaysia has dedicated itself to promoting the island and developing it as an ideal travel spot. Now, after almost 2 decades of work, the island has proven itself as one of this country's best holiday gems.

This small island also claims a Hollywood credit, as it was the backdrop for the 1999 film *Anna and the King.* Langkawi played the role of Thailand to Jodie Foster's Anna Leonowens and Chow Yun-Fat's King Mongkut (Rama IV). The Thais wouldn't allow the filmmakers to shoot on location in their kingdom, so Hollywood turned to neighboring Malaysia.

Technically, Langkawi is an archipelago of islands, the largest of which serves as the main focal point. Ask how many islands actually make up Langkawi, and you'll hear either 104 or 99. The official response? "Both are correct. It depends on the tide!" On Langkawi Island itself, the main town, **Kuah,** provides the island's administrative needs, while on the western and northern shores, the beaches have been developed with resorts. The west-coast beaches of **Pantai Cenang** and **Pantai Tengah** are the most developed; however, the concept of "development" here is quite low key. To the north, **Datai Bay** and **Tanjung Rhu** host the island's finest, and most secluded, resorts.

One final note: Malaysia has declared Langkawi a duty-free zone, so take a peek at some of the shopping in town, and enjoy RM1.50 (45¢/25p) beers!

ESSENTIALS
Getting There
BY PLANE **Malaysia Airlines** (*©* **1300/883-000;** www.malaysiaairlines.com) and **AirAsia** (*©* **03/8775-4000;** www.airasia.com) make Langkawi very convenient from either mainland Malaysia or Singapore. In addition, **Silk Air (Singapore)** flies to Langkawi International Airport (*©* **04/955-1311**).

The best way from the airport is to prearrange a shuttle pickup from your resort; otherwise, you can grab a taxi in front of the airport. To Pantai Cenang or Pantai Tengah, the fare should be about RM20 ($5.80/£3.60), while to the resorts at Tanjung Rhu and Datai Bay, it will be RM45 and RM55 ($13/£8.10 and $16/£9.90), respectively.

BY TRAIN Taking the train can be a bit of a hassle because the nearest stop (in Alor Star) is quite far from the jetty to the island, requiring a cab transfer. Still, if you prefer rail, hop on the overnight train from KL (the only train), which will put you in to Alor

13

Star at around 7am. Just outside the train station, you can find the taxi stand, with cabs to take you to the Kuala Kedah jetty for the ferry ride to Kuah.

BY BUS   To be honest, I don't really recommend using this route. If you're coming from KL, the bus ride is long and uncomfortable, catching the taxi transfer to the jetty can be problematic, and by the time you reach the island, you'll need a vacation from your vacation. Fly or use the train. If you're coming from Penang, the direct ferry is wonderfully convenient, as are a few flights per day.

BY FERRY   From the jetty at Kuala Kedah, there are about five companies that provide ferry service to the island (trip time: about 1 hr. and 45 min.; cost: RM25/$7.25/£4.50). Ferries let you off at the main ferry terminal in Kuah, where you can hop a taxi to your resort for RM20 to RM50 ($5.80–$15/£3.60–£9).

Ferries also ply between Penang and Langkawi. **Langkawi Ferry** has two early-morning ferries from Weld Quay in Georgetown for RM60 one-way ($17/£11) and RM115 round-trip ($33/£21). Call them in Penang at © **04/264-2088** or visit their office across from the clock tower. If you're heading from Langkawi to Penang, you can call them in Langkawi at © **04/966-3779.**

Visitor Information

The Tourism Malaysia office is unfortunately situated in Kuah town on Jalan Persiaran Putra, far from the beach areas. For specific queries, you can call them at © **04/966-7789.** If you're arriving by plane, there's another office at the airport (© **04/955-7155**).

Getting Around

BY TAXI   Taxis generally hang around at the airport, the main jetty, the taxi stand in Kuah, and some major hotels. From anywhere in between, your best bet is to ask your hotel's concierge to call a taxi for you. Keep in mind, if you're going as far as one side of the island to the other, your fare can go as high as RM50 ($15/£9).

CAR & MOTORCYCLE RENTAL   At the airport and from agents in the complex behind the main jetty, car rentals can be arranged starting at RM80 ($23/£14) per day. This is for the standard, no-frills model—actually, mine was more reminiscent of some of the junkers I drove throughout college, but it still got me around. Insurance policies are lax, as are rental regulations. My rental guys seemed more concerned with my passport documents than with my driver's license. If you're out on the beach at Cenang or Tengah, a few places rent jeeps and motorcycles from RM80 ($23/£14) and RM30 ($8.70/£5.40) per day, respectively. Pick a good helmet. *Note:* If you have an accident, you could be responsible for all repairs, but resorts usually rent cars that are insured.

BY FOOT   The main beaches at Cenang and Tengah can be walked quite nicely; however, don't expect to be able to walk around to other parts of the island.

Fast Facts: Langkawi

The only major **bank** branches are located far from the beach areas, in Kuah, mostly around the blocks across the street from the Night Hawker Center (off Jalan Persiaran Putra)—there is an ATM at the airport. Moneychangers keep long hours out at Pantai Cenang and Pantai Tengah, but for other resorts you'll have to change your money at the resort. Along the Pantai Cenang and Pantai Tengah main road, you'll find at least a half-dozen small **Internet** places.

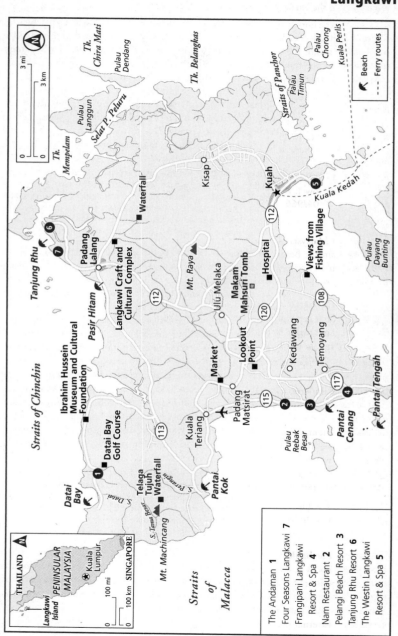

Beach
Ferry routes

The Andaman **1**
Four Seasons Langkawi **7**
Frangipani Langkawi
Resort & Spa **4**
Nam Restaurant **2**
Pelangi Beach Resort **3**
Tanjung Rhu Resort **6**
The Westin Langkawi
Resort & Spa **5**

The Andaman ★★ (Kids) You will be surprised how large this resort is, its buildings blend so perfectly with the jungle surrounding them. Andaman has a sprawl of lush grounds hugging a beautiful white beach. The temptation to clear the coastal forests has been avoided, and rooms quite pleasantly look into these forests and their native fauna, but with glimpses of the sea. The Andaman welcomes families and has special facilities, including a kid's club, and it has a safe, shallow beach. The entrance and main lobby are overpowering in size but visually quite stunning in open-air local-style architecture with vaulted roofs built from polished hardwoods. Guest rooms, in two wings that span out to either side of the main building, are big, with wall-to-wall carpeting and Western-style decor, save for a few local textiles for effect. Ground-floor lanai rooms have a private sun deck with umbrella stand. The pool is huge, with lots of shady spots, and the spa features traditional Malay herbal beauty and health treatments.

Jalan Teluk Datai, P.O. Box 94, 07000 Langkawi, Kedah. ✆ **04/959-1088.** Fax 04/959-1168. www.theandaman. com. RM990–RM1,970 ($287–$571/£178–£355) double; from RM2,250 ($653/£405) suite. Prices jump Dec–Jan. AE, DC, MC, V. **Amenities:** 3 restaurants; 2 bars; outdoor pools surrounded by gardens; golf course; 2 outdoor lighted tennis courts; health club; spa w/Jacuzzi, sauna, steam, and massage; non-motorized watersports equipment; mountain bike rental; concierge; airport transfers; room service; babysitting. *In room:* A/C, TV w/satellite programming and DVD player, minibar, hair dryer.

Four Seasons Langkawi ★★★ Every detail of this resort is perfectly exotic, influ-enced by contemporary Moorish style. Pavilion rooms are surrounded by floor-to-ceiling windows and wraparound verandas. Under soaring ceilings, huge bedrooms have wood floors, ceiling fans, carved wood detailing, and plush soft furnishings. Through double doors, huge bathrooms are majestic, with oversize terrazzo tubs built into arched nooks, separate closets for rain shower and toilet, a huge clothes closet, and a center island with double sinks. Throughout the rooms you'll find touches such as lanterns, hammered bronze work, lovely toiletries on marble pedestals, and cozy throw pillows that add an intimate Middle Eastern flavor. The resort has two infinity pools that look like they're spilling onto the beach, which is a long, wide stretch of perfect sand. Every dining venue fronts the beach. At Rhu Bar, cocktails are served with Turkish water pipes, amid Indian Moghul hanging swings, glowing lanterns, and Moorish carved latticework arches that frame the sea view gorgeously. The spa has private villas with tubs for four, space for floor and table massages, private indoor/outdoor showers, and changing rooms all encased in glass with lovely garden views. This is the most luxurious property in this whole book. Period.

Jalan Tanjung Rhu, 07000 Langkawi, Kedah. ✆ **800/332-3442** in the U.S., 800/268-6282 in Canada, or 04/950-8888. Fax 04/950-8899. www.fourseasons.com. US$600–US$685 pavilion; from US$875 villa. Prices jump Dec–Jan. AE, DC, MC, V. **Amenities:** 3 restaurants; 2 bars; 2 outdoor pools; tennis; health club; spa w/yoga and juice bar; complimentary nonmotorized watersports; children's center; concierge; air-port transfers; room service. *In room:* A/C, TV w/satellite programming and in-house movies, Wi-Fi, mini-bar, hair dryer.

Frangipani Langkawi Resort & Spa ★ This small resort packs a big punch. I like its ecological stance in setting out as a green resort, and it has already won several awards for its efforts. It's got a great location, with a 400m-long (1,312-ft.) beachfront with restaurants, shops, and bars at the front entrance. There are rooms in two-story blocks, but the best choices are the sea-facing villas with rooftop showers. All are tastefully fur-nished, and the Coco Beach Bar is the best place to view spectacular sunsets.

Jalan Teluk Baru, Pantai Tengah, 07100 Langkawi, Kedah. ℂ **04/952-0000.** Fax 04/952-0001. www.
frangipanilangkawi.com. 118 units. RM483 ($140/£87) double; from RM650 ($189/£117) suite. **Ameni-ties:** Restaurant; bar; 2 outdoor pools; watersports equipment; concierge; room service; babysitting. *In room:* A/C, TV w/satellite programming and in-house movies, minibar, hair dryer.

Pelangi Beach Resort ★

For those who prefer a more active vacation or are looking for a resort that's more family-oriented, I recommend Pelangi. A top-quality resort, this place stands out from neighboring five-star resorts for its sheer fun. A long list of orga-nized sports and leisure pastimes makes it especially attractive for families, but, surpris-ingly, I've never found children to be a distraction here. Pelangi's wooden chalets are huge inside and are divided into one, two, or four guestrooms. You'll be welcomed by vaulted ceilings, modern bathrooms, and large living spaces. But it's the little things you'll love— I didn't want to get out of bed and leave my squishy down pillows and snuggly bedding. In addition, Pelangi's location, near the central beach strip for island life, means you're not cloistered away from the rest of civilization.

Pantai Cenang, 07000 Langkawi, Kedah. ℂ **04/952-8888.** Fax 04/952-8899. www.pelangibeachresort. com. 350 units. RM1,000 ($290/£180) double; from RM1,850 ($537/£333) suite. AE, DC, MC, V. **Amenities:** 3 restaurants; 3 bars; 2 large outdoor pools w/swim-up bar; golf nearby; minigolf course; outdoor lighted tennis courts; squash courts; health club w/sauna, steam, and massage; Jacuzzi; watersports center w/ equipment rental and boating excursions; concierge; airport transfers; room service; babysitting. *In room:* A/C, TV w/satellite programming and in-house movies, minibar, hair dryer.

Tanjung Rhu Resort ★★

The beach at Tanjung Rhu is a wide crescent of dazzlingly pure sand wrapped around a perfect crystal azure bay. Tree-lined karst islets jut up from the sea, dotting the horizon. Just gorgeous. This resort claims 440 hectares (1,087 acres) of jungle in this part of the island, monopolizing the scene for extra privacy, but it has its pros and cons. The pros? Guest rooms are enormous and decorated with sensitivity to the environment, from natural materials to organic recycled-paper-wrapped toiletries. A second pool and spa facility add value. The cons? The resort is a little isolated, so guests will be locked into using the resort restaurants. This isn't all bad, as the food is good and they offer packages enabling access to all outlets and menus.

Tanjung Rhu, Mukim Ayer Hangat, 07000 Langkawi, Kedah. ℂ **04/959-1033.** Fax 04/959-1899. www. tanjungrhu.com.my. 136 units. RM1,425 ($413/£257) double; RM2,850 ($827/£513) suite. AE, DC, MC, V. **Amenities:** 3 restaurants; bar; 2 outdoor pools, 1 saltwater and 1 freshwater; golf nearby; outdoor lighted tennis courts; health club and spa w/Jacuzzi, sauna, steam, and massage; watersports equipment (non-motorized) and boat tours; concierge; airport transfers; room service; babysitting. *In room:* A/C, TV w/ satellite programming and in-room video w/movie library, CD player, minibar, hair dryer.

The Westin Langkawi Resort & Spa ★★★

The hotel has resurfaced from what was once the Sheraton Perdana Resort and has been refurbished with ultraluxurious five-star comforts. The first Westin-branded resort in Southeast Asia is located close to the township of Kuah. The resort is located along a reasonable beach, but it is the swimming pools that will appeal to most guests. It has majestic views of the Andaman Sea and several of the islands in the archipelago. It doesn't get much better than cocktails in Breeze Lounge around sunset. All rooms and villas are contemporarily designed, with the villas being my pick, as they are spacious and include a private plunge pool. All rooms feature the Westin's signature Heavenly Bed. This is a great resort for kids, who will love the pools and kids' club.

Jalan Pantai Dato Syed Omar, 07000 Langkawi, Kedah. ℂ **800/937-8461** in the U.S. and Canada, 800/656-535 in Australia, 800/490-375 in New Zealand, 800/325-95959 in the U.K., or 04/960-8888. Fax 966-3097. www.westin.com/langkawi. 222 units. AE, DC, MC, V. RM2,000 ($580/£360) double; from

Amenities: 2 restaurants; lounge; pool bar; 4 outdoor pools; 2 outdoor lighted tennis courts; health club w/Jacuzzi; spa w/bar; sauna; bikes; watersports; concierge; airport transfers; room service; babysitting. *In room:* A/C, 42-inch plasma TV w/satellite programming, DVD player and in-house movies, minibar, hair dryer.

WHERE TO DINE

If you're out at one of the more secluded resorts, chances are, you'll stay there for most of your meals. If you find yourself at Pantai Cenang, try **Nam Restaurant** (✆ **04/955-6787**), the best restaurant on Langkawi and perhaps in all of Malaysia. Located within the small and charming Bon Ton Resort, Nam serves "West meets spice" dishes along with an excellent selection of wines and dreamy desserts in a Balinese-inspired setting. Arrive at sunset for predinner drinks, and stay after your meal for drinks at the resort's fun Chin Chin bar. If you're in Kuah town looking for something good to eat, the best local dining experience can be found at the evening **hawker stalls** just along the waterfront near the taxi stand. A long row of hawkers cooks up every kind of local favorite, including seafood dishes. You can't get any cheaper or more laid back. After dinner, from here it's easy to flag down a taxi back to your resort.

ATTRACTIONS

Fifteen years ago, Langkawi was just a backwater island supporting small fishing communities. When the government came in with big money to develop the place for tourism, they thought they needed a catch, so they dug up some old moldy "legends" about the island and have tried to market them as bona fide cultural attractions. Basically, these attractions appeal more to local tourists.

In terms of beaches and watersports, most resorts are self-contained units, offering their own equipment rentals and planning their own outings.

Outside of your resort, there's some fairly decent diving to be had. **Asian Overland** (✆ **04/955-2002;** www.asianoverland.com.my) can arrange day trips with two dives to Payar Marine Park within Langkawi's extensive island network. They charge RM280 ($81/£50). You can also snorkel for the day for RM160 ($46/£29) per person. There's an interesting snorkel attraction off Langkawi—a platform in the middle of the sea that floats above a coral reef. Day trips to the platform include rides in a glass-bottomed boat, snorkeling, and lunch on the platform. It's an all-day affair for RM230 ($67/£41) per person, starting at 8am and getting you back to your resort just before dinnertime.

Asian Overland also plans round-island boat trips to "island-hop" at beaches and into mangrove swamps (interesting), with a stop at the Pregnant Maiden Lake (one of the before-mentioned overhyped places). The mangrove tours are very educational, but ask them to show you the eagles, not feed them. They'll tailor your tour so you can see the sights that most interest you.

The best thing going for Langkawi is that the island's natural assets have been preserved despite the modern infrastructure to accommodate tourists. Unlike Bali and Phuket, visitors can relax on the beaches and not be hassled by hawkers trying to sell things.

One piece of infrastructure that stands out is the cable car that extends to the summit of Mount Macinchang. It's a dramatic, near-vertical lift high above the rainforest canopy to the 706m-high (2,316-ft.) rocky summit. From here visitors can see most of the island's attractions and peer off into the distant islands of southern Thailand. The departure point for the ride is Oriental Village at Burau Bay. There is a carnival-like atmosphere here, with restaurants and souvenir shops that all seem to sell basically the same items. The 14-minute ride to the summit is one of the world's steepest, at 42 degrees, and it has the longest free-span single-rope cable in the world. At the top, there is a 125m (410 ft.) curved platform across a deep chasm. Open Monday, Tuesday, and Thursday from 10am to 6pm; Wednesday noon to 6pm; Friday to Sunday 9:30am to 7pm. Call © **04/959-4225** for more information. Prices are RM25 ($7.25/£4.50) adults, RM18 ($5.20/£3.25) children.

Sailors will enjoy visiting one of four marinas in Langkawi. The international charter company **Sunsail** (© **04/966-5869**; www.sunsailmalaysia.com) operates from Royal Langkawi Yacht Club on Jalan Dato Syed Omar, where keen sailors can rent yachts to sail around the islands or to Phuket in neighboring Thailand.

Perhaps one of the loveliest additions to Langkawi's attractions is the **Ibrahim Hussein Museum and Cultural Foundation,** Pasir Tengkorak, Jalan Datai (© **04/959-4669**). The artistic devotion of the foundation's namesake fueled the creation of this enchanting modern space designed to showcase Malaysia's contribution to the international fine-arts scene. If you can pull yourself from the beach for any one activity in Langkawi, this is the one I recommend. Mr. Hussein has created a museum worthy of international attention. Truly a gem. It's open Saturday through Thursday from 10am to 6pm; adults pay RM12 ($3.50/£2.15), children visit for free.

SHOPPING

Langkawi's designated Duty Free Port status makes shopping here quite fun and very popular. In Kuah town, two shopping malls, **Langkawi Parade** (Jalan Kelibang; © **04/966-6372**) and **Langkawi Fair** (Persiaran Putra; © **04/969-8100**), both in Kuah town, are filled with duty-free shopping. For local handicrafts, the **Langkawi Craft and Cultural Complex** (Jalan Teluk Yu; © **04/959-1913;** daily 10am–6pm) sells an assortment of *batik,* baskets, ceramic, silver jewelry, brassware, and more, and also has daily crafts demonstrations and cultural shows.

14

Peninsular Malaysia: The East Coast

Over the past 200 years, while the cities on the western coast of peninsular Malaysia preoccupied themselves with waves of foreign domination, those on the eastern coast developed in relative seclusion. Today this part of the country remains true to its Malay heritage, from small fishing *kampungs* (villages) in the south to the Islamic strongholds of the north. More recently it has developed as the nation's petroleum center.

The best attractions of the east coast are its islands. Tioman, Redang, and Perhentian attract snorkelers and divers with clear waters, diverse marine life, and comfortable accommodations. In addition, short daily flights from Kuala Lumpur (KL) make Tioman and Redang more accessible than the more renowned (and remote) dive sites of Borneo. The shoreline along the east coast of the peninsula is fringed with long stretches of sandy beaches, home to dozens of resorts. Most accommodations are budget chalets, but a few deluxe resorts stand out from the rest, notably Cherating's Club Med, Terengganu's Tanjong Aru Resort, and the Aryani.

With these few exceptions, tourism is quite laid back. For many, the lack of tourism infrastructure can sound exciting—"authentic" even—but really, although the potential for nature, adventure, and cultural tourism is here, there's just not enough creativity and investment for this area to compete with other destinations in the country. In short, if you come here, come to relax. I have, however, found some satisfying shopping, as many of Malaysia's surviving cottage industries are located in this area.

Some notes before you plan your trip: If you're looking for beach fun, the monsoon season from mid-October through late February can make the waters choppy, so avoid the island resorts and take care by the seaside. Also, try not to book during Singapore's holiday seasons, particularly during school holidays from mid-May through June and again in November and December, when resorts become crowded with fun-loving families intent on a good time.

In the north, where the locals are very conservative, it is recommended that visitors dress modestly at public beaches, although a few beach resorts and islands are relaxed about swimwear.

1 TIOMAN ISLAND

Tioman Island (pronounced *Tee*-oh-mahn), a tiny island off the south of Malaysia's east coast, is a popular destination on Malaysia's east coast, visited mostly by nearby Singaporeans; backpackers, who have a multitude of cheap chalets to flop in; and scuba enthusiasts, who have a range of coral gardens to explore. The island is only 39km (24 miles) long and 12km (7½ miles) wide, with sandy beaches that line several small bays, clear water with sea life and coral reefs, and jungle mountain-trekking trails with streams

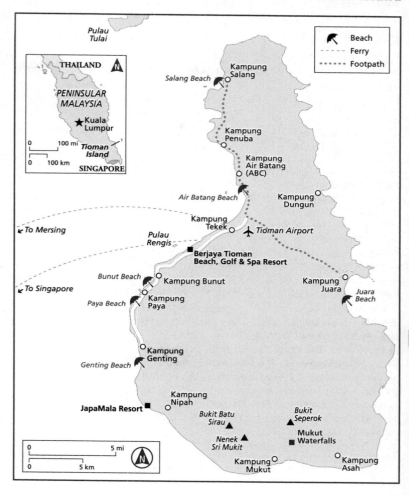

and waterfalls. So idyllic is the setting that Tioman was the location for the 1950s Hollywood film *South Pacific*.

Tioman has been snubbed by scuba enthusiasts because it was developed before its northern island neighbors, Redang and Perhentian. For many, Tioman's accessibility didn't jive with their expectation of "unspoiled" ecology. To be honest, I have many friends who have taken dive trips all over Southeast Asia and claim that diving in Tioman is as good, if not better, than in Redang and Perhentian.

Tioman has retained much of its tropical island charm, perhaps by virtue of the fact that only one modern resort has been built on it. Activity is spread throughout the kampungs, which spring up in the various bays. In **Tekek,** you'll find the airport, main ferry jetty, and some convenience shops. Other kampungs include **Air Batang ("ABC")**, and **Salang** on the west coast and **Juara** on the east coast. Each kampung has some accommodations, most of them very basic wooden chalets, with some access to simple restaurants.

ESSENTIALS

Getting There

BY PLANE   Flights to Tioman originate from KL and Singapore, operated by a private airline, **Berjaya Air,** and coordinated by the folks at the Berjaya Tioman Beach Resort. However, you need not stay at the resort to book passage on these flights. Call their KL office for reservations at *☎* **03/7846-8228.** The airport in Tioman is in Kampung Tekek, just across from the main jetty. If you're staying at Berjaya Tioman, a shuttle will fetch you; however, if you plan to stay elsewhere, you're on your own. See "Getting Around," below.

BY BOAT   Ferries and speedboats depart from the jetty just next to R&R Plaza in Mersing each day. Book passage from the many agents huddled around the jetty—they're basically all the same, each reserving trips on the same boats. Be warned about the aggressive touts at the jetty here. They are persistent and annoying, trying to lure you to less popular places with substandard facilities. Boats leave Mersing Jetty at intervals that depend on the tide. The trip takes around 1¹/₂ hours and can cost between RM35 and RM90 ($10–$26/£6.30–£16), depending on the power of the boat you hire. Avoid the cheaper ferries that take 4 hours to make the trip (snooze). Boats drop you at either the Berjaya Resort or the main jetty in Kampung Tekek. The last boat leaves for Tioman between 5 and 6pm every evening. If you miss this boat, you're stuck in Mersing for the night.

BY BUS   **Transnasional** operates five daily buses from KL's Puduraya Bus Terminal on Jalan Pudu (*☎* **03/2070-3300**). The 6-hour trip costs RM23 ($6.65/£4.15). Buses depart from Johor Bahru and Singapore for Mersing for the ferry departures to Tioman Island. **Johara Ekspres** (*☎* **07/224-8280**) and **Transasional Ekspres** (*☎* **07/222-0045**) operate buses to Mersing from Larkin Bus Station in Johor Bahru. The trip takes between 2¹/₂ and 3 hours, with departures at 8:30am, 12pm, and 1:30pm. Fares for air-conditioned buses range in price from RM8 ($2.30/£1.45) to RM13 ($3.75/£2.35). You'll arrive at R&R Plaza, the main bus depot in Mersing. The jetty is located just next door

Getting Around

There are hiking trails between kampungs along the west coast, and another trail overland to the one beach on the east coast. Other than walking, the most popular mode of transport is **water taxi.** Each village has a jetty; you can either pay your fare at tour offices located near the foot of the pier or pay the captain directly. The taxis stop operating past nightfall, so make sure you get home before 6pm. *A few sample fares:* From Tekek to ABC is RM16 ($4.65/£2.90) per person, to Salang RM25 ($7.25/£4.50), to Juara RM65 ($19/£12). Note that these guys don't like to shuttle around only one person, so if there's only one of you, be prepared to pay double.

Fast Facts: Tioman Island

Berjaya Tioman Beach, Golf & Spa Resort has modern conveniences like postal services, in-room telephones with international direct dial access, money changing, a gift shop, and other services. If you're not staying here, venture into Tekek, where you'll find these services opposite the main jetty.

(Tips) **Island Travel**

If you have not already acquired a good mosquito repellent, do so before heading to any of the islands on Malaysia's east coast. You'll need something with DEET (an active ingredient used in repellents that safely and effectively keeps bugs away from your skin). These mosquitoes are hungry. If you plan to stay in one of the smaller chalet places, you might want to invest in a mosquito net. Also, bring a flashlight to help you get around after sunset.

WHERE TO STAY

Unless you stay at the Berjaya Tioman Beach Golf & Spa Resort or JapaMala Resort, expect to be roughing it. For some travelers, a resort with wonderful modern conveniences is what it takes to make a tropical island experience relaxing. For others, though, real relaxation comes from an escape from modern distractions. Small chalets in the kampungs have minimal facilities and few or no conveniences such as hot showers and telephones. Why would you want to stay in them? Because they're simple, close to the beach, and less touristy.

Of the budget choices, the most charming is **Bamboo Hill** (© **09/419-1339**), at the northern tip of ABC. These rustic chalets are perched in the forest along a rocky hill overlooking the bay. While the beach here is too rocky, it's just a short walk to the other side of the bay, where you can swim, or you can hike over the hill to the sandy cove in Kampung Salang. Bamboo Hill's timber chalets are cozy and quiet, with balconies, refrigerators, tea kettles, and mosquito netting. Priced from RM70 to RM120 ($20–$35/£13–£22), cash only. You can also opt for air-conditioning. An Internet station and library complete the amenities. Really the only place to eat here is Nazri's Place, at the south end of the beach, which serves breakfast, lunch, and fish or chicken barbecue dinner daily.

Berjaya Tioman Beach Golf & Spa Resort ★ This is one of two Western-style resorts on the island and provides all the conveniences you'd expect from a budget chain hotel. Accommodations are provided in small blocks and private chalets, some with sea views, but most facing gardens. Inside, wood floors, flowery drapes, upholstery, and bedspreads brighten simple rattan furnishings. Each room has a small balcony, but guests are advised against hanging clothes and towels to dry. Attached bathrooms are small, tiled affairs, with combination tub/showers. The beach here is fine; however, don't expect much surf because the resort is located on the west coast of the island, protected from the open sea. One benefit is an on-site PADI scuba center, but don't come all this way for Berjaya's ho-hum golf course.

Tioman Island, Pahang Darul Makmur 86807. © **09/419-1000.** Fax 09/419-1718. www.berjayaresorts. com.my. 400 units. RM400–RM750 ($116–$218/£72–£135) chalet; RM1,500 ($435/£270) suite. Nov–Feb rates discounted 50%. AE, DC, MC, V. **Amenities:** 4 restaurants; beach bar and karaoke lounge; 2 outdoor pools; 18-hole golf course; outdoor lighted tennis courts; tiny health club; spa services; sauna; watersports equipment/rentals; airport transfers; room service; babysitting; PADI scuba center. *In room:* A/C, TV w/satellite programming, minibar, hair dryer.

JapaMala ★★ (Finds) Tioman accommodation options were limited to the large Berjaya Resort and simple chalets until the stylish boutique hotel JapaMala opened in 2004. Located on the southwest side of the island, the hotel has its own remote beach and jungle, and is in an area that's protected from monsoon winds. A member of the prestigious Relais & Châteaux group, JapaMala has rooms that are fashionably rustic and range from seaview to treetop chalets amid ancient rainforests. The hotel has five-star luxe facilities, pearly white sands, and clear waters most of the year. Guests arriving by air need to transfer to the resort via private speedboat at a fee, and those arriving from Mersing on the mainland can catch a fast speedboat that takes approximately $1^1/_2$ hours, depending upon the prevailing weather.

Kampung Lanting, 86800 Pulau Tioman, Pahang. (℗ **09/419-7777.** Fax 09/419-7979. www.japamalaresorts. com. RM600–RM1,700 ($174–$493/£108–£306). AE, DC, MC, V. **Amenities:** 2 restaurants; 2 bars; theater lounge; pool; spa; snorkeling and scuba diving. *In room:* A/C, cable TV, minibar, hair dryer.

TIOMAN OUTDOORS

Tioman's beaches can be hit-or-miss. Around Tekek, much of ABC, and spots north of the Berjaya resort, rocks spoil the beach and shallow waters. Salang's beach, a crescent of sand hugging a horseshoe-shaped cove, presents the best beach on the west side of the island. The most ideal beach, however, is on Juara, on the east side of the island. This broad sandy stretch is practically deserted half the time due to its remote location—to get there, either hop a water taxi, take the daily ferry, or hike overland. The trek from Tekek to Juara cuts across the center of the island and will take up to 2 hours to complete. Bring water and lots of mosquito repellent, and don't try it unless you are reasonably fit.

Scuba professionals **Dive Asia** (Salang and Tekek (℗ **09/419-5017;** ABC (℗ **09/419-1654;** www.diveasia.com.my) have been on Tioman over 30 years. Each day they take divers out for two dives, one at 9:30am and one at 2:30pm (at different places each day) for only RM170 ($49/£31), equipment included. A bargain. Snorkel trips can also be arranged at each beach destination for about RM45 ($13/£8.10), which includes boat transfer to the best snorkeling sites plus equipment rental.

---

2 KUANTAN & CHERATING

Pahang, covering about 35,960 sq. km (14,024 sq. miles) of mostly inland forests, is the largest state on peninsular Malaysia. Travelers come to Pahang's east-coast resorts for the long sandy beaches, which stretch all the way up the east coast along the South China Sea. Jungle forests promise adventures in trekking, climbing, and river rafting. In fact, much of **Taman Negara,** Malaysia's main peninsular national forest preserve, is in this state, although most people access the forest by traveling from Kuala Lumpur (see "Side Trips from Kuala Lumpur," in chapter 13). Kuantan, although it's the capital, doesn't have the feel of a big city; however, with the recent construction of a few big shopping malls, there's more choice for entertainment, shopping, and fast food. If you're staying at the beach at Telok Chempedak, 5km (3 miles) north of Kuantan, the atmosphere is even more relaxed.

Cherating Village has a backpacker feel to it, but unlike those in many parts of the region, there isn't the bar and party scene. This is more laid back, with few bars, and it looks a little run down these days.

ESSENTIALS
Visitor Information

A **Tourist Information Centre** (℗ 09/516-1007) is located on Jalan Penjara in the center of town. The staff is exceptionally helpful and good at answering specific inquiries. The official website for the Pahang Tourism Board is www.pahangtourism.com.my.

The most convenient way to get to Kuantan is by a quick flight from KL. **Malaysia Airlines** (℃ **1300/883-000;** www.malaysiaairlines.com) flies daily from KL, as does **AirAsia** (℃ **03/8775-4000;** www.airasia.com). Flights arrive at the **Sultan Ahmad Shah Airport** (℃ **09/667-3666**). Just outside the airport is a taxi stand where you can get a cab to Kuantan for RM35 ($10/£6.30) or to Cherating for RM60 ($17/£11).

Bus routes service Kuantan from all parts of the peninsula, and thanks to the opening in 2004 of a beautiful new highway linking Kuantan to KL, the trip is only 4 hours. **Transnasional** operates hourly buses for RM20 ($5.80/£3.60) from Puduraya Bus Terminal on Jalan Pudu (℃ **03/2070-3300**). The bus terminal in Kuantan is in Kompleks Makmur. Taxis at the stand just outside the terminal can take you to town for RM15 ($4.35/£2.70).

Outstation taxis from KL (℃ **03/2078-0213**) will cost RM200 ($58/£36) for the 3-hour trip. The outstation taxi stand in Kuantan is at the bus terminal.

Getting Around

The areas in the town's center are nice for walking. Otherwise, stick with taxis, which can be waved down on any street. There's also a stand behind the Tourist Information Centre where you'll be sure to find a cab in a pinch. Taxis here are not metered, so you must negotiate the fare before you set out. This is a good deal when you want to hire someone for a few hours to take you around the city. Rates start at about RM20 ($5.80/£3.60) per hour. Use taxis to travel to areas of interest outside the city that are covered in "Attractions Outside Kuantan," below.

Fast Facts: Kuantan & Cherating

The **area code** for Kuantan and Cherating is 09. Most major **banks and ATMs** are located appropriately along Jalan Bank, near the State Mosque. **Internet service** is available from a couple of cafes at the Kompleks Makmur; check the shopping mall adjacent to the bus terminal.

WHERE TO STAY

Kuantan is not a very large place, and most of those who vacation here prefer to stay just a little farther north, in **Cherating,** which is more established as a resort destination. If staying close to Kuantan is important to you, the Hyatt Regency, about 5km (3 miles) outside of town on the beach at Telok Chempedak, is the best choice for accommodations.

In Kuantan

Hyatt Regency Kuantan ★ The Hyatt Regency is part business hotel and part resort. Its 2 hotel blocks serve business travelers linked to Pahang and Terengganu's oil industry, which is why you'll find executive club services, a business center, and other conveniences for professionals that might seem out of place at a beachside property. On the other hand, Hyatt does front an extensive beachfront, with cool breezes and the relaxing sound of ocean waves, plus a full range of exciting watersports activities. The open-air concept of the hotel, especially the tropical reception area, shows all the efficiency of a Hyatt without the studied professionalism of a city hotel. Inside 2 large hotel blocks, guest rooms are comfortable, with modern conveniences adorned with some local decorator touches, but show some signs of wear. Each has a balcony, but not all have sea views, so be sure to inquire when booking.

Telok Chempedak, 25050 Kuantan, Pahang. © **800/233-1234** in the U.S., or 09/566-1234. Fax 09/567-7577. http://kuantan.regency.hyatt.com. 336 units. RM356–RM615 ($103–$178/£64–£111) double; RM950 ($276/£171) suite. AE, DC, MC, V. **Amenities:** 3 restaurants; 3 bars, including a pub w/live entertainment; 2 outdoor pools; 3 outdoor lighted tennis courts; 2 squash courts; health club; spa w/sauna, steam, and massage; children's center; concierge; airport transfers; room service; babysitting; smoke-free rooms on the top floors; executive-level rooms. *In room:* A/C, TV w/satellite programming and in-house movies, minibar, hair dryer.

In Cherating

Most people skip Kuantan and head straight for Cherating, some 47km (29 miles) to the north. The anchor resort, Club Med, opened in 1980. Since then a couple dozen smaller resorts have opened up, none of them coming close to Club Med's standard. Resorts here are all mostly self-contained units; to stay here means you'll most likely be dining in-house, participating in beach and watersports activities, and possibly only leaving the resort for tours planned through your resort's activities desk.

Windsurfers, take note: Cherating is world famous for excellent conditions and the home of the "Monsoon Madness" international competition, which takes place every January, when monsoon conditions make great waves. In addition to windsurfing, resorts can arrange trips through the mangroves up the Cherating River in a hired bumboat and trips to crafts shops and cultural shows.

Club Med ★★ (Kids) Typical to Club Med style, this "family village" is all about escapism—fun and relaxation. Activities include sailing, kayaking, beach volleyball, tennis, wall climbing, and rollerblading. Try bungee-bounce or take flying-trapeze lessons. For relaxation, there are yoga classes and the Mandara spa. Club Med also organizes short trips to villages outside the resort for sightseeing and can arrange golf outside the resort as well. For families, the full menu of children's activities can keep kids occupied every minute of their stay. The property itself fronts a good stretch of beachfront on 80 private hectares (198 acres). Malay-style wooden houses have contemporary furnishings, with clean wooden floors, vibrant fabrics, small balconies, and small bathrooms with standing showers. If you're new to Club Med, their pricing is a bit confusing, depending on the size of your party and the time and duration of your stay. The club works out an overall fee, which is inclusive of all meals, beverages, and most activities, in many cases including international airfare as well. For an idea, a 3-day, 2-night trip, not including transportation to and fro, will set you back RM880 ($255/£158) per night.

Correspondence through KL office only through Vacances, Suite 1.1, 1st Floor Bangunan MAS, Jalan Sultan Ismail, 50250 Kuala Lumpur. © **03/261-4599.** Fax 03/261-7229. www.clubmed.com. 323 units. Refer to text above for pricing information. AE, DC, MC, V. **Amenities:** 2 restaurants; bar; outdoor pool; outdoor lighted tennis courts; squash courts; health club; full-service spa; watersports equipment rentals; children's center; airport transfers; babysitting. *In room:* A/C, TV, hair dryer.

Swiss Garden Resort & Spa ★ Many choices of accommodations in Cherating offer basic seaside facilities for budget travelers, but you should be warned: Most are plagued by tatty rooms desperate for upgrading, substandard facilities, and disinterested service. Swiss Garden is a better choice, as it's one of the newer properties in this category and is managed by the same people behind Swiss Garden's successful leisure-class hotels in KL. This four-story horseshoe-shaped block surrounds a swimming pool fronting a very pretty beach—if you pay extra for a sea-facing room, make sure you get the top floor for the best view. Swiss Garden's rooms have good space for luggage, sport clean tile floors that make the room feel fresh, small balconies, wooden furniture, soft beds, and small TVs. Recent renovations have made rooms more stylish. The two best features of the

resort are its Balok Beach location, home to Cherating's windsurfing activities, and its **265**
Balinese spa, located in a garden courtyard with a long menu of reasonably priced relaxation and beauty treatments.

2656–2657 Mukim Sungai Karang, Balok Beach, 26100 Beserah, Kuantan, Pahang. ⓒ **09/544-7333.** Fax 09/544-955. www.swissgardenkuantan.com. 304 units. RM276 ($80/£50) double; from RM748 ($217/£135) suite. AE, DC, MC, V. **Amenities:** 2 restaurants; lounge; outdoor pool; spa; watersports equipment rental; room service; babysitting. *In room:* A/C, TV w/satellite programming and in-house movies.

WHERE TO DINE

Most folks staying in the area dine at their resorts, but if you find yourself in town during mealtime, the absolute best place to go is the **outdoor food stalls** by the beach next to the Hyatt Regency. It's a short taxi ride from the center of town, but well worth it. All varieties of very fresh seafood, including whole fish, are cooked to order and are as cheap as RM6 to RM16 ($1.75–$4.65/£1.10–£2.90) per dish. The flavors and atmosphere are about as local as you can get.

ATTRACTIONS

Kuantan can really be seen in a day. Although there are a few fun crafts shops, the place is not exactly a hotbed of culture. The main attraction in town is the huge **State Mosque,** which is quite beautiful inside and out, with a distinct dome, minarets, and stained glass. Late afternoon is the best time to see it, when the light shines through the glass. You can also have a nice walk down **Jalan Besar,** sampling local delicacies sold on the street and shopping in the smaller craft and souvenir shops.

Attractions Outside Kuantan

Pahang is home to peninsular Malaysia's oldest rainforests, but to be honest, the best way to experience them is through **Taman Negara,** Malaysia's biggest forest preserve on the peninsula. Overnight trips in decent accommodations with experienced nature guides can be organized very easily from KL (see chapter 13). A few attractions outside Kuantan can make interesting half-day or day trips if you tire of the beach. For these trips, I suggest you book through your hotel or resort—I couldn't find a single independent tour operator with suitable guides, so your resort probably has one or two they work with exclusively.

Gua Charah caves are about 25km (16 miles) outside of Kuantan. Also called Pancing caves (they're located in a town called Pancing), one of the caves in the network is a temple, home to a huge reclining Buddha. It is said that the monk caretaker, who has grown very old, is having difficulty finding another monk who will take over his duties at the caves.

Lake Chini, 12 freshwater lakes 60km (38 miles) southwest of Kuantan, claim local legends a la Loch Ness. They say that there once was an ancient Khmer city at the site of the lakes, but it is now buried deep under the water, protected by monsters. Some have tried to find both city and monsters but have come up with nothing (except litter—it's a problem). Boats take you across the lake to an *Orang Asli* (indigenous peoples) kampung to see their way of life.

Just south of Kuantan is **Pekan,** which for history and culture buffs is far more interesting than Kuantan. Called "the Royal City," it's where the Sultan of Pahang resides in a beautiful Malay-style *istana,* or palace. The **State Museum** on Jalan Sultan Ahmad has displays depicting the history of Pahang and its royal family, as well as sunken treasures from old Chinese junks.

3 KUALA TERENGGANU ★

The capital of the state of Terengganu, Kuala Terengganu has a few more exciting activities to offer a visitor than its southern neighbor, Kuantan, but suffers from the same lack of tourism investment and enthusiasm. Malaysia's east coast is best known as the country's cultural heartland. Compared to other parts of the country, the population here is overwhelmingly Malay, with conservative religious values influencing every aspect of local life. Visitors keen on exploring the culture with respect to these values will be welcomed with open arms. Those who are looking for a party will be disappointed.

Most come to Terengganu to visit the islands off its coast. Redang and Perhentian islands have excellent opportunities for divers and snorkelers to see an abundance of marine creatures. The mainland's pretty seaside also supports a couple of very atmospheric and serene resorts.

Every December, Terengganu's Pulau Duyong hosts the Monsoon Cup, the annual Malaysian leg of the Swedish Match Tour (www.monsooncup.com.my).

Kuala Terengganu is small and easy to navigate, clustered around a port at the mouth of the Terengganu River. Many livelihoods revolve around the sea, so most of the activity, even today, focuses on the areas closest to the jetties. The region is also home to many of Malaysia's crafts cottage industries, which makes shopping really fun. *One note:* In Terengganu and its northern neighbor, Kelantan, the weekend is from Friday into Saturday, with official businesses open from Sunday through Thursday. In some instances, you'll find business closings for half-days on Thursdays.

ESSENTIALS
Visitor Information
The **Tourism Information Centre** (© 09/622-1553) is on Jalan Sultan Zainal Abidin just next to the post office and across from the central market.

Getting There
Malaysia Airlines (© 1300/883-000; www.malaysiaairlines.com) and **AirAsia** (© 03/8775-4000;** www.airasia.com) fly daily from KL to Kuala Terengganu's Sultan Mahmud Airport; for local airport information, call © 09/666-4204. From the airport, a taxi to town is RM22 ($6.40/£3.95).

Transnasional operates nine daily **buses** from KL's Duta terminal on Jalan Duta (© 03/6201-3463); the trip takes 7 hours and costs RM35 ($10/£6.30).

Outstation taxis from Kuantan will cost about RM100 ($29/£18) and can be found at the Makmur Bus terminal in Kuantan.

Getting Around
Although you can stroll around the downtown areas with ease, getting to many of the bigger attractions will require a **taxi.** They're terribly inexpensive, making it well worth your while to rent by the hour or for a half- or whole day so you can go around to places and not worry how you'll get back. Your hotel's concierge can help you book. Rates will be around RM25 ($7.25/£4.50) per hour.

Fast Facts: Kuala Terengganu
Most **banks** are on Jalan Sultan Ismail. The main **post office** is on Jalan Sultan Zainal Abidin (© 09/622-7555), next to the Tourist Information Centre.

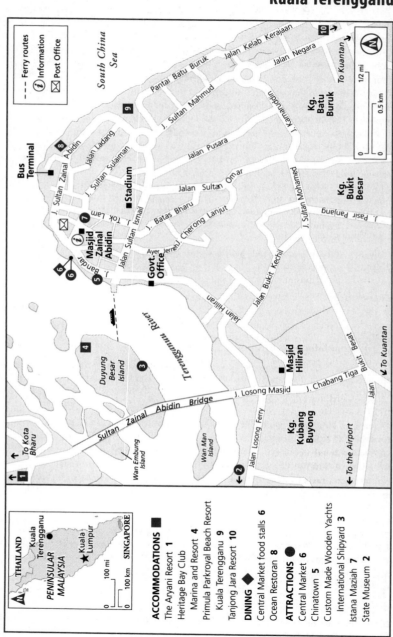

ACCOMMODATIONS

The Aryani Resort **1**
Heritage Bay Club
Marina and Resort **4**
Primula Parkroyal Beach Resort
Kuala Terengganu **9**
Tanjong Jara Resort **10**

DINING ◆

Central Market food stalls **6**
Ocean Restoran **8**

ATTRACTIONS ●

Central Market **6**
Chinatown **5**
Custom Made Wooden Yachts
International Shipyard **3**
Istana Maziah **7**
State Museum **2**

The Aryani Resort ★★ (Finds) Raja Dato' Bahrin Shah Raja Ahmad opened his dream resort here in Terengganu. A celebrated architect, he'd previously designed the State Museum (see below) and wished to translate the beautiful lines of Terengganu aesthetics into a special resort. The resulting Aryani is stunning—organic, stimulating, unique, and, best of all, peaceful. In a rural 3.6-hectare (9-acre) spot by the sea, the rooms are private bungalows situated like a village. Inside, each is masterfully decorated to suit both traditional style and modern comfort. The Heritage Suite wins the prize: a 100-year-old timber palace, restored and rebuilt on the site, it's appointed with fine antiques. The design of the outdoor pool is practically an optical illusion, and the spa (for massage and beauty treatments) is in its own Malay house. The resort's rural location has both a plus and a minus: On the plus side, it's secluded; on the minus side, it's 45 minutes from Kuala Terengganu and there's not much else around. The resort can arrange boat trips for snorkeling, tours to town, and golfing.

Jalan Rhu Tapai–Merang, 21010 Setiu, Terengganu. ℂ **09/653-2111.** Fax 09/653-1007. www.thearyani. com. 20 units. RM600–RM650 ($174–$189/£108–£117) double; RM1,200 ($348/£216) modern suite; RM1,055 ($306/£190) Heritage Suite. AE, DC, MC, V. **Amenities:** 2 restaurants; outdoor infinity pool; spa w/massage; nonmotorized watersports equipment rental; concierge; airport transfers. *In room:* A/C, TV w/satellite programming, minibar.

Heritage Bay Club Marina and Resort ★ Situated on Pulau Duyong in the middle of the Terengganu River, the club (known locally as Kelab Teluk Warisan) and resort is the newest and best hotel address in town. The facility has been developed to cater to the yachting teams and officials who attend the annual Monsoon Cup held late in the year. At other times, guests will basically have the resort to themselves. Chalets reflect traditional Malay elegance with state-of-the-art communications and entertainment facilities. It's located on the southeastern side of the small island, with most rooms overlooking the river and the city center.

Pulau Duyong, 21300 Kuala Terengganu, Terengganu. ℂ **09/627-7888.** Fax 09/622-9903. www.heritage bayclub.com. 58 units. RM450 ($131/£81) double; from RM1,020 ($296/£184) suite. AE, DC, MC, V. **Amenities:** Restaurant; poolside lounge; swimming pool. *In room:* A/C, flatscreen TV w/satellite programming, Wi-Fi, minibar, hair dryer, IDD phones.

Primula Parkroyal Beach Resort Kuala Terengganu A top pick for accommodation in Kuala Terengganu is the Primula. The first resort to open in this area, it commands the best section of beach the city has to offer and still is very close to the downtown area. It has full resort facilities, which include two excellent restaurants. Make sure you get a room facing the sea—the view is excellent. Other facilities include an outdoor pool with grassy lawn, watersports facilities, a lobby shop, and a kids' club. The beach here is reasonable and a great family venue.

Jalan Persinggahan, P.O. Box 43, 20400, Kuala Terengganu, Terengganu Darul Iman, Malaysia. ℂ **09/623-3722.** Fax 09/623-3360. www.primulaparkroyal.com 249 units. RM275 ($80/£50) double; RM570 ($165/£103) suite. AE, DC, MC, V. **Amenities:** 2 restaurants; children's center; concierge; airport transfers; room service; babysitting. *In room:* A/C, TV w/satellite programming and in-house movies, minibar, hair dryer.

Tanjong Jara Resort ★★★ Tanjong Jara exudes the most exotic of Malay traditions to create a resort that truly reflects the east coast. Its architectural character is designed after 17th-century Malay sultans' palaces, with delicate woodcarvings, hardwood floors and timber accents, tiled roofs, and other local building materials. Guest rooms come in three varieties. Serambi rooms, at ground level, are midsize double-occupancy rooms with big bathrooms, two vanities, and a huge inviting tub. These

rooms also have big private sun decks attached. Just above Serambi rooms are Bumbung
rooms, the lowest-priced category; these rooms are exactly like their downstairs neighbors, except they do not have sun decks. The ultimate accommodation here is the beachfront chalets, called Anjung, with long picture windows that open out onto a breezy veranda, big sleeping areas with separate sofa bed, and huge bathrooms that include outdoor sunken tubs within a private garden. A main attraction here is the Spa Village, a peaceful spa in a garden setting featuring traditional Malay health and beauty treatments. The resort's grounds are meticulously maintained, resonating with the sound of wind chimes and *gamelan* music, and the beach is pristine. Watersports, golf, and local tours can be arranged.

Batu 8 off Jalan Dungun, 23000 Dungun, Terengganu. 🕾 09/845-1100. Fax 09/845-1200. www.tanjong jararesort.com. 99 units. RM1,300 ($377/£234) Bumbung double; RM1,500 ($435/£270) Serambi double; RM1,870 ($542/£337) Anjung double. AE, DC, MC, V. **Amenities:** 3 restaurants; 2 outdoor pools; 2 outdoor tennis courts; health club; spa; concierge; airport transfers; room service; babysitting. *In room:* A/C, TV w/ satellite programming, minibar, hair dryer.

WHERE TO DINE

Outside of the resorts, you'll be at a loss to find Malay specialties in a pleasant restaurant setting, because most locals either cook at home or eat at hawker stalls. If you ask for the best dishes, people will point you in all sorts of directions, to roadside places with no signboards or hawkers selling treats from the back of their car even. To sample as many varieties of local Malay cuisine, your best bet is to visit the Central Market food stalls, where you'll find a variety of freshly cooked dishes for cheap. Likewise, Chinese food can be found in food stalls in Chinatown and coffee shops along Jalan Kampong Cina (pronounced *Chee*-na).

If you're in town for mealtime and want a more comfortable dining experience, **Ocean Restoran** is the best pick. Near the waterfront in what looks like a warehouse (Lot 2679 Jalan Sultan Janah Apitin; 🕾 **09/623-9154**), Ocean prepares tender prawns, light butterfish, and juicy crab in local and Chinese recipes that are very good. Don't count on much from the alfresco decor, which is simple plastic tables and chairs.

ATTRACTIONS

Central Market ★ Open daily from very early until about 7pm, the central market is a huge maze of shops selling every craft made in the region. There's basket weaving for everything from place mats to beach mats. *Batik* comes in *sarong* (with some very unique patterns), ready-made clothing, and household linens. *Songket,* beautiful fabric woven with gold and silver threads, is sold by the piece or *sarong.* Brassware pots, candlesticks, and curios are piled high and glistening. Every handicraft item you can think of is here, waiting for you to bargain for and bring home. And when you're done, venture to the back of the market and check out the produce, dried goods, and seafood in the wet market.

Jalan Sultan Zainal Abidin. Free admission. Daily early morning to 7pm.

Chinatown Although Terengganu has only a small Chinese population, its Chinatown is still quite interesting. This street of shophouses close to the water is still alive, only today many of the shops are art galleries and boutiques, showcasing only the finest regional arts. Also along Jalan Bandar you can find travel agents for trips to nearby islands.

Jalan Bandar.

Custom Made Wooden Yachts International Shipyard ★ Abdullah bin Muda's family has been building ships by hand for generations. Now Mr. Abdullah is an old-timer, but he gets around, balancing on the planks that surround the dry-docked hulls of his latest masterpieces. He makes fishing boats in western and Asian styles, as well as luxury yachts—all handmade, all from wood. Although Mr. Abdullah doesn't speak any English, he'll let you explore the boats on your own and even tell you how much money he's getting for them. You'll weep when you hear how inexpensive his fine work is. Ask your hotel's concierge to call before you plan to head out, to make sure they're open and that Mr. Abdullah is in.

3592 Duyong Besar. (**C** **09/623-2072.** Free admission.

Istana Maziah Probably one of the least ornate *istanas* in Malaysia, this lovely yellow and white royal palace, built in 1897, is today mainly only used for state and royal ceremonies. It is not open to the public, but you can catch glimpses through the gate. Tucked away down the narrow winding street is its neighbor, the Masjid (mosque) Abidin.

Jalan Masji.

State Museum ★★ The buildings that house the museum's collection were purpose-built, designed by a member of the Terengganu royal family, a renowned architect who also built the nearby Aryani resort. It reflects the stunning Terengganu architectural style. Atop stilts and with high sloping roofs, the three main buildings are connected. Inside are fine collections that illustrate the history and cultural traditions of the state.

Bukit Losong. (**C** **09/622-1444.** Adults RM5 ($1.45/90p), children RM2 (60¢/35p). Sat–Thurs 9am–5pm.

TERENGGANU'S HANDICRAFTS

Chendering, an industrial town about 40 minutes' drive south of Kuala Terengganu, is where you'll find major handicraft production—factories and showrooms of *batik* and other lovely items. All these places are located along one stretch of highway, but all are too far apart to walk. Plan to hire a taxi by the hour to shuttle you between them; they're about a 5-minute hop between each if you're driving. Also, while you're in the area, stop by the **Masjid Tengku Tengah Zahara,** which is only 5km (3 miles) outside of the town. This ornate mosque is more commonly referred to as the "Floating Mosque," as it is built in a lake and appears to be floating on the top.

Noor Arfa Noor Arfa is Malaysia's largest producer of hand-painted *batik*. This former cottage-industry business now employs 200 workers to create ready-to-wear fashions that are esteemed as designer labels throughout the country. There's also a shop in town at Aked Mara, A3 Jalan Sultan Zainal Abidin (**C** **09/623-5173**).

Lot 1048 K Kawasan Perindustrian Chendering. (**C** **09/617-5700.** Free admission. Sat–Thurs 8am–5pm.

Suteramas Suteramas specializes in *batik* painting on fine quality silks. At this, their factory showroom, you can buy their latest creations or just watch them being made. Not only do they dye the cloth, they make it from their own worm stock.

Zkawasan Perindustrian Chendering. (**C** **09/617-1355.** Free admission. Sat–Wed 9am–5pm.

Terengganu Craft Cultural Centre Operated by the Malaysian Handicraft Development Corporation, the Craft Cultural Centre, also called Budaya Craft, not only sells handicrafts, but also has blocks of warehouses where artisans create the work. See *batik* painting, brass casting, basket weaving, and woodcarving, as well as other local crafts in progress.

Lot 2195 Kawasan Perindustrian Chendering. (C) **09/617-1033.** Sat–Wed 8am–5pm; Thurs 8am–12:45pm.

TERENGGANU MARINE PARK

The first marine park in Malaysia, the Terengganu Marine Park is situated around the nine islands of the Redang archipelago, 45km (28 miles) northeast of Kuala Terengganu and 27km (17 miles) out to sea. Sporting the best coral reefs and dive conditions off peninsular Malaysia, the park attracts divers with its many excellent sites. The largest of the islands is Pulau Redang (Redang Island), where most people stay in resorts on overnight diving excursions. The recent completion of an airport on Redang makes it fabulously accessible. **Berjaya Air** (in KL (C) **03/7846-8228;** www.berjaya-air.com) flies four times a week from KL. Otherwise, you'll have to make your way from Kuala Terengganu, driving an hour north to the jetty town of Merang, followed by a speedboat trip to any one of the islands for scuba, snorkeling, and sunning on powdery beaches.

The best place to stay on Redang is the **Berjaya Redang Beach Resort ★**. It's the best, mainly because they can arrange your entire trip and activities for you—air transfers, accommodations, meals, and activities including scuba. And while Berjaya commands the best cove on the island, with powdery white-sand beaches, it also happens to be the most comfortable place here, with 152 Malay-style chalets all with en-suite bathroom, air-conditioning, phones, TVs with satellite programs and in-house movies, and mini-bars. Of their three restaurants, the beach seafood grill is the favorite. In addition to scuba and snorkeling trips to the coral reefs, they'll plan other watersports activities plus treks around the island. Their pool is a gorgeous lagoon-style affair by the beach. There is a good spa in the resort, too. Contact Berjaya Redang Beach Resort at (C) **09/630-8808,** fax 09/630-8855, or visit online at www.berjayaresorts.com. Rates are RM463 to RM930 ($134–$270/£83–£167) for a double.

PERHENTIAN ISLANDS

The Perhentian Islands (two islands; one big, one small) are part of the same archipelago within the Terengganu Marine Park. Located to the north of Redang, they are not as easy to access as Redang, because there's no easy airport access. It's about an hour's ride to the jetty from Kuala Terengganu, then a speedboat to the island.

There are many bungalow operators on these islands—most of these places are simple huts with poor excuses for beds and scarcely anything else for convenience. For some reason, these small bungalow operators have not learned how to handle waste and rubbish, and will eventually spoil the environment that draws people here in the first place.

Perhentian Island Resort is your best option on Perhantian. They have a private beach and are managed properly. Their 106 rooms, housed in cabanas, offer comfortable beds and air-conditioning. Their one restaurant serves buffet meals three times daily. Activities are organized through their PADI dive center, plus there's snorkeling, tennis, trekking, and nonmotorized sea sports. They will arrange your speedboat transfers to and from the jetty.

Note: The resort is closed during the rainy season from December through January. Contact Perhentian Island Resort at (C) **09/697-4095,** fax 09/697-8679, or visit online at www.perhentianislandresort.net. Rates are RM425 to RM572 ($123–$165/£77–£103) double chalet.

4 KOTA BHARU

In the northeast corner of peninsular Malaysia, bordering Thailand, is the state of **Kelantan.** Few tourists head this far north up the east coast, but it's a fascinating journey for those interested in seeing Malaysia as it might have been without so many foreign influences. The state is populated mostly by Malays and other Bumiputeras, with only tiny numbers of Chinese and Indian residents and almost no traces of British colonialism. Not surprisingly, Kelantan is the heart of traditional Islam in modern Malaysia. Although the government in KL constructs social policies based upon a more open and tolerant Islam, religious and government leaders in Kelantan follow a more fundamentalist line. That said, visitors who respect local conservatism are most welcome.

It is important to note that Kelantan borders Thailand's southern provinces, where, since 2004, civil unrest, including bombings in public places, has led to hundreds of deaths of Thai citizens and several international tourists. I advise travelers to use caution in this area and refrain from speaking openly about politics and religion.

Kota Bharu, the state capital, is the heart of the region. The area is rich in Malay cultural heritage, as evidenced in the continuing interest in arts like *silat* (Malay martial arts), *wayang kulit* (puppetry), *gasing* (top spinning), and *wau* (kite flying). For the record, you won't find too much traditional music or dance, as women are forbidden from entertaining in public. Also beware that the state has strict laws controlling the sale of alcoholic beverages, which cannot be purchased in many stores, hotels, or most restaurants. Chinese restaurants, however, are permitted to sell beer to their patrons but will probably not allow you to take any away.

If you take a side trip from Terengganu, plan to stay overnight. An outstation taxi from Kuala Terengganu can bring you on the 3-hour drive for around RM110 ($32/£20). Stay at the **Renaissance,** managed by Marriott; it's practically the only hint of the 21st century in all of Kelantan. Rooms are exactly what you would expect from an international business-class hotel chain, and cost RM477 ($138/£86) for double occupancy. Contact the Renaissance at Kota Sri Mutiara, Jalan Sultan Yahya Petra (© **09/746-2233;** fax 09/746-1122; www.marriott.com). You'll find the **Kelantan Tourist Information Centre** at Jalan Sultan Ibrahim (© **09/748-5534**).

Centered around the Padang Merdeka are five of the most significant sights in Kota Bharu, run by the Kelantan State Museum Corporation. They are all open Saturday to Thursday 8:30am to 4:45pm, and closed on Friday; entry charges for each are RM2 (60¢/35p) for adults and RM1 (30¢/20p) for children. At the **Istana Jahar,** Kelantan traditional costumes, antiques, and musical instruments are displayed in context of their usage in royal ceremonies. **Istana Batu** takes you through a photographic journey of Kelantan's royal family and offers a peek at their lifestyle through the past 200 years. The **Balai Getam Guri handicraft museum** showcases the finest in Kelantanese textiles, basketry, embroidery, *batik* printing, and silversmithing. You'll also be able to buy crafts in the shops within the compound. The **Islamic Museum (Muzium Islam)** teaches everything you might want to know about Islam in this state, with a focus on Islamic arts and Kelantan's role in spreading Islam in the region. Finally, there is the **War Museum (Bank Kerapu),** which tells the story of Kelantan during World War II in a 1912 bank building that survived the invasion.

The State Museum (Muzium Negeri) is located on Jalan Hospital (© **09/744-4666;** adults RM2/60¢/35p, children RM1/30¢/20p; Sat–Thurs 8:30am–4:45pm). It's been a long time since this old building served as the colonial land office, but it now houses the Kelantan Art Gallery, including ceramics, traditional musical instruments, and cultural pastimes exhibits.

For great local handicrafts shopping, visitors to Kelantan need go no farther than **Jalan PCB,** the road that leads to P.C.B. beach from Kota Bharu's Chinatown area. Hire a taxi through your hotel's concierge—it's best to hire by the hour; it should cost only about RM15 ($4.35/£2.70) per hour. Your driver will stop at every roadside factory, showroom, shop, and crafts house (the place crawls with them!), and you'll satisfy every shopping itch that needs scratching. These are all small cottage industries run out of folks' homes, so while some places actually have shops, many are very informal "look sees." You can watch women weaving *songket* cloth (fine cotton cloth with interwoven patterns in bright colors and gold or silver threads) on enormous wooden looms, see how kites are made by hand, and learn techniques for painting and dyeing *batik* cloth, along with many other crafts activities that go on in this area. Your driver can also take you to other shopping places in town for local crafts. The prices are very good—far cheaper than in KL.

East Malaysia: Borneo

Borneo for the past 2 centuries has been the epitome of adventure travel. While bustling ports like Penang, Melaka, and Singapore attracted early travelers with dollars in their eyes, Borneo attracted those with adventure in their hearts. Today the island still draws visitors who seek new and unusual experiences, and few leave disappointed. Rivers meander through dense tropical rainforests, beaches stretch for miles, and caves snake out longer than any in the world. All sorts of creatures you'd never imagine live in the rainforest: deer the size of house cats, owls only 15cm (6 in.) tall, the odd proboscis monkey, and the endangered orangutan, whose only other natural home is Sumatra. It's also home to the largest flower in the world, the Rafflesia, spanning up to a meter (3.3 ft.) wide. Small wonder this place has special interest for scientists and researchers the world around.

The people of Borneo can be credited for most of the alluring tales of early travels. The exotically adorned tribes of warring headhunters and pirates of yesteryear, some of whom still live lifestyles little changed (though both headhunting and piracy are now illegal), today share their mysterious cultures and colorful traditions openly with outsiders.

Add to all of this the fabulous tale of the White Raja of Sarawak, Sir James Brooke, whose family ruled the state for just over 100 years, and you have a land filled with allure, mystery, and romance unlike any other.

Malaysia, Brunei Darussalam, and Indonesia have divided the island of Borneo. Indonesia claims Kalimantan to the south and east, and the Malaysian states of **Sarawak** and **Sabah** lie to the north and northwest. The small sultanate of Brunei is situated between the two Malaysian states on the western coast.

1 SARAWAK ★★★

Tropical rainforest once accounted for more than 70% of Sarawak's total landmass, providing homes for not only exotic species of plants and animals, but for the myriad ethnic groups who are indigenous to the area. With more than 15 national parks and wildlife preserves, Malaysia shows its commitment to conserving the delicate balance of life here, despite extensive logging that has cleared many other natural areas. The national parks located around the state's capital Kuching provide quick access to forest life, while longer, more detailed trips to northern Sarawak lead you deeper into the jungle, to explore remote forests and extensive ancient cave networks. A number of rivers connect the inland areas to the main towns, and a boat trip from Kuching to visit tribal communities and trek into the surrounding forests is the most memorable attraction going.

The indigenous peoples of Sarawak make up more than half the state's population. Early European explorers and settlers referred to all native inhabitants of Borneo with the catchall term Dyaks, which didn't account for the variations between the more than 25 different ethnicities. Of these groups, the Iban are the largest, with more than 30% of the population overall. A nomadic people by nature, the Ibans were once located all over the region, existing on agriculture, hunting, and fishing. They were also notoriously

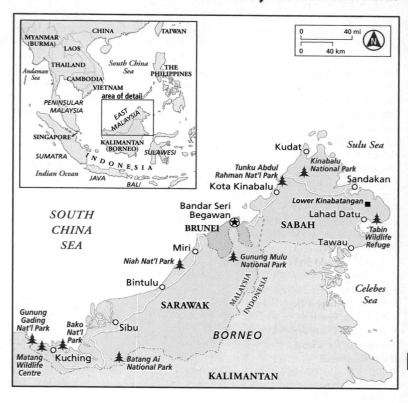

fierce warriors who would behead enemies—a practice now outlawed but that has retained its cultural significance. The Ibans fought not only with other tribes, but within their own separate tribal units as well.

The next-largest group, the Bidayuh, live peacefully in the hills. Their longhouse communities are the most accessible to travelers from Kuching. The Melanu are a coastal people who excel in fishing and boatbuilding. Finally, the Orang Ulu is an association of smaller tribes mostly in the northern parts of the state. Tribes like the Kayah, Kenyah, Kelabit, and Penan, although culturally separate entities, formed an umbrella organization to loosely govern all groups and provide representation. These groups are perhaps the least accessible to outsiders.

The indigenous people who still stay in the forest live in longhouse communities, some of which are open for visitors. Most travelers access these places with the help of local tour operators, who have trips that last from an overnight excursion to a week-long adventure. While some tours take you to well-trampled villages for the standard "gawk at the funny costumes" trips, many operators can take you to more remote places to meet people in an environment of cultural learning with a sensitivity that is appreciated by all involved. A few adventuresome souls travel solo into these areas, but I recommend that you stick with an operator. I don't care much for visitors who pop in unexpectedly, and I can't imagine why folks in one of these villages wouldn't feel the same way.

Every visitor to Sarawak starts out from **Kuching,** the capital city. With a population of some 400,000 people, it's small but oddly cosmopolitan. In addition to local tribes that gave up forest living, the city has large populations of Malays, Chinese, Indians, and Europeans, most of whom migrated in the last 2 centuries. The city sits on the Kuching River, which will be one of the arteries for trips inland. Before you head off for the river, though, check out the many delights of this mysterious colonial kingdom. The riverfront area is Malaysia's best open public space.

Sarawak was introduced to the Western world by James Brooke, an English adventurer who in 1839 came to Southeast Asia to follow in the footsteps of his idol, Sir Stamford Raffles, who settled Singapore. His wanderings brought him to Borneo, where he was introduced to the Sultan of Brunei. The sultan was deeply troubled by warring tribes to the south of his kingdom, who were in constant revolt, sometimes to the point of pirating ships to Brunei's port. Brooke provided the solution, initiating a campaign to befriend some of the warring tribes, uniting them to conquer the others. Soon the tribes were calmed. The sultan, delighted by Brooke, ceded Kuching to him for a small annual fee. In 1841, James Brooke became *raja* and set about claiming the land that is now Sarawak.

Raja Sir James Brooke became a colonial legend. Known as "the White Raja of Sarawak," he and his family ruled the territory and its people with a firm but compassionate hand. Tribal leaders were appointed to leadership and administrative positions within his government and militia, and as a result, the Brookes were highly respected by the populations they led. However, Brooke was a bit of a renegade, turning his nose up at London's attempts to include Sarawak under the crown. He took no money from the British and closed the doors to British commercial interests in Sarawak. Instead, he dealt in local trade and trade with Singapore. Still, Kuching was understood to be a British holding, though the city never flourished as did other British ports in Southeast Asia.

After his death in 1868, Raja James Brooke was succeeded by his nephew, Charles Brooke. In 1917, Charles's son, Vyner Brooke, became the last ruling Raja, a position he held until World War II, when the territory was conquered by invading Japanese. After the war, Raja Vyner Brooke returned briefly, but soon after, the territory was declared a crown colony. Eventually, Malaya was granted independence by Britain, prompting Prime Minister Tunku Abdul Rahman to form Malaysia in 1963, uniting peninsular Malaya with Singapore, Sarawak, and Sabah. Singapore departed from the union 2 years later, but Sarawak and Sabah happily remained.

KUCHING

The perfect introduction to Sarawak begins in its capital. Kuching's museums, cultural exhibits, and historical attractions will help you form an overview of the history, people, and natural wonders of the state. In Kuching, your introduction to Sarawak will be comfortable and fun; culture by day and good food and fun by night. Kuching, meaning "cat" in Malay, also has a wonderful sense of humor, featuring monuments and exhibits to its feline mascot on almost every corner.

The **Rainforest World Music Festival** (www.rainforestmusic-borneo.com) is held every second weekend of July at the Sarawak Cultural Village (see below), featuring music workshops, ethno-musical lectures, jamming sessions, and evening performances from the genre's most renowned figures. Highly recommended.

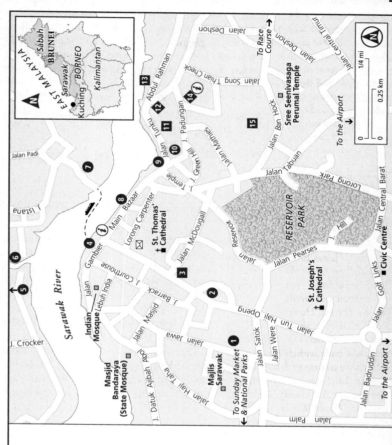

EAST MALAYSIA: BORNEO

15

SARAWAK

ACCOMMODATIONS ■
Hilton Kuching **11**
Holiday Inn Kuching **13**
Merdeka Palace Hotel **3**
Telang Usan Hotel **15**

ATTRACTIONS ●
The Astana **6**
Chinese History Museum **9**
Fort Margherita **7**
Main Bazaar **8**
Sarawak Cultural Village **5**
Sarawak Islamic Museum **1**
Sarawak Museum **2**
Square Tower **4**
Tua Pek Kong Temple **10**

DINING ◆
Dulit Coffee House **12**
Top Spot Food Court **14**

- - - Ferry routes
ⓘ Information
☒ Post Office

VISITOR INFORMATION   The **Sarawak Tourism Board's Visitor Information Centre** has literature and staff that can answer any question about activities in the state and city. This is actually the best place to start planning any trips to Sarawak's wonderful national parks, as the main office for the National Parks & Wildlife Centre operates a Visitor Information Center here as well. Both offices are incredibly informed and welcoming, so feel free to take advantage. You'll find them at the Sarawak Tourism Complex in the Old Courthouse opposite the Kuching Waterfront (Sarawak Tourism Board ℂ 082/410-944, National Parks Centre ℂ 082/248-088; www.sarawaktourism.com).

GETTING THERE   Almost all travelers to Sarawak enter through **Kuching International Airport** (ℂ 082/454-242), just outside the city. **Malaysia Airlines** (ℂ 1300/883-000; www.malaysiaairlines.com) has international flights from Singapore, with domestic service from KL, Johor Bahru, and Kota Kinabalu. **AirAsia** (ℂ 03/8775-4000; www.airasia.com) flies between Kuching and KL.

The relatively new airport is a terrific facility, with ATMs, moneychangers, restaurants, and tourist information. Taxis from the airport use coupons that you purchase outside the arrival hall. Priced according to zones, most trips to the central parts of town will be about RM20 ($5.80/£3.60).

GETTING AROUND   Centered around a *padang,* or large ceremonial field, Kuching resembles many other Malaysian cities. Buildings of beautiful colonial style rise on the edges of the field; many of these today house Sarawak's museums. The main sights, as well as the Chinatown area and the riverfront, are easily accessible on foot. Taxis are also available and do not use meters; most rides around town are quoted between RM10 and RM15 ($2.90–$4.35/£1.80–£2.70). Taxis can be waved down from the side of the road, or if you're in the Chinatown area, the main taxi stand is on Gambier Road near the end of the India Street Pedestrian Mall.

FAST FACTS   Sarawak's area code is **082**. Major **banks** have branches on Tunku Abdul Rahman Road near Holiday Inn Kuching or in the downtown area around Khoo Hun Yeang Road. There are a few **Internet** cafes around town; it's best to ask your hotel's concierge for the nearest one before you start wandering around—or use your hotel's facilities.

Where To Stay

Hilton Kuching   Located in the heart of Kuching along the riverfront, the Hilton offers panoramic views of the Sarawak River and the historic Fort Margherita on the other side. The modern white facade is the dominant structure along the city side of the river. While the hotel is a little dated, it is well maintained and offers the best international service in the city. The premier views are those facing the river and then from the 10th floor upward.

Jalan Tunku Abdul Rahman, Kuching, 93000 Sarawak. ℂ **800/HILTONS** (445-8667) in the U.S. and Canada, 800/445-8667 in Australia, 800/445-866 in New Zealand, 800/448-002 in the U.K., or 82/248-200. Fax 82/428-984. www.kuching.hilton.com. 315 units. RM410 ($119/£74) double; from RM780 ($226/£140) suite. AE, DC, MC, V. **Amenities:** 4 restaurants; bar and lobby lounge; outdoor pool; outdoor floodlit tennis courts; health club w/sauna and steam; room service; smoke-free floors. *In room:* A/C, TV w/satellite programming, high-speed Internet, minibar, hair dryer, IDD phones w/voice mail.

Holiday Inn Kuching   Holiday Inn offers Western-style accommodations at a moderate price, and you'll appreciate its location in an excellent part of town. It sits along the bank of the Kuching River, so to get to the main riverside area, you need only stroll 10 minutes past some of the city's unique historical and cultural sights, shopping, and restaurants. Catering to a diverse group of leisure travelers and businesspeople, the hotel has spacious, modern, and comfortable rooms; and although there are few bells and whistles, you won't want for convenience. The outdoor swimming pool and excellent fitness center facility will help you unwind, and the small shopping arcade has one of the best collections of books on Sarawak that can be found in the city.

P.O. Box 2928, Jalan Tunku Abdul Rahman, 93100 Kuching, Sarawak, Malaysia. ℂ 082/423-111. Fax 082/426-169. www.holidayinn-sarawak.com. 305 units. RM265 ($77/£48) double. AE, DC, MC V. **Amenities:** 3 restaurants; bar; outdoor pool; health club w/sauna; concierge; airport transfers; room service; babysitting; smoke-free rooms; executive-level rooms. In room: A/C, TV w/satellite programming and in-house movies, minibar, hair dryer.

Merdeka Palace Hotel & Suites ★

Towering over the Padang Merdeka in the center of town is the Merdeka Palace, practically a landmark in its own right (as soon as you see the easily distinguishable tower, you'll always know where you are). This is one of the most fashionable addresses in the city, for guests as well as banquets and functions. Its large marble lobby and staircase justify its reputation for elegance. Rooms range from apartment suites to hotel rooms. Large rooms come dressed in European-inspired furnishings and fabrics. Try to get a view of the padang, as the less expensive rooms face the parking lot. The rooftop outdoor swimming pool is small, but the fully equipped fitness center has sauna and steam rooms, plus massage. The English pub here is one of the most happening ones in town.

Jalan Tun Abang Haji Openg, 93000 Kuching, Sarawak, Malaysia. ℂ 082/258-000. Fax 082/425-400. www.merdekapalace.com. 214 units. RM414 ($120/£75) double. AE, DC, MC, V. **Amenities:** 2 restaurants; bar; outdoor pool; health club w/Jacuzzi, sauna, steam, and massage; concierge; airport transfers; room service; babysitting; smoke-free rooms; executive-level rooms. In room: A/C, TV w/satellite programming, minibar.

Telang Usan Hotel ★★ (Value)

While in Kuching, I like to stay at the Telang Usan Hotel. It's not as flashy as the higher-priced places, but it's a fantastic bargain for a good room. Most guests here are leisure travelers, and in fact, many are repeat visitors. The small public areas sport murals in local Iban and Orang Ulu styles, revealing the origin of the hotel's owner and operator. While rooms are small and decor is not completely up-to-date, they're spotless. Some rooms have only standing showers, so be sure to specify when making your reservation if a bathtub is important to you. The coffee shop is a fine place to try local food, but they have Western selections as well. There is an excellent tour agency under the same ownership at the hotel.

Pesiaran Ban Hock, P.O. Box 1579, 93732 Kuching, Sarawak, Malaysia. ℂ 082/415-588. Fax 082/245-316. www.telangusan.com. 66 units. RM140 ($41/£25) double. AE, DC, MC, V. **Amenities:** Restaurant; room service; Internet service. In room: A/C, TV, minibar (some rooms).

Where To Dine

Everyone ends up at the **Top Spot Food Court,** a cheap hawker center venue on Jalan Bukit Mata off Jalan Tunku Abdul Rahman just near the Holiday Inn. Various stalls cook Chinese, Malay, and Western food, all sorts of exotic dishes, and local and seafood dishes. Located on the roof of a multistory parking garage, don't expect anything but "local charm" for decor. But the food is good and cheap, and you'll be sure to find a bowl of the famous Sarawak *laksa.*

A good pick for local specialties is the **Dulit Coffee House** at Telang Usan Hotel (ℂ 082/415-588). Try their local Sarawak version of *laksa,* vermicelli noodles and seafood in a rich and spicy coconut gravy, or the Sarawak black pepper steak, which is a house specialty. Entrees are reasonably priced between RM10 and RM35 ($2.90–$10/ £1.80–£6.30).

Attractions

The Astana and Fort Margherita At the waterfront by the Square Tower, you'll find water taxis to take you across the river to see these two reminders of the White Rajas of Sarawak. The Astana, built in 1870 by Raja Charles Brooke, the second raja of Sara-wak, is now the official residence of the governor. It is not open to the public, but visitors may still walk in the gardens. The best view of the Astana, however is from the water.

Raja Charles Brooke's wife, Ranee Margaret, gave her name to Fort Margherita, which was erected in 1879 to protect the city of Kuching. Inside the great castlelike building is a police museum, the most interesting sights of which are the depictions of criminal punishment.

Across the Sarawak River from town. Fort: **✆ 082/244-232.** Free admission. Daily 9am–5pm.

Chinese History Museum Built in 1911, this old Chinese Chamber of Commerce building is the perfect venue for a museum that traces the history of Chinese communi-ties in Sarawak. Though small, it's centrally located and a convenient stop while you're in the area.

Corner of Main Bazaar and Jalan Tunku Abdul Rahman. Free admission. Daily 9am–5pm.

Main Bazaar Main Bazaar, the major thoroughfare along the river, is home to Kuch-ing's antiques and handicraft shops. If you're walking along the river, a little time in these shops is like a walk through a traditional handicrafts art gallery. You'll also find souvenir shops, tour operators, and a few restaurants.

Along the river. Free admission.

Sarawak Cultural Village ★ What appears to be a contrived theme park turns out to be a really fun place to learn about Sarawak's indigenous people. Built around a lagoon, the park re-creates the various styles of longhouse dwellings of each of the major tribes. Inside each house are representative members of each tribe displaying cultural artifacts and performing music, teaching dart blowing, and showing off carving talents. Give yourself plenty of time to stick around and talk with the people, who are recruited from villages inland and love to tell stories about their homes and traditions. Performers dance and display costumes at 11:30am and 4:30pm daily. A shuttle bus leaves at regular intervals from the Holiday Inn Kuching on Jalan Tunku Abdul Rahman.

Kampung Budaya Sarawak, Pantai Damai, Santubong. **✆ 082/846-411.** Adults RM60 ($17/£11), children RM30 ($8.70/£5.40). Daily 9am–5pm.

Sarawak Islamic Museum A splendid array of Muslim artifacts at this quiet and serene museum depicts the history of Islam and its spread to Southeast Asia. Local cus-toms and history are also highlighted. Although women are not required to cover their heads, respectable attire that covers the legs and arms is requested.

Jalan P. Ramlee. **✆ 082/244-232.** Free admission. Sat–Thurs 9am–4:30pm; Fri 9am–12:45pm and 3–5pm.

Sarawak Museum ★ Two branches, one old and one new, display exhibits of the natural history, indigenous peoples, and culture of Sarawak, plus the state's colonial and modern history. The two branches are connected by an overhead walkway above Jalan Tun Haji Openg. The wildlife exhibit is a bit musty, but the arts and artifacts in the other sections are well tended. A tiny aquarium sits neglected behind the old branch, but the gardens here are lovely.

Jalan Tun Haji Openg. ☏ **082/244-232.** Free admission. Sat–Thurs 9am–4:30pm; Fri 9am–12:45pm and 3–4:30pm.

Square Tower   The tower, built in 1879, served as a prison camp, but today the waterfront real estate is better served by an information center for travel agents. The Square Tower is also a prime starting place for a stroll along the riverside and is where you'll also find out about cultural performances and exhibitions held at the waterfront, or call the number below for performance schedules.

Jalan Gambier near the riverfront. ☏ **082/426-093.** Free admission.

Tua Pek Kong Temple   At a main crossroads near the river stands the oldest Chinese temple in Sarawak. Although officially it is dated at 1876, most locals acknowledge the true date of its beginnings as 1843. It's still lively in form and spirit, with colorful dragons tumbling along the walls and incense filling the air.

Junction of Jalan Tunku Abdul Rahman and Jalan Padungan. Free admission.

Touring Local Culture ★★★

One of the highlights of a trip to Sarawak is a visit to a longhouse community. Trips can last from simple overnight stays to 2-week intensive discovery tours. It goes without saying that shorter trips venture only as far as those longhouse villages closest to Kuching. The benefit is that these communities are at ease with foreigners and so are better able to demonstrate their culture. The drawback is that these villages are the ones most trampled by coachloads of tourists looking to gawk at "primitive tribes." Basically, the more time you have, the deeper you will venture into the interior and the more time you will have to spend with different ethnic groups, allowing greater insight into these fascinating cultures.

A typical longhouse trip starts with a van ride from Kuching followed by a longtail boat ride upriver, through gorgeous forests. If you are stopping in only for the night, you'll be welcomed, fed, and entertained—the food is generally edible and always prepared under sanitary conditions. Fruits are delicious. Your guide, through translations, will help you chat with villagers and ask questions about their lifestyle and customs. At night you will sleep in a longhouse provided especially for guests. It's basic but cool, with mosquito nets (very necessary) provided. The following day includes a very brief jungle trek, plus hunting and fishing demonstrations before your departure back from whence you came. If your trip is longer, you will probably avoid the closer villages and head straight for more remote communities, depending on how much time (and money) you have.

Your average overnight longhouse tour will set you back up to RM600 ($174/£108) per person. Good tour operators making longhouse tours are **Asian Overland Services,** 126 Green Heights Commrcial Centre (☏ **082/451-1309;** www.asianoverland.com. my), and **Telang Usan Travel & Tours,** Ban Hock Road (☏ **082/236-945;** fax 082/236-589). These agencies can also arrange trips into Sarawak's national parks.

TOURING SARAWAK'S NATIONAL PARKS

The Sarawak National Parks & Wildlife Centre has opened access to all of Sarawak's national parks to DIY (do-it-yourself) travelers. From their booking center in Kuching, you can apply for parks permits and book reservations in state-run lodging within each park. They can also advise how to travel to and from each park: Those closer to Kuching will only involve local road and river transportation, while more remote parks will require commercial flights to either Sibu or Miri, plus transfers to ground and river transportation and even chartered flights. If you have the time to plan your travel this way, you will be rewarded with the thrill of "getting there," experiencing local life a little closer to the ground.

Most people do not have the luxury of time, which is why I recommend booking trips that interest you through a tour operator who will arrange all transportation, parks permits, lodging, meals, and guides for you, freeing your time to experience the attractions themselves.

National Parks Not Far from Kuching

Both **Borneo Adventure,** 55 Main Bazaar (© **082/245-175;** www.borneoadventure. com), and **Asian Overland Services,** 126 Green Heights Commercial Centre (© **082/ 451-1309;** www.asianoverland.com.my), charge a few dollars more than many of the other local operators, but you'll get experienced guides and reliable services, and you do not need to join a huge touristy coach group. Most of these trips are for small groups. Their half-day trips from Kuching take the mystery out of local transportation—they can even be combined for longer itineraries so you can maximize your time. They can also prepare customized itineraries and special theme tours based upon your special interests—for example, crafts, flora, or tribal cultures.

Bako National Park ★★★, established in 1957, is Sarawak's oldest national park. An area of 2,728 hectares (6,738 acres), it combines mangrove forest, lowland jungle, and high plains covered in scrub. Throughout the park, you'll see the pitcher plant and other strange carnivorous plants, plus long-tailed macaques, monitor lizards, bearded pigs, and the unique proboscis monkey. Because the park is only 37km (23 miles) from Kuching, half-day trips here are extremely convenient. A day trip for two costs RM300 ($87/£54) per person.

Gunung Gading National Park, about a 2-hour drive west of Kuching, sprawls 4,106 hectares (10,142 acres) over rugged mountains to beautiful beach spots along the coast. Day-trippers and overnighters come to get a glimpse of the Rafflesia, the largest flower in the world. The flowers are short lived and temperamental, but the national parks office will let you know if any are in bloom. A day tour for two people costs RM300 ($87/£54) per person.

Semenggoh Orang Utan Sanctuary is a rehabilitation center for orangutans and other endangered wildlife species who are either orphaned or recovering from illness and are being trained for eventual release into the forest. A half-day tour for two people costs RM140 ($41/£25) per person.

National Parks a Little Farther Out

Borneo Adventure, 55 Main Bazaar (© 082/245-175; www.borneoadventure.com), and **Asian Overland Services**, 126 Green Heights Commercial Centre (© 082/451-1309; www.asianoverland.com.my), also book trips to national parks in other parts of the state. You'll have to fly to Miri or Sibu, as these two towns are the hop-off points for these excursions. Malaysia Airlines and AirAsia both service these two towns from KL and Kuching.

Gunung Mulu National Park provides an amazing adventure, with its astounding underground network of caves. The park claims the world's largest cave passage (Deer longest cave (Clearwater Cave). No fewer than 18 caves offer explorers trips of varying degrees of difficulty, from simple treks with minimal gear to technically difficult caves that require specialized equipment and skills. Aboveground are 544 sq. km (212 sq. miles) of primary rainforest, peat swamps, and mountainous forests teeming with mammals, birds, and unusual insects. Located in the north of Sarawak, Mulu is very close to the Brunei border. Borneo Adventure has a 2-day/1-night package for RM600 ($174/ £108) per person (minimum two people). The trip includes accommodations, ground transportation, longboat rides, nature guides to see Deer Cave, Sarawak Chamber, and Clearwater Cave, plus some rainforest trekking (wear a hat in the caves to protect yourself from bat droppings). They can book your flights from Kuching, but you'll have to pay extra.

2 SABAH ★★★

Sabah presents a wonderland of natural scenery, lush primary rainforest, vibrant coral reefs, and mysterious indigenous cultures. It is, in my opinion, Southeast Asia's hidden treasure. A playground for adventure seekers, extreme sportsters, and bums in search of the ultimate beach, Sabah rewards those who venture here with a holiday in an unspoiled paradise.

Covering 73,711 sq. km (28,747 sq. miles) of the northern part of Borneo, the world's third-largest island, Sabah stretches from the South China Sea in the west to the Sulu Sea in the east, both seas containing an abundance of uninhabited islands, postcard-perfect beaches, and pristine coral reefs bubbling with marine life. In between, more than half of the state is covered in ancient primary rainforest that's protected in national parks and forest reserves. In these forests, some rare species of mammals like the Sumatran rhino and Asian pygmy elephant (herds of them) take effort to witness, but other animals, such as the orangutan, proboscis monkey, gibbon, lemur, civet, Malaysian sun bear, and a host of others can be seen on jungle treks if you search them out. Of the hundreds of bird species here, the hornbills and herons steal the show.

Sabah's tallest peak is one of the highest mountains between the Himalayas and Irian Jaya. At 4,095m (13,432 ft.), it's the tallest in Malaysia, and a challenge to trek or climb. The state's interior has endless opportunities for jungle trekking, river rafting, mountain biking and 4×4 exploration for every level of excitement, from soft adventure to extreme sports.

This state holds not only mysterious wildlife and geography, but people as well. Sabahans count among their many ethnic groups some 32 different peoples whose cultures and traditions are vastly different from the Malay majority that makes up the rest of the country. In fact, ethnic Malays are a minority in Sabah.

About one-third of the population are Kadazandusun, a group that inhabits mainly the west coast and parts of the interior of Sabah. They are one of the first groups travelers come into contact with, especially during the Pesta Kaamatan, or harvest festival, held during May, where the high priest or priestess presides over a ceremony performed to appease the rice spirit. Although it's a Kadazandusun tradition, it has come to be celebrated by all cultures in the state. Although this group produces the majority of Sabah's agricultural products, most members live in towns and hold everyday jobs. The exception is the Runggus, the last group of Kadazandusun to live in traditional longhouse communities, where they produce exquisite basket weaving, fabric weaving, and beadwork in traditional designs.

The Bajau are a group of seafarers who migrated from the Philippines only a couple hundred years ago. The Bajau on the eastern coast of Sabah carry on their traditional connection to the water, living as sea gypsies and coming to shore only for burials. On the west coast, however, many Bajau have settled on dry land as farmers and cattle raisers. Known locally as the "cowboys of the east," Bajau men are very skilled equestrians. During festivals, their brilliant costumes and decorated ponies almost always take center stage.

Kota Belud, 76km (47 miles) north of Kota Kinabalu, is a town inhabited mostly by Bajau people. In the background is Mount Kinabalu, which dominates the landscape in most of Western Sabah. The town comes alive every Sunday morning with the weekly *tamu*, or market.

The third-most-prominent indigenous group, the Murut, shares the southwest corner of Sabah with the Bajau, expanding inland along the border with Sarawak and Kalimantan (Indonesia). Skilled hunters, they use spears, blowpipes, poisoned darts, and trained dogs. In past days, these skills were used for headhunting, which thankfully is not practiced today (although many skulls can still be seen during visits to longhouse settlements). One nonlethal Murut tradition involves a trampoline competition. The *lansaran* (the trampoline itself), situated in the community longhouse, is made of split bamboo. During Murut ceremonies, contestants drink rice wine and jump on the trampoline to see who can reach the farthest. A prize is hung above for the winner to grab.

Sabah also has a small community of Chinese families that settled during colonial days, and newer Filipino immigrants, many of whom are illegal plantation workers.

KOTA KINABALU

The best place to begin exploring Sabah's marine wonders, wildlife and forests, adventure opportunities, and indigenous peoples is from its capital, Kota Kinabalu. Located on the west coast, it's where you'll find the headquarters for all of Sabah's adventure-tour operators and package-excursion planners.

Essentials

VISITOR INFORMATION   The **Sabah Tourism Board** (51 Jalan Gaya; ✆ 088/212-121; www.sabahtourism.com) provides the most comprehensive information about the state. It's open daily 9am to 4pm. Although the Tourism Malaysia has a small office on Jalan Gaya a block down from the Sabah Tourism office, almost all of their information promotes travel in other parts of the country. Still, if you're interested, stop by Ground Floor Uni. Asia Building, no. 1 Jalan Sagunting (✆ **088/248-698**).

GETTING THERE   Because of Sabah's remote location, just about everybody will arrive by air through the **Kota Kinabalu International Airport** in the capital city (✆ **088/238-555**), about a 20-minute drive south of the central part of the city. A surprising number of direct international flights connect Sabah to the region. Malaysia Airlines flies from Hong Kong, Manila, Osaka, Seoul, Singapore, and Tokyo, among others (✆ **1300/883-000;** www.malaysiaairlines.com), and AirAsia flies from Bangkok (✆ **03/8775-4000;** www.airasia.com).

Both airlines also have direct domestic flights to Kota Kinabalu from KL, Johor Bahru, Kuching, Sibu, and Miri, with in-state service to Sandakan and other towns.

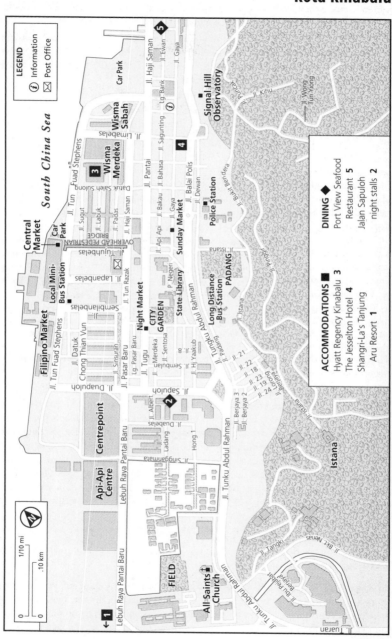

LEGEND
ⓘ Information
⊠ Post Office

South China Sea

Central Market

Filipino Market

Car Park

OVERHEAD PEDESTRIAN BRIDGE

Local Mini-Bus Station

Jl. Tun Fuad Stephens

Jl. Tun Fuad Stephens

Jl. Datuk Saleh Sulong

Jl. Tugu

Jl. Sugut

Jl. Labuk

Jl. Padas

Jl. Haji Saman

Jl. Sinsuran

Jl. Pasar Baru

Lg. Pasar Baru

Jl. Merdeka

Jl. Sembulan

Jl. Hj Yaakub

Jl. Lapanbelas

Jl. Sembilanbelas

Jl. Tujuhbelas

Jl. Limabelas

Jl. Tun Razak

Jl. Duabelas

Jl. Api Api

Jl. Bakau

Jl. Pantai

Jl. Bahasa

Jl. Sagunting

Jl. Gaya

Jl. Haji Saman

Jl. Evian

Jl. Gaya

Lg. Bank

Car Park

Jl. Bank

Wisma Sabah

Wisma Merdeka

Jl. Datuk Chong Thian Vun

Jl. Duapuloh

Centrepoint

Api-Api Centre

Lebuh Raya Pantai Baru

Jl. Albert

Jl. Duabelas

Jl. Saputoh

Ladang

Hong 1

Jl. Singgamata

Lebuh Raya Pantai Baru

Jl. Tunku Abdul Rahman

Jl. Berjaya 3
Jl. Berjaya 2

Jl. 21
Jl. 22
Jl. 18
Jl. 23
Jl. 19
Jl. 24

Jl. Hilong

Jl. P. Negeri

Jl. Padang

City Garden

Night Market

State Library

Sunday Market

Long Distance Bus Station

PADANG

Jl. Tunku Abdul Rahman

Jl. Istana

Jl. Istana

Jl. Dewan

Jl. Balai Polis

Police Station

Signal Hill Observatory

Jl. Bukit Bendera

Jl. Penjara

Jl. Pinggul

Jl. Kihu

Pekung

Jl. Kihu

Jl. Wong Tun Yiong

Istana

Jl. Bkt. Nenas

Jl. Tangki

Jl. Ibu Pejabat

Jl. Luaran

All-Saints Church

FIELD

N

0   1/10 mi
0   .10 km

15

ACCOMMODATIONS ■
Hyatt Regency Kinabalu **3**
The Jesselton Hotel **4**
Shangri-La's Tanjung
Aru Resort **1**

DINING ◆
Port View Seafood
Restaurant **5**
Jalan Sapuloh
night stalls **2**

The most efficient way to get into town from the airport is by taxi using a coupon system. You'll pay about RM15 ($4.35/£2.70) for a trip to town. Ignore the drivers that try to lure you away from the coupon counter; they will always overcharge you.

GETTING AROUND   In the downtown area, you can get around quite easily on foot between hotels, restaurants, tour operators, markets, and the tourism office. For longer trips, a taxi will be necessary; in town, trips cost about RM12 ($3.50/£2.15). Taxis are flagged down on the street or by your hotel's bellhop.

FAST FACTS   The **area code** for Sabah is **088.** While on the same time as KL, the sun rises and sets earlier than the peninsula. You'll find **banks** with ATMs conveniently located in the downtown area around Jalan Limabelas, Jalan Gaya, and Jalan Pantai. While there are no large **Internet** cafes, you'll find access in small shopfronts around the main parts of town.

Where to Stay

Hyatt Regency Kinabalu ★   One of the best international business-class hotels in town, in some ways the Hyatt seems a little out of place in cozy Kota Kinabalu. Still, it's located close to the waterfront, near major shopping and travel operators, and has a good selection of restaurants. Even if you're staying elsewhere in town, you may appreciate one of their dining options. As modern as you would expect the Hyatt chain to be, rooms here are large and have up-to-date furnishing styles that are not so Western that they take all the charm away from the room. Local tour and car-rental booking in the lobby makes the place convenient for leisure travelers. One of the high points is Shenanigan's, a lively bar, with live entertainment. It gets packed, mostly with locals and expatriates.

Jalan Datuk Salleh Sulong, 88994 Kota Kinabalu, Sabah. © **800/233-1234** in the U.S. and Canada, 800/131-234 in Australia, 800/441-234 in New Zealand, or 088/221-234. Fax 088/218-909. www.kinabalu.regency.hyatt.com. 288 units. RM368 ($107/£66) double; from RM713 ($207/£128) suite. AE, DC, MC, V. **Amenities:** 3 restaurants; bar; outdoor pool; health club; concierge; airport transfers; room service; babysitting; smoke-free rooms; executive-level rooms. *In room:* A/C, TV w/satellite programming and in-house movies, minibar, hair dryer.

The Jesselton Hotel ★★   Listen to me rave about the Jesselton. It's such a nice surprise to find this quaint boutique hotel in the center of Kota Kinabalu, just about the last real reminder in this city of a colonial presence. Even more appealing is the level of personalized service you receive and the comfort of the rooms, which, though completely modern, retain their charm with lovely Audubon-style inks and attractive wallpapers and fabrics—sort of a cross between a cozy guesthouse and a top-class hotel. Due to lack of space in the building, there's no pool, fitness center, or business center, but the staff at the front desk can help you with tour information and transportation. The coffeehouse serves local and Western food, which is quite good. Bella Italia Pizzeria Ristorante Café serves Italian and local favorites.

69 Jalan Gaya, 88000 Kota Kinabalu, Sabah. © **088/223-333.** Fax 088/240-401. www.jesseltonhotel.com. 32 units. RM247 ($72/£45) double; RM518 ($150/£93) suite. AE, DC, MC, V. **Amenities:** Restaurant; bar and lounge; coffee shop; airport transfers; room service; babysitting; smoke-free rooms. *In room:* A/C, TV (movies available), minibar, hair dryer.

Shangri-La's Tanjung Aru Resort & Spa ★★★ Kids   A short ride southwest of Kota Kinabalu and you're at Tanjung Aru, a pleasant beachside district. The Shangri-La here is located in a most impressive setting, surrounded on three sides by water. It serves the finest local Sabahan cuisine and freshest seafood you can get in the region. Book a room in the Tanjung Wing, which is nestled amid Shangri-La's signature lush garden setting, or the Kinabalu Wing, which has panoramic views of the South China Sea. Every room has a stunning view of either the sea or Mount Kinabalu, with a balcony for full appreciation. Tropical touches include furnishings in cool colors and local fabrics with wood details. Their tour desk can arrange everything from scuba to trekking and rafting. Special activities for kids make this place a good choice for families.

Locked Bag 174, 88744 Kota Kinabalu, Sabah. (C) **800/942-5050** in the U.S. and Canada, 800/222-448 in Australia, 800/442-179 in New Zealand, or 088/225-800. Fax 088/217-155. www.shangri-la.com. 499 units. RM700 ($203/£126) double; from RM1,250 ($363/£225) suite. AE, DC, MC, V. **Amenities:** 3 restaurants; beach bar and lounge; 2 outdoor lagoon-style pools; 4 outdoor lighted tennis courts; health club w/Jacuzzi, sauna, steam, and massage; concierge; airport transfers; room service; babysitting; smoke-free rooms. In room: A/C, TV w/satellite programming and in-house movies, high-speed Internet, minibar, hair dryer.

Where to Dine

One of the best local specialties, *hinava,* is a mouthwatering delicacy of raw fish marinated in lime juice, ginger, shallots, herbs, and chilies—I highly recommend trying it.

Kota Kinabalu is known for its fresh seafood, and there are a lot of places to choose from, but the locals and expatriates all agree that **Port View Seafood Restaurant,** Jalan Haji Saman across from the old Customs Wharf, near the downtown area ((C) **088/252-813**), is best. Dishes are prepared primarily in Chinese and Malay styles, are moderately priced (sold by weight), and are always succulent.

One of Malaysia's most exciting dining outlets is **@tmosphere,** on the 18th floor of Menara Tun Mustapha ((C) **088/425-100;** www.atmosphererestaurant.com), south of the city center. Arrive in style by helicopter to this revolving restaurant and dine on creative Pacific Rim cuisine. It becomes a lively night spot after dinner.

Attractions

Sabah attracts **scuba** enthusiasts from around the world who come to dive at Sipadan, an island resort off the east coast of the state. **Sipadan,** ranked as one of the top-10 dive sites in the world, is actually a tall limestone "tower" rising from the bed of the Celebes Sea, supporting vast numbers of marine species, some of which may still be unidentified. Since 2004, the Malaysian government revoked the licenses of the five dive operators that managed resorts on the tiny island, in an effort to prevent environmental degradation. The dive operators will move their base camps to surrounding islands, offering day trips to the area or running live-aboard trips.

Borneo Divers (9th floor, Menara Jubili, 53 Jalan Gaya; (C) **088/222-226;** www.borneo divers.info) was the first full-service dive operator in Borneo and the pioneering operator to Sipadan. They house divers at their resort on Mabul, along a gorgeous sandy beach with easy access to dive sites around the Mabul island and Sipadan. For RM664 ($193/£120) per night per person, you'll get accommodations, meals, airport transfers, and two dives a day. You'll have to pay extra for a round-trip flight into Tawau, which costs about RM390 ($113/£70). Booking can be made through Borneo Divers. Equipment rentals come to RM89 ($26/£16) per day. Sipadan has good diving year-round, but March through October has the best weather.

A newer spot, **Layang Layang,** located off the coast of northwest Borneo in the South China Sea, is also making a splash as an underwater bounty of marine life. **Layang Layang Island Resort** (head office in KL at Blk. A, ground floor, A-0-3, Megan Ave. II, 12 Jalan Yap Kwan Seng; (C) **03/2162-2877;** www.layanglayang.com) pioneered this area for divers. Their standard package of 6 days/5 nights runs at RM1,250 ($363/£225) per person, which includes accommodations, meals, and three dives a day. Equipment is extra, as is the chartered helicopter flight to the island, which is expensive at RM969 ($281/£174) round-trip (booked through the dive operator, flying on Tues, Thurs, Fri, and Sun). Layang Layang closes during the monsoon season (early Sept to Feb).

If you want to stay close to Kota Kinabalu, Borneo Divers (see above) makes day trips to **Tunku Abdul Rahman Marine Park.** This group of five islands about 8km (13 miles) off the coast of Kota Kinabalu has been protected since the mid-1970s. Throughout the park, waters are clear and visibility is good. Although not as lauded as Sipadan and Layang Layang, if you're looking for some quick diving excitement but you have time and money constraints, it's highly recommended. A day trip that includes two boat dives and a shore dive costs RM265 ($77/£48), not including equipment rentals. Borneo Divers has a base camp on the smallest island, from which they also conduct complete PADI scuba courses.

Sabah has many other dive sites, including sites such as Pulau Tiga, of *Survivor* TV fame. A couple of sites also offer wreck diving, so if you're interested, inquire when you make your booking.

For other types of watersports, your best bet is to either book these activities through your resort or plan a DIY trip to Tunku Abdul Rahman Park. Catch a ferry at the newly upgraded Kpta Kinabalu City Terminal, near the Sabah Ports Authority/Marine Police Jetty, to take you to the park. It costs RM30 ($8.70/£5.40) and is only 8km (13 miles) from Kota Kinabalu, so you can spend a day trip at one or more of the park's five islands sunning on the beach. **Snorkel** rentals go for around RM10 ($2.90/£1.80), and parasailing charges run RM100 ($29/£18). The latest thrill is **seawalking**—donning an enormous helmet connected to the surface with a tube, which allows you to breathe underwater without tanks. This costs RM150 ($44/£27) per person (✆ 088/249-115; www.borneoseawalking.com). *Tip for snorkelers:* Bring cotton socks to wear under your rental fins, to prevent blisters. There are cafes and toilets near the jetties, plus good accommodations on two of the islands.

Sabah's rugged terrain makes for terrific hiking, camping, biking, and rafting for any level, from soft adventure or extreme sports. **TYK Adventure** (Borneo Travel; Lot 48-2F, 2nd floor, Beverly Hill Plaza; ✆ 088/727-825; www.tykadventuretours.com) was founded by a local Chinese award-winning tour guide Tham Yau Kong, who also happens to hold records for the longest cultural walk (1998) and for leading the first group to circum-cycle Mt. Kinabalu (1999). Mountain biking trips around Papar or Penampang can be arranged for RM310 ($90/£56) per person for the day trip; the rate includes hotel transfer, mountain bike, and helmet.

Many come to Sabah to climb **Mt. Kinabalu.** It's an exhilarating trip if you are prepared and if you hit it just right, in terms of weather and timing. It can be done only on an overnight trip, which includes a 4- or 5-hour hike from the park headquarters uphill to a ranger station, where you stay the night. Groups awake at 3am to begin the 3-hour hike to the summit. This is not light trekking, as some parts are steep, altitude sickness can cause headaches and nausea, and remember—you're tooling along in the pitch darkness, the whole point being to arrive at the summit in time for the spectacular sunrise. Come prepared with cold weather snugglies, or at the very least a wool sweater or fleece, long pants, windbreaker, rain poncho, and hiking boots. Bring a good, strong flashlight and pack plenty of trail mix and sports drinks for rejuvenation. And finally, there's no guarantee that the weather will cooperate with your itinerary. You might hit rain or find the summit covered in clouds. There's pretty much nothing any tour operator can do to guarantee you'll get a clear view. But I've heard when you hit it right, it's really quite a great adventure with a rewarding view. **TYK Adventure** can also book this tour for you; a 2-day/1-night trip costs RM900 ($261/£162). Make sure you book early, because they need to make sure there's space available at park accommodations. The price includes transfer, lodging, and your guide to the summit.

TYK also plans regular trips out to Sandakan, on the eastern coast of Sabah, for trips to see the **Sepilok Orang Utan Rehabilitation Center,** the largest orangutan sanctuary in the world, with facilities to house and train hundreds of orphaned orangutans for eventual release back into the wilds, with a boat trip to see the **Marine Turtle Conservation Park and Hatchery.**

Monsopiad Cultural Village, a Kadazandusun heritage center with its creepy House of Skulls, is located in Penampang, not far from Kota Kinabalu. During the 3-hour visit to the village, you'll tour the place and be treated to a cultural performance. It's about the height of "touristy" Sabah but can be a fun half-day trip if you want to peep at a bit of local culture. Call them at *©* **088/774-337** to make a booking; RM100 ($29/£18) includes transportation to and from your hotel, the tour and show, plus a welcome drink. The tour leaves daily at 9:30am and again at 2:30pm.

In 2000, the **North Borneo Railway** (Tanjung Aru Railway; *©* **088/263-933**) revived the tradition of steam train travel with the launch of a 1954 fully renovated British Vulcan steam locomotive pulling six restored carriages. Traversing a 58km (36-mile) route from Tanjung Aru, near Kota Kinabalu, to the town of Papar, the train passes water and mangrove views, past fishermen and local sea crafts, through a mountain tunnel, and out the other side into a vast scenery of paddy fields. Carriages are open-air but comfortable, with soft seats and wood and brass accents. A swanky bar car and observation deck round out facilities that also include toilets. The train departs every Wednesday and Saturday at 10am, returning at 2pm; tickets are RM195 ($57/£35). At the time of writing, the railway was under maintenance, but do check to see if they're up and running during your visit; it's well worth it.

For another unique view of the countryside, **Touchdown Holidays Malaysia** (*©* **088/249-276;** www.touchdowncollection.com) offers thrilling **helicopter tours,** flying over Kota Kinabalu, tropical wilds, and the jewel-colored sea. They also operate luxury boats around the islands off Kota Kinabalu.

Appendix A: Singapore Fast Facts

1 FAST FACTS: SINGAPORE

AMERICAN EXPRESS The American Express office is located at 300 Beach Rd., #18-01 The Concourse (© **65/6880-1333**). It's open Monday to Friday 9am to 5pm and Saturday 9am to 1pm. There's a more convenient kiosk that handles traveler's checks and simple card transactions (including emergency check guarantee) on Orchard Road just outside the Marriott Hotel at Tangs (© **65/6735-2069**). It's open daily from 9am to 9pm. An additional foreign exchange office is open at Changi Airport Terminal 2 (© **65/6546-5456**). It's open from noon to midnight daily. See the "Money & Costs" section in chapter 3 for more on member privileges.

AREA CODES Singapore's country code is 65. Tiny Singapore has no regional area codes.

ATM NETWORKS/CASHPOINTS See "Money & Costs," p. 42.

BUSINESS HOURS Shopping centers are open Monday through Saturday from 10am to 9pm and stay open until later on some public holidays. Banks are open from 9:30am to 3pm Monday through Friday and from 9 to 11am on Saturday. Restaurants open at lunchtime from around 11am to 2:30pm, and for dinner they reopen at around 6pm and take the last order sometime around 10pm. Government offices are open from 9am to 5pm Monday through Friday and from 9am to 1pm on Saturday. Post offices conduct business from 8:30am to 5pm on weekdays and from 8:30am to 1pm on Saturday. Some keep extended hours until 8pm.

DRINKING LAWS The legal age for purchase and consumption of alcoholic beverages is 18; proof of age is rarely requested.

DRUGSTORES Guardian Pharmacy fills prescriptions with name-brand drugs (from a licensed physician) and carries a large selection of toiletries. Convenient locations include #B1-05 Centrepoint Shopping Centre (© **65/6737-4835**), #02-237 Marina Sq. (© **65/6337-4518**), and #B1-01 Raffles City Shopping Centre (© **65/6339-2137**).

ELECTRICITY Standard electrical current is 220 volts AC (50 cycles). Local electrical outlets are made for plugs with three square prongs. Consult your concierge to see if your hotel has converters and plug adapters in-house for you to use. If you are using sensitive equipment, do not trust cheap voltage transformers. Nowadays, a lot of electrical equipment—including portable radios and laptop computers—comes with built-in converters, so you can follow the manufacturer's directions for changing them over.

EMBASSIES & CONSULATES Contacts for major embassies in Singapore are as follows: U.S. Embassy, 27 Napier Rd. (© **65/6476-9100**); Canadian High Commission, One George St. #11-01 (© **65/6854-5900**); British High Commission,

Tanglin Road (© **65/6473-9333**); Australian High Commission, 25 Napier Rd. (© **65/6836-4100**).

EMERGENCIES For **police**, dial © **999.** For **medical** or **fire** emergencies, call © **995.**

HOLIDAYS See "Holidays" in chapter 3, p. 34.

HOSPITALS If you require hospitalization, the centrally located **Mount Elizabeth Hospital** is near Orchard Road at 3 Mount Elizabeth (© **65/6737-2666**); for accidents and emergencies, call (© **65/6731-2218**). You can also try **Singapore General Hospital,** Outram Road (© **65/6222-3322**); for accidents and emergencies, call (© **65/6321-4311**).

INSURANCE **Medical Insurance** For travel overseas, most U.S. health plans (including Medicare and Medicaid) do not provide coverage, and the ones that do often require you to pay for services up front and reimburse you only after you return home.

As a safety net, you may want to buy travel medical insurance, particularly if you're traveling to a remote or high-risk area where emergency evacuation might be necessary. If you require additional medical insurance, try **MEDEX Assistance** (© 410/453-6300; www.medexassist.com) or **Travel Assistance International** (© **800/821-2828;** www.travelassistance.com; for general information on services, call the company's **Worldwide Assistance Services, Inc.,** at © **800/777-8710**).

Canadians should check with their provincial health plan offices or call **Health Canada** (© **866/225-0709;** www.hc-sc.gc.ca) to find out the extent of their coverage and what documentation and receipts they must take home in case they are treated overseas.

Travelers from the U.K. should carry their European Health Insurance Card (EHIC), which replaced the E111 form as proof of entitlement to free/reduced cost medical treatment abroad (© **0845 606 2030;** www.ehic.org.uk). Note, however, that the EHIC covers only "necessary medical treatment," and for repatriation costs, lost money, baggage, or cancellation, travel insurance from a reputable company should always be sought (www.travelinsuranceweb.com).

Travel Insurance The cost of travel insurance varies widely, depending on the destination, the cost and length of your trip, your age and health, and the type of trip you're taking, but expect to pay between 5% and 8% of the vacation itself. You can get estimates from various providers through **InsureMyTrip.com.** Enter your trip cost and dates, your age, and other information, for prices from more than a dozen companies.

U.K. citizens and their families who make more than one trip abroad per year may find an annual travel insurance policy works out cheaper. Check **www.moneysupermarket.com,** which compares prices across a wide range of providers for single- and multitrip policies.

Most big travel agents offer their own insurance and will probably try to sell you their package when you book a holiday. Think before you sign. **Britain's Consumers' Association** recommends that you insist on seeing the policy and reading the fine print before buying travel insurance. **The Association of British Insurers** (© **020/7600-3333;** www.abi.org.uk) gives advice by phone and publishes Holiday Insurance, a free guide to policy provisions and prices. You might also shop around for better deals: Try **Columbus Direct** (© 0870/033-9988; www.columbusdirect.net).

Trip Cancellation Insurance Trip-cancellation insurance will help retrieve your money if you have to back out of a trip or depart early, or if your travel supplier goes bankrupt. Trip cancellation traditionally covers such events as sickness, natural

2000

disasters, and State Department advisories. The latest news in trip-cancellation insurance is the availability of **expanded hurricane coverage** and the **"any-reason"** cancellation coverage—which costs more but covers cancellations made for any reason. You won't get back 100% of your prepaid trip cost, but you'll be refunded a substantial portion. **TravelSafe** (© **888/ 885-7233;** www.travelsafe.com) offers both types of coverage. Expedia also offers any-reason cancellation coverage for its air–hotel packages. For details, contact one of the following recommended insurers: **Access America** (www.accessamerica. com), **Travel Guard International** (www. travelguard.com), **Travel Insured International** (www.travelinsured.com), or **Travelex Insurance Services** (www.travelex-insurance.com).

INTERNET ACCESS Internet cafes are common throughout the city, with usage costs about S$5 (US$3.35/£2.25) per hour (if you use the Internet in your hotel's business center, you'll pay a much higher price). Almost every shopping mall has one, and there are cybercafes in both terminals at Changi Airport. For reliability and quality, I recommend **Chills Café,** with two locations: 39 Stamford Rd., #01-07 Stamford House, open daily 9am till midnight; and 3 Temasek Blvd., #02-165/ 167/197/199, Suntec City Mall Tower 5; open daily 10am till 10pm. For both locations, call © **65/6883-1016.**

LANGUAGE Singapore's four official languages are Malay, Chinese (Mandarin dialect), Tamil, and English. Malay is the national language, while English is the language for government operations, law, and major financial transactions. Most Singaporeans are at least bilingual, with many speaking one or more dialects of Chinese, plus English and some Malay.

LEGAL AID If you find yourself in trouble in Singapore, the first thing you should do is consult your home embassy or high commission. However, for serious offences, do not expect much help. Singapore shows little leniency to foreigners who break local laws, and officials from your home country are oftentimes powerless to assist.

LOST & FOUND Be sure to tell all of your credit card companies the minute you discover your wallet has been lost or stolen, and file a report at the nearest police post. Your credit card company or insurer may require a police report number or record of the loss. Most credit card companies have an emergency toll-free number to call if your card is lost or stolen; they may be able to wire you a cash advance immediately or deliver an emergency credit card in a day or two.

To report lost or stolen credit cards within Singapore, use the following toll-free hot lines: **American Express** (© **800/ 299-1997**), **MasterCard** (© **800/110-0113**), **Visa** (© **800/110-0344**).

If you need emergency cash over the weekend, you can have money wired to you via Western Union at most SingPost branches.

MAIL Most hotels have mail services at the front counter. Singapore Post has centrally located offices that include #04-15 Ngee Ann City/Takashimaya Shopping Centre (© **65/6738-6899**); Chinatown Point, 133 New Bridge Rd. #02-41/ 42/43/44 (© **65/6538-7899**); Change Alley, 16 Collyer Quay #02-02 Hitachi Tower (© **65/6538-6899**); and Suntec City Mall #03-01/03, 3 Temasek Blvd. (© **65/6332-0289**). Plus, there are five branches at Changi International Airport.

The going rate for international airmail letters to North America, Europe, Australia, and New Zealand is S$1.10 (US75¢/ 50p) for 20 grams, plus S35¢ (US20¢/25p) for each additional 10 grams. Postcards and aerograms to all destinations are S50¢ (US30¢/20p).

Your hotel will accept mail sent for you at its address.

MAPS The STB Visitors' Centres carry a variety of free city maps and walking tour maps of individual neighborhoods.

MEASUREMENTS See the chart on the inside front cover of this book for details on converting metric measurements to nonmetric equivalents.

NEWSPAPERS & MAGAZINES Local English newspapers available are the *International Herald Tribune, The Business Times, The Straits Times, Today,* and *USA Today International.* The *Asian Wall Street Journal* has limited distribution in Singapore. Most of the major hotels carry it, though, so ask around and you can find one. *I-S Magazine* is a good resource for nightlife happenings. The STB Visitors' Centres carry a few free publications for travelers, including *Where Singapore, This Week Singapore,* and *Singapore Business Visitor.* Major bookstores and magazine shops sell a wide variety of international magazines.

PASSPORTS The websites listed provide downloadable passport applications, as well as the current fees for processing applications. For an up-to-date, country-by-country listing of passport requirements around the world, go to the "International Travel" tab of the U.S. State Department at **http://travel.state.gov**.

For Residents of Australia You can pick up an application from your local post office or any branch of Passports Australia, but you must schedule an interview at the passport office to present your application materials. Call the **Australian Passport Information Service** at ✆ **131-232,** or visit the government website at www.passports.gov.au.

For Residents of Canada Passport applications are available at travel agencies throughout Canada or from the central **Passport Office,** Department of Foreign Affairs and International Trade, Ottawa, ON K1A 0G3 (✆ **800/567-6868;** www.ppt.gc.ca). *Note:* Canadian children who

travel must have their own passport. However, if you hold a valid Canadian passport issued before December 11, 2001, that bears the name of your child, the passport remains valid for you and your child until it expires.

For Residents of Ireland You can apply for a 10-year passport at the **Passport Office,** Setanta Centre, Molesworth Street, Dublin 2 (✆ **01/671-1633;** www.irlgov.ie/iveagh). Those under age 18 and over 65 must apply for a 3-year passport. You can also apply at 1A South Mall, Cork (✆ **21/494-4700**), or at most main post offices.

For Residents of New Zealand You can pick up a passport application at any New Zealand Passports Office or download it from their website. Contact the **Passports Office** at ✆ **0800/225-050** in New Zealand or 04/474-8100, or log on to www.passports.govt.nz.

For Residents of the United Kingdom To pick up an application for a standard 10-year passport (5-yr. passport for children under 16), visit your nearest passport office, major post office, or travel agency, or contact the **United Kingdom Passport Service** at ✆ **0870/521-0410** or search its website at www.ukpa.gov.uk.

For Residents of the United States Whether you're applying in person or by mail, you can download passport applications from the U.S. State Department website at **http://travel.state.gov**. To find your regional passport office, either check the U.S. State Department website or call the **National Passport Information Center** toll-free number (✆ **877/487-2778**) for automated information

POLICE For emergencies, call ✆ **999.** If you need to call the police headquarters, dial ✆ **1800/255-0000.**

SMOKING It's against the law to smoke in public buses, elevators, theaters, cinemas, shopping centers, government offices, and taxi queues. In addition, all restaurants, hawker centers, bars, and nightclubs are smoke-free, with the exception of designated smoking areas. Establishments with outdoor seating can allocate 20% of this space for a smoking area. Nightclubs can have smoking rooms inside their premises, but this room cannot exceed 10% of the club's total floor space.

TAXES Many hotels and restaurants will advertise rates followed by "++." The first + is the goods and services tax (GST), which is levied at 7% of the purchase. The second + is a 10% gratuity charge. See chapter 8 for information on the GST Tourist Refund Scheme, which lets you recover the GST for purchases over S$100 (US$67/£45) in value.

TELEPHONES Public telephones can be found in booths on the street or back near the toilets in shopping malls, public buildings, or hotel lobbies. Local calls cost S10¢ (US7¢/5p) for 3 minutes at coin- and card-operated phones. International calls can be made only from public phones designated specifically for this purpose. International public phones will accept either a stored-value phone card or a credit card. Phone cards for local and international calls can be purchased at Singapore Post branches, 7-Eleven convenience stores, or moneychangers—make sure you specify local or international phone card when you make your purchase.

For more information, see "Staying Connected" in "Planning Your Trip to Singapore," p. 50.

TIME Singapore Standard Time is 8 hours ahead of Greenwich Mean Time (GMT). International time differences will change during daylight saving or summer time. Basic time differences are: New York –13, Los Angeles –16, Montreal –13, Vancouver –16, London –8, Brisbane +3, Darwin +1, Melbourne +2, Sydney +3, and Auckland +4. For the current time in Singapore, call ℂ **1711.**

TIPPING While tipping is not exactly discouraged at hotels, at bars, and in taxis, it is not the norm here. A gratuity is automatically added into guest checks, but servers rarely see any of it. While tipping is not expected, I typically leave the small bills behind in restaurants and bars, I tell the cabbie to "keep the change", and I always give bellhops at least S$2 (US$1.35/ 90p) per bag in all hotels. It is always appreciated.

TOILETS Clean public toilets can be found in all shopping malls, hotels, and public buildings. Smaller restaurants may not be up on their cleanliness, and beware of the "squatty potty," the Asian-style squat toilet, which you see in the more "local" places. Carry plenty of tissues with you, as they often run out.

USEFUL PHONE NUMBERS U.S. Dept. of State Travel Advisory: ℂ 202/ 647-5225 (manned 24 hr.)

U.S. Passport Agency: ℂ 202/647-0518

U.S. Centers for Disease Control International Traveler's Hotline: ℂ 404/332-4559

WATER Tap water in Singapore passes World Health Organization standards and is potable.

2 AIRLINE & HOTEL WEBSITES

MAJOR AIRLINES THAT SERVICE CHANGI INTERNATIONAL AIRPORT

Air France
www.airfrance.com

Air India
www.airindia.com

All Nippon Airways (ANA)
www.anaskyweb.com

American Airlines
www.aa.com

Asiana
http://flyasiana.com

British Airways
www.british-airways.com

Cathay Pacific
www.cathaypacific.com

China Airlines
www.china-airlines.com

Delta Air Lines
www.delta.com

Emirates Airlines
www.emirates.com

Japan Airlines
www.jal.co.jp

KLM
www.klm.com

Korean Air
www.koreanair.com

Lufthansa
www.lufthansa.com

Malaysia Airlines
www.malaysiaairlines.com

Northwest Airlines
www.nwa.com

Philippine Airlines
www.philippineairlines.com

Qantas Airways
www.qantas.com

Qatar Airways
www.qatarairways.com

Singapore Airlines
www.singaporeair.com

South African Airways
www.flysaa.com

Swiss Air
www.swiss.com

Thai Airways International
www.thaiair.com

United Airlines
www.united.com

BUDGET AIRLINES THAT SERVICE CHANGI INTERNATIONAL AIRPORT

AirAsia
www.airasia.com

Jetstar (Valuair)
www.jetstar.com
www.valuair.com

Tiger Airways
www.tigerairways.com

MAJOR HOTEL CHAINS

Crowne Plaza Hotels
www.ichotelsgroup.com/crowneplaza

Four Seasons
www.fourseasons.com

Hilton Hotels
www.hilton.com

Holiday Inn
www.holidayinn.com

Hyatt
www.hyatt.com

InterContinental Hotels & Resorts
www.ichotelsgroup.com

Marriott
www.marriott.com

Sheraton Hotels & Resorts
www.starwoodhotels.com/sheraton

Appendix B: Malaysia Fast Facts

1 FAST FACTS: MALAYSIA

AMERICAN EXPRESS The main office for American Express is located in KL at Menara Maybank, Ground Level banking hall, Jalan Perak (© **03/2050-0888**).

AREA CODES Malaysia's country code is 60. Area codes for destinations covered in this book are as follows: 03 for Kuala Lumpur; 06 for Melaka; 07 for Johor Bahru; 04 for Penang and Langkawi; 09 for Tioman, Kuantan, Cherating, Kuala Terengganu, and Kota Bharu; 082 for Sarawak; and 088 for Sabah.

ATM NETWORKS/CASHPOINTS See "Money & Costs," p. 42.

BUSINESS HOURS Banks are open from 9:30am to 3pm Monday through Friday. Government offices are open from 8am to 12:45pm and 2 to 4:15pm Monday through Friday. Smaller shops like provision stores may open as early as 6 or 6:30am and close as late as 9pm, especially those near the wet markets. Many such stores are closed on Saturday evenings and Sunday afternoons and are busiest before lunch. Other shops are open 9:30am to 7pm. Department stores and shops in malls tend to open later, about 10:30 or 11am until 8:30 or 9pm throughout the week. Note that in the states of Kelantan, Terengganu, and Kedah, the working week runs from Saturday to Wednesday, with weekends on Friday and Saturday.

DENTISTS & DOCTORS All hotels and resorts have qualified physicians on call who speak English. These doctors will come directly to your room for treatment. If your condition is serious, they can help you check into a local hospital.

DRINKING LAWS Liquor is sold in pubs and supermarkets in all big cities, or in provision stores. If you're going to a smaller island, your resort may have limited alcohol selections, so you may wish to bring your own. In Terengganu and Kelantan, liquor is strictly limited to a handful of Chinese restaurants. Pubs and other nightspots should officially close by 1am nationwide, but there are places in KL that stay open later.

The legal age for alcohol purchase and consumption is 18, but foreigners are rarely checked.

DRUG LAWS As in Singapore, the death sentence is mandatory for drug trafficking (defined as being in possession of more than 15g of heroin or morphine, 200g of marijuana or hashish, or 40g of cocaine). For lesser quantities, you'll be thrown in jail for a very long time and flogged with a cane.

ELECTRICITY The voltage used in Malaysia is 220 to 240 volts AC (50 cycles). Three-point square plugs are used, so buy an adapter if you plan to bring any appliances. Also, many larger hotels can provide adapters upon request.

EMBASSIES While in Malaysia, should you need to contact an official representative from your home country, the following contact information in Kuala Lumpur can help you out: United States Embassy, ✆ **03/2168-5000;** Canadian High Commission, ✆ **03/2718-3333;** Australian High Commission, ✆ **03/2146-5555;** New Zealand High Commission, ✆ **03/2078-2533;** and the British High Commission, ✆ **03/2170-2200.**

EMERGENCIES Call ✆ **999** for emergencies.

INSURANCE See "Insurance" in "Singapore Fast Facts," p. 291

INTERNET Service is available to most of the nation, and I have found Internet cafes in the most surprisingly remote places. Although the major international hotels will have access for their guests in the business center, charges can be very steep. I used to recommend Internet cafes in each city but found that these small places came and went overnight, making it impossible for me to provide accurate information for this book. Wherever you are, your best bet is to ask your concierge or the local tourism information office for the best places close by. Usage costs only about RM5 to RM10 ($1.45–$2.90/90p–£1.80).

LANGUAGE The national language is Malay, or Bahasa Malaysia, although English is widely spoken. Chinese dialects and Tamil are also spoken.

LEGAL AID If you encounter legal trouble in Malaysia, you should notify your home embassy immediately. They will not be able to change local laws to help you, post bail on your behalf, or offer legal advice, but they can assist you to contact family and suggest names of local legal representatives. Note that drug trafficking carries a mandatory death penalty and that conviction for certain other violent crimes can result in corporal punishment. Some aspects of Shariah (Islamic) law have been incorporated into the lawbooks of some states.

LOST & FOUND Be sure to tell all of your credit card companies the minute you discover your wallet has been lost or stolen, and file a report at the nearest police precinct. Your credit card company or insurer may require a police report number or record of the loss. Most credit card companies have an emergency toll-free number to call if your card is lost or stolen; they may be able to wire you a cash advance immediately or deliver an emergency credit card in a day or two.

In the event of a lost or stolen credit card, you can contact the following hot lines: **American Express,** ✆ 03/2050-0789; **MasterCard,** ✆ 800/804-594; and **Visa,** ✆ 800/800-159.

If you need emergency cash over the weekend when all banks and American Express offices are closed, you can have money wired to you via **Western Union** (✆ **800/325-6000;** www.westernunion.com).

MAIL Post office locations in each city covered are provided in each section. Overseas airmail postage rates are as follows: RM.50 (15¢/9p) for postcards and from RM1.40 (40¢/25p) for a 100g letter.

MEASUREMENTS See the chart on the inside front cover of this book for details on converting metric measurements to nonmetric equivalents.

NEWSPAPERS & MAGAZINES English-language papers the *New Straits Times, The Star, The Sun,* and *The Edge* can be bought in hotel lobbies and magazine stands. Of the local KL magazines, *Time Out* has great listings and local "what's happening" information for travelers.

PASSPORTS See "Passports" in "Fast Facts: Singapore," p. 293.

POLICE For emergencies, call ✆ **999.**

TAXES Hotels, with the exception of those on Langkawi, add a 5% government tax to all rates, plus an additional 10% service charge. Larger restaurants also figure the same 5% tax into your bill, plus a 10% service charge, whereas small coffee shops and hawker stalls don't charge anything above the cost of the meal. Although most tourist goods (such as crafts, camera equipment, sports equipment, cosmetics, and select small electronic items) are tax-free, a small, scaled tax is issued on various other goods such as clothing, shoes, and accessories that you'd buy in the larger shopping malls and department stores.

TELEPHONE See "Staying Connected" in "Planning Your Trip to Malaysia," p. 206.

TIME Malaysia is 8 hours ahead of Greenwich Mean Time, 16 hours ahead of U.S. Pacific Standard Time, 13 ahead of Eastern Standard Time, and 2 hours behind Sydney. It is in the same zone as Singapore. There is no daylight saving time.

TIPPING People here don't really tip, but you might want to give your bellhop something. In a nicer hotel, at least RM2 (60¢/35p) per bag should be fine. In a budget hotel, they'll probably be shocked.

TOILETS To find a public toilet, ask for the *tandas*. In Malay, *lelaki* is male and *perempuan* is female. Be prepared for pay toilets. Coin collectors sit outside almost every public facility, taking RM.20 (6¢/4p) per person, RM.30 (9¢/5p) if you want paper. Once inside, you'll find that your money doesn't go for cleaning crews. Public toilets are pure filth. They smell horrible and the floors are always an inch deep with stagnant water. While most toilets are of the "squatty-potty" variety (a porcelain bowl set into the floor), even if you find a seat-style toilet bowl, locals typically place their feet on the seat to squat. The best toilets are in hotels, upmarket shopping malls, and restaurants.

USEFUL PHONE NUMBERS See "Useful Phone Numbers" in "Singapore Fast Facts," p. 294.

WATER Water in Kuala Lumpur is supposed to be potable, but most locals boil the water before drinking it—and if that's not a tip-off, I don't know what is. I advise against drinking the tap water anywhere in Malaysia. Hotels will supply bottled water in your room. If they charge you for it, expect inflated prices, especially for premium imported water. A 1.5-liter bottle goes for RM7 (US$2.05/£1.25) in a hotel minibar, but RM2 (60¢/35p) at 7-Eleven.

2 AIRLINE & HOTEL WEBSITES

MAJOR AIRLINES THAT SERVICE KUALA LUMPUR INTERNATIONAL AIRPORT

AirAsia
www.airasia.com

Cathay Pacific
www.cathaypacific.com

China Airlines
www.china-airlines.com

EgyptAir
www.egyptair.com

Emirates Airlines
www.emirates.com

Japan Airlines
www.jal.co.jp

Jetstar (Valuair)
www.jetstar.com
www.valuair.com

KLM
www.klm.com

Korean Air
www.koreanair.com

Lufthansa
www.lufthansa.com

Malaysia Airlines
www.malaysiaairlines.com

Qatar Airways
www.qatarairways.com

Singapore Airlines
www.singaporeair.com

Thai Airways International
www.thaiair.com

MAJOR HOTEL & MOTEL CHAINS

Best Western International
www.bestwestern.com

Crowne Plaza Hotels
www.ichotelsgroup.com/crowneplaza

Four Seasons
www.fourseasons.com

Hilton Hotels
www.hilton.com

Holiday Inn
www.holidayinn.com

Hyatt
www.hyatt.com

InterContinental Hotels & Resorts
www.ichotelsgroup.com

Marriott
www.marriott.com

Sheraton Hotels & Resorts
www.starwoodhotels.com/sheraton

Westin Hotels & Resorts
www.starwoodhotels.com/westin

INDEX

See also Accommodations and Restaurant indexes, below.